The Road to Excellence

The Acquisition of Expert Performance in the Arts and Sciences, Sports, and Games

The Road to Excellence

The Acquisition of Expert Performance in the Arts and Sciences, Sports, and Games

edited by

K. Anders Ericsson
Florida State University

LEA **LAWRENCE ERLBAUM ASSOCIATES, PUBLISHERS**
1996 **Mahwah, New Jersey**

Copyright © 1996 by Lawrence Erlbaum Associates, Inc.
All rights reserved. No part of the book may be reproduced in any form, by photostat, microform, retrieval
system, or any other means, without the prior permission
of the publisher.

Lawrence Erlbaum Associates, Inc., Publishers
10 Industrial Avenue
Mahwah, New Jersey 07430

Library of Congress Cataloging-in-Publication Data

The road to excellence : the acquisition of expert performance
in the arts and sciences, sports, and games / edited by K.
Anders Ericsson.
        p. cm.
    Includes bibliographical references and index.
    ISBN 0-8058-2231-3 (alk. paper). — ISBN 0-8058-
2232-1 (pbk. : alk. paper)
    1. Expertise. 2. Excellence. 3. Gifted persons. I.
Ericsson, K. Anders (Karl Anders), 1947– .
BF378.E94R63 1996
153—dc20   95-52848
                                                CIP

Books published by Lawrence Erlbaum Associates are printed
on acid-free paper, and their bindings are chosen for strength
and durability.

Printed in the United States of America
10 9 8 7 6 5 4 3 2

Contents

Preface

The highest levels of performance and achievement in sports, games, arts, and sciences have always been an object of fascination, but only within the last couple of decades have scientists been studying these empirical phenomena within a general theoretical framework.

The origin of systematic theoretical and empirical work on expertise is linked to the seminal work on chess expertise by de Groot (1946/1978). However, the primary stimulus for the emerging interdisciplinary research on expertise is generally attributed to a paper by Chase and Simon (1973). They proposed a general theory for the structure of expertise that offered empirical predictions for the structure of expert performance in a wide range of domains of expert performance, such as "any skilled task (e.g., football, music)" (p. 279). Chase and Simon (1973) proposed that most forms of expertise were the results of vast amounts of knowledge and pattern-based retrieval mechanisms acquired over many years of experience in the associated domain. Research on solving textbook problems in physics (Larkin, McDermott, Simon, & Simon, 1980; Simon & Simon, 1978) showed that novices, that is, beginners with all the necessary knowledge, had to work backwards from the question of the problem to identify relevant formulas in a step-wise fashion. In contrast, physics experts retrieved a solution plan effortlessly as part of their initial comprehension of the problem. Subsequently, Chi, Glaser, and Rees (1982) showed that physics experts not only had more knowledge but better organized knowledge, allowing them to represent physics problems in terms of the deeper theoretical principles, whereas novices' representations were based on the presence or absence of surface features.

The first conference focusing on the interdisciplinary nature of studies of expertise was organized in 1983 by Chi, Glaser, and Farr in Pittsburgh. Their conference on The Nature of Expertise had scientists report on a wide range of pioneering research on expertise in very different domains. The presentations were later published (1988) and had a great impact on the emerging interest in the study of expertise.

In 1989, 6 years after that conference, Ericsson and Smith organized a conference in West Berlin to assess the progress of research on expertise. This conference was designed with the intent of producing an edited book systematically covering the research in the major domains where expertise had been studied. Hence, each participant in the conference had the dual obligation of reviewing progress in that domain and reporting on more recent original studies. The resulting book appeared in 1991 under the title *Toward a General Theory of Expertise: Prospects and Limits*.

As a reflection of the growing interest in expertise, two important books on specific topics of expertise have since appeared. A book based on a conference in 1988 that had focused on "expert knowledge and the application of experimental psychology to expert systems development" (p. vii) appeared in 1992 (Hoffman, 1992). A year later, Starkes and Allard (1993) published an edited book on "cognitive issues in motor expertise."

In 1993, I started to invite scientists to a conference with a new and different focus—the generalizable characteristics of the acquisition of expert performance. The previously reviewed research (Ericsson & Smith, 1991) had shown that although expert performance in different domains is behaviorally expressed in a variety of ways, the types of acquired mediating mechanisms are remarkably similar across domains. Some earlier research indicated that there may be a related set of characteristics with which expert performance is acquired within and across domains. For example, Simon and Chase (1973) proposed that individuals need to spend around 10 years of intensive preparation in the domain before they can reach international levels of performance. More recent examinations of the extended period of preparation of elite performers revealed the critical importance of training activities designed exclusively for improvement of performance (deliberate practice), which were found to be distinct from playful interactions, competition, work, and other forms of experience in the domain (Ericsson & Charness, 1994; Ericsson, Krampe, & Tesch-Römer, 1993). Expert performance in young adults was found to be closely related to the amount of deliberate practice accumulated during the individual's entire career.

The central idea for this conference was to bring together the world's foremost researchers on specific domains of expertise and related theoretical issues, such as the importance of individual differences in ability and innate talent for attaining expert levels of performance. The traditional domains of expertise were all represented at the conference: chess (Charness), music (Sloboda), sports (Starkes), and medicine (Patel). In addition, general mechanisms for acquiring expert performance in traditional domains of expertise were discussed by Herbert Simon. The issues of development and skill acquisition have been extensively studied outside the traditional areas of expertise. Hence, leading researchers in the study of creative expertise (Simonton) and reading (Wagner and Stanovich) were invited to review and integrate the findings from their domains. Finally, two presenters discussed issues concerning individual differences in early preparation and innate talent for individuals with gifts (Winner) and genius (Howe). All of the presenters were invited to summarize information about developmental trajectories and training activities of expert performers in specific domains and then to make proposals for characteristics that appear to generalize across domains. To assess the generalizability and applicability of the presented ideas, several outstanding scientists with different backgrounds were invited to be discussants: Robert Glaser (education), Lawrence Holmes (history of science), John Shea (motor learning and sports), Richard Shiffrin (experimental psychology), and Robert Sternberg (individual differences in abilities and intelligence).

A subset of these presentations were given as part of a symposium on "The acquisition of expert performance: Implications for optimal professional development" at the annual meeting of AERA in San Francisco on April 21, 1995. The main conference was successfully completed at Wakulla Springs, Florida, on April 27–30, 1995.

I hope that many readers will find the contributions in this book as exciting as the speakers at the conference found them to be. Furthermore, the findings presented in the book should be relevant on several levels. First the book summarizes our emerging knowledge of the necessary conditions for reaching international-level performance in many different domains: at least around a decade of effortful practice under optimal training conditions. The controversy over the role of innate individual differences (talent) has not been resolved, but the alternative accounts have been better articulated and range from innate general and domain-specific basic capacities to motivational differences predisposing some individuals to engage in focused learning on a regular and extended basis. Perhaps the most useful aspect of this book to researchers is that it raises numerous issues that should stimulate future research and help expand the growing field of research on expert performance.

On a more personal level the book will be relevant to all who aspire to reach their highest level of performance in their respective domain of expertise. Most everyone who has traveled on the road to excellence has reflected on how they can improve most effectively and perhaps have even generated "experiments" to identify the best daily habits and learning activities. Hopefully, this book will stimulate you to reflect on your daily activities and how you might be able to allocate more of your limited time and resources to those activities that are critical to your continued improvement and the achievement of your most desired goals. The ultimate test of the validity of theoretical ideas on expert performance is not just whether they are interesting and thought provoking and lead to new research and experiments, but also whether individuals find them effective as principles guiding the design of their own daily lives in efforts to optimize the attainment of their personal goals. In the case of expert performance, I foresee exceptional opportunities for a mutually beneficial interaction between theory and practice.

—K. Anders Ericsson

REFERENCES

Chase, W. G., & Simon, H. A. (1973). The mind's eye in chess. In W. G. Chase (Ed.), *Visual information processing* (pp. 215–281). New York: Academic Press.

Chi, M. T. H., Glaser, R., & Farr, M. J. (Eds.). (1988). *The nature of expertise.* Hillsdale, NJ: Lawrence Erlbaum Associates.

Chi, M. T. H., Glaser, R., & Rees, E. (1982). Expertise in problem solving. In R. S. Sternberg (Ed.), *Advances in the psychology of human intelligence* (Vol. 1, pp. 1–75). Hillsdale, NJ: Lawrence Erlbaum Associates.

de Groot, A. (1978). *Thought and choice and chess.* The Hague: Mouton. (Original work published 1946).

Ericsson, K. A., & Charness, N. (1994). Expert performance: Its structure and acquisition. *American Psychologist, 49*(8), 725–747.

Ericsson, K. A., Krampe, R. T., & Tesch-Römer, C. (1993). The role of deliberate practice in the acquisition of expert performance. *Psychological Review, 100*(3), 363–406.

Ericsson, K. A., & Smith, J. (Eds.). (1991). Toward a general theory of expertise: Prospects and limits. Cambridge, UK: Cambridge University Press.

Hoffman, R. R. (Ed.). (1992). *The psychology of expertise.* New York: Springer-Verlag.

Larkin, J. H., McDermott, J., Simon, D. P., & Simon, H. A. (1980). Models of competence in solving physics problems. *Cognitive Science, 4,* 317–345.

Simon, D. P., & Simon, H. A. (1978). Individual differences in solving physics problems. In R. S. Siegler (Ed.), *Children's thinking: What develops?* (pp. 325–348). Hillsdale, NJ: Lawrence Erlbaum Associates.

Simon, H. A., & Chase, W. G. (1973). Skill in chess. *American Scientist, 61,* 394–403.

Starkes, J. L., & Allard, F. (Eds.). (1993). *Cognitive issues in motor expertise.* Amsterdam: North-Holland.

Participants at the conference on "The Acquisition of Expert Performance" at Wakulla Springs Conference Center, Florida, April 27–30, 1995. Front row: John Shea, Anders Ericsson, Vimla Patel, John Sloboda, Ellen Winner, Robert Glaser, Robert Sternberg, and Lawrence Holmes. Back row: Richard Shiffrin, Herbert Simon, Neil Charness, Dean Simonton, Keith Stanovich, Richard Wagner, and Michael Howe.

1

The Acquisition of Expert Performance: An Introduction to Some of the Issues

K. Anders Ericsson
The Florida State University

In every domain of expertise, many start on the "road to excellence" but few reach the highest levels of achievement and performance. Through the centuries, a large body of historical facts, interviews, and observations have been collected about these exceptional individuals in popular and academic biographies. In many cases, the most detailed information is given retrospectively by the exceptional individuals themselves years later when their outstanding achievements have been recognized by their peers and society. For example, the famous accounts of creative experience by Kekule, Poincare, and others were first written down years or even decades after the events they describe, and consequently suffer from many of the problematic biases of recollection (Gruber, 1981b). The scarcity of relevant evidence often forces biographers to lower their standards of evidence to the point where it is difficult to separate hard facts from biased recollections and myths. Much of the popular evidence for talent and inexplicable creativity is based on accounts that cannot be subjected to scientific analysis (Ericsson & Charness, 1994). For example, many of the famous descriptions of the young genius Gauss are based on unsupported anecdotes told by Gauss himself as an old man (Bühler, 1981). The first step toward a scientific account of exceptional achievements requires rejection of unverifiable evidence and the identification and systematic accumulation of all empirical evidence that meets standard scientific criteria.

Outstanding human achievements usually consist of actual products, such as works of art or scientific publications. In these cases, the date of completion and the individual responsible for the achievement are known. However, the psychological processes that led to the achievement are far more difficult to investigate and explain scientifically. Part of the problem concerns their original and creative nature. By definition, an innovative achievement goes beyond the application of available knowledge in the domain at the time of its completion. Hence, major innovations and discoveries emerge unpredictably and often considerable time passes before they are widely accepted as valid great accomplishments. We are thus primarily limited to the evaluation of post-hoc explanations of major specific discoveries based on careful analysis of the historical records such as notebooks and earlier drafts (Gruber, 1981a; Holmes, 1989). A complementary experimental approach is to recreate the historical conditions in which a discovery of a mathematical law was made and study how individuals who are unaware of that discovery but have all the necessary knowledge are able to rediscover the original law (Qin & Simon, 1990).

An alternative approach to creative achievements involves a search for general patterns of development across exceptional individuals. This approach is well represented in this book. Simonton (chap. 8, this volume) has focused on time course of creative productivity in different domains during the life span and Howe (chap. 9, this volume) describes general characteristics of the childhoods and early careers of geniuses. Furthermore, the chapters by Richman, Gobet, Staszewski, and Simon (chap. 6, this volume) and Simonton (chap. 8, this volume) discuss related mechanisms to account for the generation of innovative ideas and creative products.

The major problem confronting the scientific investigation of extraordinary achievements and their creative nature is their uniqueness. By focusing instead on the highly replicable skills of exceptional performers (e.g., professional musicians) one can identify high (expert) levels of performance (Ericsson, Krampe, & Tesch-Römer, 1993) that correspond to phenomena that are more tractable to analysis with scientific methods.

EXPERT PERFORMANCE AS AN EMPIRICAL PHENOMENON

Empirical phenomena can be studied with scientific methods when they meet several criteria. The first and most important criterion is that the phenomenon occurs reliably in clearly specified situations with distinctive observable characteristics. Current findings on the superior performance of experts shows that it occurs reliably in many domains of expertise. Second, the phenomena should be reproducible under controlled conditions in the laboratory to allow for experimental variation and systematic observation of the mediating processes. Following Ericsson and Smith (1991), I show that many forms of expert performance can be reproduced and studied under laboratory conditions. Finally, the observed phenomena for a specific situation should be predictable and describable by objective absolute measurements. In some domains of expertise such as individual sport events (e.g., running the 100-meter dash), the performance is measured by absolute units of time. In other domains, performance is evaluated in relative terms through comparison with other contemporary performers (e.g., gymnastics). I propose methods for measuring and describing even these types of expert performance by absolute standards that are independent of the social and historical context of the studied expert performance. In the next three sections I discuss the following characteristics of expert performance: (a) its reliability, (b) its reproducibility in the laboratory, and (c) its measurement in absolute terms.

Reliability of Superior Expert Performance

There are many domains of expertise in which individuals consistently exhibit outstanding and superior performance under standardized testing conditions. In perceptual motor activities, such as individualized sports and typing, the outcome of performance can be directly measured. For competitive domains, such as tennis and chess, results from tournaments can be analyzed to rank individuals, often on an interval scale (Elo, 1978). The individual differences in recorded performance between the best and the least accomplished performers in these domains are among the largest reproducible differences in performance observed for normal adults.

Similar large differences in performance would be expected in many professional domains of expertise, such as medicine, auditing, physics, and business, in which a long period of preparatory education followed by an apprenticeship is required. Only after many years of further experience are some individuals recognized as experts in the domain. Surprisingly, the prediction that expert professionals exhibit clearly superior performance on relevant activities in the domain has not been well supported when tests are performed under standardized conditions. For example, experts in decision making and judgment have often failed to display superior accuracy of performance, especially for tasks involving prediction of future outcomes (Camerer & Johnson, 1991). Not all experts in computer programming (Doane, Pellegrino, & Klatzky, 1990) and physics (Reif & Allen, 1992) perform consistently at a superior level on representative tasks. Professional mathematicians' performance on algebra problems was not reliably superior to that of the best third of a sample of college students (Lewis, 1981). A particularly striking finding is reported by Wagner and Stanovich (chap. 7, this volume), who show that experts at speed reading can scan text rapidly but without any understanding of the content. The only validated aspect of the speed readers' skill is the high speed of turning pages.

The lack of general superiority of experts' performance has forced investigators to identify those activities that are central to experts' responsibilities. It is precisely at those activities that experts usually excel. However, expertise may never develop for some tasks, such as forecasting events. For example, it has been impossible to identify expert investors on the stock market that consistently outperform the average market indices (McClosky, 1990). There is reason to believe that the stock market is continuously adapting to publicly available information, thus making superior prediction virtually impossible in the absence of illegal information obtained from insiders. Unless one can identify at least one expert who exhibits reliably superior performance we do not know that such performance is possible.

In many types of professional expertise, most of the time is spent on relatively routine cases and complex difficult cases are encountered more rarely. In medicine, the superior diagnostic performance of experts has been readily demonstrated with difficult cases (Lesgold et al., 1988; Norman, Trott, Brooks, & Smith, 1994; Patel & Groen, 1991) even compared to medical residents with completed training and some work experience. On the other hand, evidence for performance differences with more routine medical cases has been more difficult to demonstrate (Norman, Coblentz, Brooks, & Babcook, 1992; Schmidt, Norman, & Boshuizen, 1990).

An important general finding has been that the number of years of experience in the domain is only weakly related to the level of attained performance (Ericsson, Krampe, & Tesch-Römer, 1993). Even more refined measures, such as the number of chess competitions attended (Charness, Krampe, & Mayr, chap. 2, this volume) and the number of baseball games played in the major leagues (Schulz, Musa, Staszewski, & Siegler, 1994), do not accurately predict performance in samples of skilled performers. However, the amount of time that children spend reading is related to various aspects of reading performance (Wagner & Stanovich, chap. 7, this volume).

In summary, reliably superior performance by experts is exhibited under conditions that capture the essence of expert performance of the domain, such as the conditions of competition for athletes or difficult cases in medical diagnosis for medical experts. In a later section, I explore whether insights into the necessary conditions for attaining superior performance might also explain those striking instances when experts do not outperform novices.

Reproducibility of Superior Expert Performance

In order to predict human behavior, one must take into account motivational factors. Fortunately, most expert performers face the problem of controlling motivation frequently when they have to perform at specific times during competitions or when medical doctors and other professionals have to respond to emergencies. Hence, expert performers learn to control all relevant (including motivational) factors necessary for attaining their superior performance at a time determined by external factors. This control over the elicitation of one's performance suggests that it would be possible to reproduce expert performance outside of its everyday-life context under controlled conditions in the laboratory.

In many domains of expertise, such as individual sports, the conditions for competition are already standardized for all participants and expert performance can be reproduced under similar test conditions in the laboratory. Studying expert performance in such domains as medical diagnosis and computer programming is more difficult because individual experts hardly ever encounter the same problem or cases in their normal professional practice. The standard procedure to measure expert performance in these domains has involved the collection of a set of standardized tasks. These tasks are then administered to experts and other professionals in the domain under controlled conditions that allow the researchers to study the processes mediating superior performance.

Many representative situations encountered by experts cannot be captured by fixed descriptions because they involve ongoing interaction with other experts or active participants. Patel, Kaufman, and Magder (chap. 5, this volume) review the large body of research on performance of teams of experts in complex contexts. They also propose a methodology for studying and analyzing interactions between experts in a team. A different approach to deal with the complexity of human interaction is to identify important goal-directed activities of a particular participant in the interaction (Ericsson & Smith, 1991). The relevant context of this activity and its goal can then be converted to a standardized task that can be presented to any expert responsible for that type of activity. This approach for studying expert performance has been successfully applied to chess, in which two opponents face each other during a match. Although the starting position in a chess match is always the same, the sequence of chess moves for two specific opponents is virtually never reproduced exactly. Because the index of skill in interactive domains is derived from competitions with many different opponents, it is reasonable to assume that the superior performance should be reflected in how well the performer responded to any of the individual situations within the interchange. For example, an expert chess player would be expected to select as good or better moves for each of the chess positions of a chess game (de Groot, 1946/1978). Hence, the standard method for studying expert chess players is to present them with an unfamiliar chess position from an actual chess game and ask them to select the best move. The quality of selected moves under such conditions is highly correlated with chess skill determined from tournaments (Charness, 1991).

By breaking up the interactive interchange into a sequence of its component situations, well-defined tasks can be identified that can be presented to expert performers in the corresponding domain. This methodology has been extended to analyses of expert performance within a team context. Helsen and Pauwels (1993) analyzed soccer matches in the World Cup to identify situations when a world-class soccer player got the ball and had to rapidly pass the ball to another player. Helson then carefully reconstructed the context for the situations using other soccer players so a video recording could be made from the exact view of the critical player. They then recreated the perceptual situation by projecting the video on a large screen in a gymnasium, and at the appropriate time the subject was passed a real soccer ball and the speed and accuracy of the subject's actions were recorded. Under those conditions Helsen and Pauwels (1993) were able to establish superior performance of soccer experts compared to less accomplished soccer players. How much context with prior interchanges between the players needs to be presented before the critical test situation and the degree of perceptual fidelity required raise empirical questions concerning the necessary conditions for capturing a particular type of expert performance?

It is important that each selected situation or task is associated with a correct or consensually established best action that can be objectively specified. This is not typically a problem because the investigators have access to more information and more time to analyze the situation than the participating experts. However, in some domains, such as auditing (Bedard & Chi, 1993), "experts" do not agree about the correct judgment of representative cases, which virtually precludes efforts to identify tasks measuring any associated performance.

In summary, expert performance can be reproduced in many domains for a collection of standardized tasks with consensually established best responses. Once the superior performance of experts can be reliably reproduced in the laboratory, its mediating mechanisms can be described and identified by process-tracing methodology and traditional experimental methods.

Absolute or Relative Measures of Expert Performance

Exceptional achievement and performance is a social phenomenon and virtually every major domain of expertise is associated with a hierarchical organization based on social criteria. Even for sports events, where performance is measured objectively and record-breaking performance is recorded, evaluation is primarily relative and the individual with the best performance during the final event of a given competition is considered the winner. More generally, the level of a performer is typically described by the appropriate level of competitions attended (e.g., club, district, national, and international). The number of individuals that are allowed to compete at a given level of competition becomes smaller as the level increases. At the highest level there is only a single world champion. In order to maintain this hierarchical structure, relative standards are imposed to determine the

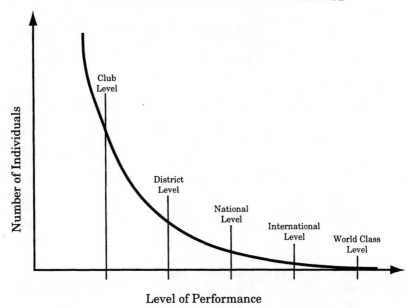

FIG. 1.1. The relation between a given level of competition and the number of active individuals at that level.

performance requirements for each level of competition (see Fig. 1.1 for an illustration).

The social organization of a domain, based on its relative levels of performance, could be almost independent of the absolute levels of performance. The absolute level of performance can substantially increase (or decrease) over historical time. In interactive abilities, such as tennis and chess, it is possible that general increases in knowledge and the speed of execution may essentially go unnoticed as expert performers must adapt to changes in the performance of their opponents. This lability in performance over historical time means that a general theory of expert performance cannot rely on relative measures of performance. Only a theory based on absolute levels of performance for a collection of specific tasks can remain invariant over historical changes in the level and structure of expert performance. Fortunately, the laboratory tasks that I discussed earlier provide data on absolute levels of expert performance.

Summary

Superior expert performance is a reliable phenomenon that can in many instances be captured by representative tasks under controlled laboratory conditions. By relying on tasks with consensually established best responses, it is possible to describe and measure performance in absolute and objective terms. The proposed methodology is an extension of the standard practices of performance measurement established as the preferred scientific procedure for data collection during a century of laboratory research in psychology (Ericsson & Hastie, 1994).

SOURCES OF DATA ON EXPERT PERFORMANCE AND ITS ACQUISITION

The study of expert performance is challenging because of the inherent complexity of the associated performance—especially when one is interested in high levels of performance in a domain. The small number of individuals performing at these levels makes it difficult to find subjects who are able and willing to participate in extended interviews and laboratory studies. Hence availability of relevant information has been an important determiner for how expert performance has been studied. The remainder of this chapter is organized around three approaches to the study of expert and exceptional performance. These approaches draw on different types of data but reach consistent conclusions.

The first approach relies primarily on available public information about the highest level of performance to infer general characteristics about its nature and acquisition. Evidence on the age of peak performance, the duration of necessary preparation for international-level performance, and the gradual increase of elite performance as a function of preparation will be reviewed. An analysis of absolute levels of performance will show significant increases over historical time. In some domains, performance at the world-class level at a given time, qualifies as club or district level performance at a later date, and thus is attained by a fairly large proportion of the individuals actively competing in the domain.

The second approach is based on studies of expert performance captured in the laboratory. I briefly summarize some of the general findings on how superior expert performance is mediated by acquired mechanisms. The final approach focuses on how expert performance is acquired during the long period of necessary preparation. The concept of deliberate practice (Ericsson, Krampe, & Tesch-Römer, 1993) is discussed and shown to account for individual differences in adult expert performance as well as for many physiological characteristics distinguishing elite performers.

Historical Data on the Highest Levels of Performance

Several important characteristics of expert performance and its development have been discovered through the analysis of publicly available records. When we restrict ourselves to extreme instances of expert performance in traditional domains, these generalizable characteristics have become apparent.

Age and Peak Performance

The highest levels of performance are attained by individuals with higher frequency at particular ages (Lehman, 1953). In vigorous sports, the age distributions for peak performance are remarkably narrow and centered in the 20s with systematic differences between various types of sports (Schulz & Curnow, 1988) as well as for different activities within a sport (Schulz et al., 1994). Age distributions for the highest achievements in fine motor skills and even predominantly cognitive activities, such as chess (Elo, 1965), are much more variable with the highest frequency of occurrence typically in the 30s (Charness & Bosman, 1990; Lehman, 1953).

The age distribution for making outstanding creative contributions to arts and science are similar with their peaks during the individuals' 30s and 40s (Lehman, 1953; Simonton, chap. 8, this volume). The outstanding achievements in the arts and science require uniqueness and creativity that make them fall outside the limits of reproducible expert performance. However, in his theory of creative expertise, Simonton (chap. 8, this volume) establishes a link between creative achievement and productivity (reproducible performance) in the same domain. He shows that the ratio between outstanding creative achievements and the total number of achievements, such as publications for scientists, is a small fraction. Hence, the probability for a given publication to report a major innovation is small and constant across different time periods within an individual's career as well as between the careers of different individuals. Given the unpredictable nature of major innovations, Simonton (chap. 8, this volume) argues that it is, thus, not possible to increase the relative proportion of innovations among the total number of publications. However, the probability that at least one of the publications written during a career of given scientists is an innovation can be influenced by the scientist by increasing his or her total number of publications. Creative expertise is thus closely connected to reproducible performance for completing papers that meet the minimal standards for publication. Simonton shows that the general shape of the productivity curve is invariant across domains and shows increasing productivity during the first decades within the domain, followed by a decline in productivity. The increases in productivity during the first phase of creative expertise are consistent with the acquisition of relevant skills and knowledge that are necessary to reliably complete publishable projects. In his commentary, Holmes (chap. 12, this volume) describes the nature of the skill development in the careers of eminent scientists.

In sum, peak performance in nonvigorous domains is typically attained over a decade later than completed physical maturation. The difference is smaller for vigorous sports where peak performance is attained on the average about 5 years after physical maturation. This discrepancy in the age of full biological maturation and that of peak performance implicates an important role of preparation.

The 10-Year Rule of Necessary Preparation

A more direct claim about the necessity for intense preparation was made by Simon and Chase (1973). They found that about 10 years of preparation was necessary to attain an international level of chess skill and they suggested similar prerequisites in other domains. Subsequent studies (Bloom, 1985a) have found support for the generalizability for the 10-year rule in several different domains, including vigorous sports. Even chess prodigies, such as Bobby Fischer, needed a preparation period of 9 years (Ericsson, Krampe, & Tesch-Römer, 1993). According to this rule, not even the most "talented" individuals can attain international performance[1] in less than about 10 years of preparation, whereas the vast majority of international-level performers have spent considerably longer. The necessity of 10 years of preparation for attaining very high levels of performance in a domain has been supported by recent research and reviews (Charness et al., chap. 2, this volume; Ericsson, Krampe, & Tesch-Römer, 1993; Patel et al., chap. 5, this volume; Richman et al., chap. 6, this volume; Simonton, chap. 8, this volume; Starkes, Deakin, Allard, Hodges, & Hayes, chap. 3, this volume). This claim has occasionally been misconstrued to mean that 10 years of relevant experience is sufficient to be considered an expert. However, as was shown earlier in this chapter, mere amount of experience is only a weak predictor of an individual's level of performance in a domain and thus 10 years of experience in a domain does not guarantee that expert performance is attained.

A critical role of preparation can be inferred from the gradual increases in performance as a function of the number of years of instruction and serious study found in several domains (Ericsson, Krampe, & Tesch-Römer, 1993). Figure 1.2 illustrates the general shape of the relation between performance and preparation.

Data from the measurement of performance in music (Watkins, 1942) and sports (Ericsson, 1990; Schulz et al., 1994) are consistent with the functional relation between performance and years of preparation shown in Fig. 1.2. Elo (1978) found similar relations between chess ratings and age for three groups of elite chess players that differed in their final level of attained chess performance. Although ratings of chess skill are relative measures of performance, it is reasonable to assume that the absolute level of chess performance remain reasonably stable over shorter time periods such as the few decades during which most players remain active.

Because most expert performers started their training at early ages, increases of performance as function of age could simply be due to physical maturation. The evidence clearly refutes that view if we exclude sport

---

[1]It is possible for child prodigies to attain an international level of performance relative to other children of comparable age. However, here we are only considering international levels of the very best performers, who are nearly always adults.

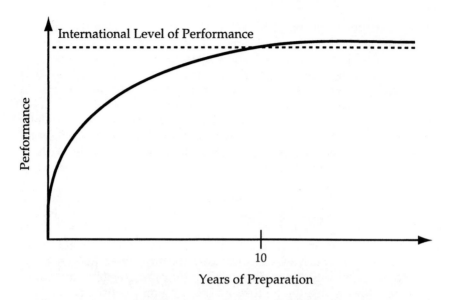

FIG. 1.2. A schematic illustration of the general form of the relation between attained performance as a function of the number of years of serious preparation. The international level of performance is indicated by the dashed line.

performances, where sufficient physical size and height are necessary for the highest levels of performance. In some domains, such as chess (Chi, 1978) and badminton (Abernethy, 1988), children and adolescents attain high levels of performance even when evaluated by adult standards. When the performance of these children and adolescents is analyzed, it is found to be mediated by the same type of acquired domain-specific skills that characterize the performance of adults at the same expert level. Further-more, the time to attain an international level in chess still exceeds 10 years even for individuals starting to play chess late between ages 11 and 17 (Krogius, 1976). Although late starters require a shorter period, on the average, to attain international status in chess than early starters, there is a reliable positive correlation between starting age and age for attaining the international level (Ericsson, Krampe, & Tesch-Römer, 1993).

Historical Development of Expert Performance

There can be no argument about the fact that the specific activities leading to outstanding performance in a domain have changed over his-torical time. The criteria for new and creative contributions in the sciences and the arts clearly rules out reproduction of earlier achievements. In-creases in relevant knowledge and prerequisite techniques have led to increased specialization in the sciences as well as the arts, such as music (Ericsson & Lehmann, 1994b). Even in domains such as chess, knowledge of what constitutes the best chess move, especially for different sequences of opening moves, has increased substantially (Charness, 1991).

In sports, objective measures show a dramatic increase in performance during this century—in some cases the world records have improved by around 50% (Schulz & Curnow, 1988). This is even true in running and swimming, where changes in equipment and rules have been minor or even negligible. The changing standards of elite athletic performance over time imply that world-class performances exhibited at the first Olympic Games are, in some events such as the marathon, attained by thousands of amateur athletes today (Ericsson, Krampe, & Tesch-Römer, 1993).

In music, Ericsson and Lehmann (1994b) found evidence that the requirements for expert performance have increased over time. By examining the recommended sequencing of piano instruction by music academies and music curricula, they found that more recently introduced techniques, such as complex polyrhythms, were judged to be more complex and to demand more years of prerequisite piano study than techniques with a longer history. Drawing on published ratings of difficulty of piano sonatas, they found a clear increase in the difficulty of such compositions over the time period from 1750 (Haydn) to 1825 (Schubert). Ericsson, Krampe, and Tesch-Römer (1993) found cases where contemporary musicians deemed new or composed music pieces to be unplayable, but today these same pieces are considered part of the standard repertoire.

In more recently introduced domains, the rapid increases in complexity over time are even more striking. In athletic events such as ice skating, platform diving, and gymnastics, the complexity and difficulty of the movement sequences have continually increased. The difficulty level of former world champions' movement sequences match today's difficulty standards at the district or national level. By contrast, the complexity of some domains such as mountain climbing cannot be similarly increased. Initially mountain climbers developed equipment and discovered accessible paths to climb challenging mountains. With increases in skill it was difficult to find sufficient challenge even on climbs involving more difficult paths. To deal with this problem, mountain climbers would deliberately avoid using helpful equipment and/or measure the time necessary to complete a given climb (Mitchell, 1983).

Summary

An analysis of publicly available information about the highest level of performance shows that peak performance is attained many years after physical maturity is reached—even in most types of sports. Evidence from several domains shows that elite performance is attained gradually and around 10 years of intense preparation are necessary to attain international-level performance in traditional domains. When performance is evaluated using absolute standards, significant increases in maximal performance over historical time are observed, even in traditional domains. The best performances of a time period are only outstanding relative to the level of other performances of that time and subsequent increases in most types of performance allow many individuals to match and even surpass those past levels.

The Laboratory Study of Mechanisms Mediating Superior Expert Performance

A different approach to the study of expert performance focuses on the mechanisms responsible for the consistently superior performance of experts on representative tasks in their domain of expertise. By instructing experts to perform these tasks under laboratory conditions, investigators have been able to reproduce many types of superior expert performance and study its mediating cognitive mechanisms by process tracing and experimental methods.

Here, the principal scientific issues concern how the superior performance of experts can be explained. These theoretical issues can be addressed without the virtually impossible project of attaining a complete description of all aspects of all different experts' performance-related characteristics and knowledge. The proposed approach involves an analysis of superior expert performance on a representative sample of tasks from a very large pool of all potential tasks defining expertise in a given domain (Ericsson & Smith, 1991). When the selected tasks are well-defined, it is possible to conduct a task analysis specifying possible general and specific methods to complete the tasks. Based on an analysis of collected verbal reports and other process-tracing data most of the alternative theoretical accounts can be rejected (Ericsson & Simon, 1993), leaving a few plausible general mechanisms that can account for the observed superior performance across all the studied tasks in the representative sample from the population.

There are several methodological challenges facing investigators of expert performance. As the highest levels of performance should provide the most difficult data to account for, one should, in most cases, strive to recruit the best available performers in the domain. However, the small number of these performers (who live all over the world) and their busy schedules make it difficult to enroll them in experiments. Hence at very high levels of performance, even very successful investigators may only be able to study a relatively small number of subjects for a couple of hours. Under these conditions it is particularly important that as much information as possible can be extracted about the processes mediating the experts' superior performance. Following de Groot (1946/1978), many investigators instruct their experts to think aloud while generating their solutions to the problem. An analysis of this record of the mediating processes compared against theoretical alternatives specified by a task analysis is a powerful tool to eliminate theoretical proposals for the mediating mechanisms (Ericsson & Simon, 1993).

The prospects of a general theory of expert performance are based on the assumption that the highly diverse forms of superior performance can be theoretically explained by a limited number of general mechanisms. The establishment of the study of expertise and expert performance as an important field is directly linked to the theoretical proposal of de Groot (1946/1978) and Chase and Simon (1973) of a general mechanism underlying expert performance across many different domains. Hence I briefly summarize this proposal and some of its supporting empirical evidence before discussing how it can be extended to accommodate more recent evidence.

The Original Mechanism Proposed by de Groot and Chase and Simon

At the time de Groot (1946/1978) started his research on chess expertise, the prevailing view was that chess experts' superior performance was due to their greater intellectual capacity for extensive search for alternative chess moves. However, de Groot (1946/1978) found that world-class chess players were able to access a couple of superior alternative chess moves during their initial perception of the chess position, which implied pattern-based retrieval from memory rather than the results of an extensive search. In their theory of expertise Chase and Simon (1973; Simon & Chase, 1973) showed how pattern-based retrieval could account for superior selection of chess moves and memory for chess positions without violating general limits of human information processing (Newell & Simon, 1972). Simon and Chase (1973) argued that very high levels of chess performance were mediated by a very large number of patterns (over 10,000) that served as retrieval cues to access appropriate chess moves for the corresponding chess positions. Recent estimates of the number of acquired patterns (chunks) are much larger and range between 100,000 and a couple of million (Richman et al., chap. 6, this volume).

Chase and Simon (1973) proposed that expert performance in "any skilled task (e.g., football, music)" (p. 279) was the result of vast amounts of knowledge and pattern-based retrieval acquired over many years of experience in the associated domain. Research on solving textbook problems in physics (Larkin, McDermott, Simon, & Simon, 1980; Simon & Simon, 1978) showed that novices (i.e., beginners with all the necessary knowledge) worked backward from the statement of the presented problem to identify relevant formulas, which, in turn, guided the calculations. In contrast, physics experts retrieved a solution plan as part of the initial comprehension of the problem. Subsequently, Chi, Glaser, and Rees (1982) showed that physics experts not only had more knowledge but their knowledge was better organized and allowed them to represent physics problems in terms of the deeper theoretical principles. Novices' representations, however, were based on the presence of surface elements, such as a pulley or an inclined plane.

This conception of expertise is consistent with theories of skill acquisition (Anderson, 1983; Fitts & Posner, 1967), based on the assumption that knowledge is first acquired and then organized into procedures for responding to encountered situations. According to these theories, practice allows appropriate actions to be accessed automatically through pattern-based retrieval. An elegant description of the structure of expert performance from this theoretical perspective is given by Richman et al. (chap. 6, this volume). They also discuss recent extensions of this theoretical model to account for a broader range of empirical phenomena associated with expert performance, which I turn to next.

Subsequent Extensions of the Original Proposal

Contrary to common expectations based on models of skill acquisition (Anderson, 1983; Fitts & Posner, 1967), high-level expert performance does not appear to be mediated solely by automated reactions. In fact, when experts are unexpectedly asked to recall information about a completed task, their memory is more accurate and complete than that of novices and less accomplished individuals in the same domain (see Ericsson & Kintsch, 1995, for a review). As part of their normal cognitive processing, experts have been found to generate a complex representation of the encountered situation, where information about the context is integrated with knowledge to allow selection of actions as well as evaluation, checking, and reasoning about alternative actions. Given that the relevant evidence has been reviewed elsewhere (Ericsson & Kintsch, 1995; Ericsson & Lehmann, 1996), I only summarize the results with a few supporting examples. The research on expertise was pioneered in the domain of chess and this has remained the primary testing ground for theories of expert performance. Hence I start by discussing evidence from the domain of chess.

Chess. There has been no reason to question de Groot's (1946/1978) basic finding that with increasing chess skill, subjects are able to rapidly access a small number of chess moves of increasingly higher quality. However, Chase and Simon's (1973) theory of the mechanism for generation of chess moves appears to have been too simple. Their mechanism was based on direct retrieval of relevant moves cued by perceived patterns of chess position stored only in short-term memory (STM). Their assumption that storage of generated products in long-term memory (LTM) is not possible during a brief (5-second) presentation has been rejected for expert performance in chess and other domains (Chase & Ericsson, 1982; see Ericsson & Kintsch, 1995, for a review). Recently, Cooke, Atlas, Lane, and Berger (1993) and Gobet and Simon (1995) found that highly skilled chess players can recall information from up to nine chess positions that have been presented rapidly one after the other without pauses.

Once one accepts storage in LTM during expert performance, one can integrate the mechanism for move generation with a number of other abilities of chess experts that Chase and Simon (1973) attributed to a different mechanism, "the mind's eye." From think-aloud protocols on the process of selecting the best move for an unfamiliar chess position, investigators have found that the depth of search in evaluating sequences increases with chess skill (Charness, 1981b; Gruber, 1991) up to the level of chess experts (Charness, 1989; de Groot, 1946/1978). Similar evidence on the ability to mentally represent chess positions comes from research showing that chess masters can play blindfold chess (without seeing an external chess board) at a level relatively close to their normal ability (Ericsson & Oliver, summarized in Ericsson & Staszewski, 1989; Holding, 1985; Koltanowski, 1985). Laboratory studies show that chess masters are able to play chess games mentally when the corresponding sequence of chess moves is read to them. The mental representation of the chess positions within the chess game is accurate because if the reading of moves is stopped, the chess masters are able to rapidly and correctly retrieve any information about the chess position corresponding to that point in the chess game (Ericsson & Staszewski, 1989). Saariluoma (1991) showed that an international chess master could mentally play out six different chess games simultaneously when the corresponding chess moves were presented on a computer screen. The capacity to represent chess positions mentally in a flexible and accessible manner suggests an acquired memory skill mediated by retrieval structures (Ericsson & Staszewski, 1989) and integrated higher level representations (Ericsson & Kintsch, 1995).

The best evidence for retrieval structures mediating storage of the locations of individual chess pieces on a chess board is reported by Saariluoma (1989). In typical tests of chess memory, a chess position is presented visually and configurations of related chess pieces can be recognized immediately. Instead, Saariluoma (1989) presented the equivalent information about the chess position verbally as a list of locations for each piece in the chess position. When a chess configuration is presented in this manner, the successful recall of the chess masters implies that they can commit the location of some of the individual chess pieces to memory without the aid of familiar relations and patterns. Chess masters could even recall a single randomly arranged chess position when it was presented in this manner. However, when several different random chess positions were presented as lists, one after the other, subsequent recall was drastically reduced. In contrast, chess masters were able to recall several regular positions from chess games under these conditions. Ericsson and Kintsch (1995) proposed that due to proactive interference only a single arrangement of chess pieces can be successfully stored in the retrieval structure. However, with a regular chess position it is possible to recode the entire position into a single integrated meaningful representation once all of the pieces have been presented. Once this recoding is completed, the retrieval structure can be used again for storage of the locations of individual pieces and patterns in a subsequently presented chess position.

The idea of two modes of representing a chess position is also consistent with the demands of search and evaluation. When a chess position is represented in memory by the retrieval structure, the chess player can explore alternative moves freely in a manner similar to having the chess position externally available. If chess positions were only represented in a highly interpreted format, then it is unclear how highly skilled chess players routinely discover new and better moves after additional search (de Groot, 1946/1978; Saariluoma, 1990, 1992).

In sum, this conception of highly skilled chess playing is consistent with the rapid access of superior chess moves that can, if necessary, be played without delay. With more available time, alternative moves can be compared and evaluated to select the best one. For highly skilled chess players it is not so much alternative moves that are accessed and compared but complete higher level approaches with associated goals and general methods (Saariluoma, 1990, 1992). Occasionally during the search and systematic evaluation of consequences of alternatives, even better chess moves and approaches can be uncovered. The highest level of chess skill appears to be attained by increasing the quality of moves through safeguards against omissions and errors.

Expert Performance in Other Domains. Consistent with Simon and Chase's (1973) argument that chess is a suitable domain to identify general mechanisms, evidence for long-term working memory (LT-WM) has been found in many other domains. However, the particular representation and its associated selective storage are closely adapted to the specific retrieval demands of the corresponding activity (Ericsson & Kintsch, 1995). In medicine (Boshuizen & Schmidt, 1992; Patel, Arocha, & Kaufman, 1994; Schmidt & Boshuizen, 1993), experts encode information about patients into a higher level representation that allows them to reason about diagnostic alternatives without the need to reinterpret basic facts. Patel et al. (chap. 5, this volume) give a detailed description of the mediating representations and cognitive processes in medical diagnosis. Similar mechanisms can also account for increased planning by experts in bridge (Charness, 1989) and in snooker (a form of billiards studied by Abernethy, Neal, & Koning, 1994).

There is substantial evidence from perceptual-motor expertise in sports that elite athletes are able to extract and recall more information after brief exposures to representative game situations (Allard & Starkes, 1991). These data suggest that elite athletes are able to internally represent complex game situations that would allow them to predict and anticipate future actions of opponents and thus select more appropriate actions. When Helsen and Pauwels (1993) recreated standardized situations from world-class soccer games, they found that expert soccer players selected more appropriate actions and were able to generate their actions faster. In racquet sports, elite athletes have been found to better anticipate the outcomes of opponents' actions, even before opponents' racquets have made contact with the ball or birdie (Abernethy, 1991). The ability to predict future events based on cues available in advance allows the experts to prepare their actions and thus essentially circumvent the need for rapid immediate reactions in many game situations. The same type of anticipatory preparation of future movements has been well documented in expert typing (Salthouse, 1991) and expert sight-reading of music (Sloboda, 1985). Similarly, Beek (1989) showed that in successful juggling, the actions of throwing the balls are constantly adjusted to maintain a steady state. The adjustment for each ball is based on information obtained earlier about the ball's deviation from its desired location at the apex of its most recent trajectory.

In conclusion, the goal of this overview has been to identify characteristics of expert performance that go beyond pattern-based automatic retrieval of appropriate actions. Contrary to many complex activities in everyday life that are highly automated, such as driving a car, experts appear to acquire and preserve highly adapted representations that aid in planning, prediction, and evaluation. These representations are an integral part of the acquired memory skills (Ericsson & Kintsch, 1995) that allow the experts to increase the functional capacity of working memory for domain-specific information by storage in LTM. In a later section, I argue that these mechanisms may be critical in supporting further improvements of performance. The traditional theories of skill acquisition assume that all the relevant knowledge is available early on and subsequent training primarily improves the efficiency of producing the appropriate actions. An extension of this type of account to expert performance has difficulty explaining increased accuracy in the selection of actions and the emergence of more complex mediating internal representations as reviewed earlier. In its standard form, the original account also has difficulty explaining improved domain-specific perceptual processing where different perceptual features and input are extracted, as well as improved flexibility and control of motor performance (see Ericsson & Lehmann, 1996, for a review). Today, a comprehensive theory appears out of reach, and my main conclusion is that expert performance offers a rich set of phenomena showing that extreme adaptations to task constraints in expert performance are mediated by more complex and diverse mechanisms than has been commonly believed.

The Study of the Acquisition of Expert Performance

In the first section of this chapter, I discussed evidence showing that peak performance was acquired after a 10-year period of intense preparation. The laboratory analyses of expert performance revealed many complex mechanisms reflecting extreme adaptation to the task demands in the respective domains of expertise. In this section, I focus on more detailed evidence regarding the nature and structure of the preparatory activities that appear necessary to attain the highest levels of performance in a given domain. In the development of expert performance it is possible to distinguish several stages in which the involvement in the domain progressively increases (Bloom, 1985b). After a discussion of these stages, I discuss different types of activities in a domain and identify those that are most relevant for improvement of performance (deliberate practice). Finally, I reconsider some of the evidence originally proposed to support innate endowment (talent) and show that it appears to reflect the results of practice and extended intense physical training.

Stages in the Development of Elite Performance

In their pioneering research, Bloom (1985a) and his colleagues were able to identify a uniform progression through several stages for the development of international-level performance in several different domains of expertise. Based on interviews with elite performers and their parents and teachers, Bloom (1985b) found that future elite performers were typically exposed to the domain initially under playful conditions as children (see

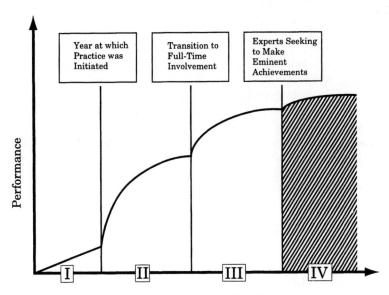

Time Since Introduction to the Domain

FIG. 1.3. Three phases of development of expert performance followed by a qualitatively different fourth phase of efforts to go beyond the available knowledge of one's teachers toward an individual creative contribution to the domain. From " Can we create gifted people?" by K. A. Ericsson, R. T. Krampe, & S. Heizmann (1993) in *The origins and development of high ability* (pp. 222–249), Chichester, UK: Wiley. Copyright © 1993 by Ciba Foundation. Adapted by permission.

Stage I in Fig. 1.3). After some time, the child would become interested and often show some promise (compared to other children in the same local environment) and parents would arrange for instruction by a teacher or coach who was skilled in working with children. During this stage (Stage II), parents helped the children to establish regular practice habits and provided enthusiastic support and encouragement in response to improvements. With further increases in performance, better qualified teachers and coaches were sought and the amount of daily practice was typically slowly increased. At some point, normally in the early or midteens, future elite performers in music and sports made a major commitment toward reaching the top level in their domain (see Stage III in Fig. 1.3). This was often associated with seeking out a master teacher and optimal training conditions, which sometimes required the family to move to a different geographical location. Across many different domains, Bloom (1985b) found that nearly all international-level performers had worked with coaches or teachers that had either themselves reached that level of performance or had instructed other students who had attained that level. Ericsson, Krampe, and Tesch-Römer (1993) suggested that in the development of elite performers one can identify a final stage (IV). At the beginning of this stage, the individuals have already mastered most of what their teachers or coaches are able to teach them and they start to search for their own innovative contribution to the domain. During this final stage, some of the experts are able to produce outstanding creative achievements by processes discussed by Richman et al. (chap. 6, this volume) and Simonton (chap. 8, this volume).

During the first three stages, the children or adolescents depend on their parents for emotional and most importantly for logistic and monetary support. It is estimated that the additional direct cost per year to develop an elite performer in some sports may exceed $5,000 (Chambliss, 1988). Furthermore, it is nearly a full-time job to help many types of future elite performers by, for example, driving to and from practice and to competitions during the weekend. The demands on the family's resources appear to be so great that Bloom (1985b) found only one elite performer per family in their sample.

Individual Differences in Expert Performance: The Role of Deliberate Practice

Even when individuals have access to a similar training environment, large individual differences in performance are still often observed. Furthermore, amount of experience in a domain is often a weak predictor of performance. Rather than accepting these facts as evidence for innate differences in ability (i.e., talent), Ericsson, Krampe, and Tesch-Römer (1993) tried to identify those training activities that would be most closely related to improvements in performance. Based on a review of a century of laboratory studies of learning and skill acquisition, Ericsson, Krampe, and Tesch-Römer (1993) concluded that the most effective learning requires a well-defined task with an appropriate difficulty level for the particular individual, informative feedback, and opportunities for repetition and corrections of errors. When all these elements are present they used the term *deliberate practice* to characterize training activities.

When these criteria are applied to the most common activities in most domains of expertise, one finds that the vast majority of active individuals in popular domains, such as tennis and golf, spend very little, if any, time on deliberate practice. Most of the time is spent on playful interaction, where the primary goal is inherent enjoyment of the activity. For example, consider someone who plays tennis and misses a backhand volley. There might be several intervening tennis matches before another similar opportunity for this shot emerges, and even then the opportunity cannot be anticipated and the chance for another miss remains high. In contrast, a tennis coach could give the individual several hundred opportunities to gradually perfect this shot in a single tennis lesson. During competitions and in work activities, the goal is to reliably produce the best possible performance and quality products. To give their best performance in competitions and work activities, individuals rely on previously well-entrenched methods rather than exploring new methods with unknown reliability. Although work activities offer some opportunities for learning, they are far from optimal for improving performance. As a further recognition of the difference between work and effective learning, employees are typically relieved of their work obligations during training and continued education.

Modern education in many domains of expertise incorporates deliberate practice. A skilled teacher designs training tasks adapted to the needs and skills of a particular student, who then goes off to practice these tasks alone to acquire the skills one by one. The student then returns to the teacher for an evaluation of performance and assignments for corrections and new tasks.

In order to identify deliberate practice activities among expert musicians, Ericsson, Krampe, and Tesch-Römer (1993) interviewed musicians and music teachers to distinguish different types of music-related activities. A group of 30 expert-level music students were then asked to rate the different activities in terms of their relevance for improvement of music performance, inherent enjoyment, and the amount of effort required. Among these activities, several were judged to be highly relevant to improvement of music performance, such as practice alone and lessons with a music teacher. Practice alone, however, was the only relevant frequent activity that the musicians could control the duration of. Furthermore, practice alone is a training activity, where the goals and training tasks are primarily designed and monitored by a supervising teacher, and thus meets the criteria for deliberate practice.

Ericsson, Krampe, and Tesch-Römer's (1993) framework for the acquisition of expert performance through deliberate practice makes several predictions. First, the quantity and quality of deliberate practice is related to the attained level of performance. I discuss more detailed aspects of quality of deliberate practice in a subsequent section of this chapter and here primarily focus on the amount of deliberate practice accumulated during the development of expert performance. The second prediction concerns the characteristics of deliberate practice, such as effort and concentration, that differentiate it from many other domain-related activities, such as playful interaction. Finally, I review evidence suggesting that people do not engage in deliberate practice because they enjoy it but because they are intent on improving their performance.

Amount of Deliberate Practice and Attained Level of Performance.

Ericsson, Krampe, and Tesch-Römer (1993) collected detailed diaries of the daily activities of expert-level musicians who had studied music for over 10 years. They found reliable differences in the weekly amount of practice alone (deliberate practice), but not in the total amount of music-related activity (experience). The expert musicians with the higher levels of performance practiced alone for about 25 hours per week, three times more than the less accomplished expert musicians. For comparison, they found that amateur musicians of the same age practiced less than 2 hours per week, which is less than 10% of the amount for the best group of expert musicians.

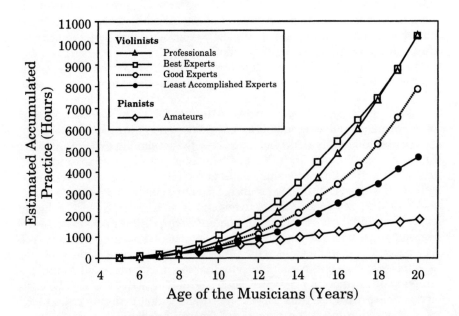

FIG. 1.4. Estimated amount of time for practice-alone as a function of age for the middle-aged (professional) violinists (triangles), the best expert violinists (squares), the good expert violinists (empty circles), the least accomplished expert violinists (filled circles) and amateur pianists (diamonds). From "The role of deliberate practice in the acquisition of expert performance," by K. A. Ericsson, R. T. Krampe & C. Tesch-Römer (1993), *Psychological Review, 100*(3), p. 379 and p. 384.
Copyright © 1993 by American Psychological Association. Adapted with permission.

The expert musicians practiced, on the average, the same amount every day including weekends. Estimates of average weekly practice for the current year, made prior to the diary study, were closely related to the amount of practice during the diary week, although the estimates were somewhat inflated. From estimates of amount of weekly practice for each year, Ericsson, Krampe, and Tesch-Römer (1993) computed the amount of accumulated deliberate practice at a given age. Figure 1.4 shows the average amounts for four groups of expert violinists differing in the attained level of violin performance along with a group of amateur pianists. At age 20, the two best groups of violinists had spent over 10,000 hours on deliberate practice. The group of expert violinists with an intermediate level expert performance had practiced on the average about 8,000 hours, and the least accomplished group of expert violinists only about 5,000 hours. For comparison, the group of amateur pianists averaged only about 2,000 hours of accumulated deliberate practice at that age. Similar relations between the amount of deliberate practice and the attained level of expert performance are reported in this volume by Starkes et al. (chap. 3), Charness et al. (chap. 2), and Sloboda (chap. 4).

In a review of estimates of deliberate practice in many domains, Ericsson, Krampe, and Tesch-Römer (1993) found a consistent patterns of results—the higher the level of attained performance, the larger amount of practice. Some studies showed a higher weekly amount of practice, others showed that the best performers started practice at younger ages. A number of studies showed that world-class athletes and musicians often started practice as young as 4 to 5 years old. The most parsimonious account of these results is that the amount of accumulated practice is monotonically related to the attained level of expert performance (Ericsson & Charness, 1994). Recent studies have shown that deliberate practice is not only important for the acquisition of expert performance but also for its maintenance. Older experts' levels of performance are correlated with their recent levels of deliberate practice in music (Krampe, 1994; Krampe & Ericsson, in press) and in chess (Charness et al., chap. 2, this volume).

Distinctive Characteristics of Deliberate Practice.   Expert performers engage in several types of activities for longer periods of time than less accomplished performers. For these activities, there will be a correlation between the amounts of time spent by individuals in the domain and their level of performance. For example, the amount of travel time to public performances and international competitions increases with level of performance, yet nobody would seriously argue that these activities cause the superior performance. Sternberg (chap. 15, this volume) and Shiffrin (chap. 14, this volume) raise the possibility that the correlations between amount of deliberate practice and attained performance might be similar and, thus, not reflect a causal relation. However, unlike most other activities, the amount of deliberate practice has been shown to lead to lawful improvements of performance, according to the power law, in a wide range of laboratory tasks with random samples of subjects (Anderson, 1982; Newell & Rosenbloom, 1981). The same type of mathematical relationship between attained level of performance and the amount of accumulated practice by expert performers has been found in music (Ericsson, Krampe, & Tesch-Römer, 1993) and chess (Charness et al., chap. 2, this volume).

A review of laboratory studies of skill acquisition by Ericsson, Krampe, and Tesch-Römer (1993) also shows that the duration of training sessions has to be limited in order for subjects to attain maximum improvement. Similarly they found that expert musicians rated practice alone as effortful. Starkes et al. (chap. 3, this volume) make the useful suggestion that one should differentiate physical effort and mental concentration for training activities in sports. They found that concentration is the most essential aspect of deliberate practice. Deliberate practice in music is consistent with the critical role of concentration. Master teachers (Auer, 1921; Galamian, 1962) argue that full concentration is essential and that when it wanes the musician should rest, because practice without full concentration may actually impair rather improve performance (Seashore, 1938/1967).

An analysis of the duration of practice sessions (extracted from the diaries of the expert musicians) is consistent with the requirement of concentration. After about an hour of practice, the experts take a break and rest. The best musicians also prefer practice in the morning when the ability to perform complex cognitive activities has been found to be the highest (Folkard & Monk, 1985). There is also indirect evidence for the effortfulness of concentration through the additional need for rest among expert performers. Ericsson, Krampe, and Tesch-Römer (1993) found that the higher levels of practice were associated with longer duration of sleep, typically in the form of afternoon naps. This pattern of napping and resting has also been found in other domains of expertise, such as sports. Furthermore, Ericsson, Krampe, and Tesch-Römer (1993) found that across a wide range of domains, expert performers only engage in about 4 hours of deliberate practice on a daily basis for extended periods. When this level is exceeded the quality of practice appears to deteriorate and the individuals will eventually experience fatigue and exhaustion. Finally, the amount of daily deliberate practice is not constant across the development of expert performance. At the commencement of practice in a domain, the weekly amount of practice is small and it is slowly increased to the maximal levels. For musicians, the relation between amount of weekly practice and age is strong (Ericsson, Krampe, & Tesch-Römer, 1993) and could be due to maturational factors. However, Starkes et al. (chap. 3, this volume) found the same increases in the amount of practice for each year of engagement in sports, where the starting ages are much older. Hence, the increase in the amount of daily practice might reflect slow adaptations to the demands of concentration during practice that are relatively independent of age.

Inherent Enjoyment of the Activity of Deliberate Practice.   How can we explain differences in the amount of deliberate practice among individuals who are active in a domain? The problem of motivating students to engage in structured learning and training has a very long history in education (Cubberley, 1920). The use of punishment as a motivator is no longer acceptable and modern educators instead stress the future value or acquired knowledge and skill, provide rewards for intermediate performance, and try to embed learning within enjoyable social activities.

Similarly, in most domains of expertise, the vast majority of active individuals do not spontaneously engage in deliberate practice but spend virtually all their time in activities involving playful social interaction. Once they have attained an acceptable level of performance, their engagement in additional practice is minimal. These amateurs typically seek out friends with a similar level of performance and rarely compete in tournaments. However, there are other individuals in these domains who actively try to reach their highest level of performance and engage frequently in competitions. Ericsson, Krampe, and Tesch-Römer (1993) argued that deliberate practice is not inherently enjoyable, but individuals engage in it as an instrumental means to improve their performance to attain the highest levels. In support of this claim, they reviewed studies showing that individuals who gave up their goal to compete in a domain shortly thereafter reduced their level of practice to that of other amateurs in the domain. Furthermore, Starkes et al. (chap. 3, this volume) found that coaches and expert performers ranked the desire to succeed as the most important factor for eventual success in a domain.

It is possible that individuals that continue to engage in high levels of deliberate practice differ from the other individuals and inherently enjoy this type of activity. Csikszentmihalyi (1990) studied inherent enjoyment and found that many individuals seek out experiences of flow. This experience is reported for skilled activities and corresponds to complete immersion and effortless mastery of the activity. However, the characteristics of flow are inconsistent with the demands of deliberate practice for monitoring explicit goals and feedback and opportunities for error correction. Hence, skilled performers may enjoy and seek out flow experiences as part of their domain-related activities, but such experiences would not occur during deliberate practice. On the other hand, flowlike states may occur during practice alone because practice alone will never consist entirely of deliberate practice (Lehmann, in press).

More direct attempts to identify enjoyable activities of expert performers have been made by Ericsson, Krampe, and Tesch-Römer (1993) and Starkes et al. (chap. 3, this volume) who asked experts to rate different activities within their domain for enjoyment. To assess inherent enjoyment of the activities, Ericsson, Krampe, and Tesch-Römer (1993) instructed their subjects to try to disregard the consequences of the corresponding activity. For example, rating of inherent enjoyment of cleaning one's house should reflect the enjoyment of the actual activity and disregard the enjoyment of the results (i.e., a clean and attractive house). This distinction should be important for ratings of deliberate practice because the enjoyment of the results of that activity (improvement of performance) could be confused with the enjoyment of the activity. Ericsson, Krampe, and Tesch-Römer (1993) found that their expert musicians rated leisure activities and playing music for fun (alone or in a group) as highly inherently enjoyable, whereas practice alone (deliberate practice) was not reliably different from the average enjoyment rating of all activities. They judged this finding to be very important because if the experts were trying to maximize their enjoyment, they should spend most of their time in leisure and playing for fun. In fact, Ericsson, Krampe, and Tesch-Römer (1993) found that the best musicians spent very little time on playing music for fun and less time on leisure than other less accomplished expert musicians and nonmusicians of the same age. Their actual allocation of time was attributed to the realization of the functional value of deliberate practice. Starkes et al. (chap. 3, this volume) found that most forms of training activity judged to be relevant for improvement of performance were not rated as highly enjoyable. However, they also found practice activities that were rated as both highly relevant and very enjoyable. These deliberate practice activities tended to involve social interaction and/or their duration could not be controlled by the athletes; even so, the elite athletes judged active leisure and sleep somewhat higher in enjoyment. These results are intriguing, but do not seem to violate the general finding that elite and expert performers appear to enjoy leisure and social interaction more than solitary activities and deliberate practice. A similar pattern of rated enjoyment of activities was found for both talented and average teenagers by Csikszentmihalyi, Rathunde, and Whalen (1993).

The weekly organization of deliberate practice and leisure in expert musicians is consistent with the different characteristics of the two types of activities (Ericsson, Krampe, & Tesch-Römer, 1993). Practice alone is organized and habitual and expert musicians can accurately estimate its weekly duration. In contrast, leisure is initiated spontaneously without much planning and its weekly duration is poorly estimated, except among the best musicians (who spend the least amount of time in leisure activities). Similarly, we find that the structure of deliberate practice among adult expert musicians has evolved during the long music development. During the first phase of musical development (Bloom, 1985b), parents help to schedule and monitor practice at fixed times during the week. They provide encouragement and show how practice leads to specific improvements. Sloboda (chap. 4, this volume) reports evidence for motivational problems in attempts to maintain a high level of practice for all music students irregardless of their eventual success in attaining music skill. He also pointed to the role of external factors influencing practice intensity. For example, students increased their level of practice in anticipation of public performances. One important variable differentiating students who dropped out, those who succeeded, and those who attained intermediate levels of mastery was the level of support and involvement of their parents in their music training. Eventually the successful music students are probably able to internalize long-term professional goals and more immediate goals, making improvements that occur during individual practice sessions meaningful and emotionally rewarding. Furthermore, music students establish new social networks with their teachers and other music students that provide them with support and encouragement for further improvements. In his commentary, Glaser (chap. 11, this volume) discusses in more detail the gradual elimination of external supports for individuals attaining expert levels of performance.

It is very likely that many factors influence and differentially predispose individuals to engage in deliberate practice, especially in its solitary form, and also allow them to sustain their rigorous practice schedule for many years. For example, Getzels and Csikszentmihalyi (1976) found that many artists were drawn to painting because it was consistent with the desire for social isolation. In other cases social isolation is imposed. Children forced to be shepherds by themselves in the mountains, individuals who become bedridden as a result of medical problems, and adults in prisons and concentration camps have sometimes acquired high levels of performance in skills, such as mental multiplication and exceptional memory (Ericsson & Faivre, 1988). In those cases, the individuals appear to try to actively ward off boredom and aversive thoughts by focusing the attention on practice of self-designed tasks. Finally, during development a majority of children develop an extreme interest in some class of objects or some activity for some period of time (DeLoache & Asmussen, 1990). However, very few of them focus on activities in prospective domains of expertise, such as drawing and music, and also sustain their obsession for extended periods to reach prodigious levels of performance in these domains (cf. Winner, chap. 10, this volume). The locus of such individual differences in obsessive interests in focused engagement in activities of a specific domain is still poorly understood. Even the "talent" of adolescents and adult expert athletes is assessed by master coaches to a large degree in terms of their perceptions of the athletes' desire to succeed and motivation to train (Starkes et al., chap. 3, this volume). Although our knowledge about motivational factors is still limited, it appears that their effect on attained performance is mediated by their influence on the individuals' activities and their engagement in deliberate practice (Ericsson & Charness, 1994). Furthermore, it is likely that heritable individual differences in personality characteristics (Bouchard, 1994) and general vocational interests (Betsworth et al., 1994) may predispose individuals to engage in practice-related activities and thus account for potential genetic influences on individual differences in the amount of practice (Sternberg, chap. 15, this volume). It is also likely that such individual differences can, at least in part, account for why some individuals drop out of physical exercise programs (Martin & Dubbert, 1985) and from training in music (Sloboda, chap. 4, this volume).

In sum, individuals who reach the highest levels in their domain have spent most of their lives improving their performance. These individuals start their training at a very young age, frequently before age 5. The large amount of focused and intense practice that they engage in approaches the maximum possible effort for any human. In light of these findings, I briefly discuss some proposed evidence for innate capacities and characteristics (talent) that might impose ultimate limits for individuals' improvement of their performance in a domain.

Do Innate Capacities and Characteristics (Talent) Impose Limits on the Level of Performance That a Given Individual Can Attain?

Expert performers react faster, perceive more accurately, and have superior memory in representative situations from their domain of expertise. It was believed that the experts' superiority reflected general unmodifiable capacities that could be measured in the laboratory by their speed to react to a light or sound (simple reaction time), the accuracy of their perceptual judgments of simple stimuli and their memory for random sequences of stimuli. Numerous studies measuring basic perceptual abilities and simple reaction time, however, have found no systematic superiority of elite athletes over control subjects (for reviews, see Abernethy, 1987; Shea & Paull, chap. 13, this volume; Starkes, 1987; Starkes & Deakin, 1984). Similarly, experts in visual medical diagnosis show no consistent basic advantage in perceptual capacities over control subjects (Norman et al., 1992). In the prior section on mechanisms meditating expert performance, it was shown that experts' superior speed, perception, and memory were domain specific and reflect acquired complex cognitive skills. These skills allow the experts to circumvent limits imposed by general capacities, but only for activities in the corresponding domain of expertise. This account is consistent with the poor predictability of adult expert performance. Individual differences in basic capacities and abilities have been found to be surprisingly poor predictors of adult expert performance in recent reviews (Ericsson, Krampe, & Tesch-Römer, 1993; Regnier, Salmela, & Russell, 1994).

There are a few potential exceptions where "basic" abilities have been related to differences in performance of experts. For example, expert musicians are more likely to have perfect pitch; that is the ability to recognize and name any of the 64 tones. World-class typists can tap their fingers faster than control subjects (Book, 1924). However, even these abilities appear to reflect acquired skills and adaptations to training. Superior tapping speed has been found to correlate with level of piano performance, but this speed advantage is correlated with individual differences in the amount of prior practice even among expert musicians. Although perfect pitch is very difficult for adults to acquire, Takeuchi and Hulse (1993) found in a recent review that normal children between the ages of 3 and 5 can relatively easily attain perfect pitch. The fact that perfect pitch occurs more often for elite musicians appears to be due to the early start of their training and to their early exposure to musical instruments. The early acquisition and use of perfect pitch appears to influence the subsequent development of the adult brain as revealed by PET scans of brains of adult musicians with and without perfect pitch (Schlaug, Jäncke, Huang, & Steinmetz, 1995). Similar critical periods have been observed for children's learning of the phonemes of second languages (Johnson & Newport, 1989; Yamada, 1991), which raises the possibility that children's phonological abilities relevant to the acquisition of reading (Wagner & Stanovich, chap. 7, this volume) might have a similar developmental origin.

The effects of extended intense training can also account for many anatomical and physiological differences in elite athletes, which have traditionally been attributed to innate factors. Everyone recognizes that physical fitness and strength can be improved by training, but they believe that the amount of possible change is limited. However, the duration and intensity of training that most people have personally experienced is very restricted compared to that which elite athletes engage in after many years of gradual increases. The intensity of elite athletes' training is often near their maximum and that level of intensity is frequently sustained until exhaustion is reached (see Ericsson, Krampe, & Tesch-Römer, 1993, for a review). A simple index of training intensity is the number of calories metabolized on a daily basis, which is much higher for elite athletes than for the normal population of modern cultures and also outside the range of the observed values for work-intensive hunter-gatherer cultures (Shephard, 1994). Recent research supports the claim that with more extreme training intensities, more extensive physiological and anatomical changes will result. Ericsson, Krampe, and Tesch-Römer (1993) reviewed evidence showing that the number of capillaries supplying blood to relevant muscles increases and the size of hearts and the metabolic properties of critical muscles (conversion of fast-twitch and slow-twitch muscles) change in response to regular intense training sustained for years. These changes are direct adaptations to training and revert back to values in the normal range when training is terminated. However, many of these acquired changes can apparently be maintained with regular intense training at lower frequency and shorter duration (Shephard, 1994).

There is some evidence suggesting that practice at young ages when the body is still developing may be necessary for certain adaptations to take place. The normal development of bones and joints is directly influenced by the intensity of mechanical stimulation and thus increased specific physical activity should influence the growth patterns (Teitz, 1989). In support of this claim, classical ballet dancers, baseball pitchers, and musicians can, through early training, change the range of motion of relevant joints in specific directions, although increases are associated with decreases in the opposite direction, keeping the overall movement range unchanged (Ericsson & Lehmann, 1996). Similarly, the increased size and density of bones in elite athletes and dancers can be accounted for by their intense training, which exposes parts of their bodies to specific mechanical stimulation well outside the normal range encountered during everyday life. Future research will identify limits on physiological adaptation—we already know that differences in height are primarily determined by genetic factors when the nutritional requirements for growth are satisfied (Ericsson, Krampe, & Tesch-Römer, 1993). However, recent research in developmental biology implies that the influence of extended activity is more far-reaching than commonly thought. For example, over the last generation, there has been a large increase in the frequency of nearsightedness, which appears to be an adapted growth response of the eye due to increased viewing of nearby objects during reading and watching television (Wallman, 1994).

Recent research shows that mechanisms mediating expert performance reflect extreme adaptations to the demands of the relevant task constraints for a given domain of expertise (Ericsson & Lehmann, 1996). These adaptations and associated complex acquired skills appear to be caused by extended daily deliberate practice, thus leaving little room for influences of innate fixed capacities. The role of any innate factors is more likely to involve motivation to engage in sustained deliberate practice.

DELIBERATE PRACTICE: A BROADER VIEW

In the earlier sections of this chapter, expert performance was shown to be acquired over an extended period and its mediating mechanisms were found to reflect major adaptations to domain-specific constraints acquired through extended intense training activities. In well-established domains with professional teachers and developed curricula, a close relationship has typically been found between the accumulated amount of supervised training (deliberate practice) and attained adult performance, even when the analysis is restricted to expert-level performers with over 10 years of study. A complete theory of the acquisition of expert performance needs to account for the development of all types of expert performance, even those attained without supervised instruction. In this section, I try to further extend the concept of deliberate practice along the lines proposed earlier (Ericsson & Charness, 1994; Ericsson, Krampe, & Tesch-Römer, 1993), to identify related types of training activities that can lead to improvement without supervision by competent instructors. In attempting to generalize the necessary conditions for improvement of performance, I first discuss how high levels of performance were attainable during earlier periods of history, before organized instruction emerged. Then I discuss the microstructure of effective supervised practice to identify sufficient conditions for deliberate practice that can be generalized to other forms of activities mediating improvement of performance. Finally, I discuss how some of the acquired mechanisms of expert performers, such as LT-WM for planning, reasoning, and anticipation, allow for effective further improvement of their performance.

Historical Development of Training

If one goes sufficiently far back in time, one will find that performance in every domain was initially acquired by individuals without instruction and only later learned through observation and imitation of a master by an apprentice. The lack of effective instruction and the resulting need for each individual to rediscover relevant knowledge and skills led to longer periods of acquisition and lower levels of attained performance. For example, in the 13th century, the famous philosopher Roger Bacon claimed that "nobody can obtain proficiency in the science of mathematics by the method hitherto known unless he devotes to its study thirty or forty years" (cited in Singer, 1958, p. 91). However, mastery of most of that mathematical knowledge can today be attained by adolescents in high school through superior instruction and better organization of the subject matter.

In the Middle Ages, the transfer of knowledge and skills required personal interaction between a master and his apprentices or, more typically, between a father and a son to convey the knowledge and techniques to carry out the craft or profession. The craft guilds typically kept their knowledge and skills secret from nonmembers. Only later were efforts made to explicate and organize the knowledge of many types of crafts in books. The emerging organization of shared knowledge based on general theories allowed individual scientists to contribute new facts and insights to the appropriate part of the knowledge base without having themselves first acquired and mastered all the available knowledge. Today, mastery of all knowledge and skills of a complete domain is virtually impossible and most elite performers in the sciences, the arts, and sports are highly specialized.

The increases in absolute levels of performance over historical time, discussed earlier, can be accounted for by the more effective organization of knowledge and skills and improvements in education and training. Within the framework of deliberate practice, it is easy to propose and account for increases in absolute levels of performance over historical time based on increased specialization of expert performance. When the goal of training is more precise, it is easier to design a training program that capitalizes on available relevant knowledge in the domain and information about effective training methods for the acquisition of the necessary skills. A clear specification of the ultimate skill makes it possible to start training with very young children using modern training methods for instrumental music, such as the Suzuki method (Hermann, 1981). Finally, there is considerable evidence showing that amount and intensity of practice have increased considerably over the last centuries, especially in sports, where the highest levels of performance are nearly always found only for full-time professional athletes.

The success of modern training in allowing many contemporary individuals to match or surpass past achievements of elite performers does not completely account for those earlier achievements. Prior to modern specialization, elite performers were trying to attain more general goals and abilities. For example, in the 18th century, musicians were expected to play many different instruments, sight-read unfamiliar music, compose, and teach, in contrast to today's solo performers who only publicly perform a small number of extensively rehearsed pieces of music. I later return with a discussion of how more general abilities, such as sight-reading, can be improved and acquired.

As the account of expert performance in terms of training and deliberate practice becomes more successful, it becomes interesting to look for counterexamples. The two most frequently cited types of evidence concern exceptional performance of autistic savants and child prodigies (for recent reviews see Howe, 1990, and Radford, 1990). Recent studies and reviews of autistic savants (Charness, Clifton, & MacDonald, 1988; Ericsson & Faivre, 1988; Sloboda, Hermelin, & O'Connor, 1985) have already found evidence for the domain-specific and acquired nature of their performance. I briefly review Ericsson and Lehmann's (1994b) analyses of famous child prodigies in music, such as Wolfgang Amadeus Mozart.

A primary obstacle in an analysis of performance of prodigies across historical time concerns the inherent relativity of such assessments. To overcome this, Ericsson and Lehmann (1994b) identified public performances by child prodigies and their age at the time of performance, as well as their age at the start of music training. The difficulty of the performed piano music was assessed by the number of years of piano study recommended prior to its mastery by conservatories and modern educational plans for piano training. Ericsson and Lehmann (1994b) then defined an index of precociousness by dividing the number of recommended years of study before mastery of a given piece by the actual number of years of study for the child prodigy before he or she performed it in public. For example, a child prodigy who played a piece requiring 6 years of music study by the average music student after only 3 years of study would get an index of 200%. They found that over time this index has increased dramatically with Wolfgang Amadeus Mozart scoring around 130% in the 18th century to prodigies in this century scoring between 300% and 500%. The observed improvement in performance is consistent with the increase of efficiency and specialization of piano training. A biographical analysis (Lehmann, in press) found that famous child prodigies started music training early. In virtually every case, it was possible to find documented evidence for adequate teachers living in their home, typically a parent. These teachers instructed the child prodigies and monitored their practice closely from an early age, thus helping them to establish focused and efficient practice. For example, Mozart was trained from a very young age by his father who was a pioneer in music education and published the first book on violin instruction in German. The amount of early supervised training appears to be a sufficient explanation for the emergence of the precocious music performance of eminent musicians.

One of the primary characteristics that sets prodigies apart from other children appears to be their capacity and motivation to sustain focused attention on domain-related activities, including extended practice and training (Winner, chap. 10, this volume). Case studies of "gifted" children (Feldman, 1986) show that these children are very active and one or both parents have to dedicate their full-time efforts to develop their child's gifts during childhood. The nature of the interactions between "gifted" children and parents is not well documented. Hence, we do not know how closely these interactions correspond to deliberate practice.

Only further research will allow us to identify potential counterexamples documenting instances of confirmed exceptional performance that cannot be satisfactorily explained by practice and training.

The Acquisition of Expert Performance and Deliberate Practice

The acquisition of expert-level performance in a domain is very difficult and takes many years, with only gradual improvement even under the best circumstances. The key problem for a beginner is to identify a sequence of training tasks with attainable learning goals that will eventually lead to the desired level of performance. This problem has been successfully addressed in established domains in which developed curricula and professional teachers provide knowledge about how to sequence instruction for individual students at all different levels. Thus the complex and ill-defined goal of acquiring expert performance is broken down into a sequence of attainable training tasks. Each of these tasks has a well-defined goal that allows the students to gain feedback about their performance and provides the students with opportunities for gradual refinement through repetition. These component tasks have all the prerequisite elements necessary for a motivated learner to improve performance, as repeatedly demonstrated in laboratory studies of learning, computer-assisted instruction, and skill acquisition (see Anderson, 1993; Ericsson, Krampe, & Tesch-Römer, 1993; and Glaser & Bassok, 1989, for reviews). If improved performance was a mechanical consequence of engaging in the assigned training tasks, the problem of skill acquisition would be essentially solved. However, to attain changes in behavior, attention is necessary to generate the correct desired action and to thus override the activation of the old habitual response. For effective learning the subjects also need to monitor their processes and performance to determine necessary adjustments and corrections. These learning activities require effort, and practice sessions are limited in duration in both successful laboratory studies and during daily practice by expert performers (Ericsson, Krampe, & Tesch-Römer, 1993). In the acquisition of expert performance, the problems of sustained concentration during training sessions become central. Many master teachers claim full concentration is necessary for effective training (deliberate practice).

Even if students are assigned appropriate training tasks, the mere duration of practice will not be a perfect predictor of attained performance. Effective learning requires attention and monitoring of goals, processes, and performance. For example, almost everyone knows about children taking piano lessons who are forced by their parents to practice for a specific duration each day. When motivation to improve is lacking, these children play the same pieces over and over without reducing the number of mistakes as the necessary effort to correct is absent. When groups of individuals with different levels of motivation are studied, it is not surprising that the correlation between amount of practice and performance is modest or even low (see Lehmann, in press, for a review). At the same time, recent research (Sloboda, chap. 4, this volume) has found that music students that progress faster per year of study and eventually reach higher levels of music performance do so by practicing more per week. Retrospective analyses showed that the best music students did not reach a given proficiency level with a smaller number of hours of practice than less accomplished music students. This finding suggests that a given duration of practice is equally effective for students attaining a high and low level of music performance and that individual differences in ability to learn music do not distinguish dropouts and more successful music students (cf. Sternberg, chap. 15, this volume). However, the relation between amount of practice and attained performance was considerably weaker within groups. Some of the problems can be avoided by restricting the study to individuals with very high levels of performance, who have made a professional commitment, and have extensive experience with effective practice (Ericsson, Krampe, & Tesch-Römer, 1993).

Sternberg (chap. 15, this volume) suggests that the definition of deliberate practice requires associated improvements of performance and thus the relation between amount of deliberate practice and attained performance is circular. To successfully address that claim it is necessary to study the microstructure of the cognitive processes during practice based on verbal reports and protocol analysis (Ericsson & Simon, 1993). Through an analysis of the cognitive processes that occur during practice, one should be able to differentiate effortless repetition from goal-directed focused learning, and thus empirically verify the occurrence of deliberate practice independent of any associated improvement. Based on a small number of studies of the detailed processes of practice (Gruson, 1988; Miklaszewski, 1989), it is clear that empirical studies of practice will be difficult but not impossible.

In preparation for future empirical studies it is useful to consider and identify necessary conditions for complex learning in musicians. Musicians who are learning a new music piece must be able to analyze and evaluate their own performance in order to attain their desired musical interpretation. It is inconceivable that a musician lacking the perceptual skills to hear the necessary distinctions could reliably produce them in performance. In addition, the musician needs to be able to listen while playing the same piece. Furthermore, the musicians need to know in considerable detail how they play critical sequences in order to know which timing and force variations could achieve the desired sound effects. They also need to be able to accomplish these changes within the limits of their current technical skill, which may involve solving problems of finding an appropriate assignment of fingers to piano keys rather than retrieval of already automated sequences of keystrokes. Sloboda (chap. 4, this volume) discusses in more detail the acquisition of skills that are necessary to attain the musical expression found at the expert level.

Perhaps the most important conclusion from this informal analysis is that expert skill requires the acquisition of refined internal representations to simultaneously image, execute, and provide feedback about their produced performance. These representations and the associated mechanisms are critical factors that allow experts to continue to generate and attain higher level goals for their performance. Efforts to more directly study these prerequisite mechanisms for expert performance are likely to reveal individual differences that might explain associated differences in attained performance. Hence, a detailed analysis of how these representations are gradually acquired is absolutely essential for a complete understanding of the attainment of expert performance.

Acquisition of Expert Performance in the Absence of Supervised Instruction

When individuals are introduced to a domain of activity they often reach an acceptable level of proficiency after a brief period of instruction followed by a limited period of effortful adaptation. During this early phase individuals typically gain immediate feedback about errors and inferior performance from more experienced participants or directly from the external environment, such as failures to return a tennis ball or to make a computer program run successfully. Under these conditions, individuals can "learn by doing" (Anderson, 1987, 1993; Greeno & Simon, 1988) and improve their performance until an acceptable level is reached. However, beyond this point improvements in measured performance are typically modest in most types of leisure, and in many jobs and professional activities. This fairly stable adaptation to the demands of a domain does not appear to be due to a fixed upper limit on performance, as the efficiency of performance in many occupations can be dramatically increased with, for example, external incentives (see Ericsson, Krampe, & Tesch-Römer, 1993, for a review). However, in other domains such as medicine, improvements in performance continue for extended periods of time. Patel et al. (chap. 5, this volume) describe and discuss many types of deliberate activities designed to increase learning and performance in that domain.

A more interesting and difficult issue is how accuracy of performance can be increased for a functionally adapted performance, where the number of instances of perceived errors is relatively low. Theorists of learning and skill acquisition, such as Newell (1990) and VanLehn (1991), argue that changes in accuracy require impasses or failures as preconditions for efforts to adjust the mechanisms mediating performance. A fairly general method of increasing "errors" is for the individual to generate internal goals and predictions that can be used to evaluate one's performance with much higher standards than those imposed by the external environment. For example, David Hemery (1976), an Olympic gold winner in hurdling, recounted in his autobiography how he converted his childhood play with stilts and a pogo stick into a competition with himself. To see how high he could eventually jump on his pogo stick, he kept records of the number of telephone directories that he could clear.

Virtually any activity, especially a solitary one, can be converted into a task where feedback on performance and repeated opportunities to improve become available. It is likely that systematic interviews with elite performers will uncover engagements in self-directed activities and interactions with parents that can explain individual differences in abilities that are found prior to the start of practice supervised by skilled teachers. It is likely that the self-directed activities of geniuses (Howe, chap. 9, this volume) and prodigies (Winner, chap. 10, this volume) directed toward their domain of expertise increase their relevant knowledge and improve aspects of their acquired skills.

Many professional activities have fairly well-defined criteria, but the nature of these criteria does not allow for immediate feedback. Most decisions refer to future events, or hidden conditions, such as in medical diagnosis, where feedback can only be attained through additional effort at a much later time when memory for the original decision-making process should be poor. Improvement of decision-making accuracy under conditions of no feedback would be expected to be minimal. In other activities it is possible for individuals to acquire increased standards for performance. The general method to deal with this problem is to identify outstanding achievements of other individuals that can be used as a model. For example, in his autobiography, Benjamin Franklin recounted how he learned to write in a clear and logical fashion by self-study. He would read a passage in a well-written book and then would try to reproduce the argument in writing from memory. By comparing his reproduction to the original, he was able to identify differences and through iteration he learned how to reproduce the original argument.

Based on informal interviews with chess players, Ericsson, Krampe, and Tesch-Römer (1993) proposed a similar mechanism for the acquisition of expert performance in chess. The best chess players in a local chess club may gain very little from playing extensively with other less skilled chess players based on the argument that their "errors" and inferior moves cannot be easily identified nor serve as a stimulus for improvement. Instead of playing chess games, serious chess players study published games between chess masters. By trying to select the best move for each position of the game and comparing their selected move to the actual move from the game, the players identify discrepancies where they must study the chess position more deeply to uncover the reason for the master's move. In support of the claim that this form of chess study improves performance, Charness et al. (chap. 2, this volume) found a high correlation between the accumulated amount of reported chess study and chess ratings for a large sample of chess players. Most importantly, Charness et al. (chap. 2, this volume) found that when the amount of chess study was statistically controlled, there was no additional influence of the amount of chess playing with others or early starting ages. These results provide strong support for the hypothesis that deliberate practice is the primary variable mediating the acquisition of expert performance (Ericsson & Charness, 1994). Ericsson, Krampe, and Tesch-Römer (1993) hypothesized that supervised instruction and coaching by a chess master would provide more effective learning than self-study based on the fact that recent world champions reportedly had studied with a chess master during their development. However, Charness et al. (chap. 2, this volume) found no effects of whether or not a chess player had been coached when the amount of chess study had been statistically controlled. Whether the amount of time of coaching or the skill level of the chess coach would provide additional information cannot be answered from Charness et al.'s data.

One of the most intriguing and challenging aspects of many types of expert performance is the requirement for generalizability. For example, chess players must be able to play against any opponent and medical doctors should be able to diagnose any patient with problems within their specialty. At the same time, we know that expert performers typically make special preparations whenever they know their opponents in advance, such as in world championship matches in chess (Botvinnik, 1960) and major-league baseball (Hanson, 1992). An analysis of a specific opponent's weaknesses, strengths, and habits allow the expert to make special adjustments. An extreme case of special preparations is found in the case of artistic performers who perform the same program many times on long tours. An international level soloist in music has a limited repertoire of pieces where the performances have been prepared and refined for months and years. The slow acquisition of technically complex pieces would not appear to account for expert skill in playing unfamiliar music at sight (sight-reading). Ericsson and Lehmann (1994a; Lehmann & Ericsson, 1993) confirmed that prediction when they measured the sight-reading ability of expert musicians specializing in solo performance and accompanying. Amount of deliberate practice did not predict sight-reading performance for this group of advanced pianists. However, they found that relevant activities, such as accompanying experience and reported size of their accompanying repertoire, predicted the observed level of sight-reading performance. They argued that playing unfamiliar music (accompanying) is likely to induce errors and problems that a skilled musician can readily identify at the time of preparation of the keystrokes or hear at the moment of production. Often accompanists get opportunities to play the same piece several times, and are thus able to make adjustments and corrections. Furthermore, as part of their deliberate efforts to increase their sight-reading repertoire, skilled accompanists identify problems for particular types of music and engage in specific practice to master them. Hence, amount of accompanying experience and time spent on deliberate efforts to increase one's accompanying repertoire provide relevant activities for increasing sight-reading performance.

There are intriguing parallels between sight-reading in music and reading. In both activities the primary mode of experience and practice consists of engaging in the actual activity. Wagner and Stanovich (chap. 7, this volume) show the importance of the amount of reading experience for the improvement of reading skill. It is likely that a more refined analysis of different types of reading activities will reveal an even closer connection to increases in reading skill. For example, the difficulty level of the texts an individual reads is important and reading texts well below the individual's reading level would not elicit problems and appropriate challenges for skill development. In addition, for children to gain significant benefits from reading alone, they must be able to monitor word recognition and the comprehension of the texts by themselves. Because children have limited skills in monitoring text comprehension (Zabrucky & Moore, 1989), they will not always be able to use feedback to determine the need to reread sentences and passages, and thus the benefits of reading alone will not be optimal for skill development.

Another general type of mechanism mediating expert performance and its improvement involves actively integrating the expert's knowledge (Glaser & Chi, 1988). By deliberately retrieving many types of relevant knowledge and experiences from memory, the expert will often discover inconsistencies among them, which in turn will serve as a stimulus for further analysis and a search for new information until an acceptable reintegration of the associated knowledge is attained. Patel et al. (1994; Patel et al., chap. 5, this volume) proposed that medical experts' efforts to fully account for all relevant information about a medical patient provides them with feedback on the sufficiency or insufficiency of the proposed diagnosis. Insufficiency of the diagnosis then leads the expert to carefully review alternatives or even to problem solving and further medical tests of the patient to arrive at a coherent understanding of the disease state. This type of reasoning requires that the experts have the necessary working memory support and the appropriate representation of their knowledge so it can be effortlessly accessed when it is relevant. The acquisition of representational systems is particularly well-documented in physics, where the representation of a problem is often externalized as a diagram (Anzai, 1991; Larkin & Simon, 1987). In addition, Chi and her colleagues (Chi, Bassok, Lewis, Reimann, & Glaser, 1989; Chi, de Leeuw, Chiu, & LaVancher, 1994) demonstrated the importance of active comprehension through the generation of self-explanations in order to attain mastery of new material in physics and biology.

A complete survey of possible self-directed learning activities of expert performers is outside the scope of this chapter and the reader is directed to recent reviews (Chipman & Meyrowitz, 1993; Glaser & Bassok, 1989; Wagner, 1991). In his commentary, Glaser (chap. 11, this volume) masterfully integrates the contributions of this volume and outlines how learning activities change during the acquisition of expert performance and how expert performers gain increasing control over their own continued development.

In general, research has focused on describing and accounting for the mechanisms mediating performance of experts. Typically, a solid understanding of the relevant performance is needed before it is feasible to study its acquisition (Newell & Simon, 1972). However, a complete description of the knowledge and mechanisms mediating expert performance does not seem to be within reach. In the case of expert performance, it is possible that empirical studies of how experts design deliberate practice activities for the sole purpose of further increasing their performance will offer a more direct path toward the identification of general principles of complex learning. The learning mechanisms available to most experts that were discussed earlier require that for effective learning the subject must acquire mechanisms supporting reasoning, planning, prediction, and expectation in order to generate feedback and effective error diagnosis with appropriate correction. In the next section, the relation between these learning mechanisms and the mechanism mediating attained performance is discussed.

Acquired Characteristics of Expert Performers and Improvement of Performance

The complex and accessible internal representations of expert performers stand in direct contrast to the nearly automatic and effortless mediation of habitual performance in work and leisure activities in everyday life. Whereas the goal for habitual performance is effortless execution of already adapted behavior, there are two quite different goals for expert performance. The first goal is to constantly improve the given level of performance and the second goal is to exhibit the best performance that is attainable given the current skill level.

I begin by considering the second goal. It is questionable if the absolute highest levels of current performance can be effortlessly produced, but in many domains slightly lower levels of expert performance can be generated so rapidly so as to virtually preclude extensive cognitive mediation. For example, under speeded conditions of chess playing, the quality of generated moves remains high, even when the available time for move selection is substantially reduced (Calderwood, Klein, & Crandall, 1988; Gobet & Simon, in press). Furthermore, there is a high correlation between chess playing ability for speed chess (around 5 seconds per move) and regular tournament chess (around 120 seconds per move) for highly skilled chess players (N. Charness, personal communication, 1995). On the other hand, many types of expert performance have to be adapted to the current conditions of weather, such as wind, rain, and sun; of equipment, such as the available grand piano or pool table; and of the particular opponent or opponents in tennis, chess, or other sports, which requires continuous attentional monitoring and control of performance.

Another more likely possibility is that individuals acquire these complex mechanisms as necessary means to improve their performance effectively. For example, when individuals study chess games between chess masters and fail to predict the next move they will only be able to learn by exploring and discovering consequences of alternative moves by planning. The acquired ability to generate and evaluate potential chess positions mentally is a prerequisite for learning from planning. The associated mechanisms allow chess masters to play blindfold chess without any specific prior training. Similarly, the ability to anticipate events in sports can also only be acquired if the athletes extract and store the relevant preconditions long enough to allow an effective analysis of discrepancies between generated expectations and the actual outcomes. The cognitive mechanisms mediating expert performance in many different domains reflect not simply the mechanisms necessary to execute the current performance, but also the means by which that performance was originally attained and further improved. If many aspects of expert performance primarily reflect the capacity for continued learning, one might predict some changes in the structure of expert performance when the goal of further improvement becomes less important or irrelevant. Simply maintaining a given level of performance in chess, for example, could probably be done with less planning and less detailed memory for the presented chess position. In support of this hypothesis, Charness (1981a, 1981b) found that older chess players attained the same level of chess skill by means of less playing and with less incidental memory for the presented chess position compared to young chess players. Although Charness (1981a, 1981b) did not collect any data on amount of deliberate practice in old or young chess players, his recent work (Charness et al., chap. 2, this volume) found a reduction in deliberate practice for older chess players. This reduction of practice with age appears to be a general phenomenon. After a maximum practice intensity typically occurring between 20 and 30 years of age, the reported amount of deliberate practice decreases with age in domains, such as music (Krampe, 1994; Krampe & Ericsson, in press) and sports (Hagberg et al., 1985).

Evidence for automatization of expert performance appears to be strongest for perceptual-motor skills, such as typing. Shaffer (1975) found that an expert typist was able to continue visual transcription typing with minimal interference from other concurrent tasks. It must thus be possible to automatize skilled typing performance even though the skilled typists look ahead at text segments that will be typed moments later (eye–hand span). Salthouse (1984) found that the relation between eye–hand span and typing speed still holds for older typists and, in fact, older typists were found to have longer eye–hand spans than young typists for the equivalent typing speed. It is likely that the performance of the older typists reflects the structure of their originally acquired typing performance, which has since been automated and declined over the years. In contrast to the effortless execution of their current typing performance, Book (1925a, 1925b) showed that improvement of typing speed beyond its current level requires full concentration and directed efforts to extend the eye–hand span. Thus, research on typing illustrates how attention to mediating mechanisms during the acquisition of improved performance can be markedly reduced once the goal is simply to maintain an already acquired level of performance.

In summary, the structure of expert performance can only be understood if the requirements for effective continued improvements are considered along with the more obvious demands for mediation of the current superior performance.

Conclusion

The principal question addressed here is how expert performers attain a successful adaptation to the demands of the critical activities in the corresponding domain. The evidence suggests that future expert performers engage in intense training activities that are especially designed to maximize improvement of a given individual's current performance (deliberate practice). In order to get maximal benefit from engaging in these activities, individuals need to remain fully concentrated on the goals of the task and on their performance in order to effectively gain feedback and make accurate adjustments to their performance. Furthermore, experts have to acquire memory skills to expand their working memory capacity to allow generation and evaluation of future potential events during planning. The accuracy of generated plans can then be evaluated against the actual observed events to obtain feedback for error correction and learning.

The requirement of continued improvement and learning may force expert performers to maintain access to many aspects of their processing, unlike the nearly automatic mediation of habitual performance in everyday life. The maintained accessibility of information in expert performance would suggest that systematic studies with verbal reports might be much more successful than previously thought. However, the accessibility of much of the information might be relatively brief for rapid perceptual-motor activities, where proactive interference would become a major factor, as Ericsson and Kintsch (1995) suggested for mental multiplication and mental abacus calculation. For these types of activities, it may be necessary to interrupt the processing at arbitrary points for retrospective reports (Ericsson & Simon, 1993) in order to assess the available information. In sum, expert performers should not only be studied for their attained performance but also for how they optimize their efforts for continued improvement.

SUMMARY AND CONCLUSIONS

Our goal of developing a general theory of the acquisition of expert performance becomes more attainable if we focus on the reliable and reproducible aspects of the superior performance of experts on representative tasks in their domains. By imposing scientific standards for verifiable facts on exceptional performance it is possible to exclude the large body of retrospective accounts and studies documenting amazing past achievements that have fueled beliefs in the magical abilities and talents attributed to exceptional individuals. Only future research will tell how many, if any, amazing facts remain when evaluated with appropriate scientific standards.

Historical and contemporary data show that the highest levels of observed public performance are only displayed after at least a 10-year period of intensive preparation in traditional domains, even in some vigorous sports such as swimming, where the age of peak performance is about 20 years old. In many domains, where normal education is not a prerequisite for specialized training, elite performers start training at very young ages, which are typically much younger than those of less proficient adult performers.

Analyses of the daily activities of future elite performers during the extended period of their preparation shows that with older ages increasingly more time and energy are spent on special activities designed to improve performance (deliberate practice). Often with the help of their parents, future elite performers seek out the best available instructors and training environments. Even in domains where professional teachers are rare, such as chess, a close relation has been found between amount of time in deliberate study activities and the attained adult performance.

To optimize the benefits of training, individuals need to remain fully focused on the training goals. The required concentration and effort limits the duration of effective practice sessions and their total daily duration. Across many different domains individuals appear to be able to maintain only 4 or 5 hours of deliberate practice per day for extended periods without reaching exhaustion and burnout, even when they increase the duration and effectiveness of rest and sleep. Adult elite performers are approaching their limits for sustainable efforts to improve their performance.

Expert performance should thus be viewed as the results of a natural experiment, where some individuals give their maximal efforts to reach their highest level of performance within the task constraints imposed by representative tasks in their domain of expertise. Laboratory analyses of the acquired mechanisms mediating their superior performance provide the best available evidence on how and to what extent the human body and mind can be modified and changed through training. Extended intense physical training of elite athletes and artistic performers was shown to lead to remarkable physical adaptations of the organs and tissue affected by the corresponding practice activities. However, most of these adaptations are mediated by the same biological mechanisms regulating the tissue and organs of all humans in response to much lower levels of physical activity. Recent evidence on the interaction between physical and mental activity and physiological development of the body and brain suggests more far-reaching effects than commonly thought possible.

Expert performance also reveals evidence for adaptation of the cognitive system through learning and skill acquisition. In addition, expert performers in most domains are able to circumvent some basic information-processing limits. For example, limits on STM are circumvented by the acquisition of memory skills based on storage in LTM. Similarly, constraints imposed by minimal reaction times for immediate reactions are relieved by anticipation based on predictive advance cues. With further research on expert performance in domains where performance is constrained by other basic capacity limits, we are likely to discover skills acquired to reduce or eliminate their adverse influence.

Studies of the acquisition of expert performance have focused on how the highest levels of performance are attained, but a complete theory also needs to account for the early phases of skill acquisition. There is currently a wide gap between the large number of laboratory studies of how performance on simple tasks improves during a single 1-to 2-hour session and the descriptive and correlational studies of expert performance after 5,000 to 50,000 hours of deliberate practice. Shiffrin (chap. 14, this volume) argues convincingly for the value of controlled studies of extended skill acquisition after 10 to 100 hours of deliberate practice. After that amount of practice, trained subjects can attain performance levels that match the speed of components of everyday skills, acceptable levels of performance in many sports and typing (Dvorak, Merrick, Dealey, & Ford, 1936), and exceptional levels of performance in, for example, memory (see Ericsson & Kintsch, 1995, for a review), mental calculation (Staszewski, 1988), and juggling (Beek & van Santvoord, 1992). Some of these skills reveal qualitative differences in the mechanisms mediating performance that are acquired after relatively short durations of practice—less than 1% of that required for the highest levels of expert performance. Many issues regarding the influence of individual differences in innate and acquired abilities (Shea & Paull, chap. 13, this volume) and the effects of other factors affecting motivation to sustain deliberate practice could be successfully investigated in extended training studies with large random samples of subjects, especially if the process-tracing methodology from expert performance research is used to monitor the detailed structure of the learning process.

A complete theory of expert performance also has to account for the extended process of improving performance and the acquisition of its mediating mechanisms. In this chapter, I have tried to argue that we should also study the expert performers as individuals who are able to effectively improve their performance. In addition to studying how they optimize their daily lives to allow maximal amounts of time and energy for deliberate practice, we need to consider how they acquire domain-specific mechanisms mediating effective improvement and learning. Many of the cognitive activities of expert performers, such as planning evaluation and anticipation, have a dual function, mediating both performance and most significantly further learning and improvement. Analysis of complex learning in expert performers who are fully committed to further improving their performance offers the potential for a new set of phenomena with significant implications for education in general as well as training of future elite performers.

ACKNOWLEDGMENTS

This research was supported by the FSCW/Conradi Endowment Fund of the Florida State University Foundation. I gratefully acknowledge the thoughtful comments on earlier drafts of this chapter by Peter Delaney, Andreas Lehmann, William Oliver, and Rolf Zwaan.

REFERENCES

Abernethy, B. (1987). Selective attention in fast ball sports II: Expert-novice differences. *Australian Journal of Science and Medicine in Sports, 19*(4), 7–16.
Abernethy, B. (1988). The effects of age and expertise upon perceptual skill development in a racquet sport. *Research Quarterly, 59*, 210–221.
Abernethy, B. (1991). Visual search strategies and decision-making in sport. *International Journal of Sport Psychology, 22*, 189–210.
Abernethy, B., Neal, R. J., & Koning, P. (1994). Visual-perceptual and cognitive differences between expert, intermediate, and novice snooker players. *Applied Cognitive Psychology, 18*, 185–211.
Allard, F., & Starkes, J. L. (1991). Motor-skill experts in sports, dance and other domains. In K. A. Ericsson & J. Smith (Eds.), *Toward a general theory of expertise: Prospects and limits* (pp. 126–152). Cambridge, UK: Cambridge University Press.
Anderson, J. R. (1982). Acquisition of cognitive skill. *Psychological Review, 89*, 369–406.
Anderson, J. R. (1983). *The architecture of cognition*. Cambridge, MA: Harvard University Press.

Anderson, J. R. (1987). Skill acquisition: Compilation of weak-method problem situations. *Psychological Review, 94*(2), 192–210.

Anderson, J. R. (1993). Problem solving and learning. *American Psychologist, 48*(1), 35–44.

Anzai, Y. (1991). Learning and use of representations for physics expertise. In K. A. Ericsson & J. Smith (Eds.), *Toward a general theory of expertise: Prospects and limits* (pp. 64–92). Cambridge, UK: Cambridge University Press.

Auer, L. (1921). *Violin playing as I teach it.* New York: Frederick A. Stokes.

Bedard, J., & Chi, M. T. H. (1993). Expertise in auditing. *Auditing, 12*(Suppl.), 1–25.

Beek, P. J. (1989). *Juggling dynamics.* Amsterdam: Free University Press.

Beek, P. J., & van Santvoord, A. A. M. (1992). Learning the cascade juggle: A dynamic systems analysis. *Journal of Motor Behavior, 24,* 85–94.

Betsworth, D. G., Bouchard, T. J., Jr., Cooper, C. R., Grotevant, H. D., Hansen, J.-I. C., Scarr, S., & Weinberg, R. A. (1994). Genetic and environmental influences on vocational interests assessed using adoptive and biological families and twins raised together. *Journal of Vocational Behavior, 44,* 263–278.

Bloom, B. S. (Ed.). (1985a). *Developing talent in young people.* New York: Ballantine.

Bloom, B. S. (1985b). Generalizations about talent development. In B. S. Bloom (Ed.), *Developing talent in young people* (pp. 507–549). New York: Ballantine.

Book, W. F. (1924). Voluntary motor ability of the world's champion typists. *Journal of Applied Psychology, 8,* 283–308.

Book, W. F. (1925a). *Learning to typewrite.* New York: Gregg.

Book, W. F. (1925b) *The psychology of skill.* New York: Gregg.

Boshuizen, H. P. A., & Schmidt, H. G. (1992). On the role of biomedical knowledge in clinical reasoning by experts, intermediates and novices. *Cognitive Science, 16,* 153–184.

Botvinnik, M. M. (1960). *One hundred selected games* (S. Garry, Trans.). New York: Dover.

Bouchard, T. J., Jr. (1994). Genes, environment, and personality. *Science, 264,* 1700–1701.

Bühler, W. K. (1981). *Gauss: A biographical study.* New York: Springer.

Calderwood, R., Klein, G. A., & Crandall, B. W. (1988). Time pressure, skill and move quality in chess. *American Journal of Psychology, 101,* 481–493

Camerer, C. F., & Johnson, E. J. (1991). The process–performance paradox in expert judgment: How can the experts know so much and predict so badly? In K. A. Ericsson & J. Smith (Eds.), *Towards a general theory of expertise: Prospects and limits* (pp. 195–217). Cambridge, UK: Cambridge University Press.

Chambliss, D. F. (1988). *Champions: The making of Olympic swimmers.* New York: Morrow.

Charness, N. (1981a). Aging and skilled problem solving. *Journal of Experimental Psychology: General, 110,* 21–38.

Charness, N. (1981b). Search in chess: Age and skill differences. *Journal of Experimental Psychology: Human Perception and Performance, 7,* 467–476.

Charness, N. (1989). Expertise in chess and bridge. In D. Klahr & K. Kotovsky (Eds.). *Complex information processing: The impact of Herbert A. Simon* (pp. 183–208). Hillsdale, NJ: Lawrence Erlbaum Associates.

Charness, N. (1991). Expertise in chess: The balance between knowledge and search. In K. A. Ericsson & J. Smith (Eds.), *Toward a general theory of expertise: Prospects and limits* (pp. 39–63). Cambridge, UK: Cambridge University Press.

Charness, N., & Bosman, E. A. (1990). Expertise and aging: Life in the lab. In T. H. Hess (Ed.), *Aging and cognition: Knowledge organization and utilization* (pp. 343–385). Amsterdam: Elsevier.

Charness, N., Clifton, J., & MacDonald, L. (1988). Case study of a musical mono-savant. In L. K. Obler & D. A. Fein (Eds.), *The exceptional brain: Neuropsychology of talent and special abilities* (pp. 277–293). New York: Guilford.

Chase, W. G., & Ericsson, K. A. (1982). Skill and working memory. In G. H. Bower (Ed.), *The psychology of learning and motivation* (Vol. 16, pp. 1–58). New York: Academic Press.

Chase, W. G., & Simon, H. A. (1973). The mind's eye in chess. In W. G. Chase (Ed.), *Visual information processing* (pp. 215–281). New York: Academic Press.

Chi, M. T. H. (1978). Knowledge structures and memory development. In R. S. Siegler (Ed.), *Children's thinking: What develops?* (pp. 73–96). Hillsdale, NJ: Lawrence Erlbaum Associates.

Chi, M. T. H., Bassok, M., Lewis, M., Reimann, P., & Glaser, R. (1989). Self-explanations: How students study and use examples in learning to solve problems. *Cognitive Science, 13,* 145–182.

Chi, M. T. H., de Leeuw, N., Chiu, M.-H., & LaVancher, C. (1994). Eliciting self-explanations improves understanding. *Cognitive Science, 18,* 439–477.

Chi, M. T. H., Glaser, R., & Rees, E. (1982). Expertise in problem solving. In R. S. Sternberg (Ed.), *Advances in the psychology of human intelligence* (Vol. 1, pp. 1–75). Hillsdale, NJ: Lawrence Erlbaum Associates.

Chipman, S., & Meyrowitz, A. L. (Eds.). (1993). *Foundations of knowledge acquisition: Cognitive models of complex learning.* Boston: Kluwer Academic.

Cooke, N. J., Atlas, R. S., Lane, D. M., & Berger, R. C. (1993). Role of high-level knowledge in memory for chess positions. *American Journal of Psychology, 106,* 321–351.

Csikszentmihalyi, M. (1990). *Flow: The psychology of optimal experience.* New York: Harper & Row.

Csikszentmihalyi, M., Rathunde, K., & Whalen, S. (1993). *Talented teenagers: The roots of success & failure.* Cambridge, UK: Cambridge University Press.

Cubberley, E. P. (1920). *The history of education.* Boston: Houghton Mifflin.

de Groot, A. (1978). *Thought and choice and chess.* The Hague: Mouton. (Original work published 1946)

DeLoache, J. S., & Asmussen, L. (1990, June). *Young children's extremely intense interests in objects and activities.* Poster presented at the American Psychological Society Conference, Dallas, TX.

Doane, S. M., Pellegrino, J. W., & Klatzky, R. L. (1990). Expertise in a computer operating system: Conceptualization and performance. *Human–Computer Interaction, 5,* 267–304.

Dvorak, A., Merrick, N. L., Dealey, W. L., & Ford, G. C. (1936). *Typewriting behavior.* New York: American Book Company.

Elo, A. E. (1965). Age changes in master chess performances. *Journal of Gerontology, 20,* 289–299.

Elo, A. E. (1978). *The rating of chessplayers, past and present.* London: Batsford.

Ericsson, K. A. (1990). Peak performance and age: An examination of peak performance in sports. In P. B. Baltes & M. M. Baltes (Eds.), *Successful aging: Perspectives from the behavioral sciences* (pp. 164–195). Cambridge, UK: Cambridge University Press.

Ericsson, K. A., & Charness, N. (1994). Expert performance: Its structure and acquisition. *American Psychologist, 49*(8), 725–747.

Ericsson, K. A., & Faivre, I. A. (1988). What's exceptional about exceptional abilities? In I. K. Obler & D. Fein (Eds.), *The exceptional brain: Neuropsychology of talent and special abilities* (pp. 436–473). New York: Guilford.

Ericsson, K. A., & Hastie, R. (1994). Contemporary approaches to the study of thinking and problem solving. In E. C. Carterette & M. P. Friedman (General Eds.) & R. J. Sternberg (Vol. Ed.), *Handbook of perception and cognition: Vol. 12. Thinking and problem solving* (pp. 37–79). New York: Academic Press.

Ericsson, K. A., & Kintsch, W. (1995). Long-term working memory. *Psychological Review, 102,* 211–245.

Ericsson, K. A., Krampe, R. T., & Heizmann, S. (1993). Can we create gifted people? In CIBA Foundation Symposium 178, *The origin and development of high ability* (pp. 222–249). Chichester, UK: Wiley.

Ericsson, K. A., Krampe, R. T., & Tesch-Römer, C. (1993). The role of deliberate practice in the acquisition of expert performance. *Psychological Review, 100*(3), 363–406.

Ericsson, K. A., & Lehmann, A. C. (1994a). The acquisition of accompanying (sight-reading) skills in expert pianists. In I. Deliege (Ed.), *Proceedings of the 3rd ICMPC, Liege, Belgium* (pp. 337–338). Liege, Belgium: ESCOM.

Ericsson, K. A., & Lehmann, A. C. (1994b, November). *Marks of genius? Re-interpretation of exceptional feats by great musicians.* Paper presented at the 35th Annual Meeting of the Psychonomic Society, St. Louis, MO.

Ericsson, K. A., & Lehmann, A. C. (1996). Expert and exceptional performance: Evidence on maximal adaptations on task constraints. *Annual Review of Psychology, 47,* 273–305.

Ericsson, K. A., & Simon, H. A. (1993). *Protocol analysis: Verbal reports as data* (rev. ed.). Cambridge, MA: MIT Press.

Ericsson, K. A., & Smith, J. (1991). Prospects and limits in the empirical study of expertise: An introduction. In K. A. Ericsson & J. Smith (Eds.), *Toward a general theory of expertise: Prospects and limits* (pp. 1–38). Cambridge, UK: Cambridge University Press.

Ericsson, K. A., & Staszewski, J. (1989). Skilled memory and expertise: Mechanisms of exceptional performance. In D. Klahr & K. Kotovsky (Eds.), *Complex information processing: The impact of Herbert A. Simon* (pp. 235–267). Hillsdale, NJ: Lawrence Erlbaum Associates.

Feldman, D. H. (1986). *Nature's gambit: Child prodigies and the development of human potential.* New York: Basic Books.

Fitts, P., & Posner, M. I. (1967). *Human performance.* Belmont, CA: Brooks/Cole.

Folkard, S., & Monk, T. H. (1985). Circadian performance rhythms. In S. Folkard & T. H. Monk (Eds.), *Hours of work* (pp. 37–52). Chichester, UK: Wiley.

Galamian, I. (1962). *Principles of violin playing & teaching.* Englewood Cliffs, NJ: Prentice-Hall.

Getzels, J. W., & Csikszentmihalyi, M. (1976). *The creative vision: A longitudinal study of problem finding in art.* New York: Wiley.

Glaser, R., & Bassok, M. (1989). Learning theory and the study of instruction. *Annual Review of Psychology, 40,* 631–666.

Glaser, R., & Chi, M. T. H. (1988). Overview. In M. T. H. Chi, R. Glaser, & M. J. Farr (Eds.), *The nature of expertise* (pp. xv–xxviii). Hillsdale, NJ: Lawrence Erlbaum Associates.

Gobet, F., & Simon, H. A. (1995). Templates in chess memory: A mechanism for recalling several boards. *Complex Information Processes* (Working paper # 513). Pittsburgh, PA: Carnegie Mellon University.

Gobet, F., & Simon, H. A. (in press). The roles of recognition processes and look-ahead search in time-constrained expert problem solving: Evidence from grandmaster level chess. *Psychological Science.*

Greeno, J. G., & Simon, H. A. (1988). Problem solving and reasoning. In R. C. Atkinson, R. J. Herrnstein, G. Lindzey, & R. D. Luce (Eds.), *Stevens' handbook of experimental psychology* (2nd ed., Vol. 2, pp. 589–672). New York: Wiley.

Gruber, H. (1991). *Qualitative Aspekte von Expertise im Schach: Begriffe, Modelle, empirische Untersuchungen und Perspektiven der Expertiseforschung* [Qualitative aspects of expertise in chess: Terminology, models, empirical studies, and outlooks on expertise research]. Aachen, Germany: Feenschach.

Gruber, H. E. (1981a). *Darwin on man: A psychological study of scientific creativity* (2nd ed.). Chicago: University of Chicago Press.

Gruber, H. E. (1981b). On the relation between "aha experiences" and the construction of ideas. *History of Science, 19,* 41–59.

Gruson, L. M. (1988). Rehearsal skill and musical competence: Does practice make perfect? In J. A. Sloboda (Ed.), *Generative processes in music: The psychology of performance, improvisation, and composition* (pp. 91–112). Oxford, UK: Clarendon.

Hagberg, J. M., Allen, W. K., Seals, D. R., Hurley, B. F., Ehsani, A. A., & Holloszy, J. O. (1985). A hemodynamic comparison of young and older endurance athletes after exercise. *Journal of Applied Physiology, 58,* 2041–2046.

Hanson, T. (1992). The mental aspects of hitting in baseball: A case study of Hank Aaron. *Contemporary Thought on Performance and Enhancement, 1*(1), 49–70.

Helsen, W., & Pauwels, J. M. (1993). The relationship between expertise and visual information processing. In J. L. Starkes & F. Allard (Eds.), *Cognitive issues in motor expertise* (pp. 109–134). New York: Elsevier.

Hemery, D. (1976). *Another hurdle: The making of an Olympic champion.* New York: Taplinger.

Hermann, E. (1981). *Shinichi Suzuki: The man and his philosophy.* Athens, OH: Ability Development Associates.

Holding, D. H. (1985). *The psychology of chess skill.* Hillsdale, NJ: Lawrence Erlbaum Associates.

Holmes, F. L. (1989). Antoine Lavoisier and Hans Krebs: Two styles of scientific creativity. In D. B. Wallace & H. E. Gruber (Eds.), *Creative people at work: twelve cognitive case studies* (pp. 44–68). New York: Oxford University Press.

Howe, M. J. A. (1990). *The origins of exceptional abilities.* Oxford, UK: Basil Blackwell.

Johnson, J. S., & Newport, E. L. (1989). Critical period effects in second language learning: The influence of maturational state on the acquisition of English as a second language. *Cognitive Psychology, 21,* 60–99.

Koltanowski, G. (1985). *In the dark.* Coraopolis, PA: Chess Enterprises.

Krampe, R. T. (1994). *Maintaining excellence: Cognitive-motor performance in pianists differing in age and skill level.* Berlin: Edition Sigma.

Krampe, R. T., & Ericsson, K. A. (in press) Maintaining excellence: Deliberate practice and elite performance in young and older pianists. *Journal of Experimental Psychology: General*

Krogius, N. (1976). *Psychology in chess.* New York: RHM Press.

Larkin, J. H., McDermott, J., Simon, D. P., & Simon, H. A. (1980). Models of competence in solving physics problems. *Cognitive Science, 4,* 317–345.

Larkin, J. H., & Simon, H. A. (1987). Why a diagram is (sometimes) worth ten thousand words. *Cognitive Science, 11,* 65–99.

Lehman, H. C. (1953). *Age and achievement.* Princeton, NJ: Princeton University Press.

Lehmann, A. C. (in press). Acquisition of expertise in music: Efficiency of deliberate practice as a moderating variable in accounting for sub-expert performance. In I. Deliege & J. A. Sloboda (Eds.), *Perception and Cognition of Music.* Mahwah, NJ: Lawrence Erlbaum Associates.

Lehmann, A. C., & Ericsson, K. A. (1993). Sight-reading ability of expert pianists in the context of piano accompanying. *Psychomusicology, 12,* 182–195.

Lesgold, A., Rubinson, H., Feltovich, P., Glaser, R., Klopfer, D., & Wang, Y. (1988). Expertise in a complex skill: Diagnosing X-ray pictures. In M. T. H. Chi, R. Glaser, & M. J. Farr (Eds.), *The nature of expertise* (pp. 311–342). Hillsdale, NJ: Lawrence Erlbaum Associates.

Lewis, C. (1981). Skill in algebra. In J. R. Anderson (Ed.), *Cognitive skills and their acquisition* (pp. 85–110). Hillsdale, NJ: Lawrence Erlbaum Associates.

Martin, J. E., & Dubbert, P. M. (1985). Adherence to exercise. *Exercise and Sport Sciences Review, 13,* 137–167.

McClosky, D. N. (1990). *If you're so smart: The narrative of economic expertise.* Chicago: University of Chicago Press.

Miklaszewski, K. (1989). A case study of a pianist preparing a musical performance. *Psychology of Music, 17,* 95–109.

Mitchell, R. G. (1983). *Mountain experience. The psychology and sociology of adventure.* Chicago: University of Chicago Press.

Newell, A. (1990). *Unified theories of cognition.* Cambridge, MA: Harvard University Press.

Newell, A., & Rosenbloom, P. S. (1981). Mechanisms of skill acquisition and the law of practice. In J. R. Anderson (Ed.), *Cognitive skills and their acquisition* (pp. 1–55). Hillsdale, NJ: Lawrence Erlbaum Associates.

Newell, A., & Simon, H. A. (1972). *Human problem solving.* Englewood Cliffs, NJ: Prentice-Hall.

Norman, D. A., Coblentz, C. L., Brooks, L. R., & Babcook, C. J. (1992). Expertise in visual diagnosis: A review of the literature. *Academic Medicine Rime Supplement.*

Norman, D. A., Trott, A. D., Brooks, L. R., & Smith, E. K. M. (1994). Cognitive differences in clinical reasoning related to postgraduate training. *Teaching and Learning in Medicine, 6*(2), 114–120.

Patel, V. L., Arocha, J. F., & Kaufman, D. R. (1994). Diagnostic reasoning and medical expertise. In D. Medin (Ed.), *The psychology of learning and motivation* (Vol. 30, pp. 187–251). New York: Academic Press.

Patel, V. L., & Groen, G. J. (1991). The general and specific nature of medical expertise: A critical look. In K. A. Ericsson & J. Smith (Eds.), *Toward a general theory of expertise* (pp. 93–125). Cambridge, UK: Cambridge University Press.

Qin, Y., & Simon, H. A. (1990). Laboratory replication of scientific discovery processes. *Cognitive Science, 14,* 281–312.

Radford, J. (1990). *Child prodigies and exceptional early achievers.* New York: The Free Press.

Regnier, G., Salmela, J., & Russell, S. J. (1994). Talent detection and development in sports. In R. N. Singer, M. Murphey, & L. K. Tennant (Eds.), *Handbook of research on sport psychology* (pp. 290–313). New York: Macmillan.

Reif, F., & Allen, S. (1992). Cognition for interpreting scientific concepts: A study of acceleration. *Cognition and Instruction, 9*(1), 1–44.

Saariluoma, P. (1989). Chess players' recall of auditorily presented chess positions. *European Journal of Cognitive Psychology, 1,* 309–320.

Saariluoma, P. (1990). Apperception and restructuring in chess players' problem solving. In K. J. Gilhooly, M. T. G. Keene, & G. Erdos (Eds.), *Lines of thought: Reflections on the psychology of thinking* (Vol. 2, pp. 41–57). London: Wiley.

Saariluoma, P. (1991). Aspects of skilled imagery in blindfold chess. *Acta Psychologica, 77,* 65–89.

Saariluoma, P. (1992). Error in chess: The apperception-restructuring view. *Psychological Research, 54,* 17–26.

Salthouse, T. A. (1984). Effects of age and skill in typing. *Journal of Experimental Psychology: General, 113*(3), 345–371.

Salthouse, T. A. (1991). Expertise as the circumvention of human processing limitations. In K. A. Ericsson & J. Smith (Eds.), *Toward a general theory of expertise: Prospects and limits* (pp. 286–300). Cambridge, UK: Cambridge University Press.

Schlaug, G., Jäncke, L., Huang, Y., & Steinmetz, H. (1995). In vivo evidence of structural brain asymmetry in musicians. *Science, 267,* 699–701.

Schmidt, H. G., & Boshuizen, H. P. A. (1993). On the origin of intermediate effects in clinical case recall. *Memory & Cognition, 21,* 338–351.

Schmidt, H. G., Norman, G. R., & Boshuizen, H. P. A. (1990). A cognitive perspective on medical expertise: Theory and implications. *Academic Medicine, 65,* 611–621.

Schulz, R., & Curnow, C. (1988). Peak performance and age among superathletes: Track and field, swimming, baseball, tennis, and golf. *Journal of Gerontology: Psychological Sciences, 43,* 113–120.

Schulz, R., Musa, D., Staszewski, J., & Siegler, R. S. (1994). The relationship between age and major league baseball performance: Implications for development. *Psychology and Aging, 9,* 274–286.

Seashore, C. E. (1967). *Psychology of music.* New York: Dover. (original work published 1938)

Shaffer, L. H. (1975). Multiple attention in continuous verbal tasks. In P. M. Rabbitt & S. Dornic (Eds.), *Attention and performance* (Vol. 5, pp. 157–167). London: Academic Press.

Shephard, R. J. (1994). *Aerobic fitness and health.* Champaign, IL: Human Kinetics.

Simon, D. P., & Simon, H. A. (1978). Individual differences in solving physics problems. In R. S. Siegler (Ed.), *Children's thinking: What develops?* (pp. 325–348). Hillsdale, NJ: Lawrence Erlbaum Associates.

Simon, H. A., & Chase, W. G. (1973). Skill in chess. *American Scientist, 61,* 394–403.

Singer, C. (1958). *From magic to science. Essays on the scientific twilight.* New York: Dover.

Sloboda, J. A. (1985). *The musical mind: The cognitive psychology of music.* Oxford, UK: Oxford University Press.

Sloboda, J. A., Hermelin, B., & O'Connor, N. (1985). An exceptional musical memory. *Music Perception, 3,* 155–170.

Starkes, J. L. (1987). Skill in field hockey: The nature of the cognitive advantage. *Journal of Sport Psychology, 9,* 146–160.

Starkes, J. L., & Deakin, J. (1984). Perception in sport: A cognitive approach to skilled performance. In W. F. Straub & J. M. Williams (Eds.), *Cognitive sport psychology* (pp. 115–128). Lansing, NY: Sport Science Associates.

Staszewski, J. J. (1988). Skilled memory and expert mental calculation. In M. T. H. Chi, R. Glaser, & M. J. Farr (Eds.), *The nature of expertise* (pp. 71–128). Hillsdale, NJ: Lawrence Erlbaum Associates.

Takeuchi, A. H., & Hulse, S. H. (1993). Absolute pitch. *Psychological Bulletin, 113,* 345–361.

Teitz, C. C. (1989). Overuse injuries. In C. C. Teitz (Ed.), *Scientific foundations of sports medicine* (pp. 299–328). Toronto, Canada: Decker.

VanLehn, K. (1991). Rule acquisition events in the discovery of problem-solving strategies. *Cognitive Science, 15,* 1–47.

Wagner, R. K. (1991). Managerial problem-solving. In R. J. Sternberg & P. Frensch (Eds.), *Complex problem solving: principles and mechanisms* (pp. 159–183). Hillsdale, NJ: Lawrence Erlbaum Associates.

Wallman, J. (1994). Nature and nurture of myopia. *Nature, 371,* 201–202.

Watkins, J. G. (1942). *Objective measurement of instrumental performance.* Teachers College, Columbia University Contributions to Education, No. 860.

Yamada, J. (1991). The discrimination learning of the liquids /r/ and /l/ by Japanese speakers. *Journal of Psycholinguistic Research, 20,* 31–46.

Zabrucky, K., & Moore, D. (1989). Children's ability to use three standards to evaluate their comprehension of text. *Reading Research Quarterly, 24,* 336–352.

2

The Role of Practice and Coaching in Entrepreneurial Skill Domains: An International Comparison of Life-Span Chess Skill Acquisition

Neil Charness
Florida State University
Ralf Krampe
Ulrich Mayr
University of Potsdam

More than a decade ago, Bloom and his colleagues (Bloom, 1985) published a book outlining the results of an interview study of talented individuals in the domains of sports (tennis, swimming), the arts (piano, sculpture) and the sciences (research biologists, mathematicians). Coaching was identified as one of the critical features for the development of skill (talent). In many cases, families, some of very modest means, went to extraordinary lengths (time and money) to find top-level coaches for their talented children.

There is a long legacy of learning by apprenticeship in human history, often with a parent or other kin member as the tutor. As society became more complex and specialized, formal structures outside the family unit arose (e.g., the guild system in medieval Europe) to train people and to protect the organization's financial interests. In modern times, much high-level professional training has been taken over by university and college systems (e.g., professional athletes, engineers, physicians).

Still, when it comes to many pastimes or hobbies such as bridge playing or chess playing, there are fewer formal organizations to turn to for the purposes of improving one's skill level. Also, the national and international organizations that have grown up around these hobbies have only begun to act as significant certification boards that dictate how and under what conditions devotees can practice their art. (Or when they do, significant figures always have the option of setting up their own organization, as did recent world chess champion, Garry Kasparov, when he broke away from FIDE and founded the PCA.) In such entrepreneurial domains, individuals can and do play a major role in their own self-development.

The purpose of this chapter is to contrast the potential effect of coaching on skill acquisition and maintenance by comparing chess players in North America (specifically, Canada) and Europe (primarily Germany). We want to examine whether coaching plays an important role in the development of chess skill. If one looks at other domains, particularly professional sports, there is a clear belief that coaching matters for both team and individual sports. (See, for instance, the rated importance of coaching in Starkes, Deakin, Allard, Hodges, & Hayes, chap. 3, this volume). Yet in entrepreneurial domains such as chess, we argue that coaching may play a more minor role, given that reliable information sources exist to support an individual's pursuit of excellence and to provide feedback on progress.

In this chapter, we first outline a broad taxonomy of important factors for skill acquisition. Next we examine chess rating data for large national and international populations. Then we analyze survey data on practicing behavior and its impact on chess rating for samples of players we contacted in Berlin, Toronto, and Moscow. We examine the impact of coaching, chess libraries, the age at which players start to play chess, age of becoming serious about chess, age of joining a chess club, the effects of different types of practice, and player calibration for effective forms of practice. To foreshadow, cumulative serious practice alone is the most important predictor of current chess rating. Surprisingly, coaching does not appear to play a significant direct role.

A TAXONOMY OF FACTORS IMPORTANT TO SKILL

To evaluate the impact of coaching, it helps to have a framework to look at skill acquisition. We have provided general overviews of important factors elsewhere (e.g., Ericsson & Charness, 1994; Ericsson, Krampe, & Tesch-Römer, 1993). Figure 2.1 provides an attempt at outlining a fairly general framework. To deal with expertise in team environments, such as the intensive care situation discussed by Patel, Kaufman, and Magder (chap. 5, this volume), we would need to find ways to encompass social skills.

Our view is that for intellectual domains, such as chess playing, skilled performance is a direct function of structures and processes comprising the

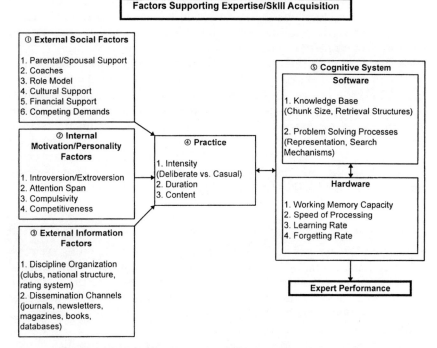

FIG. 2.1. Taxonomy of factors important to expertise/skill acquisition.

cognitive system. See Richman, Staszewski, and Simon (1995) for a simulation model of expert memory and Richman, Gobet, Staszewski, and Simon (chap. 6, this volume) for a summary of the information-processing parameters for the cognitive system of an expert. We focus here on the role of deliberate practice as the primary change mechanism. We hypothesize that the cognitive system changes through practice, both at the software and the hardware levels, enabling highly skilled individuals to bypass the normal limits on information processing (e.g., the span of immediate memory being 7 ± 2 chunks). We hypothesize that social, personality, and external factors have their impact through their influence on practicing behaviors. Each system of influences can in turn be broken down into components.

We focus here on Boxes 1 and 3. Our aim is to understand, in an admittedly indirect fashion, how coaching influences practicing behavior. There are at least two possibilities. Coaches can serve as feedback mechanisms to guide players to fill in gaps in their knowledge base. For instance, a chess coach might notice that a chess player is weak in endgame play and recommend that they work on endgame technique. The coach might also serve as an expert opponent in specific endings so that players can hone their technique against "best play." A concrete example might be how to play a king, f-pawn, h-pawn, and rook versus king and rook ending, learning the drawing technique for the weaker side and the best winning chances for the stronger side. A second possible role for a coach is as social influence, helping to maintain motivation and interest and serving as a role model. Here the coach influences the intensity of practice and techniques, rather than the content of practice.

We chose chess as the domain to examine effects of coaching because unlike almost all other skill domains, it possesses an excellent interval-level scale (Elo, 1986). Hence, we can use fairly powerful parametric statistics, such as regression analysis, to determine the weight carried by coaching in predicting a player's current skill level. We can also determine the relative weights of factors such as age and type of practice. We have outlined elsewhere (e.g., Charness, 1991) a general overview of determinants of chess skill. Our task here is to provide new data concerning the role of coaching and to contrast it with the efficacy of deliberate practice alone.

Skill in Chess

First, we review aspects of chess skill, as indexed by chess rating systems. Rating systems attempt to use a single number to summarize the panoply of skills that players bring to bear on the problem of choosing the best move from a given chess position. The number is derived from the outcome of competitions between players. Rating points are transferred from winner to loser in proportion to their pregame ratings.

Chess organizations provide their members with opportunities to play in rated chess tournaments. The most common rating system in use was devised by the late Arpad Elo (1986). Ratings in national organizations such as the United States Chess Federation (USCF) and the world chess body, Fédération Internationale des Éches (FIDE), fall on an interval scale that was intended to have a standard deviation of about 200 rating points. We present here some recent statistics for both populations.

Characteristics of the FIDE Pool of Highly Rated Players.   F I D E maintains a rating list for players who participate in FIDE-sponsored events. Such events usually attract the elite players of the world. In some cases FIDE-rated players are fairly low rated (e.g., the case of countries without strong chess infrastructures who send players to the Olympiad). The cutoff for maintaining a FIDE rating appears to be 2000. Players who fall below this rating are dropped from the list. We have been able to examine the most recent FIDE rating list, January 1995, which lists current chess rating, number of games played, and country affiliation for 15,139 players. (We thank FIDE and Eric Schiller for making the January 1995 ratings available on the Internet.)

For a subset of players, FIDE also provides date of birth information, allowing the opportunity to examine age and skill relationships. Such a cross-sectional view may not do adequate justice to the question of whether chess skill diminishes with age. Elo (1965) addressed the question longitudinally for Grandmasters (GMs, those with ratings in the 2500+ range), and we reanalyzed the data and reported a classical inverted U-shaped function (Charness & Bosman, 1990). This was done with a very small sample of GMs, however.

For this elite sample, the relationship is a slight (but with this huge sample size, highly significant) positive relationship between age and skill level: r (10,834) = .096. Age trends may be masked by the typical finding that younger players are somewhat underrated because they are on the sharply improving part of their learning function. To assess this, we filter out all players below age 30. Now we find a reduced correlation: r (6,346) = −.055, still highly significant, but the negative sign for the coefficient indicates a downward trend in rating with age.

If we filter out all players below the peak observed for GMs (mid-30s) by selecting only those players over the age of 40, we find an increased value of r (2,864) = −.071. The coefficient in a simple regression is b = −0.914, meaning that rating drops about a point for each year of age over 40. There is an increased trend for ratings to decrease with increased age. Still, trivial amounts of the variance in rating are accounted for by age. Other factors are far more important.

If we look at simple relationships between rating and activity, we note that the better players are more active in terms of games played in the past year: r (15,137) = .385. Ratings are higher by 4 points per game played. Now, with correlational data, the direction is not clear for this relationship. Many of the top players earn their livelihoods by playing in tournaments, so we may be indexing top versus bottom players.

To see if the relationship holds for those with ratings over 2499 (the Grandmaster level), we ran the regression within this subgroup. There we find no relation between number of games and current rating: r (376) = .074. This result may be due to the relatively small rating range, so we also ran the reverse selection and tested for those of less than Grandmaster strength. The correlation re-emerges in the lower than GM group, a bit reduced: r (14,759) = .283. Therefore, we can tentatively suggest that rising intermediate players account for some of this relationship and that being more highly rated is associated with playing more tournament games.

Finally, we plot these age trends as age categories in Fig. 2.2. The cross-sectional view of age trends is very similar to the one that Elo (1965) showed for Grandmasters longitudinally, and that Simonton (1988, chap. 8, this volume) showed in many other domains.

These data indicate that chronological age is a potentially important factor in skill level. In our examination of coaching effects we need to pay attention to player age.

The United States Chess Population.   Another good source of statistics for a wider range of chess ability is provided by the United States Chess Federation. We thank Dr. Mark Glickman, chair of the USCF rating commit-

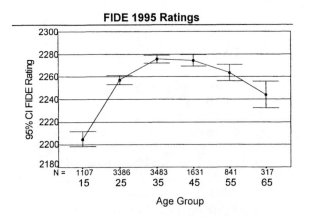

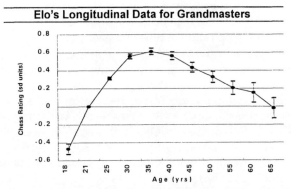

FIG. 2.2. Cross-sectional plot of age versus rating (left panel) and longitudinal plot (right panel).

tee, for making data available for analysis. It is also worth examining the cross-sectional age trends in the much less elite USCF population, shown in Fig. 2.3.

This figure presents a much kinder picture of aging for less skilled players, somewhat akin to the differences observed by Horner, Rushton, and Vernon (1986) for high- versus low-publishing psychologists. The slope of decline past the 30s is much shallower than that observed in the FIDE cross-sectional data. What we are probably observing across FIDE and the USCF is either selective attrition, with poorer players dropping out selectively from the higher age ranges, or an age-complexity finding (Cerella, Poon, & Williams, 1980) showing smaller age deficits for less demanding tasks. It is in some sense less demanding to maintain chess performance at lower skill levels than at higher skill levels.

This brief demographic survey shows that there is an enormous range of skill (0–2805 rating points, about 9 standard deviation units) even among serious chess players who go to the trouble of registering with a national organization and playing in organized tournaments. Skill level is also related to player age. Chess skill, as measured by national and international rating systems, is roughly normally distributed. Peak age is typically the mid-30s, and players often show a steep rise in their teenage years, followed by a slow decline past the peak. The cross-sectional and longitudinal data match reasonably well. One hypothesis worth considering for explaining the age-related decline in chess skill is that older players do not maintain the rigorous practice needed to maintain present levels and develop new expertise. Determining the relation among life-span practice patterns, age, and rating is an important goal for future research.

The match between cross-sectional and longitudinal age trends partially addresses a potentially serious confound in expertise research: selective attrition for "less talented" individuals. That is, we may be following only those with the "talent" to succeed (see Sternberg, chap. 15, this volume). If this hypothesis is correct, then "untalented" individuals should make less progress with their practice regimen than their "talented" counterparts, who go on to become experts. However, Sloboda (chap. 4, this volume) indicates that there is no relation between current skill level and gain with practice for young performing musicians. As he points out, if anything, the high achievers take nonsignificantly longer (deliberate practice time) than the low achievers to reach a given instrument grade level.

THE BERLIN–TORONTO–MOSCOW SAMPLE

In the summer of 1993, we developed a chess practicing behavior questionnaire while the first author was a visiting scientist at the Max Planck Institute for Human Development and Education in Berlin. The questionnaire was designed in English, then translated to German and Russian. The questionnaire

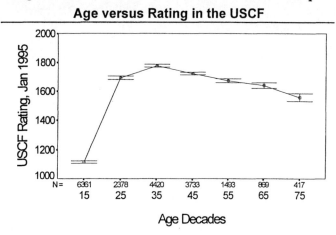

FIG. 2.3. Cross-sectional plot of age versus rating for USCF population.

was piloted with a former chess coach from East Germany, revised, and then distributed both to a sample of players in an experimental chess study and to players participating in the Berlin International August chess tournament. At the same time, it was sent to a sample of Canadian chess players who were participating in an experimental study of chess skill in Toronto. Dr. Katherine Vasiukova at the Moscow State University School of Psychology helped distribute the Russian version of the questionnaire to a small subset of top players participating in the Chess Olympiad in Moscow in December 1994.

We have received (to date) completed or partially completed questionnaires from a total of 158 players: 42 Canadians in Toronto, 94 Europeans in Berlin (primarily German nationals), and 22 (primarily Russian) players in Moscow. Rating information was provided by a subset of 136 players. One of the questions on our survey asked for education level, in terms of years of formal education. Although it is difficult to compare across different national systems, it is obvious that our sample is highly educated (M = 16 years, SD = 3.6). This result can be seen to support de Groot's (1965) and Elo's (1986) observations that top-level players are of above-average intelligence in terms of educational attainment. Our sample is much less elite in chess rating than de Groot's or Elo's, however.

The self-reported rating characteristics (Elo and Chess Federation of Canada ratings are equivalent) of the sample are shown in Fig. 2.4, along with a histogram of the distribution.

The distribution may represent two subpopulations, moderately skilled recreational players, and strong professionals. Eleven of the players have ratings of 2500 or more (Grandmaster level). Thirty-two have ratings between 2200 and 2499 (Master level). As mentioned already, the sample is generally highly educated, but there is no relationship between education level and rating: r (129) = .007. There are also quite significant differences in rating across sites, $F(2, 133) = 33$, $MSE = 53599$, $p < .001$, with the Russian players a very high-rated group, as seen in Fig. 2.5.

One advantage to having both highly skilled players (GMs) and moderately skilled players (those 2 or more standard deviations below GM level) is that we can begin to address the important issue of lack of control groups raised by Sternberg (chap. 15, this volume). One problem he notes is that when we study only the success stories (here GMs) we ignore the practice patterns of those in the "low talent" condition, who practice a great deal but still fail to make much progress.

There are also slight differences in age across sites, $F(2, 137) = 3.90$, $MSE = 229$, $p < .05$, with Toronto site players older than those at the other two sites, who do not differ. This difference was due in part to the sampling frame established for a laboratory-based experimental study in Toronto. That study investigated effects of age and skill. Given this variation across sites, we choose to analyze relationships among variables primarily using a multiple regression analysis approach.

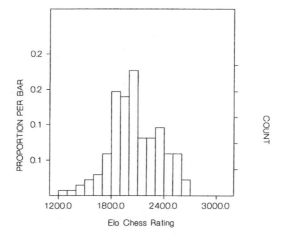

Berlin: N = 94
Moscow: N = 14
Toronto: N= 42

Elo Rating

N	136
MIN	1288
MAX	2645
MEAN	2057
SD	281
SE	24.1
MEDIAN	2026

FIG. 2.4. Histogram and statistics for ratings in the Berlin–Toronto–Moscow chess sample.

It is worth keeping in mind that we have a correlational study. Correlation does not necessarily equate with causation, as Sternberg (chap. 15, this volume) notes. We find ourselves in a position similar to that of early astronomers who could not directly manipulate planets and stars (here, deliberate practice for hundreds and thousands of hours) to ensure that their theories of celestial motion were indeed causal. Nonetheless, the patterns observed in the data can help to constrain hypotheses and theories (then about the laws of motion, now about skill acquisition processes). We also rely on nearly a century of lab-based studies of learning to help fill in the gaps and produce a plausible account of skill acquisition. We rely, too, on our commentators (Glaser, chap. 11, this volume; Holmes, chap. 12, this volume; Shea & Paull, chap. 13, this volume; Shiffrin, chap. 14, this volume; and Sternberg, chap. 15, this volume) to ensure that any confirmation biases are held up to scrutiny.

In this chapter we examine a subset of questions concerned with age, skill, practicing, and coaching. We first report on books as a knowledge

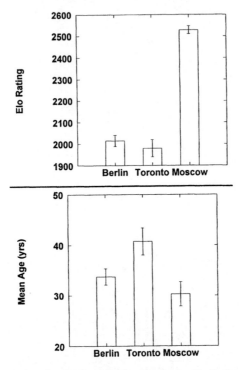

FIG. 2.5. Chess ratings by site (top panel) and ages by site (bottom panel) for chess sample.

source for acquiring skill. Then we probe when players report that they joined a chess club, a potentially important acculturation source for chess players. Next we examine the players' reports of whether they had ever had chess coaches.

Books as a Knowledge Source

In our skill acquisition model, books are seen as an important source of information for techniques to perfect chess-playing ability. One possibility is that better players make more effective use of the existing chess literature. They may purchase, then study from, more chess books or chess magazines. We did have an item that asked players to estimate the number of chess books that they owned.

15. How many chess books do you own (excluding magazines)? _____ *(number)*

This particular item may be slightly negatively biased against some of the East German and Russian players, who may not have had as much disposable income as North American players. As a check, we can see whether number of books owned is related to site. The mean books owned is 121, with a standard deviation of 251, indicating a high skew, with most players owning a moderate number of books and a very few owning several hundred each. The minimum report is 0 and the maximum is 2,000. Thus, we chose to use the logarithm (to base 10) of books owned (adding .5 to all books owned scores to obviate problems with the one score of zero) to explore bivariate and multivariate relationships.

An analysis of variance (ANOVA) by site showed that there were significant variations in book ownership, $F(2, 135) = 11.9$, $MSE = .257$, $p < .001$. However, contrary to expectations based on relative income, and possibly because of a confound with skill level, the mean log books owned was highest for Moscow ($M = 2.35$, $SE = .146$, $N = 12$), then Berlin ($M = 1.75$, $SE = .055$, $N = 84$), then Toronto ($M = 1.546$, $SE = .078$, $N = 42$).

Figure 2.6 shows that the simple relationship between the logarithm of books owned and current chess rating is $r (132) = .53$. Players possessing more books have higher ratings. As with all correlations, the directionality in this relationship is moot. The data are consistent with the hypothesis that the knowledge acquisition process is dependent on ready access to knowledge sources, such as chess books, and that stronger players do not merely collect books but also study from them and derive benefit from having a large variety. Players have "voted" many hundreds and thousands of dollars in this belief. We later examine multivariate relationships with chess book ownership.

Joining a Chess Club

Clubs provide players, particularly young ones, with reliable access to organized chess activities, chess lessons, newsletters, and often, a chess

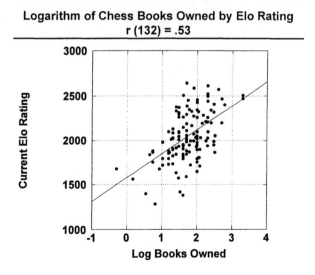

FIG. 2.6. Bivariate plot of chess books owned by chess rating.

library. Clubs are examples of Category 3 in our skill acquisition model: external information dissemination channels. Clubs also help to socialize players into the serious chess-playing subculture. In Europe, clubs sometimes also have commercial sponsors who can provide financial support to players who represent them in interclub tournaments, such as the Schach Bundesliga in Germany. Age at which players join a club is one index of when they become serious about chess. We asked one question concerning joining a club:

> 9. Did you ever join a chess club or a group where chess was played on a regular basis (club, school workshop, etc.) ? If YES, at what age for the first time _____ (Age)

As seen in Fig. 2.7 there are significant site differences for the age at which players report joining a chess club for the first time, $F(2, 137) = 7.83$, $MSE = 76.19$, $p < .01$.

Europeans affiliate with a chess club earlier than North Americans. The Russian players affiliated earlier on average than other Europeans. This finding fits with unpublished data from Doll and Mayr (1987) with 23 players (Mean Elo = 2,317, $SD = 83$, Min = 2220, Max = 2605). They had asked for the starting age ($M = 10.1$, $SD = 3.68$), and the age when joining a club ($M = 13.5$, $SD = 2.61$).

Are there advantages to joining a chess club early versus later? The simple relation between age of joining a chess club and current chess rating is $r (134) = -.38$. Those who join at an early age have higher ratings, as seen in the second panel of Fig. 2.7. The Doll and Mayr (1987) data set also shows a significant negative correlation between club-joining age and rating ($r = -.45$). Such results are consistent with the hypothesis that there may be a critical period for developing chess skill.

Coaching

In our model, coaches are seen primarily as role models, although they can also serve the function of information dissemination (external information sources). Chess coaches are comparatively rare in North America compared to Europe (although one, Bruce Pandolfini, was a central figure in a recent chess movie, *Searching for Bobby Fischer*). In our questionnaire we asked a multistep question about coaching:

> 11. Did you ever receive any formal chess instruction from a teacher or trainer? ___Yes ___No
>
> INDIVIDUALLY: from (Age) _____ to (Age) _____
>
> GROUP: from (Age) _____ to (Age) _____

There is a strong relationship between ever having a chess teacher and site, with only 16 of 41 respondents in Toronto reporting having a coach, all

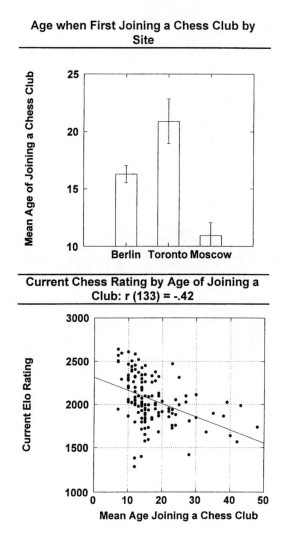

FIG. 2.7. Sample site by age of first joining a chess club (top panel) and chess rating by age of joining a chess club (bottom panel).

14 Moscow site players having had a coach, and 53 of 94 Berlin site players reporting having had a chess coach. (Note that there are missing responses from 11 questionnaires.)

A relatively small subset of players answered the two subparts to Question 11. We estimated the years of individual and group training by subtracting starting age from ending age. In the subgroups who have estimates, shown in Fig. 2.8, the mean years of group coaching varied with site, $F(2, 64) = 4.97$, $MSE = 35$, $p < .01$.

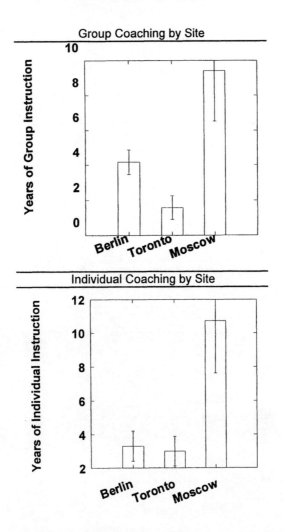

FIG. 2.8. Years of group (top panel) and individual (bottom panel) chess coaching by sample site.

A different subset of players have estimates for mean years of individual coaching. Here too, coaching years vary with site, $F(2, 30) = 5.06$, $MSE = 41.3$, $p < .02$, with Moscow players receiving many more years of individual coaching.

It is clear that European players are much more likely than North Americans to have ever had chess training or coaching. Also, the very select (highly rated) sample of Russian players are likely to have had about 10 years of both individual and group training.

Coaching and Chess Rating

Does the availability of coaching have an impact on the level of skill reached? We first examine the simple relationship between coaching and skill level, using the yes/no part of the coaching item (given that it screens in more of the sample). There is a modest positive relationship between having formal training and rating, r (133) = .26. The 56 players without formal training had a lower mean rating of 1971 (SE = 36.3) than the 79 with formal training, whose mean rating was 2121 (SE = 30.6). Coaching on average was associated with nearly half a standard deviation advantage.

As is always the case with correlational data, we cannot determine causal relations. It is possible that only highly rated players are provided with coaching, or that highly rated players seek out coaches. To try to understand the nature of this relationship we turn to the practice data.

Practicing Behavior

Reports of the intensity of practice of top players are widespread. A former chess teacher of Robert Fischer commented that Fischer practiced 5 to 10 hours a day (Collins, 1974). A biographer of the three Polgar sisters commented: "Eight to ten hours a day would be devoted to the study of its various aspects: opening theory, endgames, speed chess, and blindfold chess" (Forbes, 1992, p. 24).

Players were asked to fill out several items concerning practicing behavior. We focus primarily on the reports of hours of serious study alone, and serious study and analysis with other players (e.g., during tournament play). We created estimates of cumulative hours in each form of practice (e.g., Ericsson et al., 1993), by multiplying the reported number of hours per week by 52 and summing across years. (Note that we are probably overestimating practice time by using 52 as the multiplier. Also, players are likely to overreport the actual time spent in practice on a questionnaire, compared to the case of using a diary technique; Ericsson et al., 1993.)

Again, not all players took the time and trouble to provide these estimates. As a rough check on the representativeness of that subsample, we examined the mean ratings for players who provided the reports versus those who do not. The 126 who provided at least some practicing data (practice alone) were slightly (M = 2061, SD = 278), although not significantly, more highly rated than those (N = 10) who did not provide practicing data, M = 2003, SD = 325.

People in the sample have accumulated a very substantial amount of experience in chess, both by studying alone and by playing and analyzing games with others. We use the logarithm (base 10) of the cumulative time in hours for two reasons. First, the distributions are highly skewed (M = 6,173, SD = 9,049 for serious study alone, and M = 5,466, SD = 5,798 for tournament play and study with others). Second, skill acquisition in chess has been shown to be log-linear in time (e.g., Charness, 1989). Figure 2.9 shows the results.

The minimum time spent by any player (who provided both forms of practice data, $N = 134$) is over 100 hours for each form of activity. The maximum report is about 64,000 hours (about 7.3 years!). The expected combined time for the two forms of practice is about 11,000 hours, an estimate that is within the range of cumulative practice hours reported by serious musicians performing a classical repertoire (Ericsson et al., 1993), and at the upper end of estimates by chunking theories of chess skill acquisition (e.g., Richman et al., chap. 6, this volume; Simon & Chase, 1973).

Ericsson et al. noted that deliberate practice was the most relevant variable to differentiate the star musicians from the less skilled accompanists and amateurs. We wish to argue here that serious practice alone is probably closest in meaning to deliberate practice by musicians. We believe that serious study with others, via tournament play and postgame analysis, is probably also a useful form of practice. It is unlikely, however, to be of as great benefit to the development of skill as serious study alone.

In Fig. 2.10 we show the simple relationships between current rating and the two types of practice. As expected, the two forms of practice are fairly highly intercorrelated, $r (110) = .635$, but practice alone is more highly correlated with rating ($r = .60$) than is practice with others ($r = .35$).

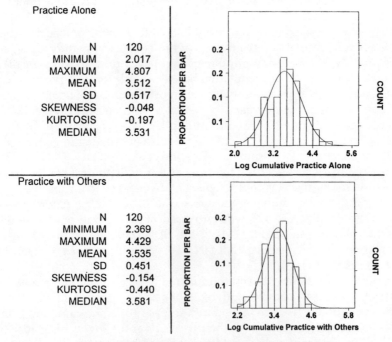

FIG. 2.9 Histogram and statistics for types of practice.

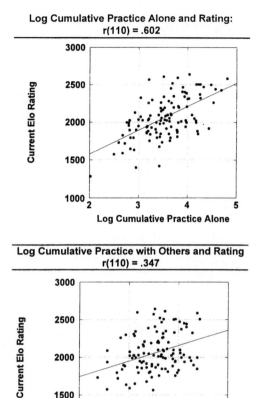

FIG. 2.10. Plot of chess rating by log cumulative hours of practice alone (top panel) and log cumulative hours of practice with others (bottom panel).

To establish the effects of age, club-joining age, coaching, log of books owned, and practice type on rating, we first examine the additive multivariate relationships among these variables. Again, not all players have data for all variables, so we will necessarily have an incomplete picture. In Table 2.1 we show that age, negatively, log cumulative practice alone, positively, and log books owned, positively, are the only significant predictors of current rating. Cumulative practice with others does not add incrementally to prediction, nor does the year when a player joined a chess club. Similarly, having a coach (formal training) also does not add significantly to rating level after accounting for the prior relationships. These variables jointly account for about 55% of the variance in rating (adjusted r-square of .551), in a highly significant prediction equation, $F(8, 100) = 20$, $p < .001$.

TABLE 2.1
Multiple Regression Predicting Elo Rating

Variable	Coefficient	SE	Beta	T	P(2-tail)
Constant	878.5	160.4	0.000	5.477	0.000
Age	−5.63	1.79	−0.315	−3.140	0.002
Log cumulative hours of serious analysis alone	309.5	47.6	0.564	6.496	0.000
Log books owned	150.1	37.1	0.291	4.043	0.000
Start year	−5.84	4.54	−0.111	−1.286	0.201
Serious year	6.70	4.94	0.221	1.358	0.178
Club joining age	−5.84	4.42	−0.209	−1.321	0.190
Trainer (0,1)	−13.8	39.6	−0.025	−0.348	0.729
Log cumulative hours of serious practice with others	21.8	52.3	0.036	0.416	0.678

Note. Significant variables are bolded.

The coefficients help put the values of these variables in perspective. Each additional accumulated log unit of serious study time alone is worth a rating gain of about 310 rating points. Each year of age decrements chess skill level by about 6 rating points. The age effect is not unexpected given the general relationships already shown between age and chess rating, and the relatively middle-aged sample of players (thereby ensuring that age to rating relationships are likely to be on the downward sloping side of the inverted backward J-shaped function). Each log unit increase in a chess library adds about 150 points.

If we include just the significant variables in the regression equation, the best predictor set is:

Chess rating = 857 + 323 Log Cumulative Hours Alone + 161 Log Books − 6.5 Age.

The detailed results for the regression are shown in Table 2.2. The nonzero intercept is probably not a bad estimate for a (young) player's initial rating in a first chess tournament (about 900 rating points).

Although there are some difficulties in assessing interaction effects with regression analysis (McClelland & Judd, 1993), we looked at a subset of two-way interactions and found two worthy of mention, as seen in Table 2.3. We first converted the predictor variables to Z-score form to avoid multicollinearity problems after creating cross-product terms. We also introduced a predictor, current deliberate practice, based on the response to a questionnaire item that asked for hours of practice in a typical week in the last year.

The interaction of age with current deliberate practice level (hours per week in the past year) has a positive coefficient, meaning that those 1 standard deviation above the sample mean in age derived 39 rating points for each hour of practice alone (hours above the mean practice level in the sample). Those at the mean age level derive no benefit, and those below the mean level (young players) have an expected negative benefit for each hour above the mean of practice alone. Older players' current ratings are particularly influenced by current practice levels, much as was the case for skilled musicians (Krampe, 1994; Krampe & Ericsson, in press). The second interaction can be interpreted to show that log cumulative practice counts less for older players. Those 1 standard deviation above the mean in age show 70 points fewer than expected from their total accumulated deliberate practice. Those at the age mean show no effect of age. Those 1 standard deviation below the mean in age show a 70-point greater gain than would be expected from the linear relation between rating and deliberate practice.

Thus, the two interactions show a net positive balance for younger players from cumulative practice relative to recent practice. They also show

TABLE 2.2
Multiple Regression Predicting Chess Rating:
Significant Predictors Only

Variable	Coefficient	SE	Beta	T	P(2-tail)
Constant	857.4	114.7	0.000	7.475	0.000
Age	−6.51	1.18	−0.376	−5.504	0.000
Log cumulative hours of serious study alone	323.4	38.11	0.618	8.487	0.000
Log books owned	161.4	35.17	0.309	4.591	0.000

Note. $F(3, 110) = 54$, $R^2 = .595$

TABLE 2.3
Multiple Regression with Select Interactions Entered
(Z-score Transformed Predictors)

Variable	Coefficient	SE	Beta	T	P(2-tail)
Constant	2080	16.9	0.000	123	0.000
Age	−56.0	22.1	−0.210	−2.532	0.013
Club-joining age	−37.5	19.8	−0.147	−1.896	0.061
Log cumulative practice alone	109.5	21.4	0.403	5.117	0.000
Log books owned	86.2	18.0	0.305	4.788	0.000
This year's practice alone (hrs/week)	70.25	16.7	0.267	4.204	0.000
Age* Current practice alone	39.2	16.8	0.154	2.335	0.021
Age* Log cumulative practice alone	−70.3	19.4	−0.241	−3.615	0.000

Note. $F(7, 104) = 32$, $R^2 = .68$

old adults to be most sensitive to current practice levels for maintaining a high current rating. It is also noteworthy that by including these interactions, explained variance rises to nearly 70%, a value so high that it is suspicious, given the inherent unreliability of self-report. Again, we need to be cautious about drawing inferences from these relationships. We do not know what would happen if the practice variable were to be systematically manipulated in younger and older players. We observe what is, not what might be.

We can also plot a simple regression equation to estimate how many hours it is expected to take a young player to become a Master (rating of 2200 points), or a Grandmaster (2500 points) based on deliberate practice alone, as seen in Fig. 2.11.

We restrict ourselves here to players below the age of 40 to avoid the negative age effect. The regression line in the figure indicates that it will take, on average, about 3.75 log cumulative hours of serious study alone to reach Master (2200) levels, and about 4.5 log cumulative hours to reach Grandmaster (2500) levels. Adding rating points as you move up the skill scale runs up quickly against a logarithmic investment in time. Such estimates fit with earlier ones (e.g., Simon & Chase, 1973) that it takes between 1,000 and 10,000 hours (3 to 4 log units) to reach strong master levels of performance, based on pattern recognition capabilities of a master player. Those estimates, however, were for all forms of practice, not deliberate study alone. Our result, showing that tournament play and deliberate practice are differentially associated with expertise, place some constraints on chunking theories of expertise (e.g., Richman et al., chap. 6, this volume).

Our estimates are somewhat higher than earlier ones, suggesting, perhaps, that our 52-week multiplier is inaccurate or that players have

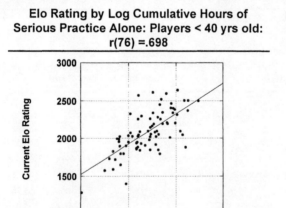

FIG. 2.11. Plot of chess rating by log cumulative hours of practice alone by players less than 40 years of age.

overestimated their practice time. Still, these predicted skill acquisition times also fit with a power law learning function in trials (e.g., Newell & Rosenbloom, 1981) for skill acquisition, showing that each increment in skill takes an additional log unit of practice. In a previous longitudinal study of one Canadian player, Charness (1989) showed power law learning in time rather than trials. Nonetheless, the average predicted time of investment necessary to reach grandmaster levels (32,000 hours) makes it clear why it is so rare an achievement.

Critical Periods for Skill?

One claim heard frequently in the anecdotal literature and mentioned by Elo (1986) is that if you do not learn the game when young, you will not become a top-ranked player. The first author has heard this claim particularly in the context of skill in speed chess, a form of chess that relies heavily on rapid perception. The advantage to learning the game when young is likened to that of learning a language as your mother tongue. We asked two questions related to the age at which players started playing chess:

1. *At what age did you learn the chess moves?* _____ *(Age)*

2. *At what age did you start playing chess seriously?* _____ *(Age)*

The mean starting year was 10 ($SD = 4.8$, $N = 139$), and the mean year when someone began to be serious about playing chess was 16.7 ($SD = 8.8$, $N = 139$). The distributions are skewed, as seen in Fig. 2.12, so medians probably provide somewhat better estimates: start age = 10, serious age = 15.

The bivariate relations between starting age, serious age, and current rating are shown in Fig. 2.13. The Doll and Mayr (1987) data set shows a nonsignificant, but comparable size ($r = -.27$) correlation between starting age and rating.

We tried adding these starting age variables into the regression equation to see whether they accounted for any additional variance beyond that explained by current age and practice alone. Neither variable added significantly to the equation. That is, starting age (either year when chess was learned, or year when chess was played seriously) did not influence development of skill. A "talent hypothesis" (e.g., Gardner, 1995; Winner, chap. 10, this volume) might predict that younger starting players would be more successful. At least in this sample, a younger starting age is not associated with greater achievement once cumulative practice hours are taken into account, in contrast to some evidence to the contrary shown in Elo (1986).

Also, Krogius (1976), looking at the relation between starting age (first learned the moves: about age 10.5 in his sample) and time to reach Grandmaster levels, argued that those starting later reached the Grandmaster

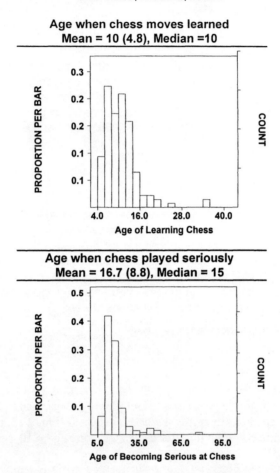

FIG. 2.12. Histograms for age when learning chess (top panel) and age when becoming serious about chess (bottom panel).

level sooner. In both cases these investigators restricted themselves to the top-ranked players (international masters and Grandmasters), unlike the case in the present sample. (Ericsson et al., 1993, argued that there may be a trend for top players of more recent cohorts to start somewhat younger. See their Table 3.) The Krogius data are plotted in Fig. 2.14.

The data in the left panel tend to support the notion that almost no one (Robert Fischer was the low point in this data set) achieves Grandmaster status with less than 10 years of experience in playing chess. The explanation for why those starting younger achieve GM status earlier in age, but take more years to do so compared to later starters is probably to be found in practice patterns. We now know that it takes a great accumulation of intensive practice to reach very high achievement levels. Those starting younger may be expected to do so at an earlier age. However, it may also be the case that it is necessary to practice efficiently. We would not expect many 4- or 5-year-old children to have the metacognitive skills to practice as effectively as a 15-year-old, so it may be that more efficient practice by later starters shortens the time to high achievement. Also, there is a major difference between learning the moves and becoming serious about chess. That lag may be greater for earlier learners. We can test the latter hypothesis by examining the correlation between start time and serious time from the questionnaire data.

The correlation between starting age and age of becoming serious is positive: r (133) = .65, meaning that those starting later also became serious

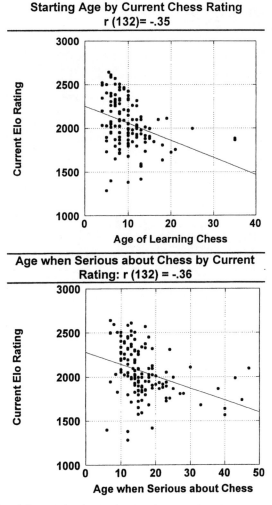

FIG. 2.13. Plot of chess rating by starting age (top panel) and age when serious about chess (bottom panel).

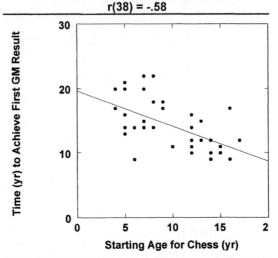

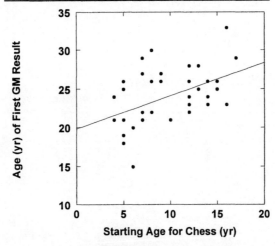

FIG. 2.14. Plot of Krogius data for starting age and time to achieve first Grandmaster result (top panel) and age of first Grandmaster result (bottom panel).

about the game later. The critical relation, though, is years to become serious with starting age, where years to become serious is the difference between age of being serious and age of starting to play chess. That correlation is r (135) = .13. (It drops to near zero if we eliminate those who started after the age of 30.) That is, starting later is not significantly associated with the amount of time elapsed before becoming serious. We can probably rule out the negative relation between starting age and years to a GM result as coming from late starters becoming serious sooner. The evidence seems more consistent with an advantage to older starters accruing from more effective study techniques.

CALIBRATION AND SKILL

Recent publications (e.g., Ericsson et al., 1993) have demonstrated the importance of deliberate practice for expert performance. How well calibrated are chess players of different skill levels to effective forms of practice? We asked players to rate the importance of a set of chess-related activities given in Table 2.4. We have also provided the correlation of importance ratings with current chess ratings. A positive correlation implies that better players differentially rated the activity as important, and a negative one means that they differentially rated the activity as unimportant. Better players are significantly better calibrated about the nature of some of the activities that lead to high-level performance. Noteworthy is the correlation for serious analysis of positions alone, despite the generally high rating given to this activity, in contrast to the case for active participation in tournaments, which also has a high rating.

TABLE 2.4
**Mean Relevance Ratings for Chess Activities and Correlation
of Relevance Ratings With Skill**

Activity for Improving Chess Skill	Mean Relevance Rating (1–7) (SE)	Correlation With Elo Chess Rating
Serious analysis of positions alone (chess books, magazines, databases, postal chess, etc.)	5.9 (.13)	.23[*]
Reading chess literature *for fun* (chess books, magazines, databases, etc.)	3.6 (.15)	.02
Active participation in chess tournaments	6.1 (.11)	.01
Blitz chess	3.2 (.13)	.07
Rapid chess (about 30 min per game)	4.1 (.12)	−.02
Playing chess games outside tournaments	3.6 (.15)	−.20[*]
Playing chess computers	3.2 (.14)	−.36[*]
Receiving formal instruction	4.4 (.18)	.15
Providing formal instruction	3.1 (.16)	.03
Analyses of positions *with others* (during tournaments, etc.)	5.1 (.14)	.12
Chess problems (chess columns, etc.)	3.9 (.15)	.08

[*] $p < .05$.

SUMMARY

Consonant with the findings for musicians, deliberate practice alone seems to carry the most weight in determining skill level. The better players are aware of this relationship. At least in this sample, tutoring by coaches seems relatively unimportant. Motivated chess players who have adequate resources (e.g., chess books) seem able to attain high levels of skill solely by deliberate study and practice alone. Older players, however, perform below the skill level predicted by cumulative hours of such deliberate practice. Such decline is mediated in part by the amount of current practice alone. Deteriorating "hardware" may also be responsible for such small, but significant, declines in skill. Finally, there is little evidence of a critical period for high-level achievement in chess, as starting age does not predict skill level beyond the prediction from cumulative hours of practice. Admittedly, there were very few players who became serious about chess past the age of 40, so we cannot be confident about this conclusion for a new retiree who wants to become an elite player. Someone starting younger can expect to reach high levels sooner given intensive practice, but a later (e.g., postpuberty) starting age is apparently not a significant barrier to high-level play.

The Role of Innate Talent?

As we outlined elsewhere (e.g., Ericsson & Charness, 1994), there is a strong historic belief that innate talent is responsible for expert performance, despite the singular lack of evidence for this construct. (See Winner, chap. 10, this volume, for some case-based evidence for the contrary position with precocious drawing by children. She argues that some child prodigies can achieve at high levels without much deliberate practice.) We think that our data on the relation between practice alone and analysis with others may provide a plausible theory for why people ought to believe in a talent factor in chess, and by extension, talent in other domains. Recall that the regression equation predicting current chess rating showed that practice alone was the most important factor, and that analyzing with others and playing in tournaments (public practice) did not add significantly to prediction.

Imagine two hypothetical players, X rated at 2200, and Y rated at 1800. Player Y notes that X plays in about the same number of tournaments, and that Player X engages in postgame analysis as often as Player Y does. Hence, their relative rating difference must be due to the fact that Player X is more talented than Player Y. The missing factor may be what X and Y do outside the chess club or tournament hall. Player X may be studying an hour per day more than Player Y, and studying in more effective ways. Publicly observable playing may not be a good enough index to more effective private practice, or so the regression equations indicate. Hence people are likely to underestimate the amount of time spent studying by other players, and attribute their greater success to "talent." In effect, this is probably not a bad definition of talent: high achievement in an unexpectedly short time.

There is a second more subtle bias that may work toward attributing success to talent. Social psychologists have observed a predilection for people to attribute their own behaviors to situation-specific factors: "I was impelled to act that way by the circumstances." However, the behavior of others is attributed to their enduring traits: "He acted that way because he is a mean person." The asymmetry in attribution patterns has been called the *fundamental attribution error* (Ross, 1977). Such a bias may also predispose people to be more willing to attribute someone else's skill level to their enduring trait of "talent" rather than to their hard work (situational explanation). People may presume "innocence" with respect to practice but rush to a hasty "guilty" verdict for talent.

What might talent represent in terms of the framework shown in Fig. 2.1? Good candidates would be individual differences in hardware that result in unique internal representations of the domain, or that result in accelerated gains in knowledge (faster chunking). Although we know of no strong evidence for either from experimental data (and have seen a negative instance for chess in Charness, 1989), such individual differences are logically possible.

CONCLUSIONS

Our survey of top-level chess players has shown one expected and one surprising result. The expected result was the influence of deliberate practice on skill. As the literature on skill in music performance revealed, high-level performance is a function of a very high investment in deliberate practice alone. This rule also applies to chess mastery. Starkes et al. (chap. 3, this volume; wrestlers, figure skaters) and Sloboda (chap. 4, this volume; instrumental music performers) provide additional support for the hypothesis that hours of deliberate practice are critical for skill acquisition.

Why is serious study alone so powerful a variable, particularly compared with tournament play and analysis with others? Serious study alone is an activity that allows the player maximal control over the amount and duration of study. Think of it as a form of self-paced versus externally paced learning. Players have finer control over the feedback and can safely try out different approaches that might be too risky in the context of the narrow goal of winning a tournament game. Studying alone is likely to be more favorable for learning than the tournament situation and it is potentially more intense than studying with others. Such intensity and striving for excellence may be a necessary feature (see Ericsson, chap. 1, this volume).

In contrast to the case for skill in music, we have been able to provide a prediction equation that makes the quantitative relationship between practice and skill (and a few other variables) more clear cut. We also have a large enough sample of players spread across both the age and skill ranges to show the negative influence of chronological age on performance. It is slight, but quite significant over the adult life cycle. An adult player can expect to lose on average about 5 to 6 rating points every year. The demographic trends presented at the beginning of this chapter suggest that this age-related rating loss accelerates. Still, this loss should be contrasted with the approximately 310-point gains for each log unit of accumulated deliberate practice. Also, the interaction of age with current practice levels, showing that older players derive a differential benefit from current serious study alone, is consistent with findings for musicians (Krampe, 1994; Krampe & Ericsson, in press).

The surprising finding was the failure to show a coaching effect. Although there were noticeable differences between North Americans and Europeans in the extent to which coaches or trainers were utilized, the presence or absence of formal training had no noticeable effect on skill acquisition, beyond any influence through deliberate practice. Perhaps most of the expected coaching effect is carried by the practice variable. Coaches may be responsible, in part, for helping players set up their rigorous practice schedules. Also, as Ericsson et al. (1993) noted, very elite musicians may have fewer coaches than less elite musicians. It may be more important to develop a good teacher–student relationship early on than to have many different coaches or many hours of coaching.

Chess is evidently more entrepreneurial than classical music performance in respect to coaching. It would be quite unusual (although not impossible) to find someone achieve very high levels of classical music performance without ever having had formal music lessons. (It would be less unusual for jazz performance; see Sloboda, 1991.) However, generalizing from this sample, it would not be terribly surprising to find a chess master who never took a chess lesson from another player.

In chess, contrary to classical instrumental music, there is more than adequate feedback from tournament results to let players know when they are on the wrong track. The critical techniques for playing well are also easily accessible through printed sources. We did show that the number of chess books owned was positively related to skill level. Learning requires feedback. In chess, evidently, adequate feedback is available with very little formal tutoring.

We do not wish to downplay the importance of tournament play and analysis with others in supporting high-level performance. Although time spent in these activities does not make an incremental prediction to current rating, beyond that for deliberate practice alone, it was one of the more important bivariate predictors of rating, and received uniformly high ratings of relevance from players. Tournament play is undoubtedly necessary for advancement, but not sufficient by itself for high achievement. The most important work seems to come in the hours away from the tournament hall.

It remains to be seen whether these findings would continue to hold as we push higher yet, toward world champion levels of play (2650-2800 ratings). Note that the most highly skilled players in the sample, the Russians, had received many years of formal coaching. At this point in time, however, we would hypothesize that chess coaches probably exert their influence on skill development through players' practicing behaviors. It takes an uncommon set of circumstances to keep people working for more than 10,000 hours at a skill, chess playing, that provides very few of them with a comfortable standard of living. Coaches may help by building and maintaining the motivation necessary to move a very good player, a Master, through the log units of cumulative practice necessary to reach Grandmaster and world championship levels.

ACKNOWLEDGMENTS

This research was supported by DAAD, the Natural Sciences and Engineering Research Council of Canada (NSERC A0790), as well as the Max Planck Institute for Human Development and Education by supporting the first author as a visiting scientist. We thank Anders Ericsson for helpful comments on an early draft.

We would like to thank Leanne Dietrich, Lianne Tan, Katherine Vasiukova, Barbara Zwikirsch, Mike Stolz, Mirko Wendland, and Horst Metzing for help in gathering data. We thank Anna and Boris Stetenko for creating the Russian translation of the questionnaire. We particularly thank Katherine Vasiukova for distributing the questionnaire during the Chess Olympiad in Moscow in December 1994. Finally, we are extremely grateful to the many chess players who took the time to fill out our questionnaire.

REFERENCES

Bloom, B. S. (Ed.) (1985). *Developing talent in young people.* New York: Ballantine.

Cerella, J., Poon, L. W. & Williams, D. M. (1980). Age and the complexity hypothesis. In L. W. Poon (Ed.) *Aging in the 1980s: Psychological issues* (pp. 332–340). Washington, DC: American Psychological Association.

Charness, N. (1989). Expertise in chess and bridge. In D. Klahr & K. Kotovsky (Eds.), *Complex information processing: The impact of Herbert A. Simon* (pp. 183–208). Hillsdale, NJ: Lawrence Erlbaum Associates.

Charness, N. (1991). Expertise in chess: The balance between knowledge and search. In K. A. Ericsson & J. Smith (Eds.), *Toward a general theory of expertise: Prospects and limits* (pp. 39–63). New York: Cambridge University Press.

Charness, N., & Bosman, E. A. (1990). Expertise and aging: Life in the lab. In T. H. Hess (Ed.), *Aging and cognition: Knowledge organization and utilization* (pp. 343–385). Amsterdam: Elsevier.

Collins, J. W. (1974). *My seven chess prodigies.* New York: Simon & Schuster.

de Groot, A. D. (1965). *Thought and choice in chess.* The Hague: Mouton.

Doll, J., & Mayr, U. (1987). Intelligenz und schachleistung—eine untersuchung an schachexperten [Intelligence and chess performance—An investigation of chess experts]. *Psychologische Beitrage, 29,* 270–289.

Elo, A. E. (1965). Age changes in master chess performances. *Journal of Gerontology, 20,* 289–299.

Elo, A. E. (1986). *The rating of chessplayers, past and present* (2nd ed.). New York: Arco.

Ericsson, K. A., & Charness, N. (1994). Expert performance: Its structure and acquisition. *American Psychologist, 49,* 725–747.

Ericsson, K. A., Krampe, R. T., & Tesch-Römer, C. (1993). The role of deliberate practice in the acquisition of expert performance. *Psychological Review, 100,* 363–406.

Forbes, C. (1992). *The Polgar sisters: Training or genius?* New York: Henry Holt.

Gardner, H. (1995). Why would anyone become an expert? *American Psychologist, 50,* 802–803.

Horner, K. L., Rushton, J. P., & Vernon, P. A. (1986). Relation between aging and research productivity of academic psychologists. *Psychology and Aging, 4,* 319–324.

Krampe, R. T. (1994). *Maintaining excellence: Cognitive-motor performance in pianists differing in age and skill level.* Berlin: Max-Planck-Institut für Bildungsforschung.

Krampe, R. T., & Ericsson, K. A. (in press). Maintaining excellence: Deliberate practice and elite performance in young and older pianists. *Journal of Experimental Psychology: General*

Krogius, N. (1976). *Psychology in chess.* New York: RHM Press.

McClelland, G. H., & Judd, C. M. (1993). Statistical difficulties of detecting interactions and moderator effects. *Psychological Bulletin, 2,* 376–390.

Newell, A., & Rosenbloom, P. S. (1981). Mechanisms of skill acquisition and the power law of practice. In J. R. Anderson (Ed.), *Cognitive skills and their acquisition* (pp. 1–55). Hillsdale, NJ: Lawrence Erlbaum Associates.

Richman, H. B., Staszewski, J. J., & Simon, H. A. (1995). Simulation of expert memory using EPAM IV. *Psychological Review, 102,* 305–330.

Ross, L. (1977). The intuitive psychologist and his shortcomings: Distortions in the attribution process. In L. Berkowitz (Ed.), *Advances in experimental social psychology* (Vol. 10) (pp. 173–220). New York: Academic Press.

Simon, H. A., & Chase, W. G. (1973). Skill in chess. *American Scientist, 61*(4), 394–403.

Simonton, D. K. (1988). Age and outstanding achievement: What do we know after a century of research? *Psychological Bulletin, 104,* 251–267.

Sloboda, J. A. (1991). Musical expertise. In K. A. Ericsson & J. Smith (Eds.), *Toward a general theory of expertise: Prospects and limits* (pp. 153–171). New York: Cambridge University Press.

3

Deliberate Practice in Sports: What Is It Anyway?

Janet L. Starkes
McMaster University
Janice M. Deakin
Queen's University
Fran Allard
University of Waterloo
Nicola J. Hodges
McMaster University
April Hayes
Queen's University

Expertise has been a research area of increasing interest to sport scientists (e.g., Housner & French, 1994; Starkes & Allard, 1993). The focus of much of this work has been on the cognitive correlates of skill in sport, with such topics as decision making (e.g., Helsen & Pauwels, 1993; McPherson & Thomas, 1989) and forms of knowledge (e.g., Allard & Starkes, 1991) being studied. This work is not simple to do because many of the tools available for the study of expertise in cognitive domains are not directly applicable to the study of sport. It is not easy to collect protocols from a basketball player who is in the process of driving to the basket. The difficulty of discovering what is in the mind of the expert athlete is balanced by the ease of observing what the athlete is actually doing while performing, and what the athlete does to prepare to perform. With the recent interest in the role of practice activities as a determinant of expertise, it is natural to turn to athletes as test cases.

In this chapter, we look at the practice activities of skilled wrestlers and figure skaters from the deliberate practice framework developed by Ericsson, Krampe, and Tesch-Römer (1993). We have looked at three tenets of this framework:

1. The definition of deliberate practice; that deliberate practice is not play, not paid work, not watching the skill being performed, not inherently enjoyable, requires effort and attention from the learner, and often involves activities selected by a coach or teacher to facilitate learning.
2. The relationship between level of deliberate practice and skill; that performance is monotonically related to the amount of deliberate practice; time spent in practice is a critical determinant of level of performance.
3. Because deliberate practice can be any activity designed to improve the current level of performance, does what constitutes deliberate practice differ across domains?

The first part of this chapter looks at practice in wrestlers of different skill levels to determine whether the framework of deliberate practice applies to an activity very different from the domain of music in which it was first investigated. The second section considers what expert coaches consider to be the most important factors in producing world-class skaters, and how they structure practices. The third section compares wrestlers and skaters to the violinists and pianists studied by Ericsson et al. (1993) with respect to biographical data, ratings of the relevance of various practice behaviors for skill development, and time spent in deliberate practice. The last section is a description of a golfer who, we argue, shows the limits to what can be accomplished purely through deliberate practice.

THE WRESTLERS

Wrestlers typically begin their careers somewhat later than musicians or even athletes in other sports. They are usually first exposed to the sport late in elementary school. To be competitive in wrestling requires extreme fitness, flexibility, endurance, and most of all, skilled technique. Because wrestlers compete within strictly controlled weight classifications, size is equalized. To be competitive, wrestlers train for fitness through running, cycling, calisthenics, stretching, and other anaerobic sport activities. Many of these are done outside of team practice time, either on their own or with others. The majority of fitness training, however, comes through actual sparring with a partner. Technique is practiced usually with a partner, sometimes in bouts performed at half-speed or effort, more usually in actual match conditions. Mat work is done in the context of team practice, although occasionally it is done with just a pair of wrestlers and a coach. Obviously part of the success in training is the ability to work with sparring partners who are close and competitive in ability.

We examined retrospective reports from four groups of wrestlers: international current (n = 15), international retired (n = 10), and current (n = 9) and retired (n = 8) club-level athletes. The wrestlers in the international group have competed at world championships and the Olympic level. The club wrestlers may or may not have competed at national championships, but their skill level is at the university or provincial level. Wrestlers were divided into retired and current categories in an attempt to evaluate the reliability of the retrospective reports of the current wrestlers, with good reliability being shown by similar estimates of practice time given by current and retired athletes within each of the international and club groups.

The demographic data for the groups show that all athletes began wrestling around 13 years of age, and started more systematic practice with a coach around age 14. By age 16 they had become involved more or less full time, on a year-round basis. For retired athletes, both international and club athletes reported the peak of their careers was around 25 years of age. The current ages of the four groups in this study were as follows: international current (IC) 24.1 yr +/- 1.9, international retired (IR) 38.2 +/- 4.2, club current (CC) 24.8 yr +/- 3.2, and club retired (CR) 35.9 yr +/- 8.5. For the retired athletes the time difference between when they began wrestling and when their career peaked was 11.4 years. Thus, the age at which the retired athletes report peaking is the same age as the current international and club athletes in the study, around 25 years.

All subjects were administered a questionnaire, either personally or by mail. In all cases subjects were asked to reflect on their careers and answer questions as best they could recall. The first section requested biographic information relating to the demographics already presented. Four sections followed that asked subjects to think back to how much time they had spent practicing alone, practicing with others, in other practice-related activities, and in everyday activities. For each section, subjects estimated the number of hours in a typical week in which they engaged in the various activities. They were also asked to recall how many hours they had engaged in these activities at the start of their career and every 3 years since. For current wrestlers this spanned the time to present; for retired wrestlers this spanned their entire career. Finally, subjects were asked the length of their off-season at each of the 3-year intervals.

Each of the four sections was further broken down into specific activities, which were determined in advance in consultation with expert wrestlers and coaches. Within *practice alone* the possible activities were weight training, flexibility training, running, work with a coach, watching wrestling videos, cycling, and swimming. For *practice with others* the activities were mat work, jogging, weight or flexibility training, running, cycling, and swimming. *Other activities related to wrestling* included diet planning, reading wrestling materials, keeping a training journal, mental rehearsal practice, watching wrestling, and professional conversation. *Everyday activities* included sleeping, studying, active leisure, work, and nonactive leisure.

Within each section, subjects were asked to rate each activity on a 10-point scale in terms of its relevance to wrestling performance, the effort required, how much they enjoyed the activity, and how much concentration it required. Effort was physical work required to perform the activity, whereas concentration was the mental work involved. This distinction was made because some activities—for example, working on a stationary bike—take a great deal of effort but little concentration, making the interpretation of a composite term very difficult. Data from ratings in the four sections are presented in Table 3.1.

In Table 3.1, data are collapsed across the various groups to give some idea of how wrestlers in general view the difficulty and relevance of the various activities. The rankings for relevance to wrestling performance, effort required, enjoyment inherent in the activity, and concentration required by the activity are all presented. The values significantly different from the grand mean for the category are indicated. For example, for relevance, a grand mean of subject responses was calculated for all 26 of the activities rated for relevance, then Bonferroni t tests were used to compare each average rating to the grand mean. To avoid inflating alpha, the value had to differ from the grand mean by $p < .05/26 = .0019$ in order to be indicated as significantly different at $p < .05$.

Several findings are important. In practicing with others, mat work is seen as the most relevant, effortful, and concentration-dependent activity. As well, next to sleeping and active leisure, it is the activity enjoyed most. Among the other findings related to practice with others, cycling and swimming are not viewed as relevant and running is very effortful. In practice alone, weight training is seen as relevant and effortful but not particularly enjoyable. Working with a coach is highly relevant, concentration dependent, and enjoyable. Watching oneself on video is enjoyable and requires concentration but is not as relevant as some other activities. Again, running is seen as relevant and effortful, but swimming and cycling are not.

A great deal of time in wrestling is spent in activities that are nonactive, yet nonetheless related to wrestling performance, such as diet planning and mental rehearsal. Surprisingly the keeping of a training journal is not seen as especially relevant, although most international coaches insist on this and see it as critical. Of the everyday activities, sleep and active leisure are seen as the most enjoyable. Studying requires the most effort and concentration. Work and nonactive leisure are not seen as relevant to wrestling performance. The fact that these average values seem reasonable in light of personal interviews with the athletes and what is known about wrestling is some reassurance of the face validity of the questionnaire.

TABLE 3.1
Ratings (0–10) for Relevance, Effort, Enjoyment, and Concentration
Required for Various Aspects of Practice and Everyday Activities.
Collapsed Across Skill (International, Club) and Time (Current, Retired)

Activity	Relevance	Effort	Enjoyment	Concentration
Practice with others				
Mat work	9.82[H]	9.59[H]	8.2[H]	9.45[H]
Jogging	5.94	5.6	4.77	4.25
Weights	7.58	8.11	5.80	6.75
Running	7.23	7.55[H]	5.30	5.99
Flexibility	5.81	5.06	4.83	4.28
Swimming	3.15[L]	5.89	4.15	4.13
Cycling	2.74[L]	4.33	4.59	3.03[L]
Practice alone				
Weights	7.89[H]	8.54[H]	5.39	6.59
Flexibility	6.73	5.33	3.72[L]	4.96
Running	7.88[H]	8.34[H]	5.00	5.31
Jogging	6.84	5.90	4.75	3.93[L]
Work with coach	9.15[H]	6.44	7.61[H]	8.21[H]
Video	7.14	4.03	7.38[H]	7.83[H]
Swimming	4.08	4.72	5.32	3.52[L]
Cycling	3.87[L]	5.94	3.37	3.73[L]
Wrestling related				
Diet planning	7.32	6.32	1.58[L]	6.12
Read wrestling	4.54	4.60	4.34	6.01
Training journal	6.74	5.74	4.29	6.37
Mental rehearsal	8.20[H]	6.01	5.81	7.82[H]
Watch wrestling	7.14	4.41	7.46[H]	6.41
Professional conversation	6.43	4.58	6.63	5.94
Everyday activities				
Sleep	7.77[H]	1.65[L]	8.45[H]	1.11[L]
Studying	4.56	8.30[H]	4.48	8.84[H]
Active leisure	5.34	4.51	8.46[H]	5.16
Work	1.76[L]	6.45	3.95	6.06
Nonactive leisure	2.80[L]	1.26[L]	7.47[H]	2.59[L]
Grand means	6.09 (1.92)	5.74 (1.92)	5.51 (1.71)	5.55 (1.95)

Note. H indicates significantly higher than overall mean. L indicates significantly lower than overall mean.

In the next stage of analysis we summed across the various aspects of wrestling training (practice alone, with others, and in wrestling-related activities) to see how many hours per week international versus club athletes were devoting to the sport at various stages of their career. In order to maximize the number of subjects analyzed (because half the athletes are still midcareer), we examined the hours per week that athletes practiced at the start of their career, and at 3 and 6 years into it. Figure 3.1 presents these data, collapsed across time (current, retired). As is apparent from Fig. 3.1, although both groups began by practicing the same number of hours, the international group devoted more hours per week to practice than did the club wrestlers even 3 years into their careers. After 9 years, the international-caliber athletes were putting in about 13 more hours per week than their club counterparts.

The next analysis was an attempt to get at the microstructure of practice. In other words, are the international athletes putting in differentially more hours in one form of practice (i.e., with others or alone) than the club athletes? To answer this question we examined cumulative hours of practice over the first 6 years for the different skill levels (international, club) and time (retired, current) with multivariate analysis of variance (MANOVA). Each MANOVA was a fixed-effects model with two between factors and analyses were conducted separately for practice alone and practice with others.

For cumulative hours of practice alone there were no significant differences between skill groups (Rao's $R = 1.08$, $df = 7, 32$, $p < .40$), or time (Rao's $R = 1.64$, $df = 7, 32$, $p < .16$). For cumulative hours of practice with others, there was no significant difference in time (retired vs. current athletes) (Rao's $R = 1.87$, $df = 7, 32$, $p < .11$). There was, however, a significant

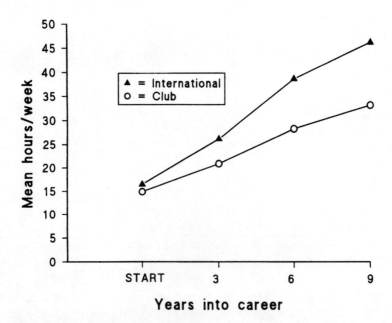

FIG. 3.1. Mean number of hours of practice per week collapsed across current and retired wrestlers.

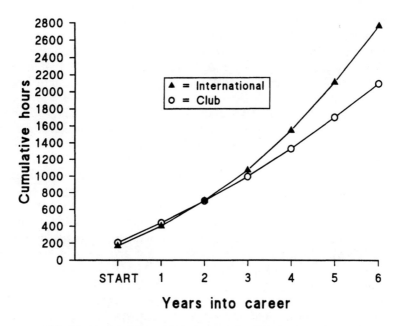

FIG. 3.2. Cumulative hours of practice with others from start of career.

difference for skill level (Rao's R = 2.34, df 7, 32, p < .05). The data are illustrated in Fig. 3.2.

Univariate analyses of variance (ANOVAs) for skill groups across each year were carried out as post hoc analyses. These revealed no significant differences between the groups at career start or for the first 5 years, with the significant differences first emerging during the sixth year, F (1, 38) = 5.38, p < .02. From this analysis, the skill groups begin to differ in the amount of cumulative practice they have with others after approximately 5 years.

What these analyses suggest is that to be competitive in wrestling at any level, one needs a basic amount of physical fitness training above and beyond what one achieves through team practices. Activities such as weight training, running, mental practice, and so on, must be done on one's own. There is no difference however, in the number of hours that more or less skilled athletes put into these activities. The big difference is in how many hours of deliberate practice the skilled athletes are devoting to team practice (primarily sparring). Because sparring also contributes substantially to fitness and flexibility and is task specific, it would seem the best form of training both for technique and skill.

Obviously questions emerge about the reliability with which subjects recall amounts and forms of practice they engaged in at various ages. We were encouraged by the fact that the average values of various forms of practice of the current athletes quite closely matched the values reported by retired athletes at the same stage of their career. We were also encouraged that average daily amounts seemed to fall in line with the kind of schedules that subjects verbally report. To examine both the reliability of recall and accuracy of practice estimates, a secondary "diary" study was conducted with 10 current members of the Canadian team (nine of whom had participated in the recollection study) and 11 current club members (four of whom had participated in Study 1). Similar to Ericsson et al.'s (1993) protocol, subjects were asked to think back and report both wrestling and everyday activities they engaged in during their most recent typical week and then to keep a diary of activities for 1 week with each day divided into 15-minute segments. Information was recorded at the end of each day. More detailed information regarding methodology and results of both studies is available in Hodges and Starkes (in press).

Surprisingly, for wrestling-related activities, the international and club wrestlers spent the same amount of hours per week in these activites (Int., M = 24.88; Club, M = 24.57). Much of this time was taken up with actual wrestling practice, which was judged as the most relevant activity to performance improvement. For the other activities judged to be highly relevant to improving performance, that is, weights alone, running alone, and mental rehearsal, there were also no significant differences between the groups (Int., M = 2.48; Club, M = 2.08). Reported fitness activities with others took up considerably less time (Int., M = .55; Club, M = .21). Although each of these was in the direction predicted, the lack of significant difference was unexpected.

Study time and travel did differentiate between the two groups. The international wrestlers reported spending 17.4 hours per week traveling compared to 6.25 hours per week for the club wrestlers. The international wrestlers also spent more time at work compared to the club wrestlers (Int., M = 17.93; Club, M = 10.18). Because the majority of club wrestlers were students, this was reflected in differences in study hours per week (Int., M = 8.1; Club, M = 19.23). Whereas club athletes tended to be students and therefore had ready access to training facilities on campus, international wrestlers worked longer hours and had to travel great distances to train in high-quality facilities with equally matched sparring partners. Because of this the international wrestlers actually engaged in fewer practice sessions per week than club athletes (Int., M = 8.80; Club, M = 11.45) but spent an average of 111 minutes per practice as opposed to 90.6 minutes by the club athletes. Analyses of practice activities showed that most training was done during the week as opposed to weekends (weekdays, M = 2.92; weekends, M = .85).

No differences were noted for active or nonactive leisure time, nor did leisure time negatively correlate with the amount of time athletes spent in wrestling activities. Number of daily hours of leisure time for both groups of wrestlers was very similar to that found by Ericsson et al. (1993) for their best violinists (Int., M = 3.07; Club, M = 3.46; best violinists, M = 3.5). As Robinson, Andreyenkov, and Patrushev (1988) reported that normal 18- to 29-year-olds spend 5.2 hours per day in leisure activities, both the wrestlers and violinists appear to sacrifice leisure time for training.

Because subjects were required to estimate the amount of time they had engaged in wrestling and everyday activites for a typical week and a diary week, it was possible to examine the reliability of these estimates. For those subjects who were part of both the retrospective recall and diary studies, estimates could also be compared between their most recent year and the diary week. For international wrestlers the correlation between a typical week and diary week was .66, for wrestling-related activities. From the retrospective study they reported spending 17.55 hours per week in practice with others, yet from the diary study they spent only 10.88 hours in practice. Club athletes estimated they spent 17.05 hours per week in practice with others, yet actually spent only 9.73 hours. In the Ericsson et al. (1993) study it was also found that musicians tended to overestimate practice hours and the authors suggested that this was probably an indication of how much time subjects aspire to train rather than actually attain. The same might be said for the wrestlers.

Although both groups overestimated the amount of time they spent in practice with others and fitness activities with others there was no difference in predicted times spent in strength training, work related to wrestling or diet and weight monitoring. For international wrestlers, comparing the most recent week and the diary week the correlation for time spent strength training with others was .98, for strength training alone was .96, and time spent attending wrestling practice was .76. These high correlations for the international group suggest that their routine was more consistent than the club athletes, who were not as accurate in predicting the amount time spent practicing.

Finally when the diary data were correlated with the most current year from the retrospective data no significant correlations were found for practice with others or alone. However the diary means and retrospective means were quite similar for practice with others (Retro., M = 15.22 hr; Diary, M = 11.36). Likewise their retrospective estimates for practice alone (.73) and practice with others (.70) also correlated with those for a typical week. It is important to note that whereas the retrospective estimates had been completed in August, diaries were not completed until 6 months later, which could reflect seasonal differences in training activities.

Although the diary study failed to yield any siginificant differences between the international and club athletes for wrestling-related activites, a number of important findings did emerge. First, given that the international athletes spend so long traveling to practice, they tend to practice less often with others but for longer periods. Clearly access to proper facilities, sparring partners and good coaches is a resource constraint that limits practice. One important difference between the musicians who served as subjects in the studies of Ericsson et al. (1993) and the wrestlers and skaters described in this chapter is in the control the performer can exert over time spent in the different practice behaviors. The wrestlers' ratings show working on the mat with another wrestler to be the most relevant practice behavior, and this form of practice cannot be done whenever the athlete has a spare minute. Skaters clearly require ice, again placing constraints on how much control the skater has over practice time and activities. In the second section of this chapter, then, we look at those individuals who are most important in determining when, what, and how much practicing the athlete does—the coaches. What do coaches look for in selecting skaters to train? How long do their skaters train in the course of a week? What do expert coaches feel are the most important factors for success in international skating competitions?

THE SKATERS

In Canada, figure skating is governed by the Canadian Figure Skating Association (CFSA), which is a member of the International Skating Union (ISU). Figure skating has three separate disciplines: figures, freestyle (singles and pairs), and dance. The emphasis in figure skating, much like music, is on the consistency and accuracy of performance rather than on the selection and execution of appropriate strategies and tactics. Progress through the disciplines is determined by objective tests, and the top skaters are identified by their placement in the annual national championships.

All skaters begin in the "test" stream, which provides an opportunity for advancement in all three disciplines. There are specific tasks that must be completed for each discipline before advancing to subsequent levels, with each level increasing in difficulty. Coaches teach the skaters the requirements for each of the levels, and guide the skater's progress through the entire CFSA system. In figures, tests range from preliminary to the first through eighth (gold) figure. The level of difficulty associated with each test is influenced by the type of turn, direction, and number of circles.

In freestyle, there are seven tests ranging from preliminary to gold. Tests consist of elements performed in isolation as well as a program (1.5–4 minutes in length) that is skated to music chosen by the skater, and must contain specific required elements. Level of difficulty of the elements is a function of the number of rotations in the jumps, the type and combination of spin positions, and the number of rotations required on each foot. Skaters are expected to be much stronger and faster at the higher test levels, and artistic impression becomes increasingly important.

At the fourth figure test and the third (Senior Bronze) freestyle test level, skaters under 16 years of age are eligible for entry to the "competitive" stream. Skaters in this stream are eligible to compete on a larger scale than skaters in the test stream, and those aspiring to the National Team and international competition must be in the competitive stream. There are three levels within the competitive stream: Novice, Junior, and Senior, and skaters must pass established freestyle tests to progress to the next level. Age restrictions are also present in the competitive stream;

the minimum age to compete at Junior is 12. In Junior competition, women must be under 18, and men must be under 19. There are no age restrictions in Senior competition.

The test and competitive streams are not mutually exclusive. The elements comprising the competitive tests are drawn from various levels in the test stream. Skaters in the competitive stream will usually continue working toward completion of the gold medals in the test stream. Figure skating is unique as a sport from the standpoint that to progress through the various levels there are specific performance criteria and tests. In this sense it is similar to the conservatoire culture in music. One advantage of this is that it is possible to plot the age and number of years or deliberate practice required to attain each successive level. In the same way that Charness, Krampe, and Mayr (chap. 2, this volume) were able to plot the age and amount of practice necessary to attain Elo point changes in chess, skating provides a sport analogy. In this case we were able to follow the career of 20 members of the Canadian figure skating team (12 males, 8 females) from preliminary to gold test levels. With age as the predictor the regression equation is $y = .516x - 2.428$, $r = .88$, and $r^2 = .77$. To attain gold test level the age was $18.27 +/- .92$. With years of practice as the predictor the equation is $y = .441x + 1.087$, $r = .81$ and $r^2 = .66$. For this group of elite athletes to attain gold test level they required 11.14 years of practice. Obviously it would be of interest in a larger heterogenous sample to examine the relationship between practice and test levels obtained. The Ericsson model might predict that those not of national team caliber could still reach the gold test level after approximately the same number of years of deliberate practice, provided that the profile of hours of practice per week was also the same. If hours per week were less, then it might take longer in terms of years for an individual to reach this level.

In competitive figure skating a generation ago, skaters typically worked with one coach during their tests and competitive careers, although skaters did change coaches periodically. These coaches were responsible for all aspects of the skater's career: teaching the figure and freestyle techniques, selecting music, and choreographing the programs. Donald Jackson, 1962 World Champion, reflected on the responsibilities of his coach at the time: "He wasn't just a coach. He did everything . . . choreographer, coach, masseur, psychologist." Jackson also commented on the secrecy associated with the teaching of techniques in this era. Coaches were solely responsible for the development of their athletes, and enjoyed the "reflected glory" associated with the competitive successes of their students.

Today, the vast majority of top figure skaters take lessons from a coaching team rather than just a single coach. Coaches are specialized to varying degrees, and other individuals with little or no skating experience also assist in the development of elite figure skaters. At major skating centers there are "skateologists" responsible for the skaters' equipment, choreographers, spin coaches, jump coaches, coaches restricted to one of the disciplines (dance, pairs, figures), and technicians. There are seminars and certification programs for coaches, and information is readily shared:

> "Everything is on a silver platter. There are no secrets anymore"

> "All the coaches on the ice . . . are lined up beside me. I run the best place I can in a team situation. I am not afraid to share anything with anybody."

Off-ice fitness specialists, sport psychologists, dance instructors, and therapists are responsible for the physical and psychological development and well-being of the athlete. Some clubs and skating centers have hired people to design costumes and select and edit music. Ultimately, however, one person—the head coach—must be responsible for the athlete.

> "Because we have a coaching team we are able to keep an eye out for all the skaters so they won't backslide and get bad habits."

> "The coaches (at the center) put in a real team effort, we have different strengths and personalities."

> "You have another coach to work with the skaters at home when you travel all over the world with the National Team skaters."

Elite Coaches and Skaters in the Present Study

Elite coaches were those who had placed at least one skater on the Canadian Junior or National teams. Currently, within Canada there is a group of about 15 coaches who consistently have skaters competing at international events. Five coaches from this group agreed to be interviewed for this investigation. The average number of years of coaching experience was 24.8 years with a range of 6 to 43 years. The average age was 48 years with a range of 35 to 72 years.

The Canadian National and Junior National teams are comprised of 40 singles skaters. Twenty of the team members responded to a request for information and participated in the study. The average age of the National team members was 21 years with a range of 19 to 24 years, and the average for the Junior National team members was 16.5 years with a range of 15 to 21 years.

The Expert Coaches

Data Collection

Individual interviews were conducted with each coach. The interviewer, herself a figure skating coach and triple-gold test skater, followed a prescribed interview format. Each coach was asked to respond to open-ended questions relating to the identification of talent, selection of skaters for their program, and the nature of training. Finally, coaches rated (10-point scale) the relative importance of items on a list of attributes thought to influence success in skating.

On the Identification of Talent.   All the coaches claimed to be able to see talent, even though they were unable to articulate what they could see: "I don't know what it is . . . you can see it." Most resorted to a list of attributes that they felt were indicative of potential skating champions. These attributes were both physical and mental, and included the following:

Physical attributes
- A certain spring in the muscles, good knees, able to jump, rhythm in the knees
- A good run of the blade (smoothly and evenly across the ice), good stroking
- Ability to rotate
- Good reflexes
- Fantastic flow . . . get speed from nowhere
- Good "snap" for height on jumps; spring, rhythm, timing
- Good posture
- Coordination
- Natural ability
- Musicality, musical flair
- Build or body type, and "whether you are physically attractive"

Mental attributes
- Persistence, motivation, dedication to hard work, the right constitution, mental stability, a no-nonsense attitude, inner strength, love of what they are doing, determination
- A "killer instinct" and a high need for control
- "Talent alone will not make you a World Champion."
- "More training, more lessons, more choreography, more money, and we have no skaters. Why? No talent. If you don't have the bodies, you can't do a damn thing."

All coaches listed determination or desire as an important part of having the potential to make it to the top. From one coach: "Sometimes hard work and a little less talent works just as well as a lot of talent and less work." And a second coach: " (. . . names a former National Champion) had very little talent but was Canadian champion because of persistence and a positive attitude."

On the Selection of Athletes.   Coaches acquire skaters in one of two ways: Either the skater simply continues within the same program for the duration of their career, or skaters who have entered the competitive stream apply to nationally recognized coaches. In either case, it is the coaches' decision whether or not to work with the particular skater.

Most coaches have an interview (either formal or informal) with the skater and the parents. The skater's and parents' goals, and what benefit the skater expects from the particular program, are typical subjects covered in the interview. The coach may give the skater a lesson or watch the skater's program as a form of audition, or may simply watch the athlete on the ice with other skaters. Several of the coaches expressed the need to establish whether or not they or their school could actually help the athlete. The important point here is that a skater cannot hope to develop without access to an excellent coaching team. At the same time, coaches must have an eye for talent to keep their programs "on the map" nationally, and not waste time and resources working with skaters who do not have the potential to succeed at the highest levels of competition. Again, desire, the ability to work hard, and motivation factor significantly in the coaches' decisions on skaters:

> Everyone has the will to win, but there are only a few who have the will to prepare to win. Preparation . . . a no nonsense attitude, a belief in yourself and a stick-to-itness and positive attitude. Winning does not mean having gold medals lined up, it means getting the best out of yourself.

On the Best Age to Start Skating. There was a general consensus among the coaches that the earlier the starting age, the better, with 8 being the latest age to begin skating and have a hope of success:

> "Twelve is too late. The last year to start is 8, and then it might be risky, but don't give up hope on that one yet."

> "Late starters are lots of work . . . you must spend lots of time with them at the beginning. Absolutely everything is crucial to a late starter and they do not have the emotional package to deal with things."

On Practice Hours. In the past, top skaters spent from 6 to 9 hours a day for 6 days of the week on the ice. The breakdown of hours was approximately 4 to 5 hours on figures and 2 to 3 hours on freestyle. Now that figures are no longer a part of international competition, it might be expected that the time formerly devoted to figures would be directed toward on-ice freestyle time. In fact, this is not done "because the body can only take so much." Because the complexity of the individual elements now performed in freestyle skating increases the chance of injury, the importance of stretching, conditioning, and proper warmup techniques is reflected in the current transition to a larger off-ice component of the overall training program. What is done in training varies widely according to the season. The competitive season lasts from mid-October until mid-February, and the remainder of the year is spent training for these competitions. Depending on the coach and the training center, most technical work is accomplished from April to August. Tapering is done before each competition, and the yearly plan for all facets of training must reflect the seasonal nature of the sport.

On-Ice Practice.   When asked how many hours the top skaters should be spending on the ice in a week, four of the five coaches responded 15 hours per week. One of the coaches described this as the minimum time requirement necessary to "get to the top," but included all practice activities, not just time on the ice, in this figure.

Coaches were reluctant to provide an "average" length of time that they (or members of their coaching team) spent in private lessons with their elite skaters during the competitive season, stressing instead the importance of flexibility, with comments such as, "Skaters receive as many lessons as necessary to get the job done," or "Many parents think that the more lessons the skaters get, the better they get. That is not true."

There was consensus among the coaches that the goal was not to "babysit" the athletes on the ice. All warned against "tutored practice" and "overlessoning." The average time spent by the coaches in private lessons with their elite skaters was estimated at 4.02 hours a week for National team skaters, and 4 hours for Junior National team members. The skaters' estimates of time spent in lessons corroborated the coaches' estimates, with National team members estimating they spend 4.08 hours per week, and Junior Nationals 3 hours per week in lessons. Thus, elite skaters are involved with lessons for as much as one third of the time they are on the ice during the competitive season.

Off-Ice Training.   Fitness training done off-ice has become more scientific in the last 10 years. Off-ice fitness testing has become standardized and the CFSA has published their own set of physical fitness guidelines for the National and Junior National team athletes. These standards are based on age and gender, and vary by discipline (free-skating, pairs, dance). National team members are tested twice a year and the Junior National team members are tested annually at a central testing center. The tests include assessment of maximum aerobic and anaerobic capacities, body composition, flexibility, and jumping capabilities.

The major training centers have permanent off-ice training facilities and personal trainers who assess the strengths and weaknesses of the athletes along with the coaching team. The trainer develops a program for the athlete, and provides brief progress reports to the coach. This is consistent with the team approach to coaching, where the head coach delegates responsibilities, and team members are responsible for their areas of expertise. Coaches in turn provide the trainer with feedback on the skater's on-ice performance for fine-tuning the training program.

The coaches indicated that they allowed for 5 to 8 hours of off-ice training per week. Although estimates of off-ice training time were consistent across the coaches, there was variability in the components of the training program. All coaches recognized the importance of strength and endurance training, and three coaches stressed the importance of dance and movement classes either off-ice or during "theatre on ice."

The Skaters

Data Collection

During October 1994, questionnaires were distributed through the CFSA to the singles skaters of the current National and Junior National teams. Skaters provided information describing their progress through the test system and their competitive history. They detailed their practice history from the time they began private lessons to the present, as well as any changes in coaches throughout their careers. Skaters also provided ratings (10-point scale) as to the relevance, effort, concentration, and enjoyment of 12 practice activities.

The skaters' data served two purposes. First, it provided an estimate of the amount of time spent by experts in a new activity, and second, it acted as a check of the coaches' estimates of skaters' practice time and activities.

Biographic Data. The average age at which the skaters began to skate was 5.3 years of age, with 7.68 years being the average age for the beginning of private lessons, and 9.95 years being the average age at which they began skating year round. The skaters had worked with an average of 4.9 coaches.

Practice Alone. The skaters' estimates of total amount of time per week spent practicing alone included time in weight training, swimming, flexibility training, lessons with a coach, and individual practice. Some skaters included activities such as dance and martial arts classes—which are for them important components of their training regime—in their estimates of total practice time. National team members reported spending an average of 28.9 hours per week practicing alone, and the Junior National team members reported an average of 19.3 hours. The weighted average of 21.2 hours per week is similar to the coaches' requirement that skaters should be spending 15 hours on-ice and 5 to 8 hours in off-ice training per week. The skaters also provided retrospective estimates of the number of hours spent in practice alone since first beginning to skate, shown in Table 3.2 normalized for starting age. The data shown at 12, 14, and last year are from senior National team skaters only.

Rating of Practice Activities. In an attempt to determine which practice activities constitute deliberate practice for skating, all National team skaters rated a series of activities on a 10-point scale for relevance, effort, concentration, and enjoyment. The mean ratings are shown in Table 3.3, with activities rated significantly higher or lower than the grand mean for

TABLE 3.2
Skaters' Hours per Week of Practice Alone Shown for Years Into Career

Start	At 2 Years	At 4 Years	At 6 Years	At 8 Years	At 10 Years	At 12 Years	At 14 Years	Last Year
5.5	7.8	11.2	14	15.5	20.33	23.67	22.67	22.18

TABLE 3.3
Skaters' Ratings of Practice Activities

Activity	Relevance	Effort	Concentration	Enjoyment
Weight training	7.5	8.5	7.1	5.5
Flexibility	8.5	6.9	6.2	5.5
Jogging	5.6	7.7	4.6	5.3
Cycling	6.4	7.4	4.8	5.7
Swimming	3.7^L	7.1	4.2	5.5
In-line skating	4.9^L	6.4	4.4	7.8
Lessons with coach	9.9^H	8.1	9.2^H	9.2^H
Choreography	9.3^H	8.2	8.9	8.9^H
On-ice training	10^H	9.4^H	9.7^H	9.3^H
Mental training	8.1	6.8	9.5^H	6.4
Video analysis	6.5	3.6^L	6.5	6.4
Other (dance, martial arts)	8.7	8.3	8.0	5.0

Note. H indicates significantly higher than overall mean. L indicates significantly lower than overall mean.

the category indicated with superscript. Note that the most relevant practice activities—on-ice training and lessons with a coach—are rated high in enjoyment as well as relevance.

Success in Figure Skating: What Does It Take?

Finally, both skaters and coaches were asked to rate a series of factors on a 10-point scale to reflect how important they judged each element to be for success in skating. The means, standard errors, and ranks of the elements for coaches and skaters are shown in Table 3.4, with the ranking being significantly correlated for the two groups ($r = .82, p < .01$).

Note that practice ranks third in importance for both coaches and skaters. Thus it seems that coaches and skaters are in agreement about both what it takes to be successful in international skating and the hours of practice required for the skaters' development. Data from this study and futher discussion of what it takes to succeed in figure skating are presented elsewhere in Hayes and Deakin (1995).

TABLE 3.4
Ratings of Importance to Success in Skating

| | *Coaches* | | *Skaters* | |
Element	Mean (SD)	Rank	Mean (SD)	Rank
Natural ability	9.1 (.50)	6	7.7 (.34)	10
Practice	9.8 (.18)	3	9.4 (.19)	3
Desire	10 (0.0)	1	9.6 (.15)	1
Musicality	8.4 (.67)	9	7.8 (.27)	9
Knowledge of skating mechanics (technique)	8.6 (.54)	8	8.3 (.27)	7
Knowledge of mental skills (controlling nerves, concentration)	7.1 (1.61)	11	8.6 (.41)	6
Equipment	9.4 (.56)	5	7.8 (.36)	8
Being consistent	9 (.56)	7	9.0 (.25)	5
Being lucky	5.2 (1.78)	12	4.4 (.67)	12
Fitness level	9.8 (.25)	3	9.0 (.23)	4
Lots of competitions and performances	8.4 (.46)	9	7.5 (.39)	11
Good coaching	9.9 (.09)	2	9.5 (.19)	2

POINTS OF CONTACT

The previous two sections have described practice activities for wrestlers and skaters. In this section, we compare the violinists and pianists studied by Ericsson et al. (1993) and the wrestlers and skaters described here. There are four points of contact between the different skill domains: starting age, ratings of practice activities to define deliberate practice for each domain, hours spent in practice, and hours spent in deliberate practice.

Biographic Information

The mean starting age of the skaters is 5.3 years, close to Ericsson et al.'s (1993) pianists (5.8), and "highest" violinists (5.0). The violinists who were subjects in the study started later, 7.7, and the wrestlers much later, at 13.

The number of teachers or coaches is very similar for all activities: violin, 4.1; piano, 4.7; international wrestlers, 4.2; and skaters, 4.9. However, the number of coaches or teachers does not differ with skill for violinists or wrestlers (club 4.9); it does for pianists, with amateur pianists reporting three teachers—but this group had 9.9 versus 19.1 years of instruction for the skilled group. It looks as if there is consistency here, but whatever produces the consistency (most likely the number of years the person has been involved in the activity) does not seem to be related to skill.

The Nature of Deliberate Practice

Defining the Term

Ericsson et al. (1993) defined deliberate practice as an activity "rated very high on relevance for performance, high on effort, and comparatively low on inherent enjoyment" (p. 373), which is "practice alone" for musicians. It is interesting to note that although practice alone is rated significantly higher than the grand mean for relevance and effort in the musicians' ratings, it is not rated significantly lower than the grand mean for pleasure; in fact, the pleasure rating is higher than the grand mean (practice alone pleasure rating 7.23, grand mean 6.52).

In both the wrestling and the skating data, there are no activities that fulfill the first requirement; that is, that are rated as highly relevant but not enjoyable. In the wrestling data, the two activities rated highest for relevance—mat work and work with coach—are also significantly higher than the grand mean in rating of enjoyment. For skating, all three of the activities rated significantly higher than the grand mean for relevance are also rated significantly higher than the grand mean for enjoyment.

The second requirement—high on relevance and high on effort—is seen in both the wrestling and the skating data, with the top two activities for relevance also being significantly higher than the grand mean for concentration (with concentration measuring mental work, and thus being equivalent to Ericsson et al.'s [1993] effort; for wrestlers and skaters, effort is physical effort).

Strictly speaking, then, we have no activities that fit the deliberate practice definition. In order to see whether wrestlers and skaters were rating in some fundamentally different way than the musicians, Spearman rhos were calculated for the rating data for the violinists in Ericsson et al.'s (1993) Table 1, eliminating "everyday activities" (not available for skaters), for wrestlers, again eliminating everyday activities, and for skaters.

For musicians, there is a significant correlation for effort and relevance (.75), a small but positive correlation between relevance and pleasure (.18), and a small but negative relationship between effort and pleasure (−.19). For skaters, there is a significant relationship between relevance and concentration (.90). For wrestlers, there are significant relationships between relevance and concentration (.83), relevance and effort (.68), relevance and enjoyment (.59), and concentration and enjoyment (.64).

The relationship that is there in full force in all sets of data is the strong positive relationship between relevance and effort/concentration. It is interesting that mental work rather than physical work is associated with most relevant practice activities by the athletes. As well, the athletes clearly enjoy the most relevant practice activities, activities which are very close to what they do in actual competition.

Nature of the Activities Rated as Deliberate Practice

If the high relevance–high effort/concentration definition is used, the top two deliberate practice activities for each of the domains are: violinists, practice alone and taking lessons; for wrestlers, mat work and work with coach; for skaters, on-ice training and lessons with coach. This shows perfect consistency across domains in that an activity almost identical to what must be done in actual performance and work with an authority are selected as most critical for improvement.

Time Engaged in All Forms of Practice

For Ericsson et al.'s violinists, the time spent in all music-related activities in one week (50.6 hours) does not differ for the three skill groups. For the wrestlers, time spent in all practice activities does differ between international and club wrestlers (Fig. 3.1), with the international group spending about 46 hours per week in all forms of practice. Pianists spend 56.75 hours per week in all forms of music activity. The group that is very different here is the skaters, who spend 28.9 hours per week in all skating activities. Because ice time is so costly, it might be expected that skaters would do as much training as possible off the ice, and put in practice hours comparable to the other skilled groups. That this does not happen could mean that skills that must be performed on the ice must be practiced on the ice—that there is little benefit for skaters from hours of off-ice practice.

Time Spent in Deliberate Practice

The comparison between skill domains for time spent in deliberate practice is complicated by the fact that time spent in deliberate practice has been counted differently in each domain. Ericsson et al. (1993) counted hours of practice alone, the wrestling data count hours of practice with others, and the skating data count practice alone. The wrestling hours then, include mat work, but also jogging, weights, running, flexibility, swimming, and cycling, with the last two activities being rated significantly lower than the grand mean for relevance. The skating hours include weight training, swimming, flexibility, lessons with a coach, and individual practice. Thus, what has been counted as deliberate practice is really very different for the three domains, with the wrestling and skating data including activities that would not be considered deliberate practice from looking at their ratings of relevance.

Ignoring the problem of what has been counted, the diary-calculated hours spent in deliberate practice per week are 24.3 for violinists (estimated time is 29.8) and 26.71 hours for pianists, and estimated hours for wrestlers are 19.1, and for skaters, 22.18.

Because these hours per week look similar, the increase in hours of deliberate practice per week over the development of skill was estimated from the retrospective accounts of the wrestlers and skaters, and estimated from the data presented in Ericsson et al.'s (1993) Figure 8 (violinists) and Figure 11. The changes in hours of deliberate practice as skill increases look similar across the domains (Fig. 3.3); despite the different starting ages for the activities (5–13 years), and despite different activities being counted, and may represent the maximum hours of effective deliberate practice that can be done in a week. These data also support the contention that the number of hours spent in deliberate practice is driven by the level of skill of the performer, not by age-related factors such as the ability to sustain concentration.

New and Different

The rating data from the five elite skating coaches for what counts in the development of success in skating are very informative. In fact, elite coaches and skaters agree on the top three ratings of what it takes for success in figure skating. Coaches rate practice and fitness (tied), whereas skaters rate practice as third most important. Both agree that coaching is second in importance, and both agree that desire is most important. Recall that practice and work with coach are the picks as most important from ratings

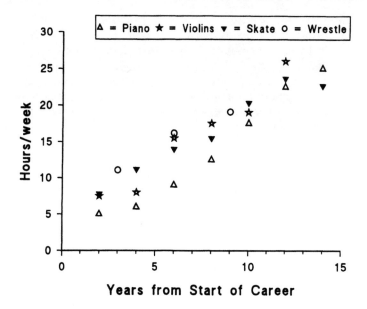

FIG. 3.3. Hours of deliberate practice per week at different career stages and across different domains. Data for piano and violins are from Ericsson et al. (1993).

of relevance and concentration or effort, and note that desire has never been included on anyone's list of what has been rated. Because the ratings have only been done for practice activities, characteristics of the subject have not been assessed.

The other new finding in the wrestling and skating data is the apparent independence of the ratings for effort and concentration, which correspond to physical effort and mental concentration for the athletes. These dimensions are not significantly correlated for either wrestlers (.36) or for skaters (.48). For wrestlers, mat work, work with coach, video work, and mental rehearsal are rated significantly higher than the mean for concentration, whereas cycling with others, swimming, cycling alone, sleep, and nonactive leisure are significantly lower than the mean. For effort, mat work, running (alone and with others), and weights are significantly higher than the mean, whereas sleep and nonactive leisure are significantly lower. For skaters, lessons with a coach, on-ice training, and mental training are significantly above the mean for concentration, with no activities differing significantly from the mean on the low side. For effort, on-ice training is high and video analysis is low. All this suggests that concentration and effort are somewhat orthogonal, with concentration being the important dimension for deliberate practice.

Why Not Just Do Deliberate Practice?

Given the great importance of deliberate practice for the acquisition of expertise, should the aspiring performer be encouraged to identify and practice only those activities that constitute deliberate practice for their particular domain? Are all other practice activities a waste of time? Does a low rating for relevance of a particular practice activity imply that the particular activity should not be done? How should ratings of relevance be interpreted? Do they simply reflect the percentage of time spent practicing each activity? Are they a reflection of the percentage of variance contributed to performance by the practice activity? The violin students studied by Ericsson et al. (1993) do not differ for the number of hours spent in music-related activities, but do differ for hours of deliberate practice. This means that the lesser skilled violinists spent more time in activities that were related to music, but not related to improving their performance in playing the violin.

For the wrestlers and the skaters, the "other" practice activities are mainly those activities that are done to develop and maintain the fitness level of the performer. The best technique in the world will not save a wrestler or skater who lacks the cardiovascular fitness to complete a bout or a program. As wrestlers of different skill levels spend the same amount of time in these other practice activities, both groups have worked to a high level of fitness, with the international wrestlers going beyond this level with their additional hours of deliberate practice. Thus the other practice activities are important, and serve as the foundation of the performance; it is just that both groups have built the same foundation.

Although there are similarities in the data from musicians and athletes, the groups differ in the positive relationship between pleasure and relevance for the athletes, and the high prominence given to a personal characteristic—desire—as a determinant of success in skating by both the coaches and athletes. Could it be that deliberate practice represents only a piece of the puzzle that must be assembled in order to understand expert performance? The last section of this chapter describes a golfer who helps understand this issue.

AN EXPERT GOLFER

Last summer we had the opportunity to interview a well-known Canadian golfer, Moe Norman, on what it takes to acquire skill in the game of golf. Now in his 60s, Norman has been a professional golfer since 1956, during which time he has won over 50 professional tournaments and set 33 course records (Rubenstein, 1991). His accomplishments include 17 holes in one, rounds of 59 three times in nontournament play, and a best tournament round of 61 (M. Norman, personal communication, September 7, 1994). In February 1995, the Chairman and CEO of the golf equipment maker Titleist and Foot-Joy announced that the company would pay Moe Norman a monthly stipend for the rest of his life (Rubenstein, 1995). Titleist is also putting up money for a video that will "show people that Moe belongs in the same category of Bobby Jones, Ben Hogan and Byron Nelson as a ball-striker" (Rubenstein, 1995, p. C12).

When asked what makes him such a great ball-striker, Norman will often show the questioner his left hand, the surface of which is so black and calloused that it looks like the tire of a race car, a clue that practice has played a large part in his success. His first exposure to golf came at the age of 11, when he caddied at a local country club to earn money for chips and sodas. He played his first rounds at the same age, taking advantage of "caddy day" at the country club. He joined a public course at 14, started systematic practice at 16, and began competing at 19. He had no real teachers, and took no formal lessons, essentially working out his swing on his own.

The systematic practice that he began at 16 was to hit 800 balls a day. From the age of 19 to 32, his routine was to hit 800 balls a day on weekdays when he had to go to work, then play 54 holes on Saturday and 72 holes on Sunday. During this time then, he was hitting 4,000 practice balls a week. Incidentally, he claims to have recorded the number of balls he has hit in practice through the years, which now totals 4 million balls. He once hit 1,540 drives in one day at a golf clinic.

According to Norman (as well as consistent with the theory of deliberate practice), he always had something he was trying to do during his practice swings. Initially, he worked out his swing, with a focus on simplicity and the need to control the fewest levers possible. Later activities involved "hitting to an image" of a specific hole that he had played, or hitting at a bucket. And what has been the consequence of all this practice? Above all, a swing that is consistent and straight, which he demonstrates by "putting a silver dollar on the ground thirty-seven inches behind the ball. The sole plate of his driver contacts the coin every time. Then he moves the coin twenty-two inches ahead of the ball and contacts it again every time. Every shot is straight, every swing a carbon copy of the one that came before. He's so accurate that he's worn a dark spot the size of a quarter in the middle of all his iron clubs" (Rubenstein, 1991, p. 124).

In short, Norman is a personification of the consequences of deliberate practice. His game is of such a high level that much of the difficulty of golf is not a factor. Most golfers need to register the location of hazards, out of bounds, areas of rough on each hole they play, and play shots that optimize the probability of not getting into trouble. Norman simply walks up to the ball and hits it where he wants it to go. He plays incredibly fast, taking in all he needs to know on the walk up to the ball. This speed of play helps him to eliminate another classic problem in golf, the fact that the stationary ball waits for the golfer to hit it. According to Boswell (1992), the stationary ball makes golf "the most mentally torturous of all sports" because "only in golf is a player given enough time as he needs to tie his own noose" (p. 250).

Moe Norman is almost always called a ball-striker—a term he uses to describe himself—rather than a golfer. This is because his undeniable skill in hitting the ball straight, with consistency, and where he wants it to go, has not produced notable success on the professional circuit. He has played in the Masters, and he did play on the U.S. professional tour in the 1950s. He left the tour after 1 year, but has spent all his years since in golf-related activities: playing lesser tournaments, giving clinics, playing for fun, even hitting balls off the dirt in golf courses that are under construction so the course architect can check the course design. Until this year, he has had no sponsor.

Given his great skill, why is Norman not an immensely wealthy individual, flying in his own plane from one seniors' tournament to the next with the likes of Jack Nicklaus and Lee Trevino? There are as many theories about this as there are people who know about Norman. He is too shy, some say; he would rather come in second than give a speech at the tournament banquet. He was unable to learn to enjoy the social events and lack of privacy that goes with being a touring professional say others. He lets small things that happen during the course of a round bother him too much, and so on. It should be said that golfers and their associations tend to be very conservative, and have not always been appreciative of the embellishments Norman has been known to throw into a round. For example, he once deliberately putted into a sand trap on the 18th hole of the last round of a tournament that he was winning by three strokes. He proceeded to chip out, sink his putt, and win by two strokes, but such activities are not seen by some as showing proper respect for the dignity of the game. Whatever the reason for the perception that Norman has not been a success, it has nothing to do with his ability to hit a golf ball.

What does the career of Moe Norman tell us about deliberate practice, you are no doubt asking? Norman has done as much deliberate practice with his clubs as any human could do, yet he has not "succeeded" in golf in the classic sense of the term. This is because such success requires an attitude, an approach to the sport that Norman does not possess, nor does he want to possess. It is intriguing to think that in golf, deliberate practice requires an individual to spend thousands of solitary hours hitting balls, yet playing professionally is best done by gregarious and highly social individuals. The point is that in sport, deliberate practice is often not enough to ensure success: There are factors of character, of luck, of the environment, and of avoiding injury that inevitably affect the outcome of competitions. These factors are one reason why sports are so interesting to perform and to watch: You just never know. Leaving the last word to Boswell (1992):

> If you work hard enough, sacrifice enough, then you will win. That's what many coaches teach. Or should we say preach? It might be more honest, and healthier, to say that if you work very hard, you will become excellent, and because of that excellence, you may do great deeds and win great prizes. Unless, of course, you don't. Because, sometimes, the other player is better or luckier. In which case you simply have to be satisfied with your excellence and the dignity of your effort. (p. 382)

ACKNOWLEDGMENTS

The authors wish to acknowledge support of Sport Canada, the Canadian Amateur Wrestling Association, and the Canadian Figure Skating Association for their assistance in carrying out these studies. A special thanks is extended to professional golfers Mike Martz and Moe Norman, and the many athletes and coaches who gave willingly of their time to serve as subjects.

REFERENCES

Allard, F., & Starkes, J. L. (1991). Motor skill experts in sports, dance, and other domains. In K. A. Ericsson & J. Smith (Eds.), *Toward a general theory of expertise* (pp. 123–152). Cambridge, UK: Cambridge University Press.

Boswell, T. (1992). *Game day.* New York: Penguin.

Ericsson, K. A., Krampe, R. T., & Tesch-Römer, C. (1993). The role of deliberate practice in the acquisition of expert performance. *Psychological Review, 100,* 363–406.

Hayes, A., & Deakin, J. (1995). *Creating elite athletes in figure skating: Fact or fiction.* Manuscript submitted for publication.

Helsen, W., & Pauwels, J. M. (1993). The relationship between expertise and visual information processing in sport. In J. L. Starkes & F. Allard (Eds.), *Cognitive issues in motor expertise* (pp. 109–134). Amsterdam: Elsevier.

Hodges, N. J., & Starkes, J. L. (in press). Wrestling with the nature of expertise: A sport specific test of Ericsson, Krampe and Tesch-Römer's theory of 'deliberate practice'. *International Journal of Sport Psychology.*

Housner, L. D., & French, K. E. (Eds.). (1994). Expertise in learning, performance, and instruction in sport and physical activity [Special issue]. *Quest, 46*(2).

McPherson, S. L., & Thomas, J. R. (1989). Relation of knowledge and performance in boys' tennis: Age and expertise. *Journal of Experimental Child Psychology, 48,* 190–211.

Robinson, J. P., Andreyenkov, V. G., & Patrushev, V. D. (1988). *The rhythm of everyday life: How Soviet and American citizens use time.* Boulder, CO: Westview.

Rubenstein, L. (1991). *Links.* Toronto: Vintage.

Rubenstein, L. (1995, February 3). Norman's huge talents finally pay off. *The Globe and Mail,* p. C12.

Starkes, J. L., & Allard, F. (Eds.). (1993). *Cognitive issues in motor expertise.* Amsterdam: Elsevier.

4

The Acquisition of Musical Performance Expertise: Deconstructing the "Talent" Account of Individual Differences in Musical Expressivity

John A. Sloboda
University of Keele

THE CURIOUS CASE OF "MUSICAL TALENT"

Considering how widespread a phenomenon music is within our society, and the fact that listening to music is an important part of so many people's daily lives, it is something of an enigma that so few people develop any significant level of music performance ability. Not only do many people never attempt to learn an instrument, but the majority of those who undertake some form of structured learning activity abandon their efforts within a few years.

In countries such as the United States and the United Kingdom, almost every child in school receives classroom music instruction from an early age. Yet the general level of musical achievement in the school-age population is surely well below that of many other skills addressed by the school curriculum.

An apparently almost irresistible popular line of explanation for this general lack of musical accomplishment in the population is the invocation of the presence or absence of "musical talent." Sloboda, Davidson, and Howe (1994) proposed the existence of a folk psychology of talent, which postulates substantial innately determined differences between individuals in their capacity for musical accomplishment. According to the folk psychology account, few people become expert musical performers because few people have the necessary talent. This folk psychology is evident in the structures and rhetoric of the music conservatoire (see, e.g., Kingsbury, 1988), and also in the beliefs of people involved in schools. For instance, O'Neill (1994) demonstrated that schoolchildren as young as 8 years old are already more likely to believe that music ability cannot be improved by effort than sporting skill. A recent survey by Davis (1994) shows that more than 75% of a sample comprised mainly of educational professionals believed that composing, singing, and playing concert instruments required a special gift or natural talent. Other activities, such as playing chess, performing surgery, and writing nonfiction, were seen as requiring talent by less than 40% of the sample, as, curiously, was orchestral conducting!

Although not wishing (or being in a position) to deny that inherited differences between individuals may play some role in determining to what extent musical skills are acquired, one major purpose of this chapter is to marshal evidence and arguments for an alternative view to the prevalent folk psychology. This alternative view holds the capacity for musical accomplishment of one sort or another to be a species-defining characteristic (along with the capacity to learn a language, develop motor skills, etc.). As with these other skills, musical development may be impeded by inherited deficiencies, but such deficiencies only cause major problems in a relatively small minority of cases. Most humans are "primed" to become musicians. Therefore, for an account of why they fail to develop significant levels of performance skill, we need to look elsewhere than lack of supposed talent.

In reviewing the state of this debate, I summarize some material and go over arguments already published elsewhere. The specific issue that I want to address in greater detail in this chapter is the distinction between technical and expressive aspects of musical performance. Those who are prepared to concede that talent might not be the best explanation of technical development are much more reluctant to concede on the issue of expressivity. Expressive musicianship is widely considered to be intuitive, spontaneous, unteachable to those who do not display it, and a prime manifestation of talent. If we can rescue expressivity from the folk psychology of talent, then the rest of musical expertise comes with it rather easily.

WHAT CAN WE KNOW ABOUT INHERITANCE OF MUSICAL ABILITY?

The usual source of evidence on heritability of psychological characteristics is, of course, the literature on twin studies. The methodological and theoretical traps of this literature are well known, particularly in the context of IQ studies, and it is outside my concerns or expertise to rehearse the arguments here. There are two points to make with respect to music. First, there exists no generally accepted psychometric measure of musical ability that has the validity and reliability of standard measures of intelligence. There are no widely accepted "MQ" tests. Second, even if all the difficulties with twin studies are set aside, such studies seem to conclude that differences in musical ability are considerably less dependent on inherited factors than are differences in IQ (Coon & Carey, 1989).

Plomin and Thompson (1993) recently offered the hope of a means of transcending the inherent difficulties of twin studies by a new technique of *allelic association*, which allows direct comparison of genetic material between large numbers of unrelated individuals varying on some known psychological property, such as IQ. This technique uses analysis of genetic material found in human blood cells. Hints that genetic correlates of high IQ have been established by this group have, however, yet to be substantiated in print, and the technique is too new to have been properly evaluated, let alone applied to music or other skill domains.

A different source of evidence concerning genetic foundations of musicality comes from direct research on the capacities of human infants pre- and postterm. Research on prenatal capacities (see Hepper, 1991; Lecanuet, 1995) and postnatal musical cognition (see Papousek, 1995; Trehub, 1990) suggests that the vast majority of human infants have rather similar, and surprisingly sophisticated, means of handling musical stimuli. These universal capacities lead to an astonishing flowering (from the sixth month on) of spontaneous premusical generativity. All but the most severely learning-disabled children display a rich vocabulary of pitch- and rhythm-modulated utterances. As in the case of language, these utterances can be shown to pass through a number of stages that can well be described in terms of different systems of underlying grammatical rules that succeed one another in an orderly way (Imberty, 1995).

Although individual differences in infant functioning are remarkably difficult to research, for methodological and practical reasons (see Colombo, 1993), it would seem that developmental research has shown that the average human infant displays musical capacities as early, if not earlier, than linguistic capacities, and in a far more developed and overt form than any capacities that might be supposed to underlie other skills such as mathematical, artistic, or athletic skills. Nothing in this literature prepares us for the dismal musical outcomes observed in our culture in late childhood and adulthood.

It would be impossible for me to address the issues of musical expertise without recurrent reference to the most recent large-scale study in which I have been involved, with colleagues Michael Howe, Jane Davidson, and Derek Moore (Davidson, Sloboda, & Howe, 1994; Howe, Davidson, Moore, & Sloboda, 1995; Sloboda & Davidson, 1995; Sloboda, Davidson, Howe, & Moore, in press; Sloboda, Davidson, Moore, & Howe, 1994). This study, named the Leverhulme Project in honor of its funding source, the Leverhulme Trust, obtained a wide variety of information, mostly biographical, on 257 young people in England. They were selected to represent a range of current performance achievement on musical instruments, from the outstandingly able through to the modal "tried an instrument but gave it up." Individuals at different levels of accomplishment were roughly matched for age, gender, instrument, and socioeconomic class. We established five major ability groups, whose rank ordering was validated by differences in objective performance measures (musical examinations set by a national U.K. examining body). Group 1 comprised 119 students of a specialist music school, where entry is by competitive audition. This group represents the highest ability level. Graduates of the school regularly win national performance competitions, and typically go on to conservatory study and careers as professional performers. Groups 2, 3, and 4 comprised current players of musical instruments, classified in terms of their levels of aspiration for excellence in musical performance. The members of Group 2 had failed the entry audition to the specialist school. The members of Group 3 had inquired about but had failed to apply for entry to the specialist school. The members of Group 4 were current "players for pleasure" in an ordinary state school, undistinguished in its general level of musical education. Group 5 comprised pupils of the same school as Group 4, who had begun to learn an instrument, but had given up study after a period of 6 months or more. Each participant was interviewed, and answers cross-checked for reliability in individual interviews with a parent of each participant.

It is very important for later steps in the argument to note that all these young people were learning musical instruments in what might be described as the "classical conservatoire culture," where emphasis is on reproduction of musical artworks within the formal classical tradition, represented by composers such as Mozart, Beethoven, Rachmaninov, and Stravinsky. The characteristics of this tradition are (a) concern with accurate and faithful reproduction of a printed score, rather than with improvisation or composition; (b) the existence of a central repertoire of extreme technical difficulty; (c) definitions of mastery in terms of ability to perform items from a rather small common core set of compositions within a culture; and (d) explicit or implicit competitive events in which performers are compared with one another by expert judges on their ability to perform identical or closely similar pieces, such judgments forming an important element in decisions about progression and reward within the culture. Other musical cultures exist, such as jazz, pop, or folk cultures, which have very different characteristics. It should not be supposed that findings from studies of conservatoire culture musicians can be straightforwardly applied to other forms of musical activity.

It has often been supposed that individual differences in musical accomplishment are prefigured by individual differences in early signs of musicality. Building on accounts of one or two legendary "geniuses" such as Mozart, and other accounts of child prodigies (e.g., Revesz, 1925/1970), commentators have often assumed that individuals displaying unusually high ability in adolescence or later must have always been unusual. We attempted to test this claim in the Leverhulme Project by asking detailed and specific questions of the parents of all participants concerning the age of occurrence of particular early manifestations of musical ability, such as the first age at which the child could reproduce by singing a recognizable tune from the culture.

The results were clear (Howe et al., 1995). Similarities between the five groups far outweighed the differences, which were nonexistent on many measures, and when present did not always favor the highest ability group. The difference most favorable to the "talent" account was a 6-month average advantage for Group 1 in singing a recognizable tune (18 months of age, as opposed to 24 months for the other groups). However, this group showed earlier parent-initiated musical activity, too, and so the result may be a consequence of differential parental behavior. We have considerable evidence from other parts of our study that the parents of the highest achieving group showed unique behavioral characteristics. Although there are obvious interpretational difficulties with retrospective studies, this study lends little credence to the notion of large individual differences in early musicality that prefigure later achievement. The results are entirely consistent with the data obtained by direct study of very young children. Most children show a variety of overt musical behaviors at an early age, and few stray far from established norms.

THE ROLE OF PRACTICE

Ericsson, Krampe, and Tesch-Römer (1993) provided compelling evidence for a conclusion of some generality with respect to acquisition of expertise. Their conclusion is that level of expertise is a direct function of the amount of effortful formal practice of that skill undertaken by an individual. Their own work on student and professional instrumental players has shown that the highest achieving individuals consistently undertook around twice as much daily practice as moderate achievers, over long periods of childhood, adolescence, and early adulthood. Similar findings have been obtained in other domains such as chess (see Charness et al., chap. 2, this volume) and sport (see Starkes et al., chap. 3, this volume).

The Ericsson position offers a strong challenge to the folk psychology of talent, which, in the case of music and many other skills, assumes that high-achieving individuals acquire their outstanding skill with the same or even less practice than others.

The Leverhulme Project has provided data that fully confirm and strengthen the practice hypothesis (Sloboda et al., in press; Sloboda et al., 1994). All participants were asked to provide estimates of average daily formal practice for each year of life since beginning to learn an instrument, with formal practice as defined as activities directly related to tasks set by the instrumental teacher in the previous lesson. A subset of the sample also kept a detailed record of practice activities over a 42-week period.

The two main subcomponents of such practice were named as scales and pieces. *Scales* is a shorthand designation for work on scales, arpeggios, and other technical exercises without musical interest or merit in their own right, but designed to provide exhaustive and repetitive opportunities for mastery of technical aspects of playing. *Pieces* designates work on items from the musical repertoire toward the end goal of polished performance.

The relationship between practice and achievement level was strongly confirmed, and extended across the entire sample. Members of Group 1 were, even by the age of 12, practicing an astonishing 800% more than the members of Group 5 (2 hours a day, as compared to 15 minutes a day). The intermediate groups fell between these extremes in exact order of achievement. The practice–achievement relationship does not, therefore, break down at low levels of achievement. We found no individuals in our sample who practiced as much as 2 hours per day yet failed to achieve high levels of skill! Such cases would surely be predicted in considerable numbers were the folk psychology view correct.

A chance feature of the U.K. instrumental education system allowed us to be even more definitive about the practice–achievement relationship than Ericsson et al. (1993). The vast majority of children learning instruments in the United Kingdom are entered by their teachers into a national system of graded instrumental examinations, which are set and examined by a nationally constituted panel of trained assessors, whose purpose is to provide equivalent measurements across the country. There is a preliminary grade, and eight main grades, which, as a very rough guide, might each represent a year's additional work on an instrument. The pedagogic practices of many teachers are totally determined by the requirements of these grade examination syllabi.

Every child in our sample had entered for these examinations, and we were able to ascertain at what age each grade level had been reached. This allowed, for each group, the calculation of the average number of hours of formal practice required to achieve each grade. This amount proved to be not significantly different between groups. The relationship between grade level and practice for the whole sample is shown in Fig. 4.1. This indicates, for instance, that, regardless of ultimate achievement level, it takes an average of 1,200 hours of formal practice in total to achieve Grade 5 standard (or 300 hours to get there from Grade 4). The reason that Group 1 members achieve grade exam successes earlier than other groups seems entirely due to accumulation of the requisite amount of practice more quickly. There is absolutely no evidence of a "fast track" for high achievers. Indeed, there is a nonsignificant trend for high achievers to practice more than low achievers to reach a particular grade.

Of course, as one might expect, there is a fairly high degree of within-group variance in amounts of practice undertaken to achieve a given grade.

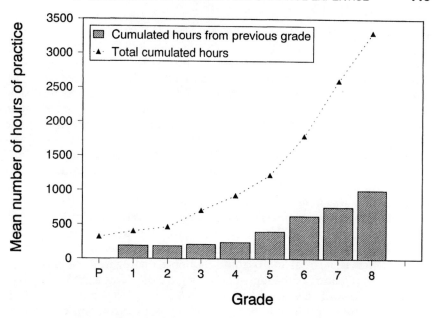

FIG. 4.1 Relationship of cumulated hours of practice to grade achievement for young instrumentalists. Data are means for 257 instrumentalists in five ability groups. There are no significant differences between groups at any grade level.

One can suppose differences in instrument, practice strategy, teaching efficiency, concentration, and other factors to account for this (see Lehmann, in press, for an elaboration of this argument). There might even be some contribution from inherited differences. The important thing for this discussion is that this variability is present at all levels of achievement, and therefore is not constitutive of achievement, as the folk psychology account would demand.

Several studies of expertise have been criticised for not including a "dropout" group (see Sternberg, chap. 15, this volume). Group 5 of this study comprises such a dropout group. The fact that this group shows exactly the same relationship between practice and achievment as any other group suggests that putative differences between persisters and dropouts (in terms of "talent," self-beliefs, and motivation) influence only the duration of practice activities, and not the effectiveness of those activities once undertaken, in improving skill.

The Leverhulme study also provided some data that helped explain why the groups differed so much in the amount of daily practice they were capable of (Davidson, Howe, Moore, & Sloboda, in press; Davidson et al., 1994). At the outset of instrumental study, groups were broadly equivalent on a crude measure or practice motivation. All reported having periods when motivation to practice was low, and when they probably would not have practiced at all without parental intervention. They displayed little of the "rage to master" reported in the case of some precocious young artists (see Winner, chap. 10, this volume). Two things marked the higher achieving children. First, the nature and level of early parental involvement was significantly different. Parents of Group 1 students were more likely to attend instrumental lessons with their children, obtain detailed feedback and instructions from teachers, and actively supervise daily practice on a moment-to-moment basis, often at some considerable cost to their own schedule. For instance, one family with three high-achieving siblings adopted a daily routine in which the father would supervise the individual practice of each child in 30-minute intervals from 6.00 a.m. until 7.30 a.m. prior to the family dispersing to school and work. Parents of low-achieving children were less likely to have meaningful contact with the teacher, and were likely to confine their domestic interventions to telling children to "go and do your practice," without any direct involvement in it. In sum, there-fore, it seems that abnormally high levels of early practice are sustained by abnormal levels of social and cognitive support, mainly from parents.

The second feature of the higher achieving children was a gradual age-re-lated move toward self-motivation for practice as adolescence progressed. These individuals appeared to be finding their own motivations for practice, although the study did not systematically probe what these were. Arguably, those who make faster progress get to work on more interesting and complex music, obtain greater mastery, perceive themselves as successful, and identify with teachers or other high-level performers as role models. All of these factors have been experimentally demonstrated in other domains to have strong effects on motivation (e.g., Amabile, 1983; Dweck, 1986), and we found exam-ples of all of these factors in the informal comments of the interviewees.

The diary study showed, however, that even among the highest achieving groups, there were large fluctuations in daily practice duration as a function of external circumstances. These individuals practiced most before important concerts, and least during school vacation. Despite these fluctuations, however, Group 1 still demonstrated the most week-to-week stability in practice dura-tion, and confirmed Ericsson et al.'s (1993) finding that high-achieving individuals tend to do more of their practice in the morning. In our sample this effect was particularly strong for scales practice. High-achieving young people tend to concentrate the more grueling repetitive technical practice at the time of day when they are physically and cognitively at their peak.

TECHNICAL VERSUS EXPRESSIVE ASPECTS
OF MUSIC PERFORMANCE

Advanced music performance requires high levels of technical skill. This is not only because much core repertoire requires extremely rapid move-ments, but also because very small differences in the positioning or timing of movements can make huge differences in the perceptual qualities of the sound. For instance, accurate tuning in violin playing can be disrupted by positioning deviations of fingers on the string of less than 1 millimeter. The technical difficulty of classical instrumental performance is recognized by the long-standing tradition of manuals, tutors, and exercises designed solely to address technical problems through highly systematic and repetitive practice. The sequences that are used for such purposes often have little or no aesthetic interest. From the very outset of instrumental learning, most teachers encourage their pupils to devote the first part of any practice period to technical exercises, before going on to work at repertoire. The teaching of technique is commonly based on some set of theoretical assumptions about optimal posture, muscle tension, transitions between different positions, and so on. These assumptions have general components that resemble those found in the pedagogy of other skills. For instance, many musical theories make general assumptions about the desirability of economies in both effort and movement, which resemble assumptions behind sporting or athletic technique. Most of the theories, however, devote the bulk of their efforts toward the peculiar problems of the interface between the human body and the particular instrument.

Because the shape, size, and sound-producing mechanisms of musical instruments are so different from one another, there is very little in common between, say, violin technique and piano technique. Perhaps even more important, musical instruments require, by and large, bodily movements of a type not common in other domains of human activity. These almost always involve small but precisely timed and located finger movements that show high degrees of independence from one another. A very fundamental issue in nearly all instrumental performance is the move toward complete independence of fingers and hands one from another. The nonmusical skill with the most similar set of requirements is typing, but even there, the level of specificity of finger movement speed and timing is of a much lower order. By and large it does not matter when a key is depressed, so long as the sequence of keys is in the correct order. Furthermore, typing rarely involves the simultaneous depression of two or more fingers. Skills such as piano playing require this routinely.

For all these reasons, we can predict that the acquisition of high levels of technical competence on an instrument will take a long time and will require much practice specifically tailored to the requirements of each instrument. People have, in effect, to learn a whole new set of motor programs for each different instrument. There are few previously learned skills that the learner can build on. We may suppose that if there is any transfer of training between different instruments it reflects either their physical similarity (e.g., piano and harpsichord, violin and viola) or other nonmotor skills (e.g., the ability to read music) that both instruments require.

It has long been recognized by musicians, and more recently confirmed by psychological research (Clarke, 1988; Gabrielsson, 1988; Shaffer, 1981; Sloboda, 1983) that mere technical prowess does not make an effective musical performer. Playing the notes as written with speed and fluency is the starting point for artistic excellence, not the finish.

High-level performers add value to the score by a range of expressive devices that affect the microstructure of timing, loudness, timbre, and other elements, resulting in notes that are equal in the notation being performed unequally in some respect. We know a number of things for certain about expressive performance:

1. The deviations from exactitude are intentional. That is, they are not unintentional by-products of technical deficiencies, or products of random noise in the motor system. We know this because a performer can (a) reproduce the same deviations on occasions that may be widely separated in time (Shaffer, 1984), and (b) produce a different expressive profile in response to changes in task demand (Palmer, 1989; Sloboda, 1983).

2. The deviations are, in part, applied without conscious awareness. Performers asked to produce expressionless "deadpan" performances are normally incapable of doing this. Reduced features of expressive performances are still present (e.g., Gabrielsson, 1974, 1988). Even when performers know they are being deliberately expressive, they do not have full conscious awareness of every detail of their performance.

3. The deviations are systematic. That is to say, a given performer applies the same type of deviation at analogous points in a musical structure, and performers within a culture tend to use the same types of expressive devices.

4. The deviations are constrained by the structure of the music. This means that expression takes account of structure, and in some situations is intended to reinforce the structure by making it more manifest or salient to a listener. Musicians can have rational debates about the relative merits of different ways of playing the same piece, because it is not the case that "anything goes" in expression.

5. The deviations are unique in some respects to a given performer. At first glance this seems to contradict the third point already given. However, even if two performers use exactly the same set of expressive devices, they can still sound quite different from one another because of their differences in frequency of use of the various devices, the distribution of magnitudes of deviations, and other "free" parameters. Hence, each performer has a distinct performing style that is recognizable to connoisseurs (Sloboda, 1985).

6. The deviations are detectable by listeners, and assist their processes of forming representations of the music. For instance, where the music is metrically ambiguous, expert performance disambiguates the meter (Sloboda, 1983).

7. Expressive skill develops over long timespans. Commentators on internationally known performers often trace significant changes in expressive character of recorded performances over a lifespan. It is generally held that "mature" interpretations are unlikely to be achieved within the first 10

years of performing an instrument. Where the issue has been studied experimentally, it has been found that performers with several decades of performing experience show distinct superiority in the consistency and effectiveness of expression, as compared to performers with only one decade of performing experience (Sloboda, 1983).

Expressive performance, unlike technical performance, is not systematically taught or acquired through the use of manuals or sets of exercises. We can observe two processes at work in the acquisition of expression. First is the use of expressive models. A teacher will play something and ask the student to imitate the expression. In later stages of development, performers avidly seek out the performances of other musicians for purposes of analysis and comparison. The second process is the encouragement of the development of an individual's own expressive style. An individual is invited to generate alternative expressive solutions and exercise some independent judgment in deciding among them.

DECONSTRUCTING THE TALENT ACCOUNT
OF EXPRESSION

When conversing with music professionals, particularly those who teach, a very common experience recounted by these professionals is the existence of young musicians who seem to be "primed" to make unusually rapid progress in the acquisition of expressive performance when compared with the norm. This unusual rapidity can be observed in both imitation and generativity. So, on the one hand, there appear to be individuals who are capable of imitating expressive models with unusual accuracy or rapidity; and on the other, there appear to be individuals who spontaneously generate appropriate expressive variations in the absence of an immediate model. To a great extent, it is such observations that support the notion of a small group of talented individuals, separated from the norm.

Imitative Expression

For the purposes of the argument, assume that these observations by teachers are reliable, accurate, and free from the kinds of biases that can so easily infect judgments of this sort. Let us first of all take the case of imitation. There is, of course, a limiting condition that must pertain if the listener is to detect an intended imitation of expression; that is, that the performance as a whole must be technically more stable than the parameters of the expressive device being detected. To take a concrete example, let us suppose that the device to be imitated is an expressive lengthening of 25% over and above the notated duration of a given note in a phrase. In this case, in order for the lengthening to be detected the average variability in note lengths over the passage as a whole must be no greater than, say, 10% (psychophysical considerations would determine the exact ratio required). If technical stability is not achieved, then we have the possibility that an individual is able to form a representation of a heard expressive device, generate a performance intention in which this device is present, and thus intended for performance, but fail to translate the intention into an adequate motor program. This has the consequence that some differences between individuals in supposed observed expressive ability are actually technical differences. Technical difficulties can be caused by many things, one of them, of course, being lack of practice. However, there are other factors at play in any individual instance. For instance, an overanxious child might well suffer technical disruption more easily than a confident child. A child who knows the piece being played, or knows pieces like it, might be able to form a representation of the notes it contains more rapidly and efficiently. Many of these factors will lead to fairly stable and reliable differences between individuals in their ability to "deliver" expressive imitation, at least in the short term, but they have nothing to do with differences in expressive ability, per se. It may not be possible for an individual informal observer to distinguish these cases of production deficiency from true differences in expressivity. Only controlled formal quasi-experimental observation may have the necessary discriminatory power.

Let us assume, however, that there is a residue of cases that do not fall foul of these problems. These cases would be individuals of equal technical capacity, in general, and in respect to the piece presented in this situation, who nevertheless show significant differences in capacity to imitate the expressive deviations being demonstrated. What account might we give of these differences that did not rely on talent?

My proposal is based on how individuals might solve the problem of storing the large amount of analog information that appears to be involved in remembering expressive details. There is a great deal of evidence that musical memory, like any other kind of memory, requires categorical structural representation that reduces the information load to manageable proportions. Most tonal music solves the problem by allowing that all musical inputs are reducible to a canonical form in which, for instance, all pitches are subsumed into one of a small number of categories (5–12 per octave according to specific genre), and all durations are likewise subsumed (usually equal subdivisions of a primary beat, 2, 4, 8, 3, and 6 being the most common). To have represented a piece of music tonally means to have extracted these categories from a much richer surface. Expressive deviations are contained in that part of the input that the categorization process must ignore, so representing it means recovering some of it before it is lost. This recovery cannot be a simple list of all the analog information present, because humans do not have the capacity to store such information, which would resemble the output from a performance to a MIDI file, containing the precise duration, loudness, and timbral qualities of every successive note.

We need to translate the expressive information into something more abstract before it can be stored. This abstract representation has two requirements: (a) it must link otherwise apparently arbitrary changes in timing, loudness, and other characteristics of successive notes one to another through some function or formula that can then be run in reverse during performance to regenerate something approximating the original pattern of deviations; and (b) it must mark the starting and end positions of a particular function or formula in the canonical representation of pitch time categories within the tonal representation of the piece. To put this in more everyday musical language, the expressive device must have a shape that has a definite location in the musical structure. We store the shape and its location rather than the analog data. Change the shape or change the location of the shape and you have a different expressive outcome.

My contention is that what bootstraps the process of representing expressive devices in music is the existence of extramusical functions and formulas that act as ready-made templates onto which musical expression can be mapped. The individual who presents as "talented" with respect to expressive imitation is the individual who has (a) acquired an appropriate repertoire of extramusical templates, and (b) has made the appropriate connections between domains that allows them to be applied "by analogy" to music.

These templates arise from a number of domains, the most plausible being those of bodily and physical motion, gesture, speech and vocal intonation, and expressions of emotion. Such linkage has been suggested by a number of studies (e.g., Clynes, 1983, 1986; Repp, 1992, 1993; Todd, 1992). There are a number of factors that can account for individual differences in the facility of this linkage:

1. Differences in nonmusical expressivity. Most theories of emotional expression (see Frijda, 1986, for instance) seem to accept that the fundamental forms of such expression are universal, innate, and species defining. What determines individual differences are cultural and social factors, concerned with repression of spontaneous expression and replacement with stylized variants. Some of these factors may be rather specific (e.g., a family environment in which emotional expression is discouraged). Others may be more general. For instance, Sloboda (1991a) provided evidence for the assertion that many children experience performance-related anxiety in music education settings, which overrides any possibility of attending to and representing the expressive characteristics of the music itself. O'Neill and Boulton (in press) and others (Abeles & Porter, 1978; Delzell & Lepplar, 1992) have demonstrated how gender-role stereotypes play a major role in determining what kind of musical engagement is thought to be appropriate

by boys and girls. These stereotypes will impact on the kind of expressive or emotional awareness that children will be prepared to bring to music.

2. Differences in the ability to identify and retain the musical location of features requiring expressive treatment. Expressive gestures in music typically have a focus, even if they are spread over a number of notes. So, for instance, a particular note may be expressively marked by a increase in volume prior to it, and a decrease in volume after it. How is someone to remember where the focus of an expressive device is? In the light of the characteristics of expert expressive performance described earlier, it is probable that events are marked for expressive treatment in virtue of their structural characteristics. Therefore, a particular note is the focus for expressive treatment because it is harmonically, rhythmically, and thematically important. The ability to locate an expressive device will therefore be affected by the extent to which those structures are encoded in the person's representation. This will be affected by the degree of experience with that particular genre of music.

3. Differences in the degree of awareness of, and elaboration of, the cross-domain analogy. It is relatively well accepted that analogies need to be noticed before they can be incorporated in cognitive strategies, and that the initial noticing of the analogy may happen quite suddenly. For instance, in Chase and Ericsson's (1981) seminal study on Falloon's digit span, they report that on Day 4 of trials he had reached an asymptote of performance, whereas on Day 5, after discovery of the "running times" analogy, he was able to dramatically increase his span. We may speculate that what caused the analogy to be noticed was some number sequence that triggered a particularly strong association to a running time that was highly salient for this subject. For another runner, it might have been a quite different number that triggered the analogy, and this may have happened sooner, later, or never. In the case of music, we can suppose that the expressive analogy is bootstrapped by the experience of an expressive gesture that evokes a strong association to a salient nonmusical gesture for that individual.

4. Differences in the degree of monitoring of one's own performance for intended expressive outcomes. There is quite clear evidence available that so-called tone deafness is nothing of the sort. Individuals identified as tone-deaf are unable to match a heard pitch by singing. This is not, however, due to any deficit in pitch perception or memory, which is just as acute as the average correct singer. Rather, it is due to an inability to monitor one's own vocal output and make appropriate adjustments. By providing enhanced feedback, for instance, computer-generated visual representation of one's own sung pitch as compared to a standard, it is possible to teach individuals to adjust their vocal pitch, and, eventually, to do so without the visual feedback (Welch, Howard, & Rush, 1989). This is essentially the same technique that is used in biofeedback to teach people to control their own heart rate or skin conductance. In relation to expressive performance, it is commonplace for teachers to observe that their pupils do not monitor the

expressive outcomes of their own performances. Rather, they seem to be monitoring their expressive intentions, and take the intention for the deed. Such a situation occurs when, for instance, a teacher asks a pupil to copy a dynamic shape (getting louder then getting softer), the pupil does something, the teacher says she cannot hear any difference, but the pupil believes that he did play louder and then softer. Such scenarios can easily lead to incorrect attributions ("the child is inexpressive"), which may not encourage the teacher to seek ways of helping the pupil monitor their own performance more appropriately.

5. Differences in degree of emotional response to the expressive device. There is considerable suggestive evidence (see Sloboda, 1991a) that the ability of individuals to experience music-generated emotional response is a function of the degree to which their emotional response is not captured by factors extrinsic to the music. Thus, where the context of music is a source of threat or anxiety, the emotional response to the situation is determined by self-related emotions (self-esteem, self-preservation, group conformity) in a way that seems to block the kind of relaxed attentiveness that is a precondition for strong aesthetically based responses to music. Such emotional blocks act as overarching factors that reduce the likelihood of noticing and internalizing the analogy between musical and nonmusical expression. In some individuals, the blocks seem to have become chronic, and independent of actual external context. Music itself triggers anxiety, by association (e.g., "Whenever I hear music I remember the humiliation of being told by my teacher that I was singing out of tune").

There are no doubt other factors that could be adduced to account for individual differences. The demonstration of their existence is a task for future empirical research, but each of them is a specific causal hypothesis in which considerations of supposed talent or its absence are really of not much help in moving toward a better understanding of individual differences.

Generative Expression

Almost all that one can say about imitation can also be said about individual differences in expressive generation, but there are some additional sources of variance. First, we need to be clear that there are two different types of generativity. One (Type 1) is closely related to imitation in that the sequence of notes is prescribed—and an expressive contour must be fitted to this pre-existent sequence. The other (Type 2) is rather different, and relates to improvisatory mode, where the notes are chosen by the performer along with their expression. This latter kind of expressivity almost never occurs in the conservatoire culture.

Type 1 generativity requires the recognition that a certain musical sequence admits of expressive treatment in the absence of the immediate presentation of a specific expressive model for that sequence. A clear example of generative expression is in the case where an individual sight-reads from an unedited score, or where an individual imitates an inexpressive model, or incorporates different expression from that offered. It is highly likely that another kind of analogical thinking is needed here. The logic would run something like this: The present sequence is similar in musical structure or form to a sequence experienced in another context; in that other context such-and-such an expressive tactic seemed to work well; therefore let us try it here. Another way of expressing this logic within musical discourse is to say that there are expressive conventions within a musical culture, and that these conventions may be learned more or less thoroughly. Nothing in this requires that a performer be able to consciously articulate the known convention. It may be entirely embodied within a nonverbal performance "habit" or "production rule," to use a more theoretically fashionable term.

Individual differences in expressive generativity may, in this case, be linked to individual differences in the opportunities that an individual has had to learn these conventions. This will be partly a matter of exposure to appropriately expressive performances of others, but also of factors such as the five adduced earlier with respect to imitative performance.

Type 2 generativity has a rather different etiology. The developmental literature shows that expressive improvisation is the norm in infants and young children. In the vocal play of young children, expressive gesture is almost the guiding force of vocalizations. Infants sigh, chortle, coo, and make other directly recognizable emotional signals, then they embellish these with pitch and temporal patterning. They also sing while engaged in physical activity, and so naturally coordinate their vocalizations with their bodily movements. What then seems to happen in midchildhood is that the formal characteristics of music separate out from the expressive. Children become very concerned with imitating recognizable tunes of their culture, and at the same time, are learning the control of emotional expression as part of socialization. By the early school years, at least in our own culture, improvisation (except where cherished and nurtured by perceptive adults) has all but dried up. Group singing and group instrumental playing, at the early stages of education, encourage this process of suppression of individual expression in favor of subordination to the group. Regrafting of expression within the elaborated formal musical structures of midchildhood represents a formidable challenge for many children. It requires going directly against the mainstream of cultural separation and repression. I believe that children require very clear enabling conditions for that to happen. We learn from music therapists that emotionally repressed individuals can discover strong and intuitive emotional expressivity within themselves when offered a music performance medium in which they come realize there are no preordained standards of correctness. Typical music therapy, at least within the United Kingdom, will not offer models that are part of the standard conservatoire culture, but might, for instance, offer an individual a large array of percussion instruments, and encourage significant bodily and sonic exploration. In such a context, for instance, anger may be gesturally expressed in a very direct way through the force with which an instrument is struck. Children may need an opportunity of a similar sort to be expressive. It is extremely significant to me that so many teachers and parents tell stories of children who appear "unmusical" (or at least unremarkable) in standard music lessons, but then are found engaging in highly expressive and creative forms of musical behavior outside the formal classroom culture, be it involvement in playground games involving singing, or in the formation of peer-organized groups, using popular forms such as pop, jazz, or folk. This seems to me to suggest key contexts in which the individual senses "permission" to be expressive. For many young people, the conservatoire culture does not provide such permission, and we may need to discover more precisely how those few that do flourish expressively within that culture are protected from the normal inhibitory processes. They are the ones who can, to some extent at any rate, feed on the wellsprings of their own primal musical expressive generativity.

CONCLUDING REMARKS

I realize that many of the comments I have made in this chapter are somewhat speculative. I believe it is appropriate in a conference of this sort to go out on a limb, and push a particular line of argument for all it is worth. I do not wish any of the arguments I put forward to be taken as conclusive, but rather suggestive. In many cases the evidence for particular kinds of processes needs to be gathered. In other cases, weaknesses in the argument need to be exposed. I hope that other participants will be merciless in this respect. We need to find the holes in each other's positions in the pursuit of scientific clarity.

What I have hoped to do is sketch out the framework of a position in which talent is not so much disproved as dissolved into a whole set of complex interacting factors and causes, each of which has its own logic and determining conditions. It is the intricacy and complexity of musical growth and development that makes for fascination and scientific discovery, not some ultimately arid dispute between oversimplistic extremes.

To summarize the steps in my argument:

1. Music seems to be biologically constitutive of early human functioning.
2. Music education in Western cultures produces a dismal yield of achievement.

3. Heritability estimates, where available, are low.
4. Technical expertise within the conservatoire culture requires practice levels far in excess of cultural norms because of its unique properties with respect to particular instruments and the specific requirements of that culture to master a technically demanding canon.
5. Such practice is sustained by external motivators in the early years, but by increasing development of internal sources through development.
6. Expressive expertise has rationality and develops through practice.
7. Significant individual differences in expression are noticed by teachers at early stages in instrumental learning.
8. Unlike technique, expression has characteristics that are similar to extramusical activities (bodily and emotional gestures).
9. This creates opportunities for learning by analogy.
10. A whole range of plausible factors can influence the ease of uptake of this analogy.
11. The articulation and investigation of these factors constitutes a progressive agenda for the scientific study of musical skill.

REFERENCES

Abeles, H. F., & Porter, S. Y. (1978). Sex-stereotyping of musical instruments. *Journal of Research in Music Education, 26,* 65–75.
Amabile, T. M. (1983). *The social psychology of creativity.* New York: Springer Verlag.
Chase, W. G., & Ericsson, K. A. (1981). Skilled memory. In J. R. Anderson (Ed.), *Cognitive skills and their acquisition* (pp. 141–189). Hillsdale, NJ: Lawrence Erlbaum Associates.
Clarke, E. F. (1988). Generative principles in music performance. In J. A. Sloboda (Ed.), *Generative processes in music: The psychology of performance, improvisation, and composition* (pp. 1–26). London: Oxford University Press.
Clynes, M. (1983). Expressive microstructure in music, linked to living qualities. In J. Sundberg (Ed.), *Studies of music performance* (pp. 76–181). Stockholm: Royal Swedish Academy of Music.
Clynes, M. (1986). Music beyond the score. *Communication and Cognition, 19,* 169–194.
Colombo, J. (1993). *Infant cognition: Predicting later intellectual functioning.* Newbury Park, CA: Sage.
Coon, H., & Carey, G. (1989). Genetic and environmental determinants of musical ability in twins. *Behavior Genetics, 19,* 183–193.
Davidson, J. W., Howe, M. J. A., Moore, D. G., & Sloboda, J. A. (in press). The role of parental influences in the development of musical performance. *British Journal of Developmental Psychology.*
Davidson, J. W., Sloboda, J. A., & Howe, M. J. A. (1994). The role of family and teachers in the success and failure of music learners. *Proceedings of the Third International Conference for Music Perception and Cognition* (pp. 359–360). University of Liege, Belgium: URPM.
Davis, M. (1994). Folk music psychology. *The Psychologist, 7*(12), 537.
Delzell, J. K., & Lepplar D. A. (1992). Gender association of musical instruments and preferences of fourth-grade students for selected instruments. *Journal of Research in Music Education, 40,* 93–103.
Dweck, C. S. (1986). Motivational processes affecting learning. *American Psychologist, 41*(10), 1040–1048.

Ericsson, K. A., Krampe, R., & Tesch-Römer, C. (1993). The role of deliberate practice in the acquisition of expert performance. *Psychological Review, 100,* 363–406.

Frijda, N. H. (1986). *The emotions.* Cambridge, UK: Cambridge University Press.

Gabrielsson, A. (1974). Performance of rhythm patterns. *Scandinavian Journal of Psychology, 15,* 63–72.

Gabrielsson, A. (1988). Timing in music performance and its relation to musical experience. In J. A. Sloboda (Ed.), *Generative processes in music: The psychology of performance, improvisation, and composition* (pp. 27–51). London: Oxford University Press.

Hepper, P. G. (1991). An examination of fetal learning before and after birth. *Irish Journal of Psychology, 12,* 95–107.

Howe, M. J. A., Davidson, J. W., Moore, D. G., & Sloboda, J. A. (1995). Are there early childhood signs of musical ability? *Psychology of Music, 23*(2), 162–176.

Imberty, M. (1995). Linguistic and musical development in pre-school and school age children. In I. Deliege & J. A. Sloboda (Eds.), *Musical beginnings: The origins and development of musical competence* (pp. 191–213). London: Oxford University Press.

Kingsbury, H. (1988). *Music, talent, and performance: A conservatory cultural system.* Philadelphia: Temple University Press.

Lecanuet, J. P. (1995). Prenatal auditory experience. In I. Deliege & J. A. Sloboda (Eds.), *Musical beginnings: The origins and development of musical competence* (pp. 3–34). London: Oxford University Press.

Lehmann, A. C. (in press). Acquisition of expertise in music: Efficiency of deliberate practice as a mediating variable in accounting for sub-expert performance. In I. Deliege & J. A. Sloboda (Eds.), *Perception and cognition of music.* Mahwah, NJ; Lawrence Erlbaum Associates.

O'Neill, S. (1994, July). *Factors influencing children's motivation and achievement during the first year of instrumental music tuition.* Paper presented at the Third International Conference on Music Perception and Cognition, Univerity of Liege, Belgium.

O'Neill, S., & Boulton, M. (in press). Boys' and girls' preferences for musical instruments: A function of gender? *Psychology of Music.*

Palmer, C. (1989). Mapping musical thought to musical performance. *Journal of Experimental Psychology: Human Perception and Performance, 15,* 331–346.

Papousek, H. (1995). Musicality and infancy research. In I. Deliege & J. A. Sloboda (Eds.), *Musical beginnings: The origins and development of musical competence* (pp. 37–55). London: Oxford University Press.

Plomin, R., & Thompson, L. A. (1993). Genetics and high cognitive ability. In G. Bock & K. Ackrill, (Eds.), *The origins of high ability: Proceedings of Ciba Symposium 178* (pp. 67–84). London: Wiley.

Repp, B. H. (1992). A constraint on the expressive timing of a melodic gesture: Evidence from performance and aesthetic judgment. *Music Perception, 10,* 221–242.

Repp, B. H. (1993). Music as motion: A synopsis of Alexander Truslit's (1938) *Gestaltung und Bewegung in der Musik. Psychology of Music, 21,* 48–72.

Revesz, G. (1970). *The psychology of a musical prodigy.* Freeport, NY: Books for Libraries Press. (Original work published 1925)

Shaffer, L. H. (1981). Performance of Chopin, Bach, and Bartok: Studies in motor programming. *Cognitive Psychology, 13,* 326–376.

Shaffer, L. H. (1984). Timing in solo and duet piano performances. *Quarterly Journal of Experimental Psychology, 36A,* 577–595.

Sloboda, J. A. (1983). The communication of musical metre in piano performance. *Quarterly Journal of Experimental Psychology, 35A,* 377–396.

Sloboda, J. A. (1985). Expressive skill in two pianists: Metrical communication in real and simulated performances. *Canadian Journal of Psychology, 39*(2), 273–293.

Sloboda, J. A. (1991a). Music as a language. In F. Wilson & F. Roehmann (Eds.), *Music and child development* (pp. 28–43). St. Louis, MO: MMB Music.

Sloboda, J. A. (1991b). Musical expertise. In K. A. Ericsson & J. Smith (Eds.), *Toward a general theory of expertise: Prospects and limits* (pp. 153–171). New York: Cambridge University Press.

Sloboda, J. A., & Davidson, J. W. (1995). The young performing musician. In I. Deliege & J. A. Sloboda (Eds.), *The origins and development of musical competence* (pp. 171–190). London: Oxford University Press.

Sloboda, J., Davidson, J., & Howe, M. J. A. (1994). Is everyone musical? *The Psychologist, 7*(8), 349–354.

Sloboda, J. A., Davidson, J. W., Howe, M. J. A., & Moore, D. G. (in press). The role of practice in the development of performing musicians. *British Journal of Psychology.*

Sloboda, J. A., Davidson, J. W., Moore, D. G., & Howe, M. J. A. (1994). Formal practice as a predictor of success or failure in instrumental learning. In *Proceedings of the Third International Conference for Music Perception and Cognition* (pp. 125–126). University of Liege, Belgium: URPM.

Todd, N. P. M. (1992). The dynamics of dynamics: A model of musical expression. *Journal of the Acoustical Society of America, 91,* 3540–3550.

Trehub, S. E. (1990). The perception of musical patterns by human infants: The provision of similar patterns by their parents. In M. A. Berkeley & W. C. Stebbins (Eds.), *Comparative perception: Vol. 1. Basic mechanisms* (pp. 429–59). New York: Wiley.

Welch, G. F., Howard, D. M., & Rush, C. (1989). Real-time visual feedback in the development of vocal pitch accuracy in singing. *Psychology of Music, 17,* 146–157.

5

The Acquisition of Medical Expertise in Complex Dynamic Environments

Vimla L. Patel
David R. Kaufman
Sheldon A. Magder
McGill University

Research investigating the nature of expertise has made significant progress towards understanding the nature of outstanding human performance. Expertise research has been one of the most active areas of inquiry in cognitive science and cognitive psychology. The investigations have characterized the factors that distinguish skilled performance from less skilled performance in a vast range of domains including chess (Charness, 1989; Chase & Simon, 1973), music (Sloboda, 1991), teaching (Leinhardt & Greeno, 1986), computer programming (Jeffries, Turner, Polson, & Atwood, 1981), and medical diagnosis (Patel & Groen, 1986). This research has also been instrumental in the shift in cognitive psychology from studies of domain-general performance in knowledge-lean tasks to semantically complex knowledge-rich domains. Despite the domain-specific nature of studies of expertise, there have been a number of characteristics of experts that have a certain degree of generality across domains. These findings, discussed in detail elsewhere (Chi & Glaser, 1988; Ericsson & Smith, 1991), pertain to factors that distinguish novices from experts, in terms of the organization of their knowledge, reasoning strategies, pattern-recognition capabilities, and metacognitive abilities. Expertise research has also contributed to understanding basic cognitive processes pertaining to memory and attentional processes (Ericsson & Staszewski, 1989) and perception and motor skills (e.g., Allard & Starkes, 1991; Ericsson, Krampe, & Tesch-Römer, 1993), and has also contributed to theories of cognitive architectures (Newell, 1990).

The findings from this body of research have advanced domain-specific models of competence that could be of considerable educational utility. Expertise research has also provided a sound methodological and theoretical basis for identifying factors that distinguish students at different levels of ability (Chi, Bassok, Lewis, Reimann, & Glaser, 1989; Thibodeau, Hardiman, Dufresne, & Mestre, 1989) and for investigating the effects of different pedagogical formats on learning and reasoning (e.g., Patel, Groen, & Norman, 1993). However, the application of expert–novice theory has only indirectly contributed to models of learning and has been of limited utility in developing innovative methods of instruction and assessment. In addition, theory and methods from expertise research have been of limited practical application in developing intelligent systems for training and have not been effectively exploited in order to study cognition in the workplace.

This has led to efforts toward investigations that expand our understanding of the conditions of learning and skill acquisition. One of the recent trends in expertise research has been toward longitudinal studies that focus on the acquisition of expertise in a given individual and in particular, the effects of practice on changes in knowledge, component skills, and improvements in performance (Charness, 1991). Another important development is reflected by an attempt to extend research from laboratory-based tasks to complex "real-world" settings (Dunbar, 1995; Orasanu, 1990). This has also necessitated a shift in emphasis from studying the cognitive processes of the solitary individual to the investigation of the collective decision-making processes involved in work groups.

The purpose of this chapter is to provide a theoretical and methodological foundation for studying the acquisition of expertise in complex dynamic environments. The chapter reports on an investigation of group decision making in a medical intensive care unit (ICU) at a local teaching hospital. The ICU is an example of a dynamic and time-pressured decision-making environment in which multiple participants contribute to the decision-making process.

The transition from studying the individual in controlled experimental situations to investigations in naturalistic environments necessitates the development of methods to characterize the complex dynamics of real-world cognition and determine how knowledge is applied in these situations. This also requires an expanded theoretical framework to account for cognition and behavior in diverse social contexts. Recently, proponents of situated action have criticized symbolic information-processing theories of cognition for their apparent inability to account for the flexibility and variability of human performance in realistic settings (e.g., Clancey, 1993). In this chapter, we argue for an extended framework of symbolic cognitive science. This framework would need to: (a) take into account singular as well as group cognitive processes; (b) reconsider the dominant role of internal mediation and plans in the context of activities; (c) shift emphasis from an exclusive focus on the individual to include cognitive processes, such as decision making, as distributed across groups and settings; and (d) develop innovative and convergent research strategies for characterizing human performance on a range of cognitive activities from dynamic work environments to educational and technological contexts. We are arguing for a genuine reconceptualization of the existing symbolic framework that has informed almost all research within the expertise paradigm. However, the suggested changes are evolutionary rather than revolutionary. In this regard, we can build on the substantial achievements of the symbolic information-processing framework.

The first part of the chapter discusses research and theoretical issues concerning the nature of expertise and medical cognition. This is followed by a review of studies that focus on dynamic decision making and cognition in the workplace. The third section of the chapter attempts to develop an integrated theoretical and methodological framework for studying medical cognition in real work settings. The section also outlines the goals of the research program we have embarked on. The final section presents results from research involving the investigation of expertise and decision making in an ICU.

THE NATURE OF MEDICAL EXPERTISE

The majority of research targeted at understanding medical expertise has focused on contrasting physicians and students in laboratory-based tasks representative of medical practice. Medicine is a semantically rich domain encompassing diverse bodies of knowledge. We can characterize two broad categories of cognitive research targeted at understanding the structure and use of basic science knowledge in medical tasks (Kaufman, Patel, & Magder, in press; Patel, Evans, & Groen, 1989) and research investigating the process of diagnostic reasoning (Patel, Arocha, & Kaufman, 1994). In this section, we review issues and research pertinent to understanding the acquisition of medical expertise in dynamic work environments.

There are two broad experimental approaches that have been used to study medical cognition. The first is a decision-making and judgment perspective in which a subject's decisions from a set of fixed alternatives are contrasted with a normative model based on probability theory, indicating optimal choices under conditions of uncertainty (Camerer & Johnson, 1991). The second one is a problem-solving approach in which the focus is on studying knowledge and cognitive processes in tasks designed to represent an aspect of medical thinking and make use of protocol-analytic techniques (Ericsson & Simon, 1993) and the development of cognitive models of performance. These two approaches offer very different characteristics of the expert. In the classical decision-making approach, the expert is viewed as a fallible predictor of outcomes whose judgmental accuracy is far from optimal (Johnson, 1988). In contrast, expert performance in problem-solving research is viewed as a kind of gold standard (not necessarily infallible) against which lesser performance is compared. The research discussed in this chapter is based in the problem-solving tradition, although the study is principally concerned with decision making in dynamic environments. Decision making can be construed as a problem-solving process in which the solution is in the form of a decision, typically leading to action (Newell, 1980). The classical decision-making approach has been criticized for its lack of applicability to real-life decision-making processes (Beach & Lipshitz, 1993; Klein, Calderwood, & McGregor, 1989). Issues pertaining to naturalistic decision making are discussed in more detail in a subsequent section of the chapter.

The Expert–Novice Continuum

Expertise in medicine, as in other domains, is a continuum from the genuine beginner to the highly trained specialist. The time period from entering medical school to becoming a board-certified specialist is, on average, 10 years. This provides a basis for differentiating between subjects at various levels in the acquisition of expertise. Expert physicians have extensive knowledge of medicine (acquired through medical school and residency training), but only a relatively narrow area of specialization. It is therefore possible to distinguish between specific (e.g., respirologist) and generic (e.g., general medicine) expertise (Patel & Groen, 1991). An individual may possess both, or only generic expertise. Medical training through medical school and internship involves the acquisition of generic expertise. Subsequently, these individuals become practicing physicians and typically enter a residency training program in which they specialize in a branch of medical practice. At this point, they acquire specific expertise and continue to develop generic expertise. The development of both kinds of expertise overlaps considerably. However, a medical resident would continue to acquire generic expertise through rotations in areas outside his specific area of specialization.

The distinction of generic and specific expertise is supported by research indicating differences between subexperts and experts in terms of reasoning strategies and organization of knowledge. In our previous work, we have emphasized the fact that expertise in complex domains cannot be characterized as a monotonic development in skill, knowledge, and problem-solving abilities. In addition, there are many kinds of expertise even within a given subspecialty. For example, certain endocrinologists are diabetes specialists and others are authorities on neuroendocrine disorders. One of the goals of studying performance in the workplace is to understand how the construct of expertise could be modified to account for the various factors introduced in these situations.

Epistemological and Theoretical Distinctions

Medical knowledge consists of two types of knowledge: clinical knowledge, including knowledge of disease entities and associated findings; and basic science knowledge, incorporating subject matter such as biochemistry, anatomy, and physiology. The role of biomedical scientific knowledge in clinical reasoning is an issue of substantial research and controversy (cf. Boshuizen & Schmidt, 1992; Patel & Kaufman, 1995).

Medicine draws on different sources of knowledge from the biomedical sciences. This knowledge can be described in terms of a hierarchical schema of the scientific sources from the most elementary molecular matter to clinical data (Blois, 1990). At each higher level in the hierarchy, there are newly emergent properties not entirely predictable from lower levels. Higher levels introduce more uncertainty and a greater degree of inexactness in ascribing causality. At the clinical level, models of disease are commonly described in terms of associations between clinical findings and diagnoses. The physician is not merely matching findings to diagnostic categories; rather, he or she is developing a model of the patient, based on a sequence of findings with a specific temporal order, and coupling this information with the patient's past medical history, family history, physical examination, and laboratory findings. Medical problems can be characterized as ill structured, in the sense that the initial states, the definite goal state, and the necessary constraints are unknown at the beginning of the problem-solving process (Simon, 1973).

To characterize clinical problem solving in medicine, Evans and Gadd (1989) proposed an epistemological framework that differentiates four levels at which clinical knowledge is organized. We have employed this framework in several studies of medical cognition (Arocha, Patel, & Patel, 1993; Leprohon & Patel, 1995; Patel, Evans, & Kaufman, 1989) to characterize how clinicians at varying levels of expertise solve medical problems. Observations are units of information that are recognized as potentially relevant in the problem-solving context. However, they do not constitute clinically useful propositions. *Findings* are comprised of observations that have potential clinical significance. Establishing a finding reflects a decision made by a physician that an array of data contains a significant cue or cues that need to be taken into account. *Facets* consist of clusters of findings that are suggestive of prediagnostic interpretations. Facets are interim hypotheses that serve to divide the information in the problem into sets of manageable subproblems and suggest possible solutions. Facets vary in terms of their levels of abstraction. A high-level facet may serve to partition the problem space and may be a reasonable approximation to a candidate solution. A low-level facet may involve a more local inference that may explain one or two findings and would not advance the problem-solving process to the same extent. Facets can be conceived as a retrieval structures (Ericsson et al., 1993) that can be used to rapidly access schemata from long-term memory (LTM) and can partition a medical problem into manageable units to facilitate the instantiation of a diagnostic hypothesis. *Diagnosis* is the level of classification that subsumes and explains all levels beneath it. The model is hierarchical, with facets and diagnoses serving both to establish a context in which observations and findings are interpreted, and also providing a basis for anticipating and searching for confirming or discriminating findings.

Diagnostic reasoning has been the principal focus of studies of medical cognition and up until recently, most research in medical artificial intelligence has been targeted at the development of diagnostic systems. There are two other major cognitive tasks in the delivery of health care: therapy and patient monitoring and management. These can be conceived of as generic tasks consisting of a distinct ontology and an inference model (Chandrasekeran, 1986; Ramoni, Stefanelli, Magnani, & Barosi, 1992). For example, diagnostic reasoning employs observed patient data as the primary evidence, which is then coordinated with one or more competing diagnostic hypotheses. Therapeutic reasoning may include the leading-edge diagnostic hypotheses as well as information about the overall condition of the patient (e.g., age, health status, allergies) as evidence toward the goal of choosing appropriate treatment. Monitoring and management is directed toward observing, controlling, and maintaining the state of the patient. This is characterized by an iterative decision–action cycle in which the course of treatment is continually adjusted as new information becomes available. Monitoring and management is the principal cognitive task in an intensive care setting.

Review of Pertinent Findings in Medical Cognition

The focus of research in medical cognition has been mainly on investigating the nature of diagnostic reasoning and the underlying structure of medical knowledge. The emphasis in this section is on themes that emerged from research conducted on individuals in laboratory tasks that have significant implications for understanding the acquisition of expertise in real-life settings. In this section, we review certain pertinent findings concerning medical expertise (for a more comprehensive review see Patel, Arocha, & Kaufman, 1994).

Diagnostic Reasoning.   One of the most robust findings in the study of medical problem solving is experts' use of forward-directed reasoning in solving routine problems in their own domains (Patel & Groen, 1986, 1991). Forward reasoning is characterized by a chain of inferences from data toward an incremental refinement of hypotheses resulting in a diagnostic solution. This reasoning method is one of the hallmarks of expert performance in other domains such as physics (e.g., Larkin, McDermott, Simon, &

Simon, 1980) and mathematics (e.g., Hinsley, Hayes, & Simon, 1977). Forward reasoning is strongly correlated with accuracy in experts.

Novices and intermediate subjects tend to employ a form of backward reasoning such as the hypothetico-deductive method, in which they develop a hypothesis and attempt to test each or most of their hypotheses against the available data (Patel & Groen, 1991). This is a less efficient strategy necessitating the use of subgoals and making heavy demands on working memory. The systematicity in which backward or mixed reasoning strategies are employed in the coordination of hypotheses and evidence is partly a function of training and experience (Arocha et al., 1993). For example, medical students in their second and third years of medical school typically generate numerous hypotheses but fail to evaluate them in a systematic fashion, whereas senior medical students are more methodical in testing each of the hypotheses they generate (Arocha et al., 1993).

Forward reasoning is a function of a highly structured knowledge base and well-developed pattern-recognition capabilities. This schema-driven strategy is highly error prone in the absence of such knowledge because there are no built-in checks for the legitimacy of inferences. Schemata, which are built up as a function of experience within a domain of expertise, guide a subject to key elements in a problem and serve to filter out irrelevant information. In a complex medical problem, there are an inordinate amount of potentially significant findings and extraneous observations. An experienced physician can rapidly access appropriate schemata and delineate a structured problem space that enables solution strategies.

We have observed that experts, when working on less familiar or more complex problems, and experts working outside their domains of expertise, tend to use a mixture of forward and backward reasoning (Patel, Groen, & Arocha, 1990). Experts typically approach these problems by employing a forward-oriented reasoning strategy to account for the parts of the problem that are readily solvable and then resort to backward reasoning to tie up loose ends or anomalies.

The process of resolving anomalies is an important issue of research in medicine (Arocha & Patel, 1995) and in many other domains of inquiry such as scientific reasoning (Chinn & Brewer, 1993; Dunbar, 1995) and in the developmental literature (Kuhn, 1989). Resolving anomalies is essential to developing globally coherent explanations. Grappling with anomalous data plays an essential role in learning and discovery in scientific reasoning (Dunbar, 1995) and in medical reasoning.

Substantive differences have been found that differentiate experts and subexperts (experts working outside their specific domain of expertise) on a range of performance tasks that support the distinction between generic and specific expertise. For example, subexperts generate many more hypotheses in their efforts to resolve anomalous data than do experts, resulting in less than maximally coherent explanations (Joseph & Patel, 1990). Similarly, subexperts tend to employ both forward and backward reasoning strategies with greater frequency and are less likely to generate completely accurate diagnoses (Patel et al., 1990). These findings may appear to be obvious to some observers; however, physicians are often confronted with problems (e.g., multisystem problems) that are at the outer edge of their area of expertise. This is especially true in hospital settings such as an ICU.

Role of Basic Science Knowledge in Diagnostic Reasoning. The primary goal of diagnostic reasoning is to classify a cluster of patient findings as belonging to a specific disease category. From this perspective, diagnostic reasoning can be viewed as a process of coordinating theory (hypothesis) and evidence, rather than one of finding fault in the system. As expertise develops, the disease knowledge of a clinician becomes more dependent on clinical experience, clinical problem solving is increasingly guided by the use of exemplars and analogy, and it is less dependent on a functional understanding of the system in question. This is consistent with Clancey's (1988) description of diagnostic reasoning as a process of heuristic classification involving the instantiation of variable slots in a disease schema. That is not to say that basic science does not play an important role in medicine; rather, the process of diagnosis, particularly in dealing with routine problems, is essentially one of classification. Basic science knowledge is important in resolving anomalies and is essential in therapeutic and management contexts.

The process of forward reasoning as exhibited by experts typically involves relating clinical findings to diagnostic solutions with minimal use of causal or biomedical reasoning. Several investigations of medical problem solving provide some evidence to support the contention that biomedical knowledge is not used optimally in clinical contexts (cf. Patel, Evans, & Groen, 1989; Patel & Kaufman, 1995). The findings suggest that basic science is used differentially in different tasks and in different medical domains (cf. Lesgold et al., 1988; Patel & Groen, 1986), that experts and novices differ in their use of basic science, and that, in some instances, basic science knowledge may even interfere with clinical problem solving (Patel, Evans, & Groen, 1989). This is most apparent in tasks where subjects, students in particular, are explicitly asked to provide a basic science explanation of a clinical problem (Patel et al., 1993). We have found that the global coherence of an explanation is often reduced when basic science concepts are employed. That is to say, the overall explanation becomes fragmented into discrete and isolated chains of inference, some correct, others partially correct, and others incorrect. It should be noted that these findings pertain to the use of basic science knowledge in diagnostic reasoning tasks. The little research there is on therapeutic reasoning suggests that basic science may play a more central role in this task (Chaturvedi & Patel, 1994; Kuipers, Moskowitz, & Kassirer, 1988). It is possible that basic science knowledge will also be employed with greater frequency in monitoring and management tasks.

COGNITION IN THE WORKPLACE

Dynamic Decision Making and the Workplace

An emerging area of research concerns investigations of cognition in dynamic real-world work environments (Klein, Orasanu, Calderwood, & Zsambok, 1993). The majority of this research combines conventional protocol analytic methods with innovative methods designed to investigate cognition and behavior in realistic settings (Rasmussen, Pejtersen, & Goodstein, 1994; Woods, 1993, 1994).

Decision-making research in naturalistic settings differs substantively from typical decision-making research, which most often focuses on a single decision event and a fixed set of alternatives in a stable environment (Klein et al., 1989). In everyday situations, decisions are embedded in a broader context and are part of a decision–action cycle. Decisions are affected by monitoring and feedback rather than a single judgment (Orasanu & Connolly, 1993).

The relevance of basic cognitive science research for understanding the dynamics of the workplace was recognized in a recent workshop on human performance in the complex workplace (Shalin, 1992). The participants also recognized the need to extend the cognitive science framework beyond typical characterizations of knowledge structures, processes, and skills to include modulating variables such as stress, time pressure, fatigue, and communication patterns in team performance.

One of the most important concerns has to do with the issues of cognitive effort and cognitive complexity (Corker, Kieras, Payne, & Reuter-Lorenz, 1992). Dynamic tasks such as air traffic control, nuclear power plant monitoring, and intensive care medicine generate rapidly changing states with multiple streams of data that must be analyzed and acted on in a short period of time. Cognitive complexity refers to the amount of cognitive activity per unit time (Corker et al., 1992). Cognitive effort can be conceived of as a subjective mental workload, reflecting deliberative processing added to automatic or routine information processing. Humans have limited attentional and working memory resources to monitor in detail and in parallel all aspects of a complex environment. There is evidence to suggest that the management of one's cognitive resources and cognitive complexity is a function of expertise (Klein et al., 1989). Individuals acquire strategies for off-loading or distributing information and workload across individuals and sometimes artifacts, attending to critical factors, and maintaining levels of vigilance as required by the situation at hand (cf. Shalin, 1992).

Some of the most innovative research on dynamic decision making in the field has been done by Klein and colleagues with fireground commanders and armed platoon leaders (Klein & Calderwood, 1991). The methods employed include field observations and retrospective accounts of actual emergency events. The types of decisions fireground commanders were required to make included whether to initiate a search and rescue, whether to initiate an offensive attack on the fire, or whether to use a more precautionary defensive strategy. Commanders acted on the basis of prior experience, immediate feedback, and careful monitoring and assessment of the situation. They used a process of serial evaluation of options, rather than systematically selecting between alternative or weighing probabilities (either subjectively or explicitly). The results indicated that expert commanders relied more extensively on recognitional strategies using minimal deliberation, whereas less experienced or novice commanders tended to employ a more deliberative decision-making approach. This kind of recognition-primed decision making appears to be characteristic of dynamic decision-making environments (Klein, 1993).

Leprohon and Patel (1995) studied the decision-making strategies used by nurses in emergency telephone triage settings. In this context, nurses are required to respond to public emergency calls for medical help (exemplified by 911 telephone service). The study analyzed transcripts of nurse–patient caller telephone conversations of different levels of urgency and complexity, and nurses were interviewed immediately following their conversations. In decision-making situations such as emergency telephone triage, there is a chronic sense of time urgency—decisions often have to be made in seconds. This may involve the immediate mobilization and allocation of resources. Decisions are always made on the basis of partial and sometimes unreliable information.

The results of the study indicate that in high-urgency situations, heuristic rules based on symptoms were used, and the decisions were mostly accurate. With an increase in problem complexity, more causal explanations were found, and the decisions were very often inaccurate. Furthermore, the explanations supporting the accurate decisions were also often inaccurate, showing a decoupling of knowledge and action. Alternative decisions were considered in moderate-to low-urgency conditions, where contextual knowledge of the situations (e.g., the age of the patient, whether the patient was alone or with others) was exploited to identify the needs of the clients and to negotiate the best plan of action to meet these needs, resulting in more accurate decisions. Decision-making accuracy was significantly higher in nurses with 10 years of experience or more than nurses with less experience, which is consistent with the acquisition of expertise in other domains.

Most decisions were based on symptoms rather than on diagnostic hypotheses, especially in urgent situations. These decisions must rely on prior instances in order to allow nurses to rapidly access a specific schema, based on minimal information; this enables them to represent the situation and to collect the information that they need to facilitate their decisions. This parallels the problem solving of expert physicians in routine cases, as exemplified by forward reasoning strategies, which typically use only clinical cues to generate diagnostic solutions. Nurses learn to recognize critical symptoms that evoke decision heuristics. They need not develop a hypothesis for explaining the underlying problem. This finding is consistent with research by Benner and Tanner (1987), who found that nurses respond on the basis of prior experiences in memory and do not decompose decisions into sets of alternatives or attempt to understand the underlying pathophysiology of a patient problem. Nurses' training, which focuses on observational skills and detection of abnormal and urgent symptoms, would contribute to the acquisition of this type of decision-making process.

The results from the Leprohon and Patel study are consistent with three patterns of decision making that reflect the perceived urgency of the situation. The first pattern corresponds to *immediate response behavior* as reflected in situations of high urgency. In these circumstances, decisions are made with great rapidity. Actions are typically triggered by symptoms or the unknown urgency level in a forward-directed manner. The nurses in this study responded with perfect accuracy in these situations. The second pattern involves *limited problem solving* and typically corresponds to a situation of moderate urgency, and to cases that are of some complexity. The behavior is characterized by information seeking and clarification exchanges over a more extended period of time. These circumstances resulted in the highest percentage of decision errors (mostly false positives). The third pattern involves and typically corresponds to low-urgency situations. These situations involved evaluating the whole situation and exploring options and alternative solutions, such as identifying the basic needs of a patient and referring the patient to an appropriate clinic. The nurses made fewer errors than in situations of moderate urgency and more errors than in situations requiring immediate response behavior. They could accurately perceive a situation as not being of high urgency.

One of the focal topics of research in the workplace involves studies of expertise and team decision making. Orasanu and Salas (1993) identified several important team characteristics in the context of decision making, including involvement of two or more individuals, multiple sources of information, interdependence and coordination among members, adaptive management of internal resources, individuals with defined roles and responsibilities, and team members possessing task-relevant knowledge. These characteristics distinguish a team from a group, which may be composed of homogenous individuals (e.g., a committee) without clearly defined roles or delineated task responsibilities.

Orasanu (1990) studied the performance of airplane pilots and flight crews trying to cope with emergency situations during simulated flight She was able to distinguish between high- and low-performing crews on the basis of their situation assessment strategies and their communication patterns. The high-performing crews gathered more relevant information, more explicitly defined problems and planned accordingly.

In addition, the captains of the superior crews more explicitly stated plans, explanations, and anticipated actions. It was observed that the captains communicated more of this information to their crews when the workload was lower. In contrast, captains in low-performing crews were more reactive to crises, planned less, and were less explicit about their assessment of the situation and their intended actions. In addition there was considerably more communication in the low-performing crews when the workload was high. Orasanu concluded that effective decision making is predicated on shared mental models that are built through patterns of skilled communication.

Gaba (1992) studied the decision-making processes of anesthesiologists in surgical settings. He is particularly concerned with how team members respond to unanticipated problems that can lead to adverse patient outcomes. In a surgical situation, any number of events can trigger problems, including the anesthesiologist's actions, the patient's underlying disease, actions of the surgeons, and equipment failures. If not detected or not appropriately and immediately acted on, a single problem can propagate, rapidly leading to an adverse outcome such as a diminished state of the patient's health or even loss of life. Consistent with the findings of Leprohon and Patel (1995), Gaba found a continuum of responses from immediate response behavior involving minimal deliberation to the use of analogical reasoning and even precompiled plans. Anesthesiologists also draw on fundamental biomedical knowledge and engage in causal reasoning to explain abnormalities and to choose the appropriate course of action. Gaba also found that expert anesthesiologists were more proactive in anticipating problems and were more willing to interact forcefully with surgeons.

Characteristics of Dynamic Decision-Making Environments

Despite the diversity in subject matter, each of these dynamic decision-making studies point to common characteristics that distinguish expert performance from novice performance. The common characteristics of decision making in naturalistic settings are summarized from Orasanu and Connoly (1993):

1. *Ill-structured problems.* Real decision problems rarely suggest themselves in well-structured alternatives. These kinds of problems frequently are made more ambiguous by uncertain dynamic information and by multiple interacting goals.
2. *Uncertain dynamic environments.* Naturalistic decision making typically takes place in a world of ambiguous and incomplete information and in an environment that may change within the time frame of the required decision.

3. *Shifting, ill-defined or competing goals.* In making decisions and taking actions, there is invariably the potential for conflicts, shifting priorities, and trade-offs over the course of time.
4. *Action–feedback loops.* Decision–action cycles are the norm in realistic settings. A certain action will cause certain effects and will provide further information to the decision makers, who will have to react and consider further decisions. Actions can frequently generate problems of their own and often it is hard to identify whether the cause of a particular problem is rooted in the original problem or is a result of a particular action.
5. *Time stress and high risk.* In many of these settings, decisions are made under significant time pressure—requiring action in minutes or seconds. Decision makers will often experience a sense of exhaustion or loss of vigilance and may opt for less complicated reasoning strategies. This is further complicated by the potential urgency and risk involved in making such a decision.
6. *Multiple players.* A decision may be distributed over a set of cooperative individuals, with distributed responsibilities who try to coordinate their activities.

Many of the findings that distinguish experts from novices are analogous to those found in studies of individuals in laboratory settings. Expert decision makers focus on evaluating a single option based on available cues and work forward until anomalies are evident, at which point they will backtrack and consider other hypotheses (Klein & Calderwood, 1991). Actions are taken on the basis of satisficing strategies (Simon, 1989) rather than a systematic comparison of alternatives. The organization of the expert's knowledge base seems to be a critical factor in the development of the rapid recognitional capabilities of expert decision makers (Klein, 1993).

Several studies also point to the fact that skilled or expert performers have superior situational communication capabilities that allow them to effectively manage and allocate resources, and convey plans and intentions to other members of their teams at the appropriate points in time (Orasanu, 1990). Another important theme relates to the cognitive control of activity in terms of appropriate response modes (Rasmussen, 1993; Rasmussen et al, 1994). Even in the most "high-velocity" environments, there is a continuum of response modes from nonreflective immediate action to analytical problem solving and deliberative planning (Gaba, 1992; Leprohon & Patel, 1995). It is not uncommon for response modes at different points of the continuum to be jointly present in a single situation. According to Rasmussen (1993), the acquisition of expertise in dynamic environments does not only necessitate the acquisition of automated or compiled skills; rather, skill acquisition involves the development and coordination of different levels of control.

Distributed Cognition

In undertaking research in a workplace, it is important to recognize that cognition is shaped by the social context as well as the technological and other artifacts that are embedded in the physical setting. One of the most compelling proposals arising from situated action perspectives has to do with a shift from viewing cognition as a property of the solitary individual to the view of cognition as distributed across groups, cultures, and artifacts (Patel, Kaufman, & Arocha, 1995). This claim has significant implications for understanding the acquisition of expertise as well as for training and instruction. In this section, we briefly attempt to define a position on distributed cognition that informs our subsequent research on cognition in the workplace.

We can characterize two distinct views on the nature of distributed cognition that differ on the appropriate level of analysis for research and theorizing. The more radical position as stated by Cole and Engeström (1993) suggests "a natural unit of analysis for the study of human behavior is activity systems, historically conditioned systems of relations among individuals and their proximal, culturally-organized environments" (p. 9). In this view, the individual, groups of individuals, and artifacts can be construed as a single indivisible cognitive system (Hutchins, 1991; Pea, 1993; Woods, 1994). Lave (1988) also claimed that activities are so embedded in context and the processes involved in an activity so varied from one context to another that the distinction between the individual's cognitions, the activity, and the context become blurred. According to this proposal, the only meaningful level of analysis is in terms of a person acting in a setting, with the individual contributors forming an integral part of the composite. This position would certainly call into question the meaningfulness of a considerable body of research within the symbolic information-processing tradition, including most research concerning the nature of expertise.

In our view, this perspective on distributed cognition underestimates the role of the individual in cognitive tasks as well as the effects of these tasks on his or her learning. We adhere to a less radical position, which, as stated by Perkins (1993), indicates that the immediate physical and social resources outside the person participate in cognition, not just as a source of input and a receiver of output, but as a vehicle of thought. The claim is that the individual and the environment are viewed as dynamically interacting, resulting in cognitive performance and learning. Interaction would mean that although the combined products of a cognitively distributed system cannot be accounted for by operation of its isolated components, each of the entities or individuals can still be seen as having qualities of his or her own, some of which are an integral part of the "distributed partnership" and others of which are not (Salomon, 1993). In this proposal, the individual is viewed as bringing to the situation his or her repertoire of skills, knowledge, and strategies, which affect the situation and are affected by the situation. This perspective maintains a continuity with symbolic information-processing theory, thereby building on a rich repository of research findings, methods, and theories.

THE DOMAIN OF INTENSIVE CARE MEDICINE

The ICU of a hospital is designed to care for seriously ill patients or patients at high risk, who are in need of very rigorous monitoring and aggressive therapy. Most of these patients are monitored both invasively and noninvasively. In addition, many of them are on ventilator support to assist them with their breathing. The primary objective in caring for these patients is monitoring, stabilization, and management. Many of these patients suffer from multisystem problems and the medications administered often produce severe side effects, necessitating careful observation and actions to diminish these adverse effects. The majority of patients whose conditions improve are transferred to other wards in the hospital that offer less intensive and less costly medical care.

We can characterize three levels of objectives and decisions in an ICU setting. The first and most immediate objective is stabilization of the patient by ensuring that the airways are protected, that respiration is maintained, that circulation is adequate, and that fluid balance (input and output of bodily fluids) is maintained. Fluid balance is affected by various medications and these need to be monitored. A second objective is to identify and treat the underlying problem, and a third is to plan a longer term course of action.

There are numerous personnel involved in the delivery of health care to ICU patients. The staff includes an attending physician (usually a respirologist, an anesthesiologist, or other internal medicine specialists), who is the senior decision maker. There are typically resident physicians from different specialist training programs (e.g., surgery, anesthesia, or generic medicine program) who do a 1- or 2-month rotation in an ICU. The residents differ in their level of training, ranging from first-year residents who have recently finished medical school and become certified physicians, to fourth-year residents who are less than a year from becoming board-certified specialists. In the ICU settings in which we conducted our research, each of the residents participates in a training program that includes lectures and work responsibilities. The program objectives are specifically targeted to their level of training. Residents are allocated responsibilities and decision-making authority commensurate with their levels of training. The staff also includes specially trained nurses, who are present at a ratio of almost one nurse per patient. In addition, the personnel may include a staff pharmacist, who carefully watches for adverse drug interactions and serves as a consultant to the attending physician.

Rather than view participants on a continuum from novice to expert, in a work setting, it is useful to consider each member from different specialties as contributing various kinds of expertise (e.g., nursing, pharmacology). However, we can view residents and attending experts on the same continuum. The residents are all practicing physicians and cannot be meaningfully construed as novices but could be considered as being between intermediates and subexperts, depending on their level of training. Each of these individuals has acquired significant degrees of generic expertise and specific expertise. The experts have considerable expertise in ICU medicine, but are frequently required to manage patients with disorders from outside their specific area of expertise, requiring them to rely on their generic knowledge of medicine. In an ICU setting, attending experts will frequently consult specialists in other domains (e.g., neurology) to provide expert opinions.

It should be noted that unlike other decision-making teams such as cockpit crews, the staff in an ICU setting are rotated with great frequency. For example, there is a day shift and a night shift for both nurses and residents. There are usually four or five attending physicians who rotate on a weekly basis. ICU settings have detailed protocols for such rotations to minimize loss of information to ensure continuity of care. The rotating team personnel can further complicate the smooth coordination of complex decisions.

THEORETICAL AND METHODOLOGICAL FRAMEWORK

The research described in this chapter departs from our studies on medical cognition in three significant ways: (a) a shift from laboratory-based studies to the workplace settings (Leprohon & Patel, 1995, is a notable exception); (b) a focus on "team cognition" or socially distributed cognition rather than on studies of the individual; and (c) a shift from studying the cognitive task of diagnosis to the study of patient monitoring and management. These changes necessitate the use of different methods and an expanded theoretical framework. In this section, we attempt to articulate our research strategy for studying dynamic decision making.

We can view research on a continuum from exploratory studies in novel areas to investigations that focus on testing and refining well-established theories. Experimental research in psychology and education is skewed toward the use of empirical methods for confirming or disconfirming hypotheses that are assumed to be well formulated rather than toward building an adequate basis for theory development (diSessa, 1991). The empirical research presented in this chapter is primarily concerned with providing a foundation for theory development. We are embarking on a new area of challenging research and this chapter outlines our first attempt toward this endeavor. However, this research builds on a rich database of previous empirical studies, theories, and well-established methods that have been widely used in studies of expertise, medical cognition, and the emerging area of naturalistic decision making. Our approach is to assemble existing methods and develop novel ones where necessary, to investigate a rather difficult and complex research problem. The study of cognition in naturalistic settings is a comparatively new endeavor and theory is at a relatively early stage of development. However, there is now a substantial body of research that can provide a sound conceptual and methodological basis to make significant scientific progress.

An intensive care medical setting is representative of work environments in which rapid decisions need to be made in coordination with multiple individuals and acted on in an iterative decision–action cycle. The overall goals of the research program are twofold: (a) to understand cognition in this unique and complex setting, and (b) to abstract generalities pertaining to understanding skilled performance and thus contribute to the emerging general theory of expertise. To be able to address the issue of generality, we need to understand the characteristics of the initial situation and then identify a class of target situations we want to generalize to (Woods, 1993).

In engaging in cognitive research in complex real settings, one must strike a balance between making the problem tractable by selecting a few relevant factors to study and trying to capture the environment in its full-blown complexity (Brown, 1992). If attempts are made to minimize complexity, researchers run the risk of eliminating critical features of the setting that result in the behaviors of interest. On the other hand, if researchers attempt to study every facet of a setting, it becomes impossible to investigate phenomena in a precise and systematic manner. This dilemma necessitates two complementary research strategies. The first strategy involves a macroscopic analysis of the setting, which in our case would include a characterization of the distribution of individual and collective responsibilities and actions, patterns of interactions, typology of cognitive tasks, and resources and constraints present in the setting. The second research approach would involve microscopic analyses, which in our domain of interest could focus intensively on in-depth characterizations of specific decisions and courses of actions pertaining to isolated situations, and investigations of individuals' development of knowledge and skills over the course of their training period. These convergent approaches should provide a basis for understanding the individual and distributed nature of cognition in a complex setting.

In naturalistic settings such as the·one in which we are conducting research, there are no shortages of data sources. According to Woods (1993), behavioral protocols can be built from diverse data sources such as direct observation of participant behavior, traces of data acquisition sequences, recorded sequences of verbal communication among team members, interviews with participants, and commentaries on individuals' performances from knowledgeable experts who did not participate in the activities under study. In our ICU research, we have collected data (and are continuing to collect data) from sources such as observations of activity patterns over the course of a work shift; recording of morning medical records; lectures given by the attending expert to residents; conference sessions in which previous decisions and actions concerning specific medical cases are dissected, analyzed, and debated; interviews with key participants; and complete patient charts. The patient charts include the nurses' report, residents' report, laboratory results, drug schedules, consulting physicians' recommendations, and the patients' medical history prior to admission. In intensive care settings, protocol requires the patient chart to be complete, so that every observation, finding, decision, and action is recorded in full detail.

The research strategy we employ focuses on both the individual and collective decision-making process. The methods that have been used to study individual cognitive processes such as protocol analytic techniques (Ericsson & Simon, 1993), and methods of semantic representation (Frederiksen, 1975; Groen & Patel, 1988; van Dijk & Kintsch, 1983) can still be employed effectively in this kind of research. In addition, methods for analyzing and categorizing knowledge, inferences, and actions that have been developed specifically for the study of medical cognition (Evans & Gadd, 1989; Hassebrock & Prietula, 1992; Patel, Arocha, & Kaufman, 1994) continue to play a central role in the analysis of data from complex medical settings.

There is a need to employ additional methods to study the collective decision-making processes that emerge from patterns of interaction. Verbal protocols obtained from a single subject are readily amenable to formal symbolic methods of propositional or semantic representation. However, the semantics of a conversation between two or more participants cannot be easily recovered from a semantic analysis of a transcript, because conventions of conversation leave much that is unsaid. In previous research investigating diagnostic reasoning during the clinical interview in medicine (Kaufman & Patel, 1991), for investigating nurse–patient conversations (Leprohon & Patel, 1995), we employed a linguistic pragmatic analysis (Levinson, 1983) to code medical dialogue. This analysis is designed to capture the pragmatic features of data acquisition and the management of data flow by the clinician(s) and specifically to characterize the information in focus and the presuppositions made by participants during the course of the conversation. We are adopting this method of pragmatic analysis for reconstructing the communication process during interactive decision making.

In undertaking research in a workplace setting, it is necessary to evaluate both the physical setting and the patterns of work activity. Toward this endeavor, we are adopting methods of work domain analysis and activity analysis developed for cognitive systems engineering (Rasmussen et al., 1994). A work domain analysis is a generalized representation of objectives, functions, activities, and resources that provide capabilities for action as well as limiting characteristics that constrain actions. Rasmussen (1993) and colleagues (Rasmussen et al., 1994) defined a three-stage strategy for characterizing activity in work settings. The first phase involves an analysis of prototypical activities, functions, and situations in work domain terms (i.e., medical language in ICU setting). The second level is analysis of activities in decision-making terms, characterizing the various functions different actors carry out during these situations. The third level of analysis involves a description of activity in cognitive terms, by identifying the various strategies and forms of knowledge used in executing the various decisions. General models of dynamic decision making can only be generated from the third level of analysis. However, the first two stages are necessary for developing an adequate understanding of these complex settings.

The research program outlined in this section is designed to address a set of issues pertaining to cognition in the complex workplace and the acquisition of medical expertise in dynamic decision-making environments. The issues of interest include: (a) the coordination of theory and evidence and the directionality of reasoning in making decisions; (b) the role of anomalies in producing shifts in reasoning strategies; (c) the prerequisite knowledge and cognitive skills necessary for different participants (e.g., residents, nurses) to function effectively in this environment; (d) the differences between trainees (residents) at various levels of training and expert physicians in reasoning and decision making; (e) the patterns of interaction and communication that determine activity; (f) the division of labor and the coordination of information among participants; and (g) characterizing the learning process as it emerges from pedagogical and work activity. The research agenda is intended to focus on both the individual and socially distributed cognition.

Data Collection and Analysis

The current research was conducted in a medical ICU at the Royal Victoria Hospital, a McGill University teaching hospital. The investigators observed the ongoing activities over a period of time to familiarize themselves with the patterns of behavior and patient care in this work setting. Subsequently, two experimenters spent a week in the ICU collecting data. The principal sources of data included audiotape recordings of morning rounds, patient charts, recordings of morning lecture series, and interviews with the major participants. This chapter focuses mainly on data collected during the morning patient rounds and related information from a specific patient's charts. The rounds are one of the most important activities in an ICU setting. During these sessions, the teams visit and evaluate each patient. Various members of the team provide patient reports, which are discussed to evaluate the patients' status, retrospectively evaluate each of the decisions and actions, and plan future courses of action. The morning rounds are also used as an instructional forum for resident trainees.

The data reported in this chapter focus on the care and management of a 71-year-old patient who was admitted to the ICU with Sudden Death Syndrome. This patient suffered a cardiac arrest at a shopping complex and was subsequently resuscitated and brought to the emergency room of a different hospital. The patient was then transferred to the study ICU setting. He received treatment for a 3-day period and recovered sufficiently to be transferred to another hospital ward. We recorded all available information on the patient's status, including medical charts and nurses' and residents' daily reports.

Each of these audiotapes were transcribed verbatim. The events of each daily round were divided into "episodes" based on the content of the discussion of each round; boundaries between episodes are based on decisions made by one of the participants to discuss some specific aspect (such as the overnight report). Each episode focused on a particular aspect of patient care and management. Within each segment, the participants discussed a number of issues relevant to laboratory data and various medical measurements. Each distinct thematic idea unit was coded as a "proposition." This differs from the micropropositional coding we normally employ in analyzing protocols. In this analysis, propositions are coded at a macro level following van Dijk and Kintsch (1983). The transcripts were examined for type of decisions, findings, and inferences.

The Process of Team Interaction

The particular ICU team that we observed during morning rounds had eight direct participants and a number of peripheral participants, including consulting physicians (e.g., a neurologist, endocrinologist, and a nephrologist) who played a role in patient management. The team "players" and their respective responsibilities are listed in Table 5.1. Each of the participants had clearly delineated roles and this division of labor is directly related to how information is monitored, managed, and reported and how specific decisions are made and actions taken. The team leader was the attending physician who was an expert cardiologist and ICU specialist. He was directly responsible for all major decisions and their consequences. Residents were principally responsible for individual patient care. Nurses played a vital role in the ICU in administering to the patient's needs and carefully monitoring the patient's status. Other participants included one nutritionist and one pharmacist.

In this section, we attempt to provide a characterization of different facets of team interaction and decision making. The analyses proceed from most general toward an increasingly detailed characterization of specific decisions and communication patterns. The process of team interaction is summarized in Table 5.2. The table describes three phases of team interaction, which involve the reporting of gathered information over a 24-hour period, followed by a systematic evaluation by the expert and the respon-

TABLE 5.1
Team Members and Their Responsibilities in the ICU Round

Participant	Functions	Length of Involvement
Attending physician: Expert	Responsible for personnel and all final decisions.	Always available (day and night) on site or by phone.
Residents: R1 opthamology R2 anesthesia R3 anesthesia R2 internal medicine	Principally responsible for individual patient care and emergency decisions. Each resident also participates in an ICU training course.	At least one present overnight, present on site throughout day.
Nurses: Nurse in charge Assistant head nurse	Responsible for routine monitoring of patient and administers medication.	There is a continuous rotation. The day nurse will present report during morning rounds.
Nutritionist:	Advises on nutritional and dietary health factors, and special food requirements based on medical conditions.	As needed.
Pharmacist:	Preparation of some drugs, monitors and advises on drug interactions.	Present in rotations of 10-hour shifts. Participates in rounds.
Respiratory Therapist:	If patient is on ventilation will be responsible for adjustments and changes to be made.	As needed.

sible resident. The medical rounds also served as a training ground for the residents. The attending physician orchestrated the sequence of the discussion and interspersed pedagogical elements in the context of discussions on patient care. Each of the team members had a specific role in gathering information, performing various actions, and reporting the results to the team.

The first of the three phases was characterized by a report from the resident who was in charge of the overnight shift. The purpose of the report is to inform the team of the patient's condition during the last 24 hours, including critical decisions that were made and actions that were taken. This was followed by a critique and evaluation of the decisions by the expert in the context of their efficacy and appropriateness for stabilizing the patient. It also served a pedagogical role in explaining the current state of the patient and why specific decisions should or should not have been made. This can include an evaluation of the resident's hypotheses and a discussion of the underlying physiology of the patient problem.

The second phase involved a report from the overnight nurse, who provided a situation assessment specifically pertaining to the vital signs and symptoms related to fluid balance and food intake, as well as the psychological status of the patient. This was followed by suggested changes made by the resident to collect more information and evaluate the appropriate future course of action. Following the nurse's report, there is a shift

TABLE 5.2
The Phases of Team Interaction During Morning Rounds

Phase I	Resident's Report	Purpose
Gathering of information	• Situation evaluation of last 24 hours	Team is informed about the patient's condition
	• Changes in specific medications and laboratory data and ancillary procedures, including reports from consulting specialists	
Evaluation by Expert	• Decisions that were made	• Changes to be made to keep the patient stable
	• Suggestions on next decisions	• Discussion on what should/should not be done

Phase II	Nurse's Report	
Gathering of information	• Observations of vital signs and symptoms (fluid balance/food intake/reactions to medications)	Update the team on the patient's current and overnight status
	• Psychological condition of patient	
Evaluation by expert and resident	• The patient status and decisions taken	• Coordination of information from residents' and nurses' reports
	• Further needed information identified	• Options evaluated
	• Advice given	
Transition between residents	• Introduction of day resident—update on patient summary and status	Training of new residents using systems evaluation—reflects organization by which decisions are made

Phase III	Team Dialogue	Evaluates
Team evaluation with expert advice	• Evaluation of current situation	• Need for more information for future decisions
	• Observations	• Sensitivities regarding specific issues are discussed and resolved
	• Further questioning	• Tasks are allocated to members
	• Requests for further information	
	• Requests for further consultations	
	• Pharmacists—evaluation of medication	
	• Nutritionist—evaluation of dietitians requirements	
	• Request for therapy evaluation of ventilators	
Summary	Expert advice and actions to be taken for the next 24 hours	• Members are updated on the patient status
		• Aware of what needs to be done

in task responsibility with another resident replacing the resident who did the previous overnight shift. The expert systematically discusses each organ system, reflecting the organization of decisions made in the ICU.

The third phase involved a dialogue among all members of the team. At this stage, all of the information gaps were filled. Further information was requested and sensitivities regarding specific issues were discussed and resolved. At this point, the pharmacist and the nutritionist evaluated the medication and the dietary requirements of the patient, respectively. The session ended with a summary by the expert, who outlined the actions to be taken for the next 24 hours. At this point, all members were updated on the patient status and were aware of their respective responsibilities.

The expert managed the flow of information in such a way as to reduce the cognitive complexity and effort for the group, but it increased the cognitive complexity for the expert himself because information from different sources had to be integrated. This was done sequentially with backtracking when necessary (e.g., if two different medications are likely to adversely interact). The expert relied on the team for maintaining evidence in a *distributed working memory,* and for analysis of data, performed mostly by the resident, who engaged in substantial analysis of findings and trends in the patient's status. This balance between coordinated information and individual decision making and data synthesis makes the process efficient.

Patterns of Information Management, Decisions, and Actions

In the following section, we present an analysis of each of the morning rounds in terms of episodes corresponding to topics of discussion. The number of propositions and clinical findings for the three morning rounds are presented in Table 5.3. The table reflects several patterns of interaction that change over the course of time. On the first morning, there was a greater need to discuss the circumstances that resulted in the patient's admission to the ICU the previous evening. His subsequent treatment was discussed, followed by a thorough and complete evaluation of his condition. This is reflected in the broad spectrum of topics discussed. The resident's and the nurse's report provided the team with most of the observations. The nurse's report and subsequent discussion generated 30 patient findings, which were then considered in detail. The resident's report provided a more analytic perspective, focusing on higher order findings, as well as on decisions and actions that were taken in the interim. He also discussed the patient's past history in order to understand his current state. There was extensive consideration of the patient's underlying pathophysiology, much more than we would normally observe in a diagnostic reasoning context. On the first day, there were a total of 185 propositions employed in the discussion, out of which 130 (78%) reflected distinct or new information introduced. The particular propositions raised by the resident formed the

TABLE 5.3
Frequency of Propositions and Findings Across Episodes For Each Day
of Medical Rounds.

Day	Episode	Total Propositions	Findings
Day 1	Overnight Report	2	1
	Resident report	33	15
	Nurse report/discussion	60	30
	Pathophysiology	64	14
	Patient visit	5	0
	Respirology issues	21	0
Total		185	60
Day 2	Overnight report	3	3
	Nurse report/discussion	27	16
	Pharmacist report	6	0
	Pathophysiology	79	9
	Resident report	10	0
	Plans/actions	20	0
Total		145	28
Day 3	Overnight report	1	0
	Nurse report	43	11
	Lab report	5	3
	Plans/actions	27	4
Total		76	18

basis of most of the subsequent discussion, and were repeatedly reviewed and evaluated. Throughout the first 2 days, there was considerable discussion of the medications that the patient was receiving and decisions were made on how to adjust them accordingly.

On Day 2, the patient's condition was changing rapidly, and there was a greater number of focused communication exchanges, suggestions, and decisions made. His overall condition had improved, as reflected in the fact that he was breathing without the assistance of a ventilator. However, complications from the medication necessitated a detailed discussion of the underlying pathophysiology. In total, there were 145 propositions, 65% of which reflected new information not previously discussed. At this point in time, the team had substantial shared knowledge about this patient and this was reflected in the level of analysis and synthesis of information.

On Day 3, the patient had been responding well to treatment, and the attending physician was planning to discharge him. There were many fewer exchanges, which included summarizing the information from the patient record and expert advice on future management. There were 76 propositions, 61% of which consisted of new information. The staff had decided to discharge the patient, based on his current state and future prognosis. The discussion in the rounds became increasingly selective over 3 days. The pattern suggests a shift from an initial focus on the patient's condition on Day 1 (generating 60 findings), to the effects of medication on Day 2, and to longer term therapeutic problems on Day 3.

Table 5.4 presents the number and types of decisions made during the morning rounds. The vast majority of treatment decisions were made on the first 2 days. Several of the more complex decisions were made on the first day, including whether to take the patient off the ventilator and whether or not to administer certain medications. On the second day, most of the medication and treatment decisions involved the adjustment of prior medication dosages and minimizing the adverse effects that result from treatment. The decisions on the final day focused on whether to discharge the patient to the cardiac care unit or a general hospital ward.

The decisions ranged from routine, on which there was no disagreement, to complex ones that involved extensive discussion. One of the most complex sets of decisions involved the potential interaction of two heart medications, Amnioderone and Digoxin. Amnioderone is a drug used to prevent cardiac arrhythmias and to diminish the likelihood of the reoccurrence of sudden death syndrome. Digoxin is used to improve cardiac function, and in higher doses can sometimes cause arrhythmias. Furthermore, the two drugs interact and each produce a range of potential side effects. In addition, there were numerous other constraints such as the effects on his underlying lung disease and whether this treatment was consistent with procedures at another hospital where he would likely be returning to after his ICU stay. This discussion generated a focused discussion of 23 exchanges on Day 1, involving the attending expert, three residents, the nurse, and the pharmacist. The final decision made by the attending staff was to start the patient on a low dosage of Amnioderone and lower the current dosage of Digoxin.

The general pattern of decision making was to consider a single solution at a time. Most often the initial decision was the only one considered. If the initial solution did not prove to be viable or if there were too many risks, the team would sequentially consider various other alternatives. For the most complex decisions, such as the Amnioderone–Digoxin problem, there were numerous constraints that limited possible alternatives. Although most decisions taken could greatly affect the patient's fragile state of health,

TABLE 5.4
Number and Type of Decisions Made in Morning Rounds
Over 3-Day Period

Day	Examination	Drug	Other Treatment	Consult	ICU Status	Totals
1	2	8	5	1	0	16
2	3	11	6	1	0	21
3	0	1	0	2	3	6

the continuous and systematic monitoring allowed the medical team to calibrate and fine-tune treatment regimens.

Plans and Actions

Planning is an integral part of the treatment process in an intensive care setting, even though conditions are dynamically changing and unanticipated consequences are routine. Treatment of any patient in an ICU setting is reflected in a recurring decision–action cycle. Every single intervention can result in adverse complications and these need to be factored into the management of the patient as well. Many of these patients receive as many as 8 to 10 different medications, many of them to counter side effects of other medications. Figure 5.1 illustrates some of the potential adverse reactions a patient may experience when placed on ventilator support. This diagram was generated from an interview protocol of an expert attending physician. Many patients in an ICU setting are placed on a ventilator, which is

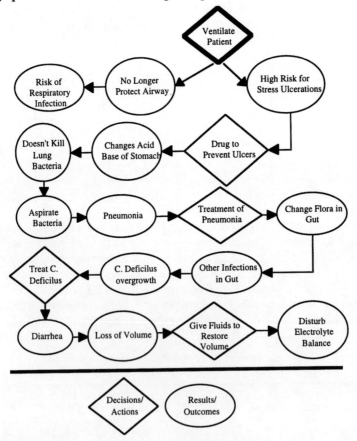

FIG. 5.1. Causal chain of events and decision action cycle for treating a ventilated patient.

designed to facilitate the breathing in patients with respiratory difficulty. These patients often suffer from multisystem complications.

The diagram partially indicates the range of complications that can ensue from ventilating a patient and the decisions that need to be made to counter these adverse effects. In a setting such as an ICU, it is apparent that physicians cannot exhaustively consider the full range of alternatives or even fully evaluate every piece of information, nor can they execute well-specified plans. However, in interviewing experienced ICU physicians, it is apparent that they can anticipate a causal sequence to a considerable degree of depth and, if needed, adjust a therapeutic plan accordingly. The important point is that plans can play an integral role even in dynamic uncertain environments, although they do not rigidly determine the sequence of actions.

The Process of Patient Care and Pedagogy

The following section focuses on the process of team discussion with specific excerpts that illustrate the respective roles played by different participants. The discussion also indicates how patient care concerns provide a vehicle for pedagogical issues. The following series of discussions were taken from Day 2 of the morning rounds, which began with the overnight nurse's report.

> Nurse: O.K., he is oriented, he knows he is in the hospital, he doesn't remember which one because he was transferred, and he doesn't remember what has happened since the cardiac arrest, before that everything is O.K., he remembers everything, he remembers that he went shopping in the morning, but didn't remember anything after, he is oriented in space, but we have to do it a lot of times. Neuro after that, good hand lifts moves all limbs. I think, he is able to go to the chair, he wants to sit in the chair, CVS, he is in sinus rhythm some PVC's, skin is O.K. with some bruising, peripherally right eye, I think it is from his fall, but he doesn't remember, let's see he has an arterial line, blood pressure is stable, around 130 and his heart rate is around 70 to 75. The peripheral IV is clean, its O.K. GI, GI, bowels sounds are positive, he still has an NG, straight drainage, around, 100 cc's each shift.

The nurse assessed the situation based on the specific observations he was expected to perform and report to the group. This includes assessment of vital signs (e.g., blood pressure, heart rate), observations of gastrointestinal (GI) status, and other bodily systems. The expert requested further information about the GI status, concerning blood. This ties in with a critical decision concerning the origin of the GI bleed, subsequent treatment, and further action. The nurse subsequently responded by providing further information concerning the bleeding status and went on to discuss respiratory and cardiovascular status in the following excerpt:

> Nurse: No blood today, he had some blood in the NG yesterday, but not today it is clear. It is O.K. for GI, he may still have a foley and rest, good air entry to bases, he breaths around 16 by minute, with high humidity mask and, he is still wheezing. Yesterday it was the same thing, after that he still has a Swan-Ganz, cardiac output of 4.8, cardiac index 2.8. It is very stable, the index is just a bit lower than yesterday when he was intubated, and blood pressure is stable, heart rate stable, he complained about pain this morning, muscular pain in his chest area, I performed an EKG and nothing changed on the EKG, and I gave him morphine, he is more comfortable with the morphine.

In the medical rounds, evaluation of bodily systems was covered by several members of the team, providing different levels of explanation. Note that the nurse's report concerning respiratory and cardiovascular function was stated as a set of observations and the inferences were kept to a minimum. The resident picked up on the nurse's observations and added another level of analysis as indicated in the following excerpt:

> Res F: From a respiratory point of view yesterday, he had wheezes and crackles in his lower bases, we'll reassess him. It's just that he showed some changes from last evening, possible atelectatic changes in the right lower lobe or possible aspirations.

> Expert: So what do you want to do about that?

> Res F: If it is just aspiration he might have a chemical pneumonitis.

> Expert: Chemical pneumonitis.

The resident commented on a few important findings concerning the patient's respiratory status, and focus on atelectatic changes (difficulty in lung expansion). The expert picked up this important piece of information and asked the resident about a proposed course of action. The goal was to determine whether the patient's respiratory problems were the result of a bacterial infection or the result of an adverse reaction to intubation because of aspiration of the stomach contents during the procedure. If the patient's respiratory difficulties were just a result of medication, then antibiotics would have no effect. A critical evaluation of the underlying pathology, that is, distinguishing a basic systemic problem from an adverse reaction to treatment, is very common in ICU medicine. The expert seized the opportunity at this point to shift the discussion toward pedagogical concerns, which resulted in the following exchange:

Res F: Chemical pneumonitis, that won't need antibiotics.

Expert: So how do you decide it is pneumonia or just a new chemical pneumonitis?

Res F: I'll wait until he strikes a fever in terms of his . . .

Expert: So, could he have a fever with pneumonitis?

Res F: He could even have a fever with pneumonitis.

Expert: So what else do you need?

Res F: White count.

Expert: You could have a rise in white count with that too although, that would be more suggestive, and finally what is going to be the most important thing?

Res F: Chills, shaking, whether he coughs sputum.

Expert: He could have aspirated, some ugly looking sputum coming out is really expanding in the lungs. When he gets the initial pneumonitis, now it gets worse over the next few days and that is a different story, it should start to clear, fairly quickly.

Res F: Chemical pneumonitis on its own doesn't need the antibiotics.

Expert: That's right, that's right, you can make him worse if you do that, so for now I would just watch him, and that may be all it is we'll see how he does. O.K., so it's pulmonary, cardiovascular, we have done uhhm, were you happy with his cardiovascular meds?

In the preceding exchange, the resident suggested a series of possibilities for discriminating between a bacterial infection or a chemical pneumonitis. The expert challenges his responses until he was able to construct the pattern of findings for discriminating between these two facets. If this were an urgent situation, the resident would have to know the cardinal signs of fever, shaking chills, and yellowish sputum to diagnose a respiratory infection. An ICU physician needs to be able to rapidly access the conditions of applicability for identifying classes of patients' states. Treating a chemical pneumonitis as a bacterial infection could complicate the patient's course of recovery.

Explanations are provided by the residents in terms of forward-oriented inferences, leading from the data to the hypothesis (e.g., if fever, then infection). In addition, "deeper" causal reasoning about mechanisms is not employed when describing routine problems. This pattern shifts when anomalies or unanticipated changes in the patient's condition are raised. This induces participants to explore possible underlying causes. Pedagogical discussions also shift the reasoning pattern toward justification and evaluation in the coordination of hypothesis and evidence.

Distributed and Individual Expertise in Action

The decision making–action–feedback cycle involving the various participants is summarized in Fig. 5.2. There are a number of parallels between the findings concerning the problem-solving behavior of experts in laboratory settings and naturalistic settings. There is a selective processing of relevant information leading to forward-oriented reasoning patterns and the evaluation of a single hypothesis. In the diagnostic setting, the data is collected most often by the expert in a sequential format (Patel, Evans, & Kaufman, 1989), whereas in the ICU setting, sets of data are collected by different "experts" based on the distribution of information gathering, management, and processing by various members of the team. Each individual team member does a task-specific situation assessment, attends to any immediate problems, and then coordinates the information with the person at the next level of the hierarchy. The situation assessment involves identification and classification of the current state of the patient. The nurse is responsible for making continuous observations of the patient's condition and noting any changes in the patient's status. The nurse communicates pertinent information to the resident, who will take appropriate action and then communicate with the expert. The goal for each person is to work toward stabilizing, maintaining, and improving the patient's state. Finally, it is the attending expert physician who coordinates and evaluates the relevant data for adequate action and subsequent planning for future management.

In a situation requiring immediate concern, the evidence is evaluated in order to take rapid action without providing an underlying justification. When the situation is under control and there is no time pressure or urgency, the decisions are evaluated carefully using another level of reasoning. Such situations also provide an opportunity for resident training and a means of checking the adequacy of one's decisions.

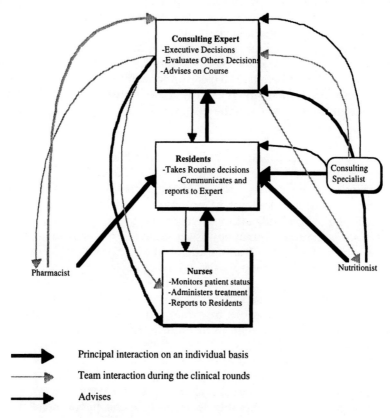

FIG. 5.2. The hierarchical process of information gathering, situation assessment and decision making in an ICU team.

We can characterize the distribution of cognitive complexity in terms of the epistemological framework, concerning the distinctions of observations, findings, and facets, described earlier in the chapter (Evans & Gadd, 1989). Nurses are chiefly responsible for gathering observations and they also report on selected findings. Residents synthesize and organize observations into findings and generate a set of organ-system specific facets (e.g., gastrointestinal bleed), whereas the attending expert must consider the patient as a whole and generate appropriate plans. There is an increase in the complexity of analyses at each level in the hierarchy. There is also a reduction in information management; the nurse is responsible for recording all observations, and the resident focuses on significant benchmark values (e.g., cardiac index) and anomalous findings. Although the expert is chiefly responsible for synthesizing information and planning future courses of action, he or she need only attend to the significant findings.

It appears that even with the increased resources of the team, the process of decision making in this real-life situation was performed using a strategy similar to that of an individual expert problem solver. It also appears that the whole team is not "acquiring" information in the same way. One may "pick up" and use a particular piece of information, depending on task allocation, but all members have a clear understanding of the overall task, allowing the team to function efficiently. There is also a distinct allocation of tasks and division of labor in the team work.

DISCUSSION AND CONCLUSIONS

One of the central aims of research on expertise has been to discover how knowledge of complex domains is represented and how to facilitate the acquisition of this knowledge through instruction. In this chapter, we have given accounts of some of our attempts to extend our research on the nature and acquisition of expertise from laboratory-based to real-world dynamic settings. We also shifted our emphasis from studying the cognitive processes of the solitary individual to investigations of the collective decision-making and problem-solving processes involved in the medical workplace.

The study of expertise seeks to explain the cognitive attributes that distinguish outstanding human performance from less outstanding performance (Ericsson & Smith, 1991). According to Ericsson (chap. 1, this volume), an important criterion for selecting dimensions of expert phenomena for inquiry is that they should occur reliably in clearly specified situations with distinctly observable characteristics. He went on to suggest that investigators should be able to reproduce the phenomena under controlled conditions in the laboratory. Although a range of expert phenomena has been systematically studied under controlled conditions, there is still a need to identify a range of distinctive characteristics of expertise and the situations in which expertlike performance is actualized. Naturalistic research is an effective means for identifying and characterizing situations in which expert performance is manifested.

In this chapter, we outline a framework for studying cognitive performance in a naturalistic medical decision-making context and present results from an investigation in an intensive care clinical setting. We view this research as part of a broader research program in which laboratory research and naturalistic cognitive research reciprocally interact to broaden and deepen our understanding of medical expertise. Dunbar (1995) and Gaba (1992) successfully employed complex simulation environments in laboratory settings to study phenomena uncovered in naturalistic settings. In our view, this is a promising research strategy for investigating the acquisition of expert-level performance. Naturalistic studies provide a basis for characterizing the context of activity and learning, whereas carefully controlled laboratory studies can explore the mechanisms of learning in greater detail.

The analysis of results presented in this chapter parallels Rasmussen's (1993) three-stage strategy for investigating performance in work settings. The first phase involved an analysis of everyday activities and situations in terms of medical language typical of the intensive care setting. The second level of analysis required a characterization, describing the various tasks, in decision-making terms, and actions carried out by the various team members and the process of coordination. The third level of analysis involved a description of activity in cognitive terms, specifically identifying the various strategies and forms of knowledge evidenced in expert performance in dynamic decision environments. The third level of analysis is essential to the development of models of expert decision making. In our view, we have made substantial progress toward completing the first two stages of analysis and some progress toward the third. We briefly expand on this cognitive level of analysis, and on the acquisition of expertise in dynamic decision-making environments in the following paragraphs.

Given the diversity of team players involved in ICU activities, the acquisition of expertise can be viewed from multiple perspectives. In this research, our focus has been on the development of expert performance by resident trainees. The demands of this environment can promote the acquisition of a range of skills and knowledge, including technical abilities, clinical reasoning skills, and rapid decision-making capabilities under conditions of great uncertainty. In the residency training program, there are conventional learning activities such as lectures, seminars, and clinical rounds. In addition, residents also devote considerable time to reviewing clinical research literature and medical references. However, the vast majority of learning takes place in the context of clinical practice where learning by doing (Anzai & Simon, 1979) is one of the principal learning mechanisms. This is also a clear example of a cognitive apprenticeship learning situation, where residents are closely guided by expert role models. An effective role model not only demonstrates correct procedures, but models ways of thinking about particular problems, and challenges counterproductive reasoning strategies. The morning rounds provide an effective vehicle for the attending expert to evaluate a trainee's level of understanding and decision-making competency. As we observed in this study, the expert attempt to guide the resident to generate the conditions of applicability for delimiting certain decision choices.

Instructional opportunities often arise from anomalous or unanticipated findings. These findings suggest that a specific decision has not yielded the expected results. The error is analyzed in great detail during posthoc evaluation sessions, and this provides an excellent avenue for failure-driven learning. This results in the acquisition of clinical exemplars that can be transferred to other patient problems. As stated earlier, there are three levels of objectives and decisions in an ICU setting. The foremost objective is the stabilization of the patient. Faulty decisions for meeting this objective can jeopardize the patient's life. Expert-level performance requires a sensitivity to subtle changes in the patient's state. The continuous monitoring provides some opportunity for one to recalibrate a treatment regimen and respond to any emergency situations. Expert decision making involves a selective processing of information and the ability to distinguish signal from noise, because ICU patient data are so voluminous. The second objective in an ICU setting is to diagnose and treat the underlying medical problem. This is a very complicated process, because most of these patients suffer from multisystem disorders, and it is sometimes difficult to disambiguate symptoms resulting from the underlying disease and those that are caused by the aggressive therapy regimen. The third objective is to plan a longer term course of action for the patient. This involves considerations such as the prognosis of the patient and the anticipated course of recovery as well as several extramedical constraints, such as the availability of beds in other wards and the wishes of the family.

In the intensive care working environment, a mixture of both the time-pressured decision making and deliberate evaluation of actions and future plans, were identified. This is reflected in the predominant use of two different kinds of strategies under urgent and less urgent conditions, which is consistent with the work of Leprohon and Patel (1995) and Gaba (1992). The first is characterized by the use of high-level organization of knowledge such that reasoning is driven in a forward direction toward action. Little or no use is made of any underlying justification. In the second condition, there is an attempt to use causally directed backward reasoning to explain the relevant patient information with the use of detailed pathophysiology. Both of these strategies use satisficing principles based on explanatory coherence criteria. Individual and collective reasoning is targeted toward finding a reasonable explanation for a particular aspect of a patient's condition such that appropriate actions can be taken. We seldom observed any deliberations over alternative courses of action.

As Ericsson (chap. 1, this volume) has pointed out, the majority of expertise research has focused too narrowly on the automatization of skill that enables superior skilled performance. Although this is an important component in the acquisition of expertise in dynamic decision-making tasks, it is only one dimension of expertise. Rasmussen (1993) identified three levels of cognitive control including skill-based, rule-based, and knowledge-based behavior. Skill-based level response mode involves smooth execution of data-driven processes. This allows for rapid pattern recognition and the triggering of immediate decisions leading to action. Rule-based control involves a more conscious level of activity involving some deliberate preparation and planning in order to adapt learned rules to specific contexts. It is in this response mode that experts can make use of the highly adapted representations, referred to by Ericsson (chap. 1, this volume), that facilitate planning, prediction, evaluation, and expansion of working memory. Knowledge-based control requires the greatest cognitive effort and it is triggered most commonly in unfamiliar situations. This demands a consideration of goals in the context of the environment and available resources. The acquisition of expertise requires the development of each mode of cognitive control as well as the ability to shift between the various response modes.

The traditional hierarchical organization of the role of team members based on social structure of the environment interacts with the cognitive processes, both of which appear to influence the decision-making behavior of the team. The expertise in this context can be viewed in two ways: One is where the resident is viewed as a trainee, and the attending physician as an expert. Another way of looking at this is to view nurses, residents, pharmacists, and so forth as individual experts who contribute their specific expertise, both individually and collectively, to the decision-making process. Thus each expert's ability to function flexibly and adaptively in a rapidly changing situation is essential.

Acquisition of information by a team is rather different from the process of individual data acquisition in that: (a) there are multiple streams of information that are too much for a single individual to process and maintain in working memory; (b) teams require communication and coordination between individuals; and (c) a broader context is provided for interpreting commands or information requests, leading to appropriate courses of action at specific times.

An investigation of the acquisition of expertise even in a team context requires a focus on the development of individual knowledge and cognitive skills. The attainment of expert-level performance in the workplace is also predicated on subjects' ability to function smoothly in an environment in which the coordination of tasks, decisions, and information is essential. The attainment of expertise necessitates the ability to employ and engineer the distribution of resources (e.g., knowledge and working memory) as well as the ability to communicate and off-load information. In settings where activities and decisions are socially distributed, there is still a need to develop individual competencies. We concur with Salomon (1993) that the locus of change predominantly resides in the individual, rather than the more contextualized view of distributed cognition as the person acting in a setting. This indicates a necessity to focus on the singular and distributed dimension of expert performance.

The chapters in this volume have contributed to both a refined understanding of the mechanisms involved in the acquisition of expertise and a broadened perspective on expert—novice research. Expanding the boundaries of expertise research provides answers to some questions, also raising challenging new problems. Although a comprehensive theory of expert performance seems somewhat elusive at the moment, the road map for future research is becoming more clearly charted.

ACKNOWLEDGMENTS

The research reported in this chapter was supported by a grant from Fonds pour la Formation de Chercheurs et L'Aide à la Recherche (ER1177) to Vimla L. Patel. We would like thank the subjects who participated in this study. We wish to acknowledge Michael Leccisi for his assistance in the collection and the analysis of data, and for his help in editing this manuscript, and Eric Poole for his assistance in data analysis. André Kushniruk and José Arocha provided constructive comments and valuable suggestions on an earlier draft of this chapter.

REFERENCES

Allard, F., & Starkes, J. L. (1991). Motor skill experts in sports, dance and other domains. In A. Ericsson & J. Smith (Eds.), *Toward a general theory of expertise: Prospects and limits* (pp. 126–152). New York: Cambridge University Press.

Anzai, Y., & Simon, H. A. (1979). The theory of learning by doing. *Psychological Review, 86,* 124–140.

Arocha, J. F., & Patel, V. L. (1995). Novice diagnostic reasoning in medicine: Accounting for clinical evidence. *Journal of the Learning Sciences, 4,* 355–384.

Arocha, J. F., Patel, V. L., & Patel, Y. C. (1993). Hypothesis generation and the coordination of theory and evidence in novice diagnostic reasoning. *Medical Decision Making, 13,* 198–211.

Beach, L. R., & Lipshitz, R. (1993). Why classical decision theory is an inappropriate standard for evaluating and aiding most human decision making. In G. A. Klein, J. Orasanu, R. Calderwood, & C. E. Zsambok (Eds.), *Decision making in action: Models and methods* (pp. 21–35). Norwood, NJ: Ablex.

Benner, P., & Tanner C. (1987). Clinical judgment: How expert nurses use intuition. *American Journal of Nursing, 87,* 23–31.

Blois, M. S. (1990). Medicine and the nature of vertical reasoning. *New England Journal of Medicine, 318,* 847–851.

Boshuizen, H. P. A., & Schmidt, H. G. (1992). On the role of biomedical knowledge in clinical reasoning by experts, intermediates, and novices. *Cognitive Science, 16,* 153–184.

Brown, A. L. (1992). Design experiments: Theoretical and methodological challenges in creating complex interventions in classroom settings. *The Journal of The Learning Sciences, 2,* 141–178.

Camerer, C. F., & Johnson, E. J. (1991). The process-performance paradox in expert judgment: How can experts know so much and predict so badly? In A. Ericsson & J. Smith (Eds.), *Toward a general theory of expertise* (pp. 195–217). New York: Cambridge University Press.

Chandrasekeran, B. (1986). Generic tasks in knowledge-based reasoning: High level building blocks for expert system design. *IEEE Expert, 1*(3), 23–30.

Charness, N. (1989). Expertise in chess and bridge. In D. Klahr & K. Kotovsky (Eds.), *Complex information processing: The impact of Herbert A. Simon* (pp. 183–208). Hillsdale, NJ: Lawrence Erlbaum Associates.

Charness, N. (1991). Expertise in chess: The balance between knowledge and search. In A. Ericsson & J. Smith (Eds.), *Toward a general theory of expertise: Prospects and limits* (pp. 39–63). New York: Cambridge University Press.

Chase, W. G., & Simon, H. A. (1973). Perception in chess. *Cognitive Psychology, 4,* 55–81.

Chaturvedi, R. K., & Patel, V. L. (1994). *Therapeutic decision making by physicians and students: Role of knowledge and reasoning strategies* (Tech. Rep. No. CME94–CS3). Montreal, Canada: McGill University, Centre for Medical Education.

Chi, M. T. H., Bassok, M., Lewis, M. W., Reimann, P., & Glaser, R. (1989). Self-explanations: How students study and use examples of learning to solve problems. *Cognitive Science, 13,* 145–182.

Chi, M. T. H., & Glaser, R. (1988). Overview. In M. T. H. Chi, R. Glaser, & M. J. Farr (Eds.), *The nature of expertise* (pp. xv–xxviii). Hillsdale, NJ: Lawrence Erlbaum Associates.

Chinn, C. A., & Brewer, W. F. (1993). The role of anomalous data in knowledge acquisition: A theoretical framework and implications for science instruction. *Review of Educational Research, 63*(1), 1–49.

Clancey, W. J. (1988). Acquiring, representing and evaluating a competence model of diagnostic strategy. In M. T. H. Chi, R. Glaser, & M. J. Farr (Eds.), *The nature of expertise* (pp. 343–418). Hillsdale, NJ: Lawrence Erlbaum Associates.

Clancey, W. J. (1993). Situated action: A neuropsychological interpretation response to Vera and Simon. *Cognitive Science, 17,* 87–116.

Cole, M., & Engeström, Y. (1993). A cultural-historical approach to distributed cognition. In G. Salomon (Ed.), *Distributed cognitions: Psychological and educational considerations* (pp. 1–46). New York: Cambridge University Press.

Corker, K., Kieras, D., Payne, J., & Reuter-Lorenz, P. (1992). Cognitive effort and cognitive complexity. In V. Shalin (Ed.), *Human performance in the complex workplace: Implications for basic research in cognitive science* (pp. 17–23). Buffalo: State University of New York at Buffalo.

diSessa, A. A. (1991, October). If we want to get ahead, we should get some theories. In *Proceedings of the Thirteenth Annual Meeting of the International Group for Psychology of Mathematics Education* (pp. 220–239). Blacksburg: Virginia Tech.

Dunbar, K. (1995). How scientists really reason: Scientific reasoning in real-world laboratories. In R. J. Sternberg & J. Davidson (Eds.), *The nature of insight* (pp. 365–395). Cambridge, MA: MIT Press.

Ericsson, K. A., Krampe, R. T., & Tesch-Römer, C. (1993). The role of deliberate practice in the acquisition of expert performance. *Psychological Review, 100*(3), 363–406.

Ericsson, K. A., & Simon, H. A. (1993). *Protocol analysis: Verbal reports as data.* Cambridge, MA: MIT Press.

Ericsson, K. A., & Smith, J. (1991). Prospects and limits of the empirical study of expertise: An introduction. In K. A. Ericsson & J. Smith (Eds.), *Toward a general theory of expertise: Prospects and limits* (pp. 1–38). New York: Cambridge University Press.

Ericsson, K. A., & Staszewski, J. J. (1989). Skilled memory and expertise: Mechanisms of exceptional performance. In D. Klahr & K. Kovotsky (Eds.), *Complex information processing: The impact of Herbert A. Simon* (pp. 235–267). Hillsdale, NJ: Lawrence Erlbaum Associates.

Evans, D. A., & Gadd, C. S. (1989). Managing coherence and context in medical problem-solving discourse. In D. A. Evans & V. L. Patel (Eds.), *Cognitive science in medicine: Biomedical modeling* (pp. 211–255). Cambridge, MA: MIT Press.

Frederiksen, C. H. (1975). Representing logical and semantic structure of knowledge acquired from discourse. *Cognitive Psychology, 7,* 371–458.

Gaba, D. (1992). Dynamic decision-making in anesthesiology: Cognitive models and training approaches. In D. A. Evans & V. L. Patel (Eds.), *Advanced models of cognition for medical training and practice* (pp. 123–148). Heidelberg, Germany: Springer-Verlag.

Groen, G. J., & Patel, V. L. (1988) Relationship between comprehension and reasoning in medical expertise. In M. Chi, R. Glaser, & M. Farr (Eds.), *The nature of expertise* (pp. 287–310). Hillsdale, NJ: Lawrence Erlbaum Associates.

Hassebrock, F., & Prietula, M. J. (1992). A protocol-based coding scheme for the analysis of medical reasoning. *International Journal of Man-Machine Studies, 37,* 613–652.

Hinsley, D. A., Hayes, J. R., & Simon, H. A. (1977). From words to equations: Meaning and representation in algebra word problems. In M. A. Just & P. A. Carpenter (Eds.), *Cognitive processes in comprehension* (pp. 89–108). Hillsdale, NJ: Lawrence Erlbaum Associates.

Hutchins, E. (1991). The social organization of distributed cognition. In L. B. Resnick, J. M. Levine, & S. D. Teasley (Eds.), *Perspectives on socially shared cognition* (pp. 283–307). Washington, DC: American Psychological Association.

164   PATEL, KAUFMAN, MAGDER

Jeffries, R., Turner, A. A., Polson, P. G., & Atwood, M. E. (1981). Processes involved in designing software. In J. R. Anderson (Ed.), *Cognitive skills and their acquisition* (pp. 255–283). Hillsdale, NJ: Lawrence Erlbaum Associates.

Johnson, E. J. (1988). Expertise and decision under certainty: Performance and process. In M. T. H. Chi, R. Glaser, & M. J. Farr (Eds.), *The nature of expertise* (pp. 209–228). Hillsdale, NJ: Lawrence Erlbaum Associates.

Joseph, G.-M., & Patel, V. L. (1990). Domain knowledge and hypothesis generation in diagnostic reasoning. *Medical Decision Making, 10,* 31–46.

Kaufman, D. R., & Patel, V. L. (1991). Problem solving in the clinical interview: A cognitive analysis of the performance of physicians, residents, and students. *Teaching & Learning in Medicine: An International Journal, 3,* 6–14.

Kaufman, D. R., Patel, V. L., & Magder, S. (in press). The explanatory role of spontaneously generated analogies in reasoning about physiological concepts. *International Journal of Science Education.*

Klein, A. (1993). A recognition-primed decision (RPD) model of rapid decision making. In G. A. Klein, J. Orasanu, R. Calderwood, & C. E. Zsambok (Eds.), *Decision making in action: Models and methods* (pp. 138–147). Norwood, NJ: Ablex.

Klein, G. A., & Calderwood, R. (1991). Decision models: Some lessons from the field. *IEEE Transactions on Systems, Man, and Cybernetics, 21*(5), 1018–1026.

Klein, G. A., Calderwood, R., & McGregor, D. (1989). Critical decision method for eliciting knowledge. *IEEE Systems, Man, and Cybernetics, 19*(3), 462–472.

Klein, G. A., Orasanu, J., Calderwood, R., & Zsambok, C. E. (Eds.) (1993). *Decision making in action: Models and methods.* Norwood, NJ: Ablex.

Kuhn, D. (1989). Children and adults as intuitive scientists. *Psychological Review, 96,* 674–689.

Kuipers, B. J., Moskowitz, A. J., & Kassirer, J. P. (1988). Critical decisions under uncertainty: Representation and structure. *Cognitive Science, 12,* 177–210.

Larkin, J. H., McDermott, J., Simon, H. A., & Simon, D. P. (1980). Expert and novice performances in solving physics problems. *Science, 208,* 1335–1342.

Lave, J. (1988). *Cognition in practice: Mind, mathematics, and culture in everyday life.* Cambridge, UK: Cambridge University Press.

Leinhardt, G., & Greeno, J. G. (1986). The cognitive skill of teaching. *Journal of Educational Psychology, 78,* 75–95.

Leprohon, J., & Patel, V. L. (1995). Decision making strategies for telephone triage in emergency medical services. *Medical Decision Making, 15,* 240–253.

Lesgold, A. M., Rubinson, H., Feltovich, P. J., Glaser, R., Klopfer, D., & Wang, Y. (1988). Expertise in a complex skill: Diagnosing x-ray pictures. In M. T. H. Chi, R. Glaser, & M. J. Farr (Eds.), *The nature of expertise* (pp. 311–342). Hillsdale, NJ: Lawrence Erlbaum Associates.

Levinson, S. C. (1983). Pragmatics. New York: Cambridge University Press.

Newell, A. (1980). Reasoning, problem solving, and decision processes: The problem space as a fundamental category. In R. Nickerson (Ed.), *Attention and performance VIII* (pp. 693–718). Hillsdale, NJ: Lawrence Erlbaum Associates.

Newell, A. (1990). *Unified theories of cognition.* Cambridge, MA: Harvard University Press.

Orasanu, J. (1990). *Shared mental models and crew decision making* (Tech. Rep. No. 46). Princeton, NJ: Princeton University, Cognitive Sciences Laboratory.

Orasanu, J., & Connoly, T. (1993). The reinvention of decision making. In G. A. Klein, J. Orasanu, R. Calderwood, & C. E. Zsambok (Eds.), *Decision making in action: Models and methods* (pp. 3–20). Norwood, NJ: Ablex.

Orasanu, J., & Salas, E. (1993). Team decision making in complex environments. In G. A. Klein, J. Orasanu, R. Calderwood, & C. E. Zsambok (Eds.), *Decision making in action: Models and methods* (pp. 327–345). Norwood, NJ: Ablex.

Patel, V. L., Arocha, J. F., & Kaufman, D. R. (1994). Diagnostic reasoning and expertise. *Psychology of Learning and Motivation, 31,* 137–252.

Patel, V. L., Evans, D. A., & Groen, G. J. (1989). On reconciling basic science and clinical reasoning. *Teaching and Learning in Medicine, 1*(1), 116–121.

Patel, V. L., Evans, D. A., & Kaufman, D. R. (1989). Cognitive framework for doctor-patient interaction. In D. A. Evans, V. L. Patel (Eds.), *Cognitive science in medicine: Biomedical modeling* (pp. 253–308). Cambridge, MA: MIT Press.

Patel, V. L., & Groen, G. J. (1986). Knowledge-based solution strategies in medical reasoning. *Cognitive Science, 10*, 91–116.

Patel, V. L., & Groen, G. J. (1991). Developmental accounts of the transition from medical students to doctor: Some problems and suggestions. *Medical Education, 25*, 527–535.

Patel, V. L., Groen, G. J., & Arocha, J. F. (1990). Medical expertise as a function of task difficulty. *Memory & Cognition, 18*(4), 394–406.

Patel, V. L., Groen, G. J., & Norman, G. R. (1993). Reasoning and instruction in medical curricula. *Cognition & Instruction, 10*(4), 335–378.

Patel, V. L., & Kaufman, D. R. (1995). Clinical reasoning and biomedical knowledge. In J. Higgs & M. Jones (Eds.), *Clinical reasoning strategies* (pp. 117–128). Oxford, UK: Butterworth Heinemenn.

Patel, V. L., Kaufman, D. R., & Arocha, J. F. (1995). Steering through the murky waters of a scientific conflict: Situated and symbolic models of clinical cognition. *Artificial Intelligence in Medicine, 7*, 413–438.

Pea, R. D. (1993). Practices of distributed intelligence and designs for education. In G. Salomon (Ed.), *Distributed cognition: Psychological and educational considerations* (pp. 47–87). Cambridge, MA: Cambridge University Press.

Perkins, D. N. (1993). Person-plus: A distributed view of thinking and learning. In G. Salomon (Ed.), *Distributed cognition: Psychological and educational considerations* (pp. 88–110). Cambridge, MA: Cambridge University Press.

Ramoni, M., Stefanelli, M., Magnani, L., & Barosi, G. (1992). An epistemological framework for medical knowledge based systems. *IEEE Transactions on Systems, Man and Cybernetics, 22*, 1361–1375.

Rasmussen, J. (1993). Deciding and doing: Decision making in natural contexts. In G. A. Klein, J. Orasanu, R. Calderwood, & C. E. Zsambok (Eds.), *Decision making in action: Models and methods* (pp. 158–171). Norwood, NJ: Ablex.

Rasmussen, J., Pejtersen, A. M., & Goodstein, L. P. (1994). *Cognitive systems engineering*. New York: Wiley.

Salomon, G. (1993). No distribution without individuals' cognition: A dynamic interactional view. In G. Salomon (Ed.), *Distributed cognition: Psychological and educational considerations* (pp. 111–138). New York: Cambridge University Press.

Shalin, V. (Ed.). (1992). *Human performance in the complex workplace: Implications for basic research in cognitive science* (Working Paper No. 94–001). Buffalo: State University of New York at Buffalo.

Simon, H. A. (1973). The structure of ill-structured problems. *Artificial Intelligence, 4*, 181–201.

Simon, H. A. (1989). The scientist as a problem solver. In D. Klahr & K. Kotovsky (Eds.), *Complex information processing: The impact of Herbert A. Simon* (pp. 375–398). Hillsdale, NJ: Lawrence Erlbaum Associates.

Sloboda, J. (1991). Musical expertise. In A. Ericsson & J. Smith (Eds.), *Toward a general theory of expertise: Prospects and limits* (pp. 153–171). Cambridge, UK: Cambridge University Press.

Thibodeau, P., Hardiman, P. T., Dufresne, R., & Mestre, J. P. (1989). The relation between problem categorization and problem-solving among experts and novices. *Memory & Cognition, 17*, 627–638.

van Dijk, T. A., & Kintsch, W. (1983). *Strategies of discourse comprehension*. New York: Academic Press.

Woods, D. D. (1993). Process-tracing methods for the study of cognition outside of the experimental psychology laboratory. In G. A. Klein, J. Orasanu, R. Calderwood, & C. E. Zsambok (Eds.), *Decision making in action: Models and methods* (pp. 228–251). Norwood, NJ: Ablex.

Woods, D. D. (1994). Observations from studying cognitive systems in context. In *Proceedings of the Sixteenth Annual Conference of the Cognitive Science Society* (pp. 961–964). Hillsdale NJ: Lawrence Erlbaum Associates.

6

Perceptual and Memory Processes in the Acquisition of Expert Performance: The EPAM Model

Howard B. Richman
Fernand Gobet
James J. Staszewski
Herbert A. Simon
Carnegie Mellon University

The performance of experts in various domains has become an important topic of psychological research, especially since the pioneering study of chessmasters by de Groot (1946). This research has shown that expertise depends on acquiring large stores of relevant knowledge that are then accessible for use within the expert domain. The magnitude and nature of this knowledge has been investigated, as well as the way in which experts come to acquire it (Ericsson & Staszewski, 1989). Today we know that expert behavior combines (a) the abilities to recognize key features of situations and to access information in memory that is relevant to them with (b) the ability to solve problems by heuristic search in appropriate problem spaces (Newell & Simon, 1972).

The first ability underlies expert capacity for solving problems of familiar types rapidly and without much explicit analysis (the terms *instantly* and *intuitively* are often applied). The second ability underlies expert capacity for solving problems that require more systematic, and sometimes very extensive, analysis. In practice, most problems that an expert encounters call on a closely interwoven combination of recognition and search processes. Because both kinds of processes draw extensively on domain knowledge, experts are usually unable to behave "expertly" when confronted with problems outside their domains.

This general, but not very precise, characterization of expertise as revealed by research explains the general mechanisms and processes that make expert behavior possible. It does not explain how the mechanisms and processes of the human brain support the expert's functioning; nor does it explain how expert knowledge and processes are learned. To link the phenomena of expertise with the mechanisms for their implementation and with the expert's knowledge base, we need more than a description of the phenomena; we need rigorous models of cognitive processes that are consistent with both what is known about expertise and our general knowledge of human perception, memory, problem solving, and learning. Such models now exist, in rather extensive form, at the level of information processes (symbolic processes). As yet, we have little knowledge about how the information-processing models are implemented neurologically.

In the first section of this chapter, we enlarge the very broad picture we have just sketched of the nature of expertise. In the second section, we describe a model of human perception, learning, memory, and search that provides an explanation for expert behavior, and of the learning processes that are used in the acquisition of expertise. The models of expert performance and learning employ information-processing mechanisms whose presence, parameters, and functioning in human cognition have been validated by a substantial body of converging evidence, most of it not derived directly from research on expertise. (For the perception and memory part of the picture see especially Feigenbaum & Simon, 1984, and Richman, Staszewski & Simon, 1995; for the problem-solving part, see Newell & Simon, 1972, and Newell, 1990).

We have little to say, except by way of occasional comment, about the realization of these cognitive processes in the physiological mechanisms of the human brain, for, as we have remarked, the linkage between the information-processing level and the level of neuronal structures and processes is still very sketchy and incomplete.

THE NATURE OF EXPERT PERFORMANCE

Definition of Expertise

In research on expertise, an expert is usually defined in a very pragmatic way as someone who performs at the level of an experienced professional: an MD in medicine, a Master or Grandmaster in chess, an experienced systems programmer, a practicing attorney, an engineer employed in design, and so on. The difference between the performance of experts defined in this way and of novices, who lack the training and experience of the experts, is so great that it is easy to observe and characterize expert–novice differences even with this crude division; in fact, the performance of the two groups seldom overlaps.

Chess has been a very valuable domain for research on expertise because, among other reasons, there exists a standard quantitative scale for measuring differences in chess skill. The ELO rating, which is assigned to all persons throughout the world who play in tournaments, measures the player's results from competitive play against other rated players.[1] A rating of 1,800 to 1,999 assigns a player to Class A, 2,000 to 2,199 to Expert, 2,200 to 2,499 to Master, and 2,500 and over to Grandmaster rank. The ratings are so adjusted that a player whose rating exceeds another's by 200 points should defeat the latter in about two games out of three. In most research on expertise in chess, Masters and Grandmasters are regarded as experts and players of Class A and below as novices, but the research is not limited to simple expert–novice distinctions, for it can observe differences all along the scale and confirm the fact that there are not discontinuities, but a smooth gradient to the very top levels.

Some researchers on expertise (e.g., Simonton, chap. 8, this volume) would distinguish two levels of experts: those who represent state of the art practice, and those who are the discipline's creators, continually changing the discipline by contributing new knowledge, theories, and techniques. We later have some comments on this distinction between experts and creators, but work mostly with a simple distinction between experts and novices, as most of the research has been reported in those terms.

Performance of Experts

Quality of Performance

The tasks put to experts in experiments generally involve making decisions or solving problems. We combine both activities under the term *problem solving*. The consistent (and unsurprising) finding of research is that experts can solve problems in their domain that novices cannot solve, or, in the case of problems solvable by novices, experts can solve them much more rapidly and accurately. When think-aloud protocols are taken of problem solving, experts' protocols are generally briefer than novices', probably reflecting the fact that many of the experts' subprocesses have been automated so that they no longer require conscious attention. Novices tend to work backward from the problem goal, whereas on problems that are very easy for them, experts work forward, simply noticing and reporting conse-

---

[1]There are both international and national ELO ratings, which differ slightly, but we do not need to be concerned with these differences.

quences of the "givens" of the problem until a solution appears. On more difficult problems, experts usually revert to working backward, or at least to working in a goal-directed manner (Simon & Simon, 1978).

On problems of kinds that experts encounter frequently in professional practice, they reach rapid, sometimes "instantaneous," solutions, and are often unable to report intermediate steps in the process that led to the solution. In such cases, they commonly report that they solved the problem by intuition. In medical diagnosis, physicians often announce a tentative diagnosis immediately on initial presentation of some symptoms, but usually call for additional information before reaching a final conclusion. Similarly, in chess, experts are frequently aware of a possible move within seconds of gaining sight of a board, but will spend time—sometimes as much as a quarter of an hour—in verifying or revising the initial intuition. Similar intuitive expert behavior can be seen in other domains.

The same basic representation of a problem is frequently shared by all experts—as a product of the experts' training and experience. For example, when confronted with a problem in dynamics, expert physicists will usually try at once to express the problem in terms of differential equations. Operations research experts will classify a problem as a "linear programming problem," a "queuing problem," an "integer programming problem," and so on. Research has shown that experts generally sort and characterize problems according to the basic representations and methods relevant to solving them, whereas novices sort them in terms of surface features that often do not cue the representations that are effective for solving them (Chi, Feltovich, & Glaser, 1981).

In so-called "insight problems," the initial representation that most people adopt when presented with the problem is inappropriate. (This is what makes the problem an insight problem.) There is usually a long period during which the solver attempts to use this initial representation, followed by frustration and then attempts to find a better representation. If one is found, its discovery may be accompanied by an "aha!" (literally), and the "aha" soon followed, in turn, by a solution to the problem (Kaplan & Simon, 1990). Of course what is an insight problem to a novice may not be an insight problem to an expert, who may recognize at once from the problem statement what representation will lead to a solution. In general, subjects are unable to report the reasoning (if that is what it is) that leads them to discover the correct problem representation. The "aha" is evidence that the solution obtained suddenly was unanticipated before the change in representation was made.

Speed of Performance. Experts not only solve domain problems that novices cannot solve, but they generally solve them much more rapidly. Protocol data indicate that many subtasks that require novices to carry out a sequence of steps and to engage in heuristic search are solved by experts in a single step triggered by recognition of the appropriate cue. Thus, the expert has replaced the sequence of operations used by the novice by some kind of macro-operation. In fact (although this may not hold for some kinds of motor tasks), superior speed in performance can generally be accounted for by "chunking" of this general kind, and does not require that the primitive processes (reaction times, times to apply simple arithmetic operators, and so on) of the expert be speedier than those of the novice.

For example, from think-aloud protocols, information can be obtained about the processes used by lightning calculators, and about the differences between those processes and the ones used by people with ordinary abilities in calculation. When allowance is made for the differences in strategy (differences that are based in large part on numerical knowledge that the lightning calculator possesses and novices do not), most of the difference in overall speed can be accounted for without postulating that the lightning calculator adds or subtracts single digits substantially more rapidly than novices do, or has unusual memory capacity (Dansereau, 1969).

Performance on Extradomain Tasks. The superior performance of experts does not carry over, in general, to tasks lying outside the domain. Of course if the extradomain tasks share common elements at an abstract level with tasks in the domain of expertise, there may be more or less extensive transfer of heuristics. (A physicist will probably have an easier time reading a text in mathematical economics than will a person without training in calculus.) But unless identifiable opportunities for transfer are present (common elements), the expert is likely to perform only a little better, or no better, than the novice.

A classical demonstration of this fact that has received much attention compares the respective abilities of chess experts and novices to replace the chess pieces on a board that they have seen for only a short interval (5 seconds, say). The boards used in these experiments typically have about 25 pieces on them, either (Condition 1) arranged as they were in a game between strong players or (Condition 2) arranged at random. In the game positions, the experts show an enormous advantage over novices: Masters and Grandmasters are usually able to replace the pieces with 90% or more accuracy (23–25 pieces, say), whereas Class A players will generally replace only 6 or 7 pieces. In the random positions, novices (Class A players) will do a little more poorly than with the game positions (3 or 4 pieces replaced correctly), and experts will average only about 1 piece more than the novices (Chase & Simon, 1973; Gobet & Simon, in press).

This experiment refutes the hypothesis that the superior performance of the experts is due to a superiority of domain-independent perception and/or memory. Instead, it appears that novices see individual pieces on the board, whereas experts see familiar constellations (chunks) of pieces—a half dozen of them, say. If short-term memory (STM) is limited by the number of chunks (familiar patterns) that can be held, then the results of this experiment can be explained without positing any difference in the capacities of the expert and novice STMs: Both can hold six or seven chunks in memory, and when familiar chunks are rare (as on the random boards), experts do nearly as badly as novices. This same effect of chunking on STM capacity has been demonstrated for a variety of other tasks besides chess.

The Knowledge of Experts

We have already suggested that, to a major degree, the superior performance of experts can be explained in terms of their superior domain knowledge. There have been a few direct estimates of the extent of that knowledge, the estimates being all of the same order of magnitude. First, we have some measurements of native language vocabularies of children and adults. In round numbers, the measured vocabulary of a college-educated adult is usually in the range of 100,000 to 200,000 lexical items whose meanings would be understood if they were seen in the context of text. This estimate is consistent with the vocabulary size of good bilingual dictionaries, typically in the neighborhood of 60,000 words, which need to be supplemented by technical vocabularies in special domains. Estimates have also been made, by several more or less indirect routes, of the number of chunks (familiar patterns of pieces) held in memory by chess experts. These estimates lie in the range from 50,000 to 100,000.[2]

Of course, the knowledge of the expert is surely not limited to a vocabulary of familiar patterns. It also includes a more or less extensive store of representations that can be used in solving problems, actions that can be taken in the solution process, and a variety of other components. The important overall point is that the expert's ability to perform in his or her domain of expertise rests solidly on a large accumulation in long-term memory of knowledge that is (often) evoked when it is relevant for solving the problem at hand. If we broaden the definition of chunk to encompass knowledge of all of these kinds, then we can estimate that the expert holds in memory hundreds of thousands, or even a few million, of such chunks.

Becoming an Expert

The empirical studies of how someone becomes expert in a domain proclaim loudly and consistently that experts are made, not born. This is not to say that there are not innate differences among people in "talent" or ability. Of course there are. No training regimen is likely to make someone born with an IQ of 50 (using any standard measure of IQ) into a competent attorney, aircraft mechanic, flute player, or research mathematician. However, innate talent or ability only becomes expertise when it is nourished by

---

[2]Holding (1985) argued that the number is much smaller, but Gobet and Simon (1995), on the basis of a re-examination of the evidence, found strong evidence for the earlier estimates.

extensive training and practice. This fact has been confirmed at the highest level of expertise by studies of more than a dozen expert domains, including chess playing, musical performance, swimming, tennis, musical composition, experimental science, mathematical research, and others (Bloom, 1985; Ericsson & Charness, 1994).

World-class experts may be defined as the top few hundred persons in any domain: Olympic winners in sports, concert pianists who win international prizes, strong chess Grandmasters, Nobel Prize winners in science, members of national academies, and the like. The central research finding is that no one becomes a world-class expert without 10 years or more of intense attention to training and practice in the domain of expertise (Bloom, 1985; Hayes, 1988). Einstein, for example, was studying physics (and had even written an unpublished paper on electromagnetism) 10 years before the famous year (1905) in which he published, at age 26, his first paper on special relativity.

Moreover, even at very high levels in a domain, there is a strong correlation between acknowledged expertise and cumulated learning time (Ericsson & Charness, 1994). It has gradually become clear that neither child prodigies nor so-called "idiot savants" are exceptions to this rule: When their histories are studied, it is found that they have put in their 10 years before reaching world-class levels. Mozart, for example, was composing at age 4 or 5, but his first works that would be regarded as world class were composed when he was at least 17 (and perhaps none written before he was 21 really qualify as world class)—an interval of 12 or more years. The same is found to be the case for other prodigies.

Idiot Savants. As for idiot savants (who may form an exception to the "tested-IQ-of-50 rule" proposed already), the "idiocy" stems from the fact that almost all of their efforts have been directed toward their domain of pre-eminence, hence they know little about anything else. Their expertness is almost always acquired in domains (arithmetic is one example, music another) in which they can increase their knowledge by constant, and usually solitary, mental activity (e.g., memorizing large numbers of prime numbers and various short-cut computations that use such knowledge, or memorizing both specific pieces of music and characteristic "chunks" that lie at the basis of musical pattern). They do this without necessarily being instructed explicitly or having access to books. When information is available about the ways in which savants spend their time, there is always a history of intense preoccupation with the domain of expertise. In the rare cases where they are world class in that domain, their histories do not violate the 10-year rule.

In contrast to idiot savants, most persons who become world-class experts receive a great deal of instruction along the path, first from parents, teachers, or coaches available in the immediate environment, then from progressively more sophisticated teachers and coaches combined with immersion in a culture that provides many opportunities for competition and collaboration with other experts, and observation of their performances.

Talent and Expertise. Sternberg (chap. 15, this volume) has argued passionately and persuasively that innate talent is essential to acquiring high levels of expertise. We must emphasize again that the empirically based 10-year rule of thumb and the 50,000-chunk estimate for the acquisition of world-class expertise set necessary conditions for these attainments, but we do not claim that they are sufficient conditions.

To establish sufficient conditions for expert performance, we have to conduct experiments, either with human subjects or computer problem-solving simulators or both, that start with rather complete information about initial memory inputs and abilities and show that these were adequate to produce some kind of expert behavior. We mention two examples where this strategy has been employed to some extent, one involving computer simulation, the other involving human subjects.

The computer program BACON (Langley, Simon, Bradshaw, & Zytkow, 1987), given exactly the same data as Kepler had available (periods of the solar planets and their distances from the sun), and no other knowledge or hypotheses about astronomy, concluded, within a short time and after generating and testing only four different hypotheses, that the data were described by the law: Period = (Distance)$^{3/2}$, which is precisely Kepler's Third Law, a major landmark in the history of astronomy. We know exactly what knowledge BACON had. In addition to the data (identical with Kepler's), it had only some heuristics (rules of thumb) for generating simple functions and modifying them successively on the basis of the kind of fit or misfit it observed between function and data. Therefore, we can conclude that any system possessing these data and these simple heuristics has sufficient "talent" to make some discoveries of this kind and magnitude. Of course BACON did not only find Kepler's Third Law but, under exactly the same conditions and using exactly the same heuristics with the appropriate data set, rediscovered a whole host of important basic laws of physics and chemistry (Ohm's Law, Black's Law, conservation of mass, etc.).

To calibrate this performance against human capabilities, Kepler's data were given to 14 college students in the laboratory. The variables were simply labeled x and y, no interpretation was provided in terms of periods and distances, and no mention made that these were astronomical data. Nevertheless, 4 of the 14 students arrived at the law stated earlier within an hour. The 10 who failed to do so either (a) generated only a small set of candidate functions (exclusively linear functions), or (b) generated functions without using feedback from the previous attempts to guide construction of the next function (Qin & Simon, 1990).

As we do not know in detail what was stored in the students' memories prior to the experiment, we cannot make as confident a statement as we can for BACON about the sufficient conditions for successful performance; but the experiment could easily be extended to discover what percentage of students having various backgrounds and histories of academic proficiency could be trained in a shorter or longer period of time to behave in the general manner of BACON and to achieve comparable success in law-discovery problems. Until experiments like these are carried out, we cannot make confident statements about the relative importance of talent and training in attaining high-level performance, or in determining the speed with which high levels can be reached.

Motivation and Cognition in Expert Performance

The histories of world-class experts show that high levels of expertise require not only learning but also the motivation (innate or acquired) that produces the necessary patience and persistence in training and practice. Even when the tasks on which the expertise is demonstrated are wholly cognitive, the attainment of this expertise can only be explained with proper attention to motivation. As this topic lies largely outside our own domain of expertise, we do not have much to say about it. In this case, silence does not imply unimportance.

A MODEL OF EXPERTISE AND ITS ACQUISITION

Having described some of the main characteristics of expertise that have been revealed by research, we wish to show (a) how the facts we have recounted can be explained in terms of a small number of information-processing structures and mechanisms, and (b) that these structures and mechanisms are not peculiar to the phenomenon of expertise but are the basic mechanisms that have been used to explain cognition generally—whether of experts or novices. Experts simply employ, at a very high level of skill in their domains of expertise, the basic information processes that other human beings employ at lower levels of skill, but the experts have access to much richer knowledge bases than are available to nonexperts. What we aim at, then, is a parsimonious account of expert behavior within the framework of a general account of cognition; in the words that Newell used to title his last book, at "unified theories of cognition" (Newell, 1990).

We need such a model for several reasons. The first is to demonstrate that our explanations are not being constructed ad hoc for each distinct phenomenon: that a modest number of basic mechanisms can account for them all. The second is to show that parameters of the model that have been estimated from one experimental paradigm (not necessarily related to expertise at all) retain the same values in the other paradigms, thereby providing the parsimony that is necessary if the theory is to be refutable or testable. Splintered accounts of individual phenomena do not have this parsimony or this testability.

As the mechanisms that we need for our purposes have not yet been wholly encapsulated in a single unified theory, we have to settle for a little less: two interrelated information-processing models, one of them, EPAM, dealing primarily with perception, memory, and the processes of recognition that depend on them; the other, embodied either in GPS or Soar, an expert system that solves problems by searching heuristically through problem spaces. These models also incorporate learning mechanisms that acquire the expert knowledge and problem-solving processes, as well as the processes for generating and altering problem representations. We focus most of our attention on EPAM, for its role in expertise is perhaps less familiar than the role of problem-solving mechanisms.

The EPAM Model

The EPAM model of elementary perception and memory was built initially by Feigenbaum (1961) to account for the processes of knowledge acquisition and recall, and has since been expanded by Feigenbaum, Gregg, Richman, Simon, and others to model a wide variety of memory phenomena that have been studied in the laboratory (Feigenbaum & Simon, 1984; Gobet, 1993; Richman et al., 1995). In acquiring new knowledge, as EPAM becomes familiar with simple stimuli, it groups these stimuli into larger units called chunks, a phenomenon whose importance was first recognized by Miller (1956). A chunk is any unit of information that has been familiarized and has become meaningful (e.g., the words and phrases in one's natural language vocabulary, the objects that can be recognized when seen and named, etc.). The familiarity of a chunk relates to the ability to recognize it; meaningfulness to the information that is stored in association with it in long-term memory (LTM).

Chunking is recursive, so that chunks at any level can be grouped again into chunks at the next level above (visual features into letters, letters into words, words into familiar phrases, etc.). By testing EPAM in a wide range of experimental tasks, estimates have been obtained, and confirmed by converging evidence, for the latencies of the basic processes required to recognize a familiar item (about 0.5 s), learn the recognition tests for a new chunk (about 8 s), add a new piece of information to a LTM chunk (about 1-2 s) and retrieve stimuli (about 200 ms–2 s).

Short-Term Memory.   EPAM models both STM and LTM. The most important STM for our purposes is the articulatory loop (Baddeley, 1986), whose capacity has been shown to equal the number of chunks that can be rehearsed in about 2 seconds, where the time required to rehearse each chunk is about 300 ms for the first syllable and 80 ms for each additional syllable (Zhang & Simon, 1985). What appears to be held in STM is a pointer to each chunk, so that the contents of the memory can be rehearsed by accessing the articulatory image of each chunk via the pointer, thereby recovering its syllables. Information stored in the articulatory loop at any given time can be attended to, and this information is subject to learning—that is, gradual transfer to LTM. The time required for transfer is about 8 seconds for each new chunk, as EPAM's discrimination net is elaborated to distinguish it from chunks already familiar.

From the standpoint of expert memory, the principal significance of the parameters of STM lies in the constraint that they place on the time required to acquire new recognizable chunks. At 8 seconds per chunk, the 50,000 chunks we have estimated for the chessmaster's memory store could be acquired in a little more than 100 hours, smaller, by two orders of magnitude, than the 10 years required to reach world-class skill. How do we account for the remaining time? First, the 8-second parameter for storing a new chunk in LTM is derived from standard verbal learning experiments, where ability to recall memorized items is tested only a few minutes after they have been stored. It is well known that information stored under these conditions, without redundancy, decays very rapidly, so that only a small fraction is available after 24 hours has elapsed. The relearning and over-learning required for long-term retention can easily account for one order of magnitude more learning time, or a total of 1,000 hours.

Second, the 50,000 chunks estimated for the chess expert includes only patterns of pieces that will be recognized when they occur in a game position (including templates, which we discuss later, of typical positions that appear frequently in opening play). The expert must retain many other kinds of knowledge as well—in particular, knowledge of moves that may be appropriate when a particular pattern appears in a game, strategies for look-ahead analysis of moves, and so on. Again, it is not unreasonable to allow another factor of 10 in learning time to account for all of this additional information that must be stored in LTM. Finally, not all of the time spent in study is available for learning new chunks; in fact, as the learner becomes more and more expert, novel information that can be added to the knowledge store is encountered less and less frequently. We conclude that the parameters of learning speed that have been estimated from verbal learning studies are consistent with the estimate of 20,000 learning hours available during a 10-year period of work. (We conservatively estimate a 40-hour week!)

Visual Short-Term Memory. Most of the measurements on rates of learning have dealt with auditory material and the articulatory loop. The parameters of visual STM (the "mind's eye") are less well known, but there is no reason to suppose that the time required to transfer a familiar chunk of information from the mind's eye to LTM is very different from the time required to transfer an auditory chunk. Hence, our earlier comments about the time required to acquire the recognition capabilities that the expert possesses can be applied to both auditory and visual chunks. For purposes of studying expertise and its acquisition, little specification is needed of the details of STM, auditory or visual, beyond the phenomenon of chunking and the time required to transfer new chunks to LTM.

Long-Term Memory.   EPAM's LTM can be thought of as an indexed encyclopedia. On presentation of a visual or auditory stimulus, perceptual processes (not represented in the present EPAM or in most other current models of perception) extract a list of features from the stimulus and these features are then sorted down through a discrimination net to a terminal or "leaf" node. The different leaf nodes of the EPAM net represent the different stimuli that EPAM is able, at any given time, to discriminate. At each leaf node is stored an "image" of the stimulus, containing partial information about it (including the information that was used to sort it) and containing, also, associational links to other information about it that is held in LTM (semantic LTM). The EPAM net, then, is the index to the semantic LTM, providing access, through the associational links, to the information held in the latter. The net is not a simple tree but a network, for many paths may lead to the same leaf node, providing the redundancy that is required to recognize objects when they are observed from different angles and under varying circumstances.

Learning: Growth of the EPAM Net.   When a stimulus is sorted to a leaf node of EPAM, its features may be compared with the features of the image stored there. If there are discrepancies between the two sets of features, EPAM can construct a new test node that tests for the nonidentical feature, and a new leaf node to accommodate the new stimulus, retaining the old leaf for the original stimulus (Simon, 1976). By this means, the EPAM net and the corresponding set of leaf nodes grow continually as they learn new patterns, performing the same function that is performed by the "hidden layers" of connectionist learning systems. Each new pattern that is discriminated gains its own leaf node, identifying a new chunk.

Large discrimination nets have been acquired in this manner. EPAM, in simulating a human subject who learned to repeat back sequences of 100 digits that were read to him at the rate of one digit per second, gradually "grew" a discrimination net with more than 3,000 leaf nodes (Richman et al., 1995). CHREST, an EPAM-like system for simulating the acquisition of chess expertise has acquired nets as large as 70,000 leaf nodes on being exposed to a large number of chess positions with the goal of retaining the patterns contained in them (Gobet, 1993; Gobet & Simon, 1995).

Acquiring Templates and Retrieval Structures.   It has been found that human chess experts store in memory templates of many thousands of opening positions—the positions at which the game typically arrives after sequences of 10 or 20 "standard" opening moves. The templates of these positions generally contain information about the locations of 10 or more pieces, and the presumptive locations of perhaps another half dozen. When an expert is given a brief view of a game position, he or she can then usually recognize it as corresponding to one of these templates, and thereby retain information about the locations of nearly half the pieces on the board. Moreover, information about additional pieces can be added rapidly by noticing whether they do or do not conform to their presumptive locations. We call these presumptive locations the template's *slots,* or variable places. It appears from experiments in which experts replace pieces on a briefly exposed board that information about the location of a piece can be stored in a slot in a fraction of a second.

An important technique of mnemonists, known and taught from Greek and Roman times, is to learn deliberately a *retrieval structure* that contains a great many slots in a determinate relation with each other. Once the retrieval structure is in place, each of its slots, like the slots of the chess expert's templates, can be filled with a chunk of information in a second or less. Classically, the retrieval structure took the form of a "memory palace." The mnemonist memorized the room plan of a palace, with various pieces of furniture permanently stationed in each room. Then, to store a particular list of chunks rapidly, the mnemonist simply assigned each item, in order, to one of these locations. Subsequently, they were recalled by accessing one room after another and noticing (in the mind's eye) what items had been placed there. The retrieval structure resided permanently in LTM, and could be used repeatedly to store new lists in its slots.

The expert, mentioned earlier, who recalled long lists of digits used a retrieval structure of a slightly more abstract kind (Chase & Ericsson, 1981; Richman et al., 1995). He simply imagined a hierarchy of slots, grouped by threes and fours, and assigned the digits to the successive leaf nodes at the bottom of this hierarchy. He also associated groups of digits (again groups of three or four) with long-distance running times he had previously stored in semantic memory as a result of his extensive experience and knowledge of running. As each three or four digits were read to him for the recall task, he assigned them to successive retrieval structure slots, and at the same time associated them with a familiar running time. Although the process was subject to some forgetting (it is estimated that he almost immediately forgot about 25% of the items stored) the redundancy of storage of information in more than one place allowed him to recover most of the information, and thereby to recall long lists without error.

The critical parameters in this kind of performance are (a) the ability, over some period of time, to build templates or retrieval structures in LTM, at a rate of perhaps 8 seconds for each new chunk, and (b) the ability to fill the slots in these structures with information (to be retained for a matter of hours) at a rate of less than 1 second per chunk. EPAM and CHREST, which embody such parameters, simulate closely the performance of chess and digit-memory experts in recall tasks, thus reconciling these "exceptional" performances with what has been learned about human memories in the standard laboratory tasks on verbal learning. The effectiveness of the chunking/retrieval structure mechanisms embodied in EPAM to explain expert memory has thus been demonstrated in two quite different environments, in one of which the acquisition of retrieval structures was a deliberate mnemonic strategy, in the other, a by-product of practice and the study of chess.

Recognition and Expertise. The indexed knowledge base that is EPAM provides the mechanisms that we require to explain the commonly observed ability, discussed in a previous section of this chapter, of experts who solve many problems and deal with many situations "intuitively." The basis of EPAM's intuitions is simply its ability to recognize familiar cues (by sorting stimulus features through its discrimination net), thereby gaining access to the relevant knowledge associated with them. The physician recognizes symptoms and "intuitively" concludes (subject, perhaps to additional tests) that the patient is suffering from a particular disease; the attorney recognizes features of a contract and "intuitively" concludes that it subjects her client to certain risks. It is not a question of whether these intuitions are always reliable; they are often reliable enough to permit the expert to proceed with the task vastly more rapidly and reliably than the novice, who must employ much more tedious step-by-step search processes. The information recovered by such recognitions of cues can be very extensive; the physician may access not only the name of the disease but a large store of information about prognosis, methods of treatment, and so on. We no longer need to regard intuition as an unexplained phenomenon. It is synonymous with the familiar process of recognition, and we can simulate its workings with EPAM and other models of memory.

Insight and Learning Representations. Closely related to intuition, but perhaps requiring a slightly more elaborate mechanism for explanation, is the phenomenon of *insight*. Like intuition, insight involves sudden solution of a problem, usually accompanied by inability of the solver to explain how the solution was found, and often punctuated by a figurative or literal "aha!" What distinguishes occasions of insight from the much more common occurrences of intuition is that insight is often preceded by a shorter or longer period during which no problem solution is found, and often no plausible steps for moving toward a solution. When the insight finally occurs, it usually can be seen that the representation of the problem had to be changed in order to find the solution, but that the solution was found easily (perhaps even became "obvious") as soon as the new representation was available (Kaplan & Simon, 1990).

The key to the insight is the process of discovering a new problem representation. This new representation can already be present in the memory of the problem solver, or it can be unfamiliar. In the former case, the reason for the delayed solution is that no clue is recognized in the situation that associates with the effective representation, so that the latter is simply not evoked, and hence is unavailable. In these situations, it is usually easy to produce the insight by providing the problem solver with a clue (often a very simple one) that produces the recognition, and thereby leads quickly to the change in representation. With experience, EPAM adds a new path from cues characterizing a class of situations to knowledge of one or more representations effective for dealing with it.

Where a representation is required that is not already familiar, insight requires problem-solving activity as well as recognition. The new representation must be discovered, then added to LTM along with the cues for its recognition. Lack of an effective representation was the principal reason for the failure of Newton's contemporaries, who were unfamiliar with the calculus, to demonstrate the law of universal gravitation. Although several of them (e.g., Hooke, Wren) conjectured a gravitational force that varied inversely with the square of the distance, none was able to demonstrate that such a force could account for the planetary motions. Once the calculus representation was available, the derivation was quite straightforward—today, students in first-year physics carry it out routinely. We have a little more to say about insight and invention in the next section.

The Problem-Solving Model

EPAM's indexed memory, the body of knowledge stored in it, and its processes for acquiring new knowledge by learning can account for a considerable part of the expert's superior abilities in memory retrieval and problem solving in the domain of expertise (and the absence of that superiority outside the domain). However, to complete the story, we must look at problem solving that requires more than recognition processes—situations in which more or less extensive heuristic search is also required. Here again, existing models of problem-solving processes like GPS and Soar provide most of the answers we need; but to see this we have to discuss the search process in a little more detail (Newell, 1990; Newell & Simon, 1972).

Solving a simple problem, say the Tower of Hanoi, is usually described as a search through the space of possible ("legal") arrangements of the disks on the pegs, from the starting arrangement to the arrangement specified as the goal. Successive states in the problem space are reached by moves, each of which, in this puzzle, amounts to changing the location of a single disk. The search is almost never random, but is guided by various heuristic rules that seek to guide the selection of the proper moves. The heuristic rules may be more or less complete, more or less correct.

When we come to more complex tasks, however, even tasks like finding the concept an experimenter has in mind to distinguish one set of objects from another, the search becomes more complex, usually involving interaction between two or more distinct problem spaces: the space of "instances" and the space of "hypotheses" (Simon & Lea, 1974). Suppose, for example, that a subject is presented with a succession of objects and asked to designate each one as belonging or not belonging to the concept by which the experimenter classifies them. The succession of objects constitutes the instance space, the hypotheses that the subject generates as possible classifiers constitute the hypothesis space. When the subject is told that he or she has made an incorrect judgment, the current hypothesis is usually rejected and a move made to another point in the hypothesis space. Again, this move may be guided by heuristics that are based on information collected from the previous choices and reinforcements. It has been shown that the behavior of subjects in concept attainment experiments can be explained in terms of search in the dual instance and hypothesis spaces.

Finding a scientific law that describes data obtained in a similarly cumulative fashion has been modeled in the same way by computer programs like BACON and others, using a dual search in the space of possible laws and the space of possible data observations. But why limit the process to two spaces? A scientist may search in a space of instruments, a space of experiments, a space of possible descriptive laws, a space of explanatory mechanisms, a space of problem representations, a space of research problems, and perhaps others (Langley et al., 1987).

Krebs, for example, in his search for the mechanism of urea synthesis in living organisms, selected that problem as one already recognized as important but unsolved, selected instruments and experimental procedures that he had acquired as a postdoctoral student in the laboratory of Otto Warburg, searched a space of substances as possible sources for the nitrogen in the urea, and when he discovered that ornithine and ammonia were implicated in the process, searched a space of chemical reactions to find a reaction path from inputs of these substances to the output of urea (Holmes, 1980).

Knowledge of this multitude of spaces as well as some knowledge of their structure is required for an expert approach to the research problem. As with every problem, progress will depend on processes of recognition (of possible representations, instruments, experiments, theoretical hypotheses, etc.), combined with search processes in the several spaces whenever recognition does not give an answer to the current question and a new one must be synthesized. The programs that have been built in recent years to accomplish these recognitions and searches are, again, recognizable kinfolk of programs like EPAM and the General Problem Solver (or Soar)—EPAM to make use of the knowledge base to achieve recognition of relevant information, GPS or Soar to conduct the searches in the many problem spaces. As an integral part of these processes, new learning goes on: New chunks are constructed, stored in LTM, and indexed by the cues that permit them to be recognized.

Acquisition of Problem-Solving Skill

It is clear from this account that the expert needs to acquire much more than knowledge in declarative form. Expert skill is heavily dependent on efficient processes, including strategies, planning processes, and representation-generating processes. If the processes in the expert system take the form of productions (i.e., If <cue>, then <action>), as they do in such problem-solving systems as GPS (Newell & Simon, 1972), Soar (Newell, 1990), and Act* (Anderson, 1983), then the learning mechanisms must create new productions that can be added to LTM and evoked, via the discrimination net, when the appropriate cues are present. Soar, for example, accomplishes this by storing information about the paths it has followed during problem solving so that it can recover these paths without search when the same or a similar problem later presents itself.

It is not yet clear whether learning schemes of this kind are sufficient to account fully for expert skill acquisition or whether additional mechanisms are required, but the power of learning by elaboration of a discrimination net combined with storage of knowledge schemas and new productions has been demonstrated in numerous contexts.

Expertise and Creativity

Simonton (chap. 8, this volume) hypothesizes that there may be a special group of experts in each domain who have not only exceptional knowledge and skill but also unusual capacities for inventing and adding new representations and other knowledge to the domain. These especially creative individuals may or may not be the very best performers. In chess, for example, Reti and Niemzovich were great and influential innovators who, although they were strong Grandmasters, never reached the very top of the ladder in chess competition. On the other hand, Morphy, Steinitz, Alekhine, and Botvinnik, each a world champion, also introduced important innovative ideas, whereas few important new ideas appear to have been contributed by Lasker, Capablanca, or Euwe, all world champions.

In this domain, as in others, we observe that certain experts do play a more innovative role than others without being the most highly regarded performers. In fact (one thinks of a Kandinsky in painting, a Schoenberg in musical composition) an expert may take innovating as his or her special role, and in domains like science, innovation (contributing new knowledge) actually defines the expert's central professional task. Moreover, we would, in fact, expect more than an average number of innovators among the top ranks of experts for, once the existing state of the art has been mastered, employing new ideas and practices is the principal remaining route to pre-eminence. The chess master has no choice but to display his innovations in his games (but they may be misunderstood by this contemporaries), whereas in other domains innovators may gain more permanent advantage through patenting or secrecy.

Do we require special mechanisms to account for these innovators? It appears that we do not, for as we have seen in the previous section of this chapter, innovating (e.g., finding new representations and new strategies) is itself a problem-solving task to which the tools of recognition and heuristic search in the spaces of possible representations, possible strategies, and so on, can be applied. The innovator, from this standpoint, is simply a problem solver (and "recognizer") who applies his or her efforts to changing the problem spaces in which recognition and search are carried on. The "great" innovators are those who solve the problem of bringing about the largest changes: Newton's calculus, Planck's quantum, Harvey's blood circulation, and so on.

If the tasks of innovation are problem-solving tasks, then we should be able to model them using the same mechanisms that have been used to model problem solving generally, and we have seen that this has in fact been done in such discovery systems as AM, BACON, EURISKO, LIVE, MECHEM, and the many others that can now be found in the psychological and artificial intelligence literatures (see, e.g., Langley et al., 1987). Nor are the examples limited to science. Hiller and Isaacson (1959) produced a very early program that composed original (and sometimes musically interesting) music, and the painter, Harold Cohen, has produced the Aaron program, which makes original drawings (both nonrepresentational and representational) that are aesthetically sophisticated and pleasing (McCorduck, 1991).

Of course, we can consider these programs simply as models of performance: They solve problems. But we must also take into account the extent to which discovery models incorporate learning processes and modify themselves in ways I have described earlier. Perhaps the simplest form of self-modification is EPAM's elaboration of its discrimination net, so that a program can progressively recognize a wider and wider range of stimuli. A related procedure, incorporated, for example, in theorem-proving systems, is the ability to store problem solutions and to use them in solving subsequent problems. Beyond even this are systems that can modify their own representations, processes, and strategies. In this category, I have mentioned Soar, which stores and uses strategies that have been successful in solving previous problems (Newell, 1990); and I would also call attention to the UNDERSTAND system, capable of constructing problem representations from verbal problem instructions (Hayes & Simon, 1974).

In the light of the experience we have already had with systems of these kinds—incorporating the basic capabilities of recognizing and of solving problems by search through multiple problem spaces and of learning—it is not unreasonable to hypothesize that creativity is "simply" unusually competent or admirable problem solving that accomplishes its tasks by the use of these very mechanisms. We sometimes produce work that is creative if we explore the space of problem representations, of instruments, or strategies, and so on, not limiting ourselves to the problem spaces that the current state of the art presents to us.

CONCLUSION

Research in information processing psychology began in the middle 1950s, with the construction of theories, in the form of computer simulations, of human performance on relatively simple and well-structured tasks, most of them tasks that were already familiar from the psychological laboratory. Two of these early theories, both in operation before 1960, were EPAM, a model of elementary perceptual and memory processes that was tested against the data from verbal learning experiments, and GPS, a model of problem-solving processes (emphasizing means–ends analysis) that was tested against the data from various puzzlelike tasks. As the mechanisms that were needed to explain these phenomena gradually became clearer, it began to appear that EPAM and GPS could go a long way toward accounting for the behavior of experts and explaining why experts are so much more competent than novices on tasks belonging to the expert domain. In particular, it became clear that expertise depends heavily on the possession of, and access to, large bodies of domain knowledge. Having in hand a number of systems capable of expert performance, it proved possible to devise learning schemes that showed how the expertness could be acquired.

The early models were improved and extended, and new models (e.g., ACT*, Soar, BACON) emerged in an effort to give a better account of the phenomena, but these and other systems that describe and explain how experts behave expertly are recognizable descendants of EPAM and GPS. The knowledge-accumulating and knowledge-accessing mechanisms of EPAM-like systems explain the expert's use of "intuition" in the form of recognition processes. The search mechanisms, extended to multiple search spaces and making extensive use of means–ends analysis and other heuristics, explain the expert's capabilities for solving scientific problems, including the subsidiary problems of finding appropriate representations, instruments, experiments, data, and hypotheses.

Although we do wish to convey a picture of continuity and cumulation in this chronicle of research, for we think these are fully documented by the vast and continually growing body of phenomena that have been successfully described and explained, we do not wish to convey a picture of completeness or even near completeness (no one would be fooled if we did). Lots of things have been demonstrated "in principle" that still need to be demonstrated in detail. A great many tasks (e.g., tasks in realms like language behavior and language learning, representation change, uses of visual imagery—an endless list) have only been touched. There are new challenges posed by the discovery of alternative mechanisms—connectionist systems and neural networks currently the most prominent among them.

In short, we are in a fast-flowing stream of normal science, which is rapidly gaining a broader and deeper understanding of human thinking in general and the thinking of experts in particular; and we may even expect this stream to bring us closer to a solid linkage with neuropsychology, which up to the present has been a rather separate, and even distant world. As symbolic processes must be implemented by neuronal structures, getting a better understanding of that linkage is one of the important tasks before us—although, we hasten to add, not the only one.

The symbolic level itself continues to present us with innumerable research opportunities. It will be most interesting, as we watch these developments in the future to see how far the basic processes of recognition of familiar chunks and heuristic search through multiple problem spaces, supported by the learning processes that create the underlying stored knowledge and skill, will continue to stand at the core of our understanding of the competencies of experts.

REFERENCES

Anderson, J. R. (1983). *The architecture of cognition.* Cambridge, MA: Harvard University Press.
Baddeley, A. (1986). *Working memory.* Oxford, UK: Oxford University Press.
Bloom, B. S. (1985). *Developing talent in young people.* New York: Random House.
Chase, W. G., & Ericsson, K. A. (1981). Skilled memory. In J. R. Anderson (Ed.), *Cognitive skills and their acquisition* (pp. 141–190). Hillsdale, NJ: Lawrence Erlbaum Associates.
Chase, W. G. & Simon, H. A. (1973). Perception in chess. *Cognitive Psychology, 4,* 55–81.
Chi, M. T. H., Feltovich, P. J., & Glaser, R. (1981). Categorization and representation of physics problems by experts and novices. *Cognitive Science, 5,* 121–125.
Dansereau, D. (1969). *An information processing model of mental multiplication.* Unpublished doctoral dissertation, Carnegie Mellon University, Pittsburgh, PA.
de Groot, A. D. (1946). *Het denken van den schaker* [Thought and choice in chess]. Amsterdam: North-Holland.
Ericsson, K. A., & Charness, N. (1994). Expert performance: Its structure and acquisition. *American Psychologist, 49,* 725–747.
Ericsson, K. A., & Staszewski, J. (1989). Skilled memory and expertise: Mechanisms of exceptional performance. In D. Klahr & K. Kotovsky (Eds.), *Complex information processing* (pp. 235–268). Hillsdale, NJ: Lawrence Erlbaum Associates.
Feigenbaum, E. A. (1961). The simulation of verbal learning behaviors. *Proceedings of the 1961 Western Joint Computer Conference,* 121–132.
Feigenbaum, E. A., & Simon, H. A. (1984). EPAM-like models of recognition and learning. *Cognitive Science, 8,* 305–336.
Gobet, F. (1993). A computer model of chess memory. *Proceedings of the 15th Annual Meeting of the Cognitive Science Society* (pp. 463–468). Hillsdale, NJ: Lawrence Erlbaum Associates.
Gobet, F., & Simon, H. A. (in press). Recall of random and distorted positions: Implications for the theory of expertise. *Memory & Cognition*
Gobet, F., & Simon, H. A. (1995). *Role of presentation time in recall of game and random positions* (Tech. Rep. C.I.P. 524). Pittsburgh, PA: Carnegie Mellon University, Department of Psychology.
Hayes, J. R. (1988). *The complete problem solver* (2nd ed.). Hillsdale, NJ: Lawrence Erlbaum Associates.
Hayes, J. R., & Simon, H. A. (1974). Understanding written problem instructions. In L. W. Gregg (Ed.), *Knowledge and cognition* (pp. 167–200). Hillsdale, NJ: Lawrence Erlbaum Associates.
Hiller, L. A., & Isaacson, L. M. (1959). *Experimental music.* New York: McGraw-Hill.
Holding, D. H. (1985). *The psychology of chess skill.* Hillsdale, NJ: Lawrence Erlbaum Associates.

Holmes, F. L. (1980). Hans Krebs and the discovery of the ornithine cycle. *Federation Proceedings, 39*(2), 216–225.

Kaplan, C. A., & Simon, H. A. (1990). In search of insight. *Cognitive Psychology, 22*(3), 374–419.

Langley, P., Simon, H. A., Bradshaw, G. L., & Zytkow, J. M. (1987). *Scientific discovery: Computational explorations of the creative processes.* Cambridge, MA: MIT Press.

McCorduck, P. (1991). *Aaron's code.* New York: W. H. Freeman.

Miller, G. A. (1956). The magical number seven, plus or minus two: Some limits on our capacity for processing information. *Psychological Review, 63,* 81–97.

Newell, A. (1990). *Unified theories of cognition.* Cambridge, MA: Harvard University Press.

Newell, A., & Simon, H. A. (1972). *Human problem solving.* Englewood Cliffs, NJ: Prentice-Hall.

Qin, Y., & Simon, H. A. (1990). Laboratory replication of scientific discovery processes. *Cognitive Science, 14,* 281–312.

Richman, H. B., Staszewski, J. J., & Simon, H. A. (1995). Simulation of expert memory using EPAM IV. *Psychological Review, 102,* 305–330.

Simon, D. P., & Simon, H. A. (1978). Individual differences in solving physics problems. In R. S. Siegler (Ed.), *Children's thinking: What develops?* (pp. 325–348). Hillsdale, NJ: Lawrence Erlbaum Associates.

Simon, H. A. (1976). The information storage system called "human memory." In M. R. Rosenzweig & E. L. Bennett (Eds.), *Neural mechanisms of learning and memory* (pp. 79–96). Cambridge, MA: MIT Press.

Simon, H. A., & Lea, G. (1974). Problem solving and rule induction: A unified view. In L. W. Gregg (Ed.), *Knowledge and cognition* (pp. 105–127). Hillsdale, NJ: Lawrence Erlbaum Associates.

Zhang, G., & Simon, H. A. (1985). STM capacity for Chinese words and idioms: Chunking and the acoustical loop hypothesis. *Memory and Cognition, 13,* 202–207.

7

Expertise in Reading

Richard K. Wagner
Florida State University
Keith E. Stanovich
Ontario Institute for Studies in Education

The programmatic study of expertise over the last quarter century has resulted in remarkable progress. By coaxing the phenomenon of expertise into the laboratory, and by following it into the field using reproducible scientific methods, a growing body of substantiated facts and theory have begun to displace popular mythology about experts and expert performance.

Given our topic of the acquisition of expert performance, one of the best and most important examples of the displacement of myths by facts and theory is advances in our knowledge about the necessity of long-term, intense training for the development of expert levels of performance. Beginning with Simon and Chase's (1973) observation that no one attains the level of Grandmaster in chess without a decade of intense preparation, and now extending across a wide range of domains (Bloom, 1985; Ericsson & Charness, 1994; Ericsson, Krampe, & Tesch-Römer, 1993), it is clear that even the most eminent individuals required an extended period of intense preparation before exhibiting expert levels of performance—despite popular folk accounts to the contrary.

This important finding has implications that extend beyond the study of expertise proper. If the situation were otherwise, and experts were freaks of nature whose achievements in the womb surpassed what 99.9% of us could ever hope to achieve in our lifetime, and who possessed qualitatively different supermechanisms of acquisition, there would seem to be few implications of the study of expertise to the study of normal human development. The suggestion that expert performance requires years of hard work and involves perhaps a more intense and more sustained application of the same acquisition mechanisms responsible for the attainment of more ordinary levels of performance (Ericsson et al., 1993) implies that the study of expertise is directly relevant to the study of human development broadly defined, providing an opportunity to observe developmental mechanisms functioning at maximal efficiency.

However, if a decade of intense preparation is necessary for expert levels of performance, is it sufficient? Were any of us to be switched at birth with Bobby Fischer or Bo Jackson or Steffi Graf, would we come at all close to duplicating their accomplishments? Despite the remarkable progress just alluded to in our understanding of the necessity of an extended period of intense preparation for the attainment of expert levels of performance, largely intractable limitations in existing data make attempts to answer the question of the sufficiency of such preparation speculative at best.

One cannot really do a prospective, developmental study of 50 million individuals to obtain an ultimate sample of 50 individuals whose level of performance is 1 in a million. Consequently, the majority of expertise studies begin at the end, identifying experts and then either working backward via retrospective, correlational studies, or working laterally via expert–novice comparisons or individual difference analyses.

The main problem with drawing sufficiency conclusions from such data is selection bias. Individuals who do well in the early phase of training may self-select, or be selected by authorities who limit access to elite training and performance opportunities. If individuals at increasingly advanced levels of training and performance represent an increasingly selective sample, it becomes problematic to make inferences about causal influences from correlations between level of performance and variables representing either environmental (e.g., practice) and genetic (e.g., genetic similarity) influences.

Because of limitations in the existing data for drawing conclusions about the sufficiency of particular environmental or genetic influences for the attainment of expert levels of performance, a more realistic goal for the conference on which the volume is based with respect to this issue would seem to be to identify what kind of program of study would be required potentially to contribute to current knowledge.

Individuals who scan the table of contents of this volume might be surprised by the inclusion of a chapter on reading. Reading is not the prototypic domain of expert performance that is represented by domains such as chess, music, art, mental calculation, and various sports. Why include a chapter on reading? Frankly, we initially asked ourselves the same question. We agreed to participate more on the basis of the challenge and novelty associated with the enterprise relative to what we and other reading researchers typically do, than we did because we thought that reading belonged. Although it may well be a rationalization in response to taking on this challenge, we have emerged believing the field of reading does have something to offer the study of expertise. With perhaps more than a little imagination and suspension of usual levels of critical disbelief, one can view schooling as providing the natural developmental study previously described, in which millions of children undergo years of preparation to achieve fluent levels of reading. We also believe that the study of expertise, and the results of this conference in particular, have something to offer the field of reading. A comparison of what is known about the acquisition of expertise in various domains with how reading is taught may suggest ways in which reading instruction might be improved.

By way of organization, our chapter is divided into four parts. In the first part, we address basic issues about defining expertise in the domain of reading. In the second part, we consider evidence that individual differences in prerequisite language abilities result in children being differentially prepared to profit from beginning reading instruction and achieving differential success at early reading. In the third part, we consider evidence of the effects of differential learning experiences—due in part to differential early success and in part to other factors—on subsequent reading skill. In the fourth and final part, we consider more general issues that arise when viewing reading from the perspective of the acquisition of a domain of expertise.

AN INTRODUCTION TO EXPERTISE IN READING

Because reading is not a typical domain for the study of expertise, we begin by taking up the issue of a working definition of expertise in reading. This requires attention to defining expertise and reading.

Defining Expertise

The predominant strategy for defining an expert has been in terms of individual differences. For example, an expert might be defined as someone who falls in the top 5% of performers in a domain. Thus, Ericsson and Smith (1991) suggested that nearly all human endeavors are characterized by some who stand out from the majority, and they characterized the study of expertise in terms of seeking to "understand and account for what distinguishes outstanding individuals in a domain from less outstanding individuals in that domain, as well as from people in general" (p. 2).

A working definition of expertise based on individual differences is sensible under assumptions about the fundamental nature of expertise that are common to traditional domains of expertise, but may be less sensible under assumptions that apply to the domain of reading. For example, seeking to understand what distinguishes outstanding individuals from the majority as an approach to studying expertise is sensible if one assumes that (a) expertise is largely inherited rather than acquired, and that the distribution of the inherited characteristics that result in expert performance is narrow rather than broad based; or (b) expertise is largely acquired, but access to the environmental conditions or training opportunities necessary for the development of expertise is restricted rather than universal. In either case, one would expect to find a small percentage of individuals who would stand out from the majority, and what distinguishes these individuals from the majority would be central to understanding their expertise.

However, what if expertise is largely inherited, but the distribution of inherited characteristics that result in expert performance is broad based? Or what if expertise is largely acquired, but nearly everyone has access to the requisite environmental conditions or training opportunities required to develop expert levels of performance? The resources required to develop expert levels of performance are considerable, and society at large has no reason to ensure that all of its members can, say, play a scratch game of golf or a competitive hand of bridge. In contrast, basic skills such as literacy are highly valued in modern societies, to the point that 13 or more years of free public school instruction are made available to nearly everyone in a number of countries.

Expertise demonstrated by the majority of individuals, as opposed to a small minority, is precluded by working definitions of expertise based on individual differences. Yet to the extent that expertise is acquired, and to the extent that requisite environmental conditions or training opportunities are provided broadly, there is no reason to expect that a small percentage of individuals would stand out from the majority for any reason other than random error. Consequently, one would not want to base the field of expertise on the study of what distinguishes such individuals from the majority.

Regardless of the truth or falsity of any one set of fundamental assumptions about the nature of expertise, the important point is that working definitions of expertise are rooted in sometimes tacit assumptions about the fundamental nature of expertise. If it should turn out that these tacit assumptions are wrong for a particular domain, what are the alternatives?

For the case of reading, two additional approaches to defining expertise would appear equally sensible to one based on individual differences. The first is to define expertise in terms of developmental, as opposed to individual differences. For example, we might define expert performance to be performance at a level that is 5 (or 10 or 15) standard deviations above the mean performance shown by individuals with a year of training. A second approach is to define expertise in terms of mastery of performance-based criteria, such as reading material of a given level of readability with a specified reading rate and level of comprehension. Neither of these approaches would preclude expert levels of performance attained by a majority of participants in a domain.

Defining Reading

Defining reading has been a surprisingly contentious undertaking. On the one hand, some have argued that the primary subject matter for the study of reading is the process of decoding print (Crowder & Wagner, 1992). Of course, reading nearly always is done for comprehension, but a lot of comprehension occurs without reading, as when understanding speech. Similar comprehension processes appear to operate regardless of whether the communication channel involves print, oral language, or pictures. What is unique to reading is decoding printed words on a page. Were we to pick up a book on Braille, we would not expect it to contain chapters on metaphor, inference, and story comprehension, despite the fact that readers of Braille do all of these things when reading.

On the other hand, some have argued that the primary subject matter for the study of reading is comprehension, and that reading is best conceptualized as thinking with a book in one's hand (Goodman, 1967; Smith, 1971, 1973; Thorndike, 1917).

From the point of view of the acquisition of expertise, there is no compelling reason to exclude either prelexical decoding processes—the part of reasoning that involves translating print to pronunciation and meaning—or postlexical comprehension processes—the part of reading that involves understanding and other kinds of reasoning about what has been read (Stanovich & Cunningham, 1991).

In the next two sections, we review evidence about the acquisition of reading skill. In a nutshell, we suggest that children begin reading instruction being differentially prepared to profit from it, primarily due to individual differences in prerequisite language abilities. These differences play a role in differential early success at learning to read. Differential early success and other factors result in differences in learning experiences that affect subsequent success at reading.

DIFFERENTIAL ABILITY TO PROFIT FROM INSTRUCTION

When children begin reading instruction, they vary on any number of intellectual, linguistic, personality, and background variables. Among these many variables, individual differences in phonological processing appear to be particularly important determiners of the ease with which beginning reading skills will be acquired.

Phonological processing refers to using the phonological or sound structure of oral language when processing oral and written language (Jorm & Share, 1983; Wagner & Torgesen, 1987). Spoken words represent combinations of basic sounds or *phonemes*. Taking English for example, there are roughly 30 to 45 basic phonemes, depending on the classification system used. Of the nearly infinite number of possible combinations of phonemes, only a relatively small number actually occur, and most combinations of phonemes occur in multiple words. Thus, *bat* and *cat* each contain three phonemes, the latter two of which are shared. This fact is represented by their spellings, which have different initial letters and identical medial and final letters, because the spellings in alphabetic orthographies such as English represent sound as well as meaning.

Developmental Studies of Normal Acquisition

Developmental and individual differences in phonological processing abilities appear to be causally related to the acquisition of reading skills, although the direction, magnitudes, and underlying mechanisms responsible for such causal relations have yet to be established (Ball & Blachman, 1988; Brady & Shankweiler, 1991; Bradley & Bryant, 1985; Bryant, Bradley, MacLean, & Crossland, 1989; Byrne, Freebody, & Gates, 1992; Ehri, 1987; Ehri & Wilce, 1980; Lundberg, Frost, & Petersen, 1988; Perfetti, Beck, Bell, & Hughes, 1987; Stanovich, 1986; Treiman, 1991; Tunmer & Nesdale, 1985; Vellutino & Scanlon, 1987; Wagner, 1988; Wagner, Torgenson, Laughon, Simmons, & Rashotte, 1993; Wagner, Torgenson, & Rashotte, 1994; Wagner et al., 1995; Wagner & Torgesen, 1987).

We investigated causal relations between individual differences in phonological processing abilities and word-level reading skills were examined in a longitudinal correlational study of 216 children (Wagner et al., 1995). Three kinds of phonological processing abilities were assessed: phonological awareness (i.e., one's awareness and access to the phonological structure of oral language), phonological naming (i.e., retrieving and producing pronunciations for common stimuli), and phonological memory (i.e., phonological coding of information for brief storage). The three kinds of phonological processing abilities, word-level reading skills, and vocabulary were assessed annually from kindergarten through fourth grade, as the children developed from nonreaders to beginning readers and finally to fluent readers.

Individual differences in phonological processing abilities were remarkably stable from kindergarten through fourth grade. Structural equation models were constructed to assess the causal influences of individual differences in phonological processing abilities on subsequent individual differences in word-level reading for the time periods from kindergarten to second grade, first grade to third grade, and second grade to fourth grade. The results of primary interest are the structure coefficients presented in Table 7.1. The structure coefficient for a given exogenous causal variable represents the predicted change in word-level reading associated with a one-unit change in the causal variable, when the values of the other causal variables in the model are constant. In other words, structure coefficients provide estimates of the unique causal influence of each exogenous cause.

The proportion of variance accounted for indicates the proportion of total variance in word-level reading accounted for by the set of exogenous variables. The structural equation models included all of the exogenous causes listed in Table 7.1 as simultaneous predictors.

There were four main results of interest. First, for every time period, individual differences in phonological awareness exerted a causal influence on subsequent individual differences in word-level reading. Second, individual differences in naming and vocabulary exerted independent causal influences on subsequent individual differences in word-level reading initially, but with development, these influences faded in the face of the increasing stability of individual differences in word-level reading (i.e., the increasing autoregressive effect of prior word-level reading on subsequent word-level reading). Third, individual differences in phonological memory did not exert an independent causal influence on subsequent individual differences in word-level reading for any time period. Fourth, the proportion of total variance in word-level reading accounted for by the phonological processing and control variables was considerable for each time period, and it increased as children developed from beginning to fluent readers.

Quantifying and Analyzing Growth. Quantifying and analyzing growth in performance would seem to be an essential tool for testing alternative theories about the acquisition of expertise. The view that talent plays a primary role in the acquisition of expertise would imply that individuals would be characterized by marked individual differences in rates of growth that could not be accounted for by environmental variables such as amount of deliberate practice. Conversely, the view that environ-

TABLE 7.1
Causal Influences of Individual Differences in Phonological Processing Abilities, Vocabulary, and the Autoregressive Effect of Prior Reading (at K, 1st, and 2nd Grades) on Subsequent Individual Differences in Word-Level Reading (at 2nd, 3rd, and 4th Grades)

	Time Period		
Exogenous Causes	*K to 2nd*	*1st to 3rd*	*2nd to 4th*
Phonological processing variables			
Awareness	$.37^{***}$	$.29^{**}$	$.27^{***}$
Memory	.12	−.03	.07
Naming	$.25^{**}$	$.21^{**}$	.07
Control variables			
Vocabulary	.10	$.22^{***}$	−.01
Autoregressor	.02	$.27^{**}$	$.57^{***}$
Proportion of variance accounted for	.48	.64	.77

$*p < .05.$ $**p < .01.$ $***p < .001$

mental variables such as amount of deliberate practice play a primary role in the acquisition of expertise would imply that observed individual differences in rates of growth would be accounted for by such environmental variables.

Traditionally, attempts to quantify and analyze growth have relied on only two measurement points (i.e., pretest and posttest), with growth represented by a difference score or a residual change score. Although such scores provide unbiased estimates of growth, they often suffer from poor reliability for individual difference analyses and provide little information about the nature of growth (Rogosa, Brandt, & Zimowski, 1982; Willett, 1988), both of which are detrimental to understanding the acquisition of expert performance.

Growth curve modeling (also known as multilevel analysis or hierarchical linear modeling) has proven to be a powerful new method for quantifying and analyzing growth that largely overcomes the problems associated with difference scores and residual change scores (Bryk & Raudenbush, 1987; Rogosa et al., 1982; Willett, 1988; Willett & Sayer, 1994). Instead of having only two measurement points, multiple waves of data are collected. Three or more waves are sufficient for fitting linear growth curve models; four or more waves are sufficient for fitting nonlinear models.

Just as variability in observed scores obtained on a single occasion can be divided into true score variance and measurement error, growth in observed performance can be divided into true growth (i.e., true score change) and measurement error. Estimates of true growth parameters, their variances, and their reliabilities can be obtained.

Conceptually, growth curve modeling involves two levels of analysis. At the within-person level, growth parameters are calculated for each subject by regressing performance on an algebraic function of time, training trials, or some other relevant index. At the between-person level, individual differences in growth parameters over subjects are analyzed, and attempts are made to account for these individual differences by examining potential correlates of growth. Computationally, both levels of analysis proceed simultaneously, yielding more reliable estimates of growth parameters than would be obtained by performing separate ordinary least-squared regressions to solve with within-person and between-person models.

Growth curve modeling has proven to be a powerful new tool in developmental studies of the acquisition of reading skill. An example of the application of growth curve modeling applied to the development of word-level reading skills is provided by our longitudinal study of 216 children from kindergarten through fourth grade described previously. Five waves of annual assessment data were available. One reading variable of particular interest is decoding nonwords, which assesses children's mastery of the alphabetic code that links letters and sounds in alphabetic languages such as English. The results of growth curve modeling of children's development of nonword reading are presented in Table 7.2.

TABLE 7.2
Growth Curve Analysis for Nonword Decoding (Longitudinal Sample)

	Parameter Estimate		Parameter Variance		
	Value (SE)	p <	Value (SE)	p <	Reliability
Intercept	11.99 (0.42)	.001	33.08 (1.07)	.001	.93
Linear growth	6.65 (0.17)	.001	6.29 (0.13)	.001	.72
Quadratic growth	0.99 (0.09)	.001	0.59 (0.00)	.001	.20

The values in the parameter estimate column are the growth curve parameters. The intercept parameter is the true status (level of nonword reading) when time is equal to zero. In many studies, there is no actual origin of time, so the researcher can define time zero at some interesting or convenient point of the study. In the present analyses, time zero represents the midpoint of the study (i.e., performance in second grade), at which point the data indicate that students got about 12 items correct. The linear growth rate parameter represents the average yearly linear increase in true score, which is between six and seven items per year, and the quadratic growth rate parameter represents yearly nonlinear change in true score, which is about one item per year on average. The values in the parameter variance column represent the amount of true variance in growth curve parameters across subjects. This represents variance that might be accounted for by predictors representing characteristics of the children and their reading instruction. The results suggest substantial variability in both status and linear growth. The values in the reliability column represent the reliability of the growth curve parameters. Reliabilities are substantial for the intercept and linear growth, but not for quadratic growth. The reliability for linear growth is higher than the typical reliabilities for difference scores, showing the advantage of multiple waves of data collection.

We are carrying out many analyses to determine what accounts for individual differences in growth curve parameters. For present purposes, we just present results for two predictors obtained in kindergarten: phonological awareness (a phoneme elision task in which children listen to a word and then say it after deleting a target phoneme), and for control purposes, verbal aptitude (Stanford–Binet Vocabulary score). We used these variables to predict individual differences in the two reliable growth curve parameters—intercept and linear growth. Variability in the intercept was predicted by both initial levels of phonological awareness (.857, $p < .001$) and of verbal aptitude (.438, $p < .01$), with both variables being used in a simultaneous regression model. Thus, the effects of initial level of phonological awareness on second-grade status in nonword decoding were independent of those of verbal aptitude. Variability in linear growth also was predicted by both variables (.232, $p < .01$, and .192, $p < .05$, respectively).

Developmental Studies of Dyslexic Readers

Despite documented provision of adequate instruction, adequate aptitude, socioeconomic opportunity, and no known visual, hearing, motor, or emotional handicaps, a small percentage of children (i.e., 3–5%) have a remarkably difficult time learning to read. The most seriously impaired will fail to develop a functional level of literacy during their lifetime.

For many years, the consensus was that children with reading disabilities (a) had problems that resulted from minimal brain dysfunction or damage, (b) were three times more likely to be male than female, (c) were represented by a lump in the bottom of the normal distribution of readers, and (d) demonstrated "signature" behaviors such as reversing the letters b and d and "scatter" in cognitive profiles from tests such as the Wechsler scales. These characteristics suggested that children with reading disabilities were different from children who did not have reading problems and from children whose reading problems were accompanied by generalized poor performance (i.e., garden-variety poor readers).

After many years of hard work, it is clear that many aspects of the traditional view of reading disabilities are incorrect (Calfee, 1977; DeFries, Olson, Pennington, & Smith, 1991; Share, McGee, McKenzie, Williams, & Silva, 1987; Shaywitz, Escobar, Shaywitz, Fletcher, & Makugh, 1992; Vellutino, 1979). For example, children with reading disabilities are no more likely to reverse letters such as *b* and *d* than are normal readers who are matched with the reading-disabled children in reading level. Reversing letters is something commonly done by children who are just learning to read. Recent large-scale epidemiological studies indicate that the incidence of reading disabilities is more comparable for males and females than suggested by the three-to-one ratio of males to females, the latter being an artifact of referral rates. Boys who have reading problems are more likely to be noticed and be referred for evaluation than are girls, perhaps because of concomitant behavior problems. It also appears to be the case that reading-disabled children do not represent a discontinuous lump in a normal distribution of reading skill, but rather just the bottom end of a normal distribution.

The main problems of reading-disabled children have been localized to the level of word reading, as opposed to reading in context or comprehension (Perfetti, 1985; Stanovich, 1988b; Vellutino, 1979). The most likely origin of these word-level reading problems is a deficit in phonological processing, and poor readers have similar phonological processing problems regardless of whether their reading level is discrepant from their IQ (i.e., the classic, specifically impaired child) or not discrepant from their IQ (i.e., the garden-variety poor reader; Fletcher et al., 1994; Stanovich & Siegel, 1994). That a deficit in phonological processing is a hallmark of poor readers provides further evidence of causal relations between the development of phonological processing abilities and the acquisition of beginning reading skills.

A theoretical framework that incorporates the main results of the literature on the phonological basis of disabled reading is the phonological core–variable difference model of individual differences in reading (Stanovich, 1988a). The phonological core refers to the fact that poor readers have deficits in phonological processing, regardless of whether their reading performance is discrepant from their IQ. The variable difference refers to the fact that what differentiates poor readers who are not IQ discrepant from those who are is the presence of additional, broad linguistic and cognitive deficits relative to their chronological age-match peers.

A phenomenon of the complexity of reading disabilities obviously represents the long-term joint actions, and probable interactions, of a multitude of genetic and environmental influences (Plomin & Bergman, 1991). We briefly consider genetic influences here, reserving the issue of environmental influences on the development of reading skill for the next section.

The familial nature of reading disabilities was recognized at the turn of the century by Thomas (1905, cited in DeFries & Gillis, 1993), when he noted the frequency with which more than one member of a family was affected. For example, one severely impaired child who was unable to learn to read had five siblings and a parent who were also unable to learn to read.

The familial nature of reading disabilities has been demonstrated by a number of family studies and twin studies (see DeFries & Gillis, 1993, for a review of this literature). Olson, Forsberg, and Wise's (1994) latest analysis of the Colorado reading-disabled twin study provides evidence of the joint effects of genetic and environmental influences on basic reading skills. This large data set includes data from 459 twin pairs with at least one twin having evidence of a reading problem, with another 297 twin pairs with no evidence of reading problems available as controls. For word reading, the genetic influences ($h^2g = .47$, $SE = .09$) and shared environmental influences ($c^2g = .48$, $SE = .11$) were significant and comparable in magnitude. Variance attributable to nonshared environmental influences and test error was negligible. For nonword reading, a task that is particularly difficult for children with reading disabilities, genetic influences ($h^2g = .59$, $SE = .12$) were greater than shared environmental influences ($c^2g = .27$, $SE = .12$), although both were significant. Variance attributable to nonshared environmental influences and test error again was negligible. These results, along with those of a large number of other studies (see DeFries & Gillis, 1993), indicate important roles for genetic and environmental influences on the development of basic reading skills among children with reading disabilities.

Recent work has focused on localizing the origin of genetic influences to particular chromosomes. The approach involves searching for quantitative trait loci by comparing patterns of reading performance over family members with patterns of characteristics (e.g., levels of a particular serum protein) linked to known DNA markers. Results from a kindred sibling sample of 358 individuals from 19 families isolated a quantitative trait locus on a small region of Chromosome 6. A follow-up study using 50 families drawn from the Colorado twin study confirmed this result (Cardon et al., 1994; Gayan et al., in press).

The Case of Expert Reading

The picture that we have described so far about the acquisition of reading skills is limited to basic skill acquisition for normally developing or impaired readers. Is the picture different for the case of expert reading?

As in most areas, examples exist of kinds of readers whose performance is remarkably different from most others. In this section we review two examples of expert reading performance, and consider the issue of whether individuals who demonstrate such performance show qualitative as well as quantitative differences in acquisition or performance.

Speed Reading.   Advertisements for speed-reading courses routinely guarantee that an individual can triple his or her reading rate with no loss of comprehension. A typical adult reads material of average difficulty for comprehension at a rate of roughly 250 words per minute. Wood (1963) claimed that graduates of her speed reading program routinely read at a rate of 1,300 words per minute with no loss in comprehension. Even more staggering claims have been made, including reading rates as high as 100,000 words per minute. This would correspond to reading *Gone With the Wind* in about 6 minutes.

How is such performance possible? Most speed reading programs employ one or more of the following strategies: (a) learning to see larger areas of print in a single fixation than readers do normally; (b) eliminating subvocalization (i.e., pronouncing words to oneself); (c) using the index finger to guide the eyes down the page, often in a zigzag motion, in support of the first two strategies; and (d) reading aggressively, by making inferences about what will come next and by not being obsessed about understanding every point.

How fast should it be possible to read? Crowder and Wagner (1992) used data from various eye-movement studies of normal readers to provide a ballpark answer to this question. When reading, the eyes do not move smoothly but rather are characterized by fixations, during which information is available to the eyes, and rapid ballistic jumps called saccades, during which little if anything on the page is in focus. Normal fixations last about 240 milliseconds, or roughly 4 per second. During a fixation, information is available as far as from 5 to 10 letter positions to the right of the fixation point (for orthographies that are read left to right such as English), depending on the kind of information (i.e., letter identity vs. word length). These data come from normal readers; perhaps some readers can do better. Let us be generous then and allow for the possibility of making five fixations per second, and access to 15 letter positions or three words at each fixation.

This would result in an estimated reading rate of 15 words per second, or 900 words per minute as an upper limit on performance.

Typical observed reading rates are much less. Carver (1990) analyzed the performance of the college senior normative sample of the Nelson–Denny Reading Test, reporting mean rates of 300 and 290 words per minute, respectively, for Forms E and F. With corresponding standard deviations of 103 and 81 words per minute for the two forms of the test, less than 2% read at a rate greater than 480 words per minute, and less than 1% exceeded 600 words per minute.

Perhaps the best study of speed readers yet to be reported is a study by Carver (1985). Carver began with a nationwide search to find the best speed readers. He followed up newspaper articles about reading feats and contacted advocates of speed-reading programs. Potential subjects were offered honoraria of $200 to $500 plus paid expenses as inducements to participate in a reading study. Some well-known speed readers refused the offer. S. B., a speed reader shown in a Paul Harvey film reading at a rate of 90,000 words per minute declined because she was out of practice. G. P., who had been described in a newspaper article as having a rate of 203,000 words per minute, refused to participate, citing possible eye strain.

Carver was able to persuade some speed readers to participate in his study, including an individual whose records from a speed-reading program indicated a reading rate of 81,000 words per minute with 65% accuracy in comprehension. For comparison purposes, three groups of superior readers were added to the study: college readers who achieved the highest scores on a reading screening test, professionals such as copyeditors and journal editors whose jobs required a great deal of reading, and individuals who had obtained perfect scores on the reading sections of the Graduate Record Exam or the Scholastic Aptitude Test.

The results of an extensive battery of testing were that the reading rates for the four groups ranged from 250 to 450 words per minute, when subjects knew their comprehension would be tested. Note that these figures fall well below our upper bound estimate of 900 words per minute. One exception to these results was that the reading rate of the speed readers matched the upper bound estimate of 900 words per minute, but only when the speed readers knew that their rate was being measured and that their comprehension would not be tested.

Just and Carpenter (1987) studied eye movements of graduates of the Evelyn Wood Reading Dynamics course. They found that, compared to normal readers who fixate just about every word, speed readers skipped over words in an unselective fashion, ignoring crucial and trivial words alike. The speed readers read at a rate of 700 words per minute, but at a cost of impaired comprehension relative to a group of normal readers.

Finally, Homa (1983) tested two graduates of the American Speedreading Academy whose reported reading rates were in excess of 100,000 words per minute. On the reading tasks they were given, the two speed readers recorded rates of 15,000 and 30,000 words per minute. Unfortunately, they exhibited almost no comprehension. Homa concluded that the "only note-worthy skill exhibited by the two speed-readers was a remarkable dexterity in page-turning" (p. 126; cited in Carver, 1990).

Precocious Reading.   Most of us learned to read sometime after our fifth birthday. In the United States, reading instruction begins in earnest at 6 years of age. Some other industrialized nations begin reading instruction a year or two later. However, some precocious readers either learn to read at a remarkably earlier age or acquire reading skills at a remarkably faster rate than their peers once formal reading instruction has begun.

What differentiates such precocious readers from their nonprecocious age-mates and from older, reading-matched samples? Compared to age-mates, precocious readers are likely to be somewhat above average in verbal aptitude, short-term memory, and letter naming speed (Jackson, 1992; Jack-son, Donaldson, & Cleland, 1988). However, children who are precocious with respect to verbal language (e.g., early talkers) show only a low incidence of precocious reading (Crain-Thoreson & Dale, 1992; Jackson, 1992).

In an ambitious and comprehensive study, Jackson, Donaldson, and Mills (1993) compared the performance of 116 postkindergarten precocious readers with that of 123 second-grade children who were mostly above-av-erage readers who matched the precocious readers in reading level. A total of 29 measures of reading or reading-related variables were obtained. The data were analyzed using confirmatory factor analysis and structural equa-tion modeling in an effort to determine the extent to which the precocious readers differed from reading-matched controls. The results were no differ-ences between the groups. In other words, the structure of precocious readers' reading and reading-related abilities is identical to that of older nonprecocious readers.

Precocious readers are likely to remain above-average readers during their elementary school years but their advantage in reading compared to their peers diminishes over the years. Individual differences are apparent, with some precocious readers maintaining a considerable advantage in reading over their peers, and others not. Precocious readers most likely to maintain their reading advantage are those with the highest kindergarten levels of verbal aptitude and reading skill (Mills & Jackson, 1990). In general, precocious readers appear to become literate in much the same way as their peers, only faster.

In summary, our analysis of the cases of speed reading and precocious reading and disabled reading suggests that these examples of atypical reading performance do not represent different patterns of skill acquisition with the exception of rate. Speed readers show no evidence of superhuman reading powers (with the possible exception of skill at page turning). Precocious readers appear to acquire reading skills much the same way that nonprecocious readers do with the exception of a faster rate of learning.

THE ROLE OF DIFFERENTIAL LEARNING
EXPERIENCES

Much of the research on the acquisition of reading skill has focused on relations between various cognitive characteristics and reading performance, or on the differential effectiveness of different approaches to teaching reading. However, relatively little research has been carried out that attempts to quantify amount of reading practice and instruction, and then examines the effects of absolute amounts of instruction and practice on reading performance and on other cognitive characteristics.

Part of the problem for those seeking to do such studies is the difficulty associated with quantifying amounts of reading instruction and practice, relative to the ease with which cognitive characteristics and reading performance have been measured using brief tasks and tests. One cannot simply use number of days or years of school attended as a proxy for amount of reading instruction and practice. For example, despite the emphasis on reading in the elementary school years, it has been estimated that less that 10 minutes per day involves reading on the part of a child that is monitored by a teacher who provides feedback. This is an outgrowth of the reading group approach to reading instruction, in which the teacher works with a small group of children at a time. When the teacher is working with one reading group, the other children in the class are given worksheets to complete. A second problem with quantifying reading instruction and practice is that a good bit of reading practice happens outside the classroom, at least for some children.

Attempts to quantify amounts of reading activity outside the classroom have relied on one of three approaches. The first approach involves standard questionnaire techniques that ask children and/or their parents to provide estimates of the amount of reading outside the classroom (Ennis, 1965; Nell, 1988; Stanovich & West, 1989; Walberg & Tsai, 1984). Unfortunately, such questionnaires have been plagued by a number of problems (Cunningham & Stanovich, 1991), chief among them being poor reliability and a tendency to overestimate the amount of reading that actually takes place because it is socially desirable to do so (Ennis, 1965; Sharon, 1973–1974).

A second approach involves the use of diaries (Allen, Cipielewski, & Stanovich, 1992; Anderson, Wilson, & Fielding, 1988; Greaney, 1980; Greaney & Hegarty, 1987). In these studies, daily diaries were filled out by children in order to estimate amounts of time spent reading. When carefully implemented, the diary method can minimize the reliability problem noted for the standard questionnaire techniques because the method involves recording minutes of time spent in reading and other activities rather than making a more subjective ballpark estimate. However, the diary method would appear to be susceptible to socially desirable responding. Self-reports of book reading by adults are known to be distorted by social desirability, but the extent of such effects for children's diary records of reading is unknown. An additional problem associated with the diary method is the extensive cooperation, commitment, and effort required.

A third approach involves using checklists that employ a signal detection methodology. Stanovich and West (1989) developed two such measures, the Author Recognition Test (ART) and the Magazine Recognition Test (MRT). The measures involved lists of either authors or magazine titles embedded among foils (i.e., names of nonexistent authors or magazines). The subject's task is to identify the true authors or magazine titles. Relative to the two previous approaches, the checklist approach avoids the problem of socially desirable responding and, unlike the diary method, can be completed in a single 5- to 10-minute session.

The results of studies employing these approaches indicate that amounts of reading practice affect subsequent reading performance. For example, Anderson et al. (1988) reported a study that related amount of reading during nonschool hours to growth in reading skills. Fifth-grade children maintained diary records of the amount of time spent reading and performing other out-of-school activities. The data were analyzed using a hierarchical regression approach in which the first step was to predict the criterion variable of fifth-grade reading comprehension, with second-grade reading comprehension as the sole predictor. In a second step, amount of diary-recorded reading experience was added as a second predictor. This logic controls for spurious additional variables such as IQ that might covary with amount of reading and reading comprehension, and avoids the problem that the most able readers tend also to be the most voracious readers. The results were that amount of reading explained a significant amount of variance in fifth-grade reading independent of the predictive power of second-grade reading. Note that this approach provides a conservative assessment of the effects of reading experience. Second-grade reading skill presumably might already have been influenced by differences in reading experience, and by entering reading experience second in the regression equation, some variance that might have been attributable to print exposure if a fully specified longitudinal design beginning in kindergarten were used is attributed to the second-grade reading predictor erroneously (Cipielewski & Stanovich, 1992).

These results were replicated in a study of fifth graders by Allen et al., (1992) that used a diary method designed to be easier to use than that used by Anderson et al. (1988; e.g., required less time to complete; minimized need to add or subtract minutes or to convert hours to minutes). Time spent per day for the activities that were recorded are presented in Table 7.3. In addition to providing interesting information about how fifth graders spend their out of school time, the distributions were highly skewed. Consequently, median time for a variable such as reading books (5.0) was about half of the mean time (10.2), with the standard deviation (15.0)

TABLE 7.3
Time Spent per Day by Fifth-Grade Students in Various Activities

Activity	Minutes per Day		
	Mean	Medium	SD
Reading	21.3	16.0	19.4
Books	10.2	5.0	15.0
Comics	2.1	0.0	4.0
Other	5.8	3.5	8.4
Television	83.2	68.0	65.5
Eating	52.9	54.6	19.1
Homework	49.0	45.0	26.0
Fooling around	35.7	26.0	32.7
Playing outdoor games	25.7	18.0	25.2
Talking	17.0	13.6	12.9
Family activities	18.0	13.9	18.2
Playing indoor games	14.5	8.6	19.1
Practices	14.3	8.0	18.4
Hobbies	7.9	0.0	17.5
Dhores	6.6	5.0	6.4
Lessons	4.5	0.0	7.0
Others	62.6	60.0	35.0

Note. Adapted from Allen, Cipielewski, and Stanovich (1992).

exceeding the mean. The results of main importance from this study were that book reading time was predictive of vocabulary even after general academic performance was partialed out.

Some idea of how the highly skewed individual differences in self-chosen reading activities cumulate into differential exposure to words was provided in the Anderson et al. (1988) study. Table 7.4 presents the amount of book reading (in minutes) that children at various percentiles in self-chosen reading were engaged in. For example, the table indicates that the child at the 50th percentile in amount of book reading time was reading approximately 4.6 minutes per day, over six times as much as the child at the 20th percentile in amount of reading time (less than a minute daily). Or, to take another example, the child at the 80th percentile in amount of book reading time (14.2 minutes) was reading over 20 times as much as the child at the 20th percentile.

Anderson et al. (1988) estimated the children's reading rates and used these, in conjunction with the amount of reading in minutes per day, to extrapolate a figure for the number of words that the children at various percentiles were reading. These figures, presented in the far right of the table, illustrate the enormous differences in word exposure that are generated by children's differential proclivities toward reading. For example, the

TABLE 7.4
Variation in Amount of Independent Book Reading

%	Minutes	Words per Year
98	65.0	4,358,000
90	21.1	1,823,000
80	14.2	1,146,000
70	9.6	622,000
60	6.5	432,000
50	4.6	282,000
40	3.2	200,000
30	1.3	106,000
20	0.7	21,000
10	0.1	8,000
2	0.0	0

Note. Adapted from Anderson, Wilson, and Fielding (1988).

average child at the 90th percentile in book exposure reads almost 2.5 million words per year outside of school, over 46 times more words than the child at the 10th percentile, who is exposed to just 51,000 words outside of school during a year. Or, to put it another way, the entire year's out-of-school exposure for the child at the 10th percentile amounts to just 8 days' reading for the child at the 90th percentile!

What are the cognitive consequences of these enormous differences in practice? One such consequence was already mentioned—practice builds expertise in reading comprehension itself. The Anderson group demonstrated this using a hierarchical regression logic and employing the activity diary method of measuring individual differences in print exposure. Cipielewski and Stanovich (1992) replicated this finding using the recognition checklist methodology. The participants in the latter investigation were 82 children in the third grade (8–9-year-olds) who had been administered the comprehension subtest of the Iowa Tests of Basic Skills (ITBS). Two years later as fifth graders, these same children were administered the reading comprehension section of the Stanford Diagnostic Reading Test and again the ITBS. Measures of exposure to print were also administered to the children in Grade 5.

Table 7.5 displays the results of a hierarchical forced-entry regression analysis in which fifth-grade reading comprehension is the criterion variable. Third-grade reading comprehension was entered first into the equation, followed by a measure of the children's exposure to print outside of school. Thus, the analyses essentially address the question of whether exposure to print can predict individual differences in growth in reading comprehension from third grade to fifth grade. In the first analysis, with the Stanford reading comprehension test as the criterion variable, the measure of print exposure accounted for 11.0% unique variance after the third-grade comprehension level had been partialed. In the second analysis, with the Iowa comprehension subtest as the criterion variable, print exposure accounted for 7.4% unique variance. In both cases the unique variance accounted for by print exposure was statistically significant.

It is important to emphasize again the conservatism of the analyses that have been presented. If print exposure does indeed contribute to growth in comprehension ability, then some of its effects are already in the covariate (third-grade comprehension ability) because it is highly unlikely that the effects of print exposure begin only after the third-grade year. Thus, the analysis is focused on growth from third to fifth and fifth grade only. Longer time periods would probably apportion more variance to print exposure than did these analyses.

The Role of Reading Experience in Building Vocabulary and Declarative Knowledge

The findings of Anderson et al. (1988) and Cipielewski and Stanovich (1992) indicate a unique contribution of print exposure to the explanation of reading comprehension differences. However, reading comprehension is an extremely broad skill. A large body of research has demonstrated that reading comprehension is linked to a wide range of verbal abilities: Vocabulary, syntactic knowledge, metalinguistic awareness, verbal short-term memory, phonological awareness, speech production, inferential comprehension, semantic memory, and verbal fluency form only a partial list (Cunningham, Stanovich, & Wilson, 1990; Gathercole & Baddeley, 1993; Gernsbacher, 1993; Kamhi & Catts, 1989; Oakhill & Garnham, 1988; Siegel & Ryan, 1988; Stanovich & Cunningham, 1991; Stanovich, Nathan, & Zolman, 1988; Vellutino & Scanlon, 1987; Wagner & Torgesen, 1987). This raises the question of whether print exposure can be linked to any of these specific

TABLE 7.5
Hierarchical Regressions Predicting Fifth-Grade Reading
Comprehension

Step	Variable	R	R^2	R^2 Change
Fifth Grade Stanford Reading Comprehension				
1. Iowa Comprehension (3rd)	.645	.416	.416	54.06[*]
2. Print Exposure	.725	.526	.110	17.38[*]
Fifth Grade Iowa Reading Comprehension				
1. Iowa Comprehension (3rd)	.545	.297	.297	33.78[*]
2. Print Exposure	.609	.371	.074	9.25[*]

[*]$p < .01$.

subcomponents of reading skill. In this section, we consider how reading experience has been linked to various knowledge bases and verbal skills that support efficient comprehension. In the next section, we review evidence indicating that reading experience may be differentially linked to the subprocesses that support efficient word recognition.

In certain domains, reading is especially likely to be a substantial contributor to cognitive growth. For example, as a mechanism for building content knowledge structures (Glaser, 1984), reading seems to be unparalleled (Goody, 1977). The world's storehouse of knowledge is readily available for those who read, and much of this information is not usually obtained from other media (Comstock & Paik, 1991; Huston, Watkins, & Kunkel, 1989; Postman, 1985; West, Stanovich, & Mitchell, 1993; Zill & Winglee, 1990). Additionally, if we consider vocabulary to be one of the primary tools of verbal intelligence (Olson, 1986), then we have another mechanism by which print exposure may influence cognition because reading appears to be a uniquely efficacious way of acquiring vocabulary (Nagy & Anderson, 1984; Nagy & Herman, 1987; Stanovich, 1986, 1993). This is because there are differences in the statistical distributions of words that have been found between print and oral language (see Hayes, 1988; Hayes & Ahrens, 1988).

Thus, there are sound theoretical reasons for believing that print exposure is a particularly efficacious way of expanding a child's vocabulary and declarative knowledge. Indeed, there are significant zero-order correlations between exposure to print and performance on a variety of vocabulary and declarative knowledge measures (e.g., Allen et al., 1992; Anderson et al., 1988; West & Stanovich, 1991). But how should we interpret such correlations? There are numerous inferential problems when trying to assess the consequences of print exposure. Avid readers tend to be different from nonreaders on a wide variety of cognitive skills, behavioral habits, and background variables. Attributing any particular outcome uniquely to print exposure is extremely difficult. This problem is not dissimilar from the debate about the connection between domain knowledge and component processes in a variety of areas. As Keating and Crane (1990) stated it:

> The key finding from extensive work on various kinds of expertise is that level of expertise is closely related to higher performance on most measures of these underlying processes, from simple memory to advanced reasoning. . . . But this is precisely where the theoretical conflict arises: Which is causally primary—superior expertise or superior cognitive processes? The domain-specificity argument (at this level) is that as expertise is acquired, the cognitive processes which subserve it become more sophisticated. The domain-generality argument is that broadly superior cognitive processes give rise to the acquisition of various kinds of expertise. (pp. 413–414)

Thus, we are led to ask, analogously, what is causally prior—extensive reading experience or the reading comprehension and vocabulary skills that are associated with extensive experience? So, for example, one view is that an extensive vocabulary is simply a concomitant of basic information-processing skills that are associated with superior reading ability. Sternberg (1985) stated such a view thusly: "Simply reading a lot does not guarantee a high vocabulary. What seems to be critical is not sheer amount of experience but rather what one has been able to learn from and do with that experience. According to this view, then, individual differences in knowledge acquisition have priority over individual differences in actual knowledge" (p. 307).

As illustrated earlier, a regression logic can be used to deal with the directionality and spurious variable problems illustrated in the Sternberg and Keating and Crane quotes. For example, measures of general cognitive ability can be regressed out before examining the relationship between print exposure and criterion variables. Or alternatively, reading comprehension ability can be used as an autoregressor and as a criterion variable as illustrated in the Cipielewski and Stanovich (1992) study discussed earlier and in Anderson et al. (1988). The logic of this analytic strategy is quite conservative because many times the analyses partialed out variance in abilities that are likely to be developed by print exposure itself (Stanovich, 1986, 1993). However, the explanatory ambiguities surrounding a variable such as print exposure seem to suggest that in the early stages of investigation the analyses should be structured in a "worst case" manner, as far as print exposure is concerned.

An example of investigation structured according to this logic is provided by Cunningham and Stanovich (1991) who studied 134 fourth-, fifth-, and sixth-grade children (9- to 13-year-olds) in order to examine whether print exposure accounts for differences in vocabulary development once controls for both general and specific (i.e., vocabulary-relevant) abilities were invoked. The analyses displayed in Table 7.6 illustrate some of the outcomes of this study. Three different vocabulary measures were employed as dependent variables: a word checklist measure of the written vocabulary modeled on the work of Anderson and Freebody (1983), a group-administered version of the Peabody Picture Vocabulary Test (PPVT), and a verbal fluency measure where the children had to output as many words as they could that fit into a particular category (e.g., things that are red; see Sincoff & Sternberg, 1987). Age was entered first into the regression equation, followed by scores on the Raven Progressive Matrices as a control for general intelligence.

As a second ability control more closely linked to vocabulary acquisition mechanisms, we entered phonological coding ability into the equation. A variable such as phonological coding skill might mediate a relationship between print exposure and a variable like vocabulary size in numerous ways. High levels of decoding skill—certainly a contributor to greater print exposure—might provide relatively complete verbal contexts for the induction of word meanings during reading. Decoding skill might also indirectly

TABLE 7.6
Unique Print Exposure Variance After Age, Raven,
and Phonological Coding Are Partialed

	R	R^2 Change	F to Enter
Written vocabulary			
Age	.103	.011	1.41
Raven	.457	.198	32.57*
Phonological coding	.610	.163	33.49*
Print exposure	.683	.094	22.52*
Oral Vocabulary			
Age	.230	.053	7.29*
Raven	.393	.101	15.60*
Phonological coding	.403	.008	1.21
Print exposure	.516	.104	18.19*
Verbal fluency			
Age	.043	.002	0.24
Raven	.231	.051	6.89*
Phonological coding	.477	.175	28.47*
Print exposure	.582	.111	21.02*

*$p < .01$.

reflect differences in short-term phonological storage that are related to vocabulary learning, particularly in the preschool years (Gathercole & Baddeley, 1989, 1993). Thus, print exposure and vocabulary might be spuriously linked via their connection with decoding ability: Good decoders do more reading and have the best context available for inferring new words. This spurious linkage is controlled by entering phonological coding into the regression equation prior to print exposure. If print exposure were only an incidental correlate of vocabulary because of its linkage with phonological coding skill, then print exposure would not serve as a unique predictor of vocabulary once phonological coding was partialed out. The results of the analyses displayed in Table 7.3 indicate that for each of the vocabulary measures, print exposure accounted for significant variance after the variance attributable to performance on the Raven and the phonological coding measure had been removed.

Stanovich and Cunningham (1992) conducted an even more stringent test of whether exposure to print is a unique predictor of verbal skill in a study of college students (see also Stanovich & Cunningham, 1993). Table 7.7 presents the results of this study. Here, two nonverbal measures of general ability were entered first in a hierarchical regression analysis—performance on a figural analogies test and on the Raven Matrices. Next, performance on the Nelson–Denny reading comprehension test was entered subsequent to the two nonverbal ability tasks but prior to the measure of print exposure. Here we have an example of the extreme conservatism of the analyses. As demonstrated in the Cipielewski and Stanovich (1992) study, contemporaneous comprehension ability carries some of the variance associated with print exposure at earlier periods in time. Thus, in some sense, these analyses are deliberately causally misspecified.

The results illustrated in Table 7.7 indicate that print exposure was able to account for additional variance in two measures of vocabulary (the Nelson–Denny vocabulary subtest and the PPVT), two measures of general knowledge (a measure of history and literature knowledge taken from the National Assessment of Educational Progress and a cultural literacy test), spelling, and verbal fluency, even after reading comprehension ability had been partialed along with nonverbal ability. In some cases, the unique variance explained was quite substantial. These results suggest that people who reading extensively are likely to be generic knowledge "experts" as well.

In the Stanovich and Cunningham (1992) study, the sample size was large enough to allow us to explore the consequences—in a correlational sense—of pitting general comprehension ability against print experience as predictors of cognitive outcomes in the verbal domain. The analysis takes advantage of the fact that, although print exposure is positively correlated with Nelson–Denny comprehension performance, the relationship is far from perfect. There are individuals who, despite having modest comprehension skills, seem to read avidly; and there are other individuals who, despite very good comprehension skills, seem not to exercise their abilities—so-called aliterates. This particular partitioning raises some interesting issues regarding the definition of expertise in the domain of reading. Who is the expert, someone who reads avidly but scores low on a test of reading comprehension or someone who scores highly on such a test but does not exercise their ability? We are tempted to react that the former person seems not to qualify for the term expert because they are not executing the target performance well (a fact we infer from the outcome of

TABLE 7.7
Unique Print Exposure Variance After Nonverbal Abilities and Reading Comprehension Ability Are Partialed Out

	R^2 Change					
Dependent Variable	1	2	3	4	5	6
1. Figural Analogies	.100[*]	.077[*]	.079[*]	.073[*]	.057[*]	.042[*]
2. Raven	.138[*]	.087[*]	.057[*]	.059[*]	.074[*]	.017
3. Comprehension	.230[*]	.129[*]	.222[*]	.227[*]	.208[*]	.045[*]
4. Print Exposure	.076[*]	.180[*]	.100[*]	.286[*]	.052[*]	.075[*]

Dependent Variables: 1 = Nelson–Denny Vocabulary, 2 = PPVT, 3 = History and Literature Knowledge (NAEP), 4 = Cultural Literacy Test, 5 = Spelling Composite, 6 = Verbal Fluency.
[*]$p < .001$.

the comprehension test). One would not consider a poor musician who practiced a lot to be an expert. On the other hand, reading is a very special sort of interface with the environment, providing unique opportunities to acquire declarative knowledge. It may be unique among the domains of expertise in having profound secondary effects.

What are the cognitive consequences for people who read frequently but are not good at it? In the Stanovich and Cunningham (1992) study, the sample of adults was classified according to a median split of performance on the Nelson–Denny comprehension subtest and a composite print exposure variable. The resulting 2 × 2 matrix revealed 82 subjects who were discrepant: 38 subjects who were low in print exposure but high in comprehension (LoPrint/HiComp) and 44 subjects who were high in print exposure but low in comprehension (HiPrint/LoComp). These two groups were then compared on all the variables in the study (see Table 7.8). Despite comprehension differences favoring the LoPrint/HiComp group, as well as nonverbal cognitive abilities favoring this group (they were also higher on the Raven), LoPrint/HiComp individuals were not superior on any of the other variables assessed in the study. In fact, on one measure of vocabulary (the PPVT) and one measure of general knowledge (a cultural literacy test) the HiPrint/LoComp group performed significantly better. As far as these declarative knowledge domains are concerned, avid readers who are poor comprehenders are as much "experts" as good readers who do not exercise their ability. Although inferences from these correlational analyses must be tentative, the results do suggest that low ability need not necessarily hamper the development of vocabulary and verbal knowledge as long as the individual is exposed to a lot of print.

In another study suggesting a compensatory role for print exposure in building knowledge bases for individuals with suboptimal basic processes, Stanovich, West, and Harrison (in press) compared the performance of 133

TABLE 7.8
Differences Between Subjects High in Comprehension Ability
but Low in Print Exposure (*N* = 38) and Subjects Low
in Comprehesion Ability but High in Print Exposure (*N* = 44)

Variable	LoPrint/HiComp	HiPrint/LoComp	t(80)
N–D Comprehension	25.3	20.9	−11.47**
Raven Matrices	10.7	9.0	−2.44*
Nelson–Denny Vocabulary	15.1	14.4	−0.94
Peabody Vocabulary	10.6	12.1	2.06*
History & Lit (NAEP)	12.7	13.4	0.99
Cultural Literacy	.396	.483	3.86**
Spelling Composite	.16	−.05	−1.12
Verbal Fluency	31.6	32.0	0.30

*$p < .05$. **$p < .001$.

college students (mean age = 19.1 years) and 49 older individuals (mean age = 79.9 years) on two general knowledge tasks, a vocabulary task, a working memory task, a syllogistic reasoning task, and several measures of exposure to print. The older individuals outperformed the college students on the measures of general knowledge and vocabulary, but did significantly less well than the college students on the working memory and syllogistic reasoning tasks. These results are consistent with the trend in the literature for crystallized abilities (knowledge and vocabulary) to continue to grow with age and for measures of fluid ability (e.g., working memory, syllogistic reasoning) to decline with age (Baltes, 1987; Horn, 1982, 1989; Horn & Hofer, 1992). However, a series of hierarchical regression analyses indicated that when measures of exposure to print were used as control variables, the positive relationships between age and vocabulary and age and declarative knowledge were eliminated (in contrast, the negative relationships between age and fluid abilities were largely unattenuated). The results suggest that, in the domain of verbal abilities, print exposure helps to compensate for the normally deleterious effects of aging.

Reading Experience and the Microprocesses of Word Recognition

Declarative knowledge bases and vocabulary are knowledge sources that serve central processes, according to the dichotomy between central and modular process popularized by Fodor (1983). In contrast, as indicated in our brief overview of the literature on reading disability, the proximal cause of reading disability resides largely in the process of word recognition, and word recognition in adult readers has been shown to have the properties of acquired modularity (Perfetti & McCutchen, 1987; Stanovich, 1990; Stanovich & Cunningham, 1991). We might thus ask whether reading experience also impacts the microprocesses that support efficient word recognition. Here it is useful to distinguish between phonological and orthographic coding processes—a distinction that looms large in the so-called dual-route theories that have been so influential in the area of reading disability (Olson et al., 1984; Olson, Kliegl, Davidson, & Foltz, 1985; Wagner & Barker, 1994). Phonological coding refers to the ability to turn orthographic segments into phonological codes and is indexed by such tasks as pseudoword naming (see Stanovich & West, 1989; Wagner & Barker, 1994). Orthographic coding refers to the ability to use familiar letter sequences to directly access the mental lexicon without phonological mediation and it is indexed by such tasks as having subjects select the correct homophone (e.g., rows, rose) for a particular context (see Stanovich & West, 1989; Wagner & Barker, 1994). Research has indicated that these two forms of processing are separable in analyses of individual differences (Barker, Torgesen, & Wagner, 1992; Cunningham & Stanovich, 1990, 1993; Stanovich & West, 1989: Wagner & Barker, 1994).

There is some suggestive research indicating that reading experience has a differential impact on these two subprocesses of word recognition. Olson and colleagues (Olson et al., 1994) included an index of print exposure—a checklist measure of book title recognition—in the battery of tasks given to the twins in the Colorado Reading Project. Of the four factors that emerged, two reflected the phonological coding and orthographic coding processes mentioned previously. The other two factors were an IQ dimension and a rapid naming factor. The measure of print exposure—the title recognition test—had its primary loading on the orthographic factor rather than the phonological factor.

The Olson et al. (1994) findings are consistent with other studies indicating that print exposure almost always displays significant correlations with orthographic tasks, but that its association with phonological processing is often nonsignificant. The results presented in Table 7.9 indicate that in a series of studies, the correlation of print exposure with phonological processing has consistently been quite small. This finding—that exposure to print is only modestly linked with the primary proximal mechanism (phonological coding) that is associated with reading disability—is consistent with the finding that reading disability is refractory to interventions that simply involve more exposure to print (Hatcher, Hulme, & Ellis, 1994; Lovett, Warren-Chaplin, Ransby, & Borden, 1990). Additionally, although difficulties in phonological processing have been unequivocally linked to reading disability (Fletcher et al., 1994; Share, 1995; Stanovich & Siegel, 1994), the existence of a subtype of reading disability with specific orthographic deficits has been a more controversial hypothesis (Berninger, 1994; Bowers & Wolf, 1993; Stanovich, 1992). A disability subtype defined by orthographic problems will clearly be a secondary subtype in quantitative terms. Likewise, the variance across the normal continuum that is explained

TABLE 7.9
Correlations Between Print Exposure and Phonological Processing

Study	Correlation
Barker, Torgeson, and Wagner (1992)	.02
	.24
Cunningham and Stanovich (1993)	.01
	.16
	−.04
Cunningham and Stanovich (1990)	.12
	−.04
Cipielewski and Stanovich (1992)	.31
	.17
Stanovich and West (1989)	.27
	.35

by orthographic factors is clearly smaller than that associated with phonological processing.

The relatively mild associations between print exposure and phonological coding may also relate to some discouraging facts about attempts to remediate the word deficits of poor readers through exposure. For example, Hogaboam and Perfetti (1978) gave third graders who were poor readers 18 exposures to pseudowords, which they pronounced after hearing the experimenter pronounce them. Even after 18 exposures, these less skilled readers were still several hundred milliseconds slower in naming the pseudoword than were skilled readers who saw the pseudoword for the first time! Lemoine, Levy, and Hutchinson (1993; see also Ehri & Wilce, 1983) observed an analogous outcome in a study in which third graders were trained on words rather than pseudowords.

READING AS A DOMAIN OF EXPERTISE

The results of these training studies do seem to indicate that, with regard to the word recognition processes of disabled readers, we are running into some relatively "hard-wired" cognitive limitations (this, of course, is not to deny the efficacy of treatment, which has been proven; see Clark, 1988; Felton, 1993; Hatcher et al., 1994). The issue of deficits in a (perhaps) modular subsystem that prevents some proportion of the population from ever attaining the level of expert performance (by either a developmental or a performance-based criterion) provokes thought about the question (raised in our introduction) of how definitions of reading might interact with notions of expertise in reading.

In two classic papers published over 50 years apart, both E. L. Thorndike (1917) and R. L. Thorndike (1973–1974) urged that, for most the most part, reading was best thought of as reasoning. Stanovich and Cunningham (1991) reviewed contemporary theories of reading and used this question—Is reading like reasoning?—as a framework for their survey. They argued that current theories of reading—as well as general theories of linguistic processing in cognitive science—strongly demarcate word recognition from comprehension processes (Fodor, 1983; Perfetti & McCutchen, 1987; Rayner & Pollatsek, 1989; Seidenberg, 1985; Stanovich, 1990; Stanovich & West, 1983). Although processes of word recognition interface—and undoubtedly overlap temporally—with comprehension processes, the theoretical conceptualization of these different levels of processing is divergent and serves to demarcate those aspects of reading that do resemble reasoning processes from those that do not.

Fodor's (1983) differentiation between modular and central processes is typical of the nature of this demarcation in cognitive science. According to Fodor (1983), a modular process is one that is informationally encapsulated:

The operation of the process is not controlled by higher level operations or supplemented by information from knowledge structures not contained in the module itself. All nonmodular processes—those that are not encapsulated—are termed *central processes*. Fodor (1983) viewed processes such as basic speech perception and face perception as candidates for modular input systems, but several theorists have advanced the concept of acquired modularity (Humphreys, 1985; Sternberg, 1985). Others have applied the modularity concept to the process of word recognition and its development (Perfetti & McCutchen, 1987; Stanovich, 1990; Stanovich & West, 1983).

Using these Fodorian distinctions, Stanovich and Cunningham (1991) argued for a revised version of Thorndike's (1973–1974) suggestion that we view "reading as reasoning." In the fluent reader, prelexical mechanisms are very stimulus constrained, and mainly execute via noncontrolled processing. Subsequent to input processing (to use Fodor's terms), reading begins to look much more like reasoning, but it is reasoning of a special type, because of the sequential arrangement of pre- and postlexical processes. That is, the modular input processes deliver the data that central processes of text-model construction must work with. The lexical entries activated by the input processes put severe constraints on the nature of the text model that can be constructed. Thus, if we conceive of processes such as text-model construction based on knowledge integration as "reasoning" processes, then they are subject to prior constraints that are unusually strong compared to the type of central processes that we might identify as involved in reasoning or problem solving. Stanovich and Cunningham (1991) argued that the proper metaphor would be to conceive of reading as a type of "constrained reasoning."

The key to optimal reading performance under this framework is an encapsulated and efficient word recognition module that rapidly delivers the contents of lexical entries to higher level comprehension processes. Of course, the encapsulation of the word recognition module is unlike some of Fodor's other domains (e.g., face recognition) in that it is acquired, and it is acquired through practice. However, as we have seen in the results of Lemoine et al. (1993), due to underlying phonological processing limitations, the attainment of expertise will be inordinately difficult for some people even with extensive practice (Ben-Dror, Pollatsek, & Scarpati, 1991; Bruck, 1992; Campbell & Butterworth, 1985). Thus, in reading, as in many of the other domains considered in this volume, some people will not become experts (even using developmental or performance-based criteria rather than individual differences criteria) despite extensive practice. But in some respects the situation in reading is very different. First, we have a much better handle on why this is the case (we have a great deal of knowledge about the developmental course, genetics, and environmental determinants of phonological processing; see Olson et al., 1994; Wagner et al., 1994). Second, we have done the natural experiment. Enough people have been given the requisite environmental conditions so that we know that a very large number of people can achieve developmental and/or performance-based criteria of expertise.

Two points we leave more as questions. First, to what extent does the model of reciprocal effects of practice that appears to characterize reading skill development characterize other areas as well? That is, in reviewing the work on the effects of print exposure, we seem to have traced a model whereby reading skill leads to greater engagement in reading activity, which in turn serves to develop some (but not all) of the subprocesses that subserve further increases in reading skill (vocabulary, developmental of an orthographic lexicon, etc.). It is fairly easy to imagine this feedback pattern working in other domains as well.

What is more difficult to conceptualize is how we should view some of the cognitive consequences of print exposure that may in turn have implications for other aspects of cognition. For example, we saw in several experiments illustrated earlier that print exposure is uniquely and strongly associated with increases in declarative knowledge. Recent theories of cognitive development have strongly emphasized the importance of domain knowledge as a determinant of information-processing efficiency (Alexander, 1992; Bjorklund, 1987; Ceci, 1990; Chi, 1985; Hoyer, 1987; Keil, 1984; Scribner, 1986). Research has amply demonstrated that it is difficult to accurately gauge information-processing efficiency without some knowledge of the subject's depth of familiarity with the stimulus domain (Ceci, 1990; Charness, 1989; Chi, Hutchinson, & Robin, 1989; Hall & Edmondson, 1992; Recht & Leslie, 1988; Schneider, Korkel, & Weinert, 1989; Walker, 1987; Yekovich, Walker, Ogle, & Thompson, 1990). Some basic processes can become so dependent on prior knowledge of the stimulus domain that it seems almost a misnomer to call them basic (see Ceci, 1990).

To the extent that we endorse cognitive theories that view individual differences in basic processing capacities as at least partly determined by differences in knowledge bases (e.g., Ceci, 1990), then print exposure becomes strongly implicated in such theories because it is a major mechanism determining individual differences in declarative knowledge. Thus, domain knowledge theories indirectly provide a mechanism through which print exposure influences cognitive efficiency in general. Print is simply a more distal factor that determines individual differences in knowledge bases, which in turn influence performance on a variety of "basic" information-processing tasks (see Ceci, 1990).

Such theorizing leads us to ponder again those subjects who read a considerable amount but who have very modest reading comprehension abilities as indicated by standardized tests. Chances are that the individuals who happen to be at the 49th percentile in level of trombone skill are not practicing the trombone hundreds of hours a year. These nonexpert trombone players will, due to their lack of practice, undoubtedly remain nonexpert trombone players. Furthermore, even if they were to engage in such practice, it is unclear what other cognitive effects playing the trombone would have. The case of reading is entirely different. Many individuals who are at the 49th percentile of reading skill do practice the skill hundreds of hours a year, and they expose themselves to millions of words a year. Whatever cognitive processes are engaged over word or word-group units (phonological coding, semantic activation, parsing, induction of new vocabulary items) are being exercised hundreds of times a day for these people. The research we reviewed here indicates that this amount of cognitive muscle flexing does have some effects on many aspects of verbal information processing.

Thus, the conjunction of two things makes reading as a domain somewhat unique. Individuals with very modest levels of reading ability practice an inordinate amount (at least compared to other domains) and this practice serves to develop a host of verbal skills. It remains to be explicated what this means for how we classify reading in the matrix of domains of expertise. Much remains to be learned, in addition, about the nature of reading practice that readers engage in and about the effects of such practice on differing aspects of reading performance (i.e., word-level decoding vs. comprehension). One promising approach to further our limited knowledge of the effects of practice on reading would be to design studies that apply frameworks for categorizing different kinds of practice and its effects on other domains (e.g., Ericsson, chap. 1, this volume; Charness et al., chap. 2, this volume) to the domain of reading.

Despite remarkable progress in our understanding of what is necessary for the attainment of expert levels of performance—most notably, an enduring period of intense preparation—limitations in existing studies leave unanswered the question of the sufficiency of particular experiences or characteristics of individuals for such attainment. An example of a potential limitation is selection bias, in which those who do well in the early phase of training may self-select, or be selected by others, for admission to elite training and performance opportunities.

For each new domain of expertise examined, it is advisable to be sure that assumptions implicit in one's working definition are acknowledged and defensible. For example, the traditional working definition based on individual differences precludes the possibility of a domain in which a majority of participants reach expert levels of performance. Alternatives to definitions based on individual differences include definitions based on developmental differences or on mastery criteria.

Our analyses of examples of expert performance in the domain of reading, including the cases of speed reading and precocious reading, suggest that these examples of atypical reading performance do not represent different patterns of skill acquisition beyond differences in rate. Speed readers show no evidence of astonishing performance that transcends limitations associated with eye movement patterns and visual perception. Precocious readers differ from typical readers primarily in rates of acquisition, which appear to be determined jointly by genetic and environmental influences.

We have suggested that children begin reading instruction being differentially prepared to profit from it, due in part to individual differences in prerequisite language abilities. These differences play a role in differential early success at learning to read. Differential early success and other factors result in differences in learning experiences that affect subsequent success at reading.

Our view, then, is that whereas an extended period of effortful training or deliberate practice (Ericsson, chap. 1, this volume) is necessary for the development of expert levels of performance, the results we have reviewed from the domain of reading do not support the sufficiency of such training for attaining expert performance. Were cumulative amount of deliberate practice the sole determiner of expert performance, there would be no explanation of the inevitable decline in performance associated with aging (see Charness et al., chap. 2, this volume, and Simonton, chap. 8, this volume, for evidence of declines in function associated with aging). The worst-case scenario, in which an expert completely stops all deliberate practice, would result in a predicted stable level of performance in perpetuity because the cumulative amount of practice can never decline. If we acknowledge the role of developmental differences associated with aging as a codeterminer of levels of performance, as the data appear to force us to do, it is a small rather than a large step to posit a similar role for individual differences in skill-related underlying processes or prerequisites.

We see no inconsistency in the coexistence of large effects of effortful practice on the acquisition of expertise and individual differences in ability to profit from such practice. Even individual differences that appear to have minimal influence in performance in the near term can have large ultimate effects if the effects of individual differences on acquisition cumulate over time (Abelson, 1985). The upshot, as noted by Shiffrin (chap. 14, this volume), is that whereas a decade of effortful practice is guaranteed to improve level of performance dramatically, it may not be enough to join the elite level of world-class performers.

ACKNOWLEDGMENTS

Preparation of this manuscript was supported in part by Grant No. 410-95-0315 from the Social Sciences and Humanities Research Council of Canada to Keith E. Stanovich, and by Grants HD23340 and HD30988 from the National Institute of Child Health and Human Development to Richard Wagner.

REFERENCES

Abelson, R. P. (1985). A variance explanation paradox: When a little is a lot. *Psychological Bulletin, 97*, 129–133.

Alexander, P. A. (1992). Domain knowledge: Evolving themes and emerging concerns. *Educational Psychologist, 27*, 33–51.

Allen, L., Cipielewski, J., & Stanovich, K. E. (1992). Multiple indicators of children's reading habits and attitudes: Construct validity and cognitive correlates. *Journal of Educational Psychology, 84*, 489–503.

Anderson, R. C., & Freebody, P. (1983). Reading comprehension and the assessment and acquisition of word knowledge. In B. Huston (Ed.), *Advances in reading/language research* (Vol. 2, pp. 231–256). Greenwich, CT: JAI.

Anderson, R. C., Wilson, P. T., & Fielding, L. G. (1988). Growth in reading and how children spend their time outside of school. *Reading Research Quarterly, 23*, 285–303.

Ball, E., & Blachman, B. (1988). Phonological segmentation training: Effects of reading readiness. *Annals of Dyslexia, 38*, 208–225.

Baltes, P. B. (1987). Theoretical propositions of life-span developmental psychology: On the dynamics between growth and decline. *Developmental Psychology, 23*, 611–626.

Barker, K., Torgesen, J. K., & Wagner, R. K. (1992). The role of orthographic processing skills on five different reading tasks. *Reading Research Quarterly, 27*, 334–345.

Ben-Dror, I., Pollatsek, A., & Scarpati, S. (1991). Word identification in isolation and in context by college dyslexic students. *Brain and Language, 40*, 471–490.

Berninger, V. (Ed.). (1994). *Varieties of orthographic knowledge: Theoretical and developmental issues* (Vol. 1). Dordrecht, The Netherlands: Kluwer.

Bjorklund, D. F. (1987). How age changes in knowledge base contribute to the development of children's memory: An interpretive review. *Developmental Review, 7*, 93–130.

Bloom, B. S. (Ed.). (1985). *Developing talent in young people*. New York: Ballantine Books.

Bowers, P. G., & Wolf, M. (1993). Theoretical links among naming speed, precise timing mechanisms and orthographic skill in dyslexia. *Reading and Writing: An Interdisciplinary Journal, 5*, 69–85.

Brady, S. A., & Shankweiler, D. P. (Eds.). (1991). *Phonological processes in literacy*. Hillsdale, NJ: Lawrence Erlbaum Associates.

Bradley, L., & Bryant, P. E. (1985). *Rhyme and reason in reading and spelling*. Ann Arbor: University of Michigan Press.

Bruck, M. (1992). Persistence of dyslexics' phonological awareness deficits. *Developmental Psychology, 28*, 874–886.

Bryant, P. E., Bradley, L., MacLean, M., & Crossland, D. (1989). Nursery rhymes, phonological skills and reading. *Journal of Child Language, 16*, 407–428.

Bryk, A. S., & Raudenbush, S. W. (1987). Application of hierarchical linear models to assessing change. *Psychological Bulletin, 101*, 147–158.

Byrne, B., Freebody, P., & Gates, A. (1992). Longitudinal data on the relations of word-reading strategies to comprehension, reading time, and phonemic awareness. *Reading Research Quarterly, 27*, 141–151.

Calfee, R. (1977). Assessment of independent reading skills: Basic research and practical applications. In A. S. Reber & D. L. Scarborough (Eds.), *Toward a psychology of reading* (pp. 289–323). Hillsdale, NJ: Lawrence Erlbaum Associates.

Campbell, R., & Butterworth, B. (1985). Phonological dyslexia and dysgraphia in a highly literate subject: A developmental case with associated deficits in phonemic processing and awareness. *Quarterly Journal of Experimental Psychology, 37A*, 435–475.

Cardon, L. R., Smith, S. D., Fulker, D. W., Kimberling, W. J., Pennington, B. F., & De Fries, J. C. (1994). Quantitative trait locus for reading disability on chromosome 6. *Science, 266*, 276–279.

Carver, R. P. (1985). How good are some of the world's best speed readers? *Reading Research Quarterly, 20*, 389–419.

Carver, R. P. (1990). *Reading rate: A review of research and theory*. New York: Academic Press.

Ceci, S. J. (1990). *On intelligence . . . more or less: A bio-ecological treatise on intellectual development.* Englewood Cliffs, NJ: Prentice-Hall.

Charness, N. (1989). Age and expertise: Responding to Talland's challenge. In L. W. Poon, D. C. Rubin, & B. A. Wilson (Eds.), *Everyday cognition in adulthood and late life* (pp. 437–456). Cambridge, UK: Cambridge University Press.

Chi, M. T. H. (1985). Changing conception of sources of memory development. *Human Development, 28,* 50–56.

Chi, M. T. H., Hutchinson, J. E., & Robin, A. F. (1989). How inferences about novel domain-related concepts can be constrained by structured knowledge. *Merrill-Palmer Quarterly, 35,* 27–62.

Cipielewski, J., & Stanovich, K. E. (1992). Predicting growth in reading ability from children's exposure to print. *Journal of Experimental Child Psychology, 54,* 74–89.

Clark, D. B. (1988). *Dyslexia: Theory & practice of remedial instruction.* Parkton, MD: York Press.

Comstock, G., & Paik, H. (1991). *Television and the American child.* San Diego, CA: Academic Press.

Crain-Thoreson, C., & Dale, P. S. (1992). Do early talkers become early readers? Linguistic precocity, preschool language, and emergent literacy. *Developmental Psychology, 28,* 421–429.

Crowder, R. G., & Wagner, R. K. (1992). *The psychology of reading.* New York: Oxford University Press.

Cunningham, A. E., & Stanovich, K. E. (1990). Assessing print exposure and orthographic processing skill in children: A quick measure of reading experience. *Journal of Educational Psychology, 82,* 733–740.

Cunningham, A. E., & Stanovich, K. E. (1991). Tracking the unique effects of print exposure in children: Associations with vocabulary, general knowledge, and spelling. *Journal of Educational Psychology, 83,* 264–274.

Cunningham, A. E., & Stanovich, K. E. (1993). Children's literacy environments and early word recognition skills. *Reading and Writing: An Interdisciplinary Journal, 5,* 193–204.

Cunningham, A. E., Stanovich, K. E., & Wilson, M. R. (1990). Cognitive variation in adult students differing in reading ability. In T. Carr & B. A. Levy (Eds.), *Reading and development: Component skills approaches* (pp. 129–159). San Diego, CA: Academic Press.

DeFries, J. C., & Gillis, J. J. (1993). Genetics of reading disability. In R. Plomin & G. E. McClearn (Eds.), *Nature, nurture, & psychology* (pp. 27–68). Washington, DC: American Psychological Association.

DeFries, J. C., Olson, R. K., Pennington, B. F., & Smith, S. D. (1991). The Colorado reading project: An update. In D. Duane & D. B. Gray (Eds.), *The reading brain: The biological bases of dyslexia* (pp. 53–87). Parkton, MD: York Press.

Ehri, L. C. (1987). Learning to read and spell words. *Journal of Reading Behavior, 19,* 5–31.

Ehri, L. C., & Wilce, L. (1980). The influence of orthography on readers' conceptualization of the phonemic structure of words. *Applied Psycholinguistics, 1,* 371–385.

Ehri, L. C., & Wilce, L. (1983). Development of word identification speed in skilled and less skilled beginning readers. *Journal of Educational Psychology, 75,* 3–18.

Ennis, P. H. (1965). *Adult book reading in the United States* (National Opinion Research Center Report No. 105). Chicago: University of Chicago Press.

Ericsson, K. A., & Charness, N. (1994). Expert performance: Its structure and acquisition. *American Psychologist, 49,* 725–747.

Ericsson, K. A., Krampe, R. T., & Tesch-Römer, C. (1993). The role of deliberate practice in the acquisition of expert performance. *Psychological Review, 100,* 363–406.

Ericsson, K. A., & Smith, J. (Eds.) (1991). *Toward a general theory of expertise: Prospects and limits.* Cambridge, UK: Cambridge University Press.

Felton, R. H. (1993). Effects of instruction on the decoding skills of children with phonological-processing problems. *Journal of Learning Disabilities, 26,* 583–589.

Fletcher, J. M., Shaywitz, S. E., Shankweiler, D., Katz, L., Liberman, I., Stuebing, K., Francis, D. J., Fowler, A., & Shaywitz, B. A. (1994). Cognitive profiles of reading disability: Comparisons of discrepancy and low achievement definitions. *Journal of Educational Psychology, 86,* 6–23.

Fodor, J. (1983). *Modularity of mind.* Cambridge, MA: MIT Press.

Gathercole, S. E., & Baddeley, A. D. (1989). Evaluation of the role of phonological STM in the development of vocabulary in children: A longitudinal study. *Journal of Memory and Language, 28*, 200–213.

Gathercole, S. E., & Baddeley, A. D. (1993). *Working memory and language.* Hove, UK: Lawrence Erlbaum Associates.

Gayan, J., Olson, R. K., Cardon, L. R., Smith, S. D., Fulker, D. W., Kinberling, W. J., Pennington, B. F., & DeFries, J. C. (in press). Quantitative trait locus for different measures of reading disability. *Behavior Genetics.*

Gernsbacher, M. A. (1993). Less skilled readers have less efficient suppression mechanisms. *Psychological Science, 4*, 294–298.

Glaser, R. (1984). Education and thinking: The role of knowledge. *American Psychologist, 39*, 93–104.

Goodman, K. S. (1967). Reading: A psycholinguistic guessing game. *Journal of the Reading Specialist, 6*, 126–135.

Goody, J. (1977). *The domestication of the savage mind.* New York: Cambridge University Press.

Greaney, V. (1980). Factors related to amount and time of leisure time reading. *Reading Research Quarterly, 15*, 337–357.

Greaney, V., & Hegarty, M. (1987). Correlates of leisure-time reading. *Journal of Research in Reading, 10*, 3–20.

Hall, V. C., & Edmondson, B. (1992). Relative importance of aptitude and prior domain knowledge on immediate and delayed posttests. *Journal of Educational Psychology, 84*, 219–223.

Hatcher, P., Hulme, C., & Ellis, A. W. (1994). Ameliorating early reading failure by integrating the teaching of reading and phonological skills: The phonological linkage hypothesis. *Child Development, 65*, 41–57.

Hayes, D. P. (1988). Speaking and writing: Distinct patterns of word choice. *Journal of Memory and Language, 27*, 572–585.

Hayes, D. P., & Ahrens, M. (1988). Vocabulary simplification for children: A special case of 'motherese'? *Journal of Child Language, 15*, 395–410.

Hogaboam, T., & Perfetti, C. (1978). Reading skill and the role of verbal experience in decoding. *Journal of Educational Psychology, 70*, 717–729.

Homa, D. (1983). An assessment of two extraordinary speed readers. *Bulletin of the Psychonomic Society, 21*, 123–126.

Horn, J. L. (1982). The theory of fluid and crystallized intelligence in relation to concepts of cognitive psychology and aging in adulthood. In F. I. M. Craik & S. Trehub (Eds.), *Aging and cognitive processes* (pp. 847–870). New York: Plenum.

Horn, J. L. (1989). Cognitive diversity: A framework for learning. In P. Ackerman, R. Sternberg, & R. Glaser (Eds.), *Learning and individual differences* (pp. 61–116). Norwood, NJ: Ablex.

Horn, J. L., & Hofer, S. (1992). Major abilities and development in the adult period. In R. J. Sternberg & C. A. Berg (Eds.), *Intellectual development* (pp. 44–99). Cambridge, UK: Cambridge University Press.

Hoyer, W. (1987). Acquisition of knowledge and the decentralization of *g* in adult intellectual development. In C. Schooler & K. W. Schaie (Eds.), *Cognitive functioning and social structure over the life course* (pp. 120–141). Norwood, NJ: Ablex.

Humphreys, G. W. (1985). Attention, automaticity, and autonomy in visual word processing. In D. Besner, T. Waller, & G. MacKinnon (Eds.), *Reading research: Advances in theory and practice* (Vol. 5, pp. 253–309). New York: Academic Press.

Huston, A., Watkins, B. A., & Kunkel, D. (1989). Public policy and children's television. *American Psychologist, 44*, 424–433.

Jackson, N. E. (1992). Precocious reading of English: Origins, structure, and predictive significance. In P. S. Klein & A. J. Tannenbaum (Eds.), *To be young and gifted* (pp. 171–203). Norwood, NJ: Ablex.

Jackson, N. E., Donaldson, G., & Cleland, L. N. (1988). The structure of precocious reading ability. *Journal of Educational Psychology, 80*, 234–243.

Jackson, N. E., Donaldson, G., & Mills, J. R. (1993). Components of reading skill in postkinder-garten precocious readers and level-matched second graders. *Journal of Reading Behavior, 25,* 181–208.

Jorm, A. F., & Share, D. L. (1983). Phonological recoding and reading acquisition. *Applied Psycholinguistics, 4,* 103–147.

Just, M. A., & Carpenter, P. A. (1987). *The psychology of reading and language comprehension.* Newton, MA: Allyn & Bacon.

Kamhi, A., & Catts, H. (1989). *Reading disabilities: A developmental language perspective.* Boston: College-Hill Press.

Keating, D. P., & Crane, L. (1990). Domain-general and domain-specific processes in propor-tional reasoning. *Merrill-Palmer Quarterly, 36,* 411–424.

Keil, F. C. (1984). Mechanisms of cognitive development and the structure of knowledge. In R. Sternberg (Ed.), *Mechanisms of cognitive development* (pp. 81–99). New York: Freeman.

Lemoine, H. E., Levy, B. A., & Hutchinson, A. (1993). Increasing the naming speed of poor readers: Representations formed across repetitions. *Journal of Experimental Child Psychology, 55,* 297–328.

Lovett, M., Warren-Chaplin, P., Ransby, M., & Borden, S. (1990). Training the word recognition skills of reading disabled children: Treatment and transfer effects. *Journal of Educational Psychology, 82,* 769–780.

Lundberg, I., Frost, J., & Petersen, O. (1988). Effects of an extensive program for stimulating phonological awareness in preschool children. *Reading Research Quarterly, 23,* 263–284.

Mills, J. R., & Jackson, N. E. (1990). Predictive significance of early giftedness: The case of precocious reading. *Journal of Educational Psychology, 82,* 410–419.

Nagy, W. E., & Anderson, R. C. (1984). How many words are there in printed school English? *Reading Research Quarterly, 19,* 304–330.

Nagy, W. E., & Herman, P. A. (1987). Breadth and depth of vocabulary knowledge: Implications for acquisition and instruction. In M. McKeown & M. Curtis (Eds.), *The nature of vocabulary acquisition* (pp. 19–35). Hillsdale, NJ: Lawrence Erlbaum Associates.

Nell, V. (1988). The psychology of reading for pleasure: Needs and gratification. *Reading Research Quarterly, 23,* 6–50.

Oakhill, J., & Garnham, A. (1988). *Becoming a skilled reader.* Oxford, UK: Basil Blackwell.

Olson, D. R. (1986). Intelligence and literacy: The relationships between intelligence and the technologies of representation and communication. In R. J. Sternberg & R. K. Wagner (Eds.), *Practical intelligence* (pp. 338–360). Cambridge, UK: Cambridge University Press.

Olson, R. K., Forsberg, H., & Wise, B. (1994). Genes, environment, and the development of orthographic skills. In V. Berninger (Ed.), *Varieties of orthographic knowledge: Theoretical and developmental issues* (pp. 27–71). Dordrecht, The Netherlands: Kluwer.

Olson, R. K., Kliegl, R., Davidson, B., & Foltz, G. (1985). Individual and developmental differences in reading disability. In G. E. MacKinnon & T. Waller (Eds.), *Reading research: Advances in theory and practice* (Vol. 4, pp. 1–64). London: Academic Press.

Perfetti, C. A. (1985). *Reading ability.* New York: Oxford University Press.

Perfetti, C. A., Beck, I., Bell, L., & Hughes, C. (1987). Phonemic knowledge and learning to read are reciprocal: A longitudinal study of first grade children. *Merrill-Palmer Quarterly, 33,* 283–319.

Perfetti, C. A., & McCutchen, D. (1987). Schooled language competence: Linguistic abilities in reading and writing. In S. Rosenberg (Ed.), *Advances in applied psycholinguistics* (Vol. 2, pp. 105–141). Cambridge, UK: Cambridge University Press.

Plomin, R., & Bergman, C. S. (1991). The nature of nurture: Genetic influence on "environ-mental" measures. *Behavior and Brain Sciences, 14,* 373–427.

Postman, N. (1985). *Amusing ourselves to death.* New York: Viking Penguin.

Rayner, K., & Pollatsek, A. (1989). *The psychology of reading.* Englewood Cliffs, NJ: Prentice-Hall.

Recht, D. R., & Leslie, L. (1988). Effect of prior knowledge on good and poor readers' memory of text. *Journal of Educational Psychology, 80,* 16–20.

Rogosa, D. R., Brandt, D., & Zimowski, M. (1982). A growth curve approach to the measure-ment of change. *Psychological Bulletin, 90,* 726–748.

Schneider, W., Korkel, J., & Weinert, F. (1989). Domain-specific knowledge and memory performance: A comparison of high and low-aptitude children. *Journal of Educational Psychology, 81,* 306–312.

Scribner, S. (1986). Thinking in action: Some characteristics of practical thought. In R. J. Sternberg & R. K. Wagner (Eds.), *Practical intelligence* (pp. 13–30). Cambridge, UK: Cambridge University Press.

Seidenberg, M. (1985). Lexicon as module. *Behavioral and Brain Sciences, 8,* 31–32.

Share, D. L. (1995). Phonological recoding and self-teaching: Sine qua non of reading acquisition. *Cognition, 55,* 151–218.

Share, D. L., McGee, R., McKenzie, D., Williams, S., & Silva, P. A. (1987). Further evidence relating to the distinction between specific reading retardation and general reading backwardness. *British Journal of Educational Psychology, 5,* 35–44.

Sharon, A. T. (1973–1974). What do adults read? *Reading Research Quarterly, 9,* 148–169.

Shaywitz, S. E., Escobar, M. D., Shaywitz, B. A., Fletcher, J. M., & Makugh, R. (1992). Evidence that dyslexia may represent the lower tail of a normal distribution of reading ability. *The New England Journal of Medicine, 326,* 145–150.

Siegel, L. S., & Ryan, E. B. (1988). Development of grammatical-sensitivity, phonological, and short-term memory skills in normally achieving and learning disabled children. *Developmental Psychology, 24,* 28–37.

Simon, H. A., & Chase, W. G. (1973). Skill in chess. *American Scientist, 61*(4), 394–403.

Sincoff, J. B., & Sternberg, R. J. (1987). Two faces of verbal ability. *Intelligence, 11,* 263–276.

Smith, F. (1971). *Understanding reading.* New York: Holt, Rinehart & Winston.

Smith, F. (1973). *Psycholinguistics and reading.* New York: Holt, Rinehart & Winston.

Stanovich, K. E. (1986). Matthew effects in reading: Some consequences of individual differences in the acquisition of literacy. *Reading Research Quarterly, 21,* 360–407.

Stanovich, K. E. (1988a). Explaining the differences between the dyslexic and the garden-variety poor reader: the phonological-core variable-difference model. *Journal of Learning Disabilities, 21,* 590–612.

Stanovich, K. E. (1988b). The right and wrong places to look for the cognitive locus of reading disability. *Annals of Dyslexia, 38,* 154–177.

Stanovich, K. E. (1990). Concepts in developmental theories of reading skill: Cognitive resources, automaticity, and modularity. *Developmental Review, 10,* 72–100.

Stanovich, K. E. (1992). Speculations on the causes and consequences of individual differences in early reading acquisition. In P. Gough, L. Ehri, & R. Treiman (Eds.), *Reading acquisition* (pp. 307–342). Hillsdale, NJ: Lawrence Erlbaum Associates.

Stanovich, K. E. (1993). Does reading make you smarter? Literacy and the development of verbal intelligence. In H. Reese (Ed.), *Advances in child development and behavior* (Vol. 24, pp. 133–180). San Diego, CA: Academic Press.

Stanovich, K. E., & Cunningham, A. E. (1991). Reading as constrained reasoning. In R. Sternberg & P. Frensch (Eds.), *Complex problem solving: Principles and mechanisms* (pp. 3–60). Hillsdale, NJ: Lawrence Erlbaum Associates.

Stanovich, K. E., & Cunningham, A. E. (1992). Studying the consequences of literacy within a literate society: The cognitive correlates of print exposure. *Memory & Cognition, 20,* 51–68.

Stanovich, K. E., & Cunningham, A. E. (1993). Where does knowledge come from? Specific associations between print exposure and information acquisition. *Journal of Educational Psychology, 85,* 211–229.

Stanovich, K. E., Nathan, R. G., & Zolman, J. E. (1988). The developmental lag hypothesis in reading: Longitudinal and matched reading-level comparisons. *Child Development, 59,* 71–86.

Stanovich, K. E., & Siegel, L. S. (1994). The phenotypic performance profile of reading-disabled children: A regression-based test of the phonological-core variable-difference model. *Journal of Educational Psychology, 86,* 24–53.

Stanovich, K. E., & West, R. F. (1983). On priming by a sentence context. *Journal of Experimental Psychology: General, 112,* 1–36.

Stanovich, K. E., & West, R. F. (1989). Exposure to print and orthographic processing. *Reading Research Quarterly, 24,* 402–433.

Stanovich, K. E., West, R. F., & Harrison, M. (in press). Knowledge growth and maintenance across the life span: The role of print exposure. *Developmental Psychology.*

Sternberg, R. J. (1985). *Beyond IQ: A triarchic theory of human intelligence.* Cambridge, UK: Cambridge University Press.

Thorndike, E. L. (1917). Reading as reasoning: A study of mistakes in paragraph reading. *Journal of Educational Psychology, 8,* 323–332.

Thorndike, R. L. (1973–1974). Reading as reasoning. *Reading Research Quarterly, 9,* 135–147.

Treiman, R. (1991). Phonological awareness and its roles in learning to read and spell. In D. J. Saywer & B. J. Fox (Eds.), *Phonological awareness in reading: The evolution of current perspectives* (pp. 159–189). New York: Springer-Verlag.

Tunmer, W. E., & Nesdale, A. R. (1985). Phonemic segmentation skill and beginning reading. *Journal of Educational Psychology, 77,* 417–427.

Vellutino, F. R. (1979). *Dyslexia: Theory and research.* Cambridge, MA: MIT Press.

Vellutino, F., & Scanlon, D. (1987). Phonological coding, phonological awareness, and reading ability: Evidence from a longitudinal and experimental study. *Merrill-Palmer Quarterly, 33,* 321–363.

Wagner, R. K. (1988). Causal relations between the development of phonological processing abilities and the acquisition of reading skills: A meta-analysis. *Merrill-Palmer Quarterly, 34,* 261–279.

Wagner, R. K., & Barker, T. (1994). The development of orthographic processing ability. In V. Berninger (Ed.), *Varieties of orthographic knowledge: Theoretical and developmental issues* (pp. 243–276). Dordrecht, The Netherlands: Kluwer.

Wagner, R. K., & Torgesen, J. K. (1987). The nature of phonological processing and its causal role in the acquisition of reading skills. *Psychological Bulletin, 101,* 192–212.

Wagner, R. K., Torgesen, J. K., Laughon, P., Simmons, K., & Rashotte, C. A. (1993). The development of young readers' phonological processing abilities. *Journal of Educational Psychology, 85,* 1–20.

Wagner, R. K., Torgesen, J. K., & Rashotte, C. A. (1994). Development of reading-related phonological processing abilities: New evidence of bidirectional causality from a latent variable longitudinal study. *Developmental Psychology, 30,* 73–87.

Wagner, R. K., Torgesen, J. K., Rashotte, C. A., Hecht, S., Barker, T. A., Burgess, S. R., Donahue, J., & Garon, T. (1995). *Causal relations between phonological processing abilities and reading as children develop from beginning to fluent readers: A five-year longitudinal study.* Manuscript submitted for publication.

Walberg, H. J., & Tsai, S. (1984). Reading achievement and diminishing returns to time. *Journal of Educational Psychology, 76,* 442–451.

Walker, C. H. (1987). Relative importance of domain knowledge and overall aptitude on acquisition of domain-related information. *Cognition and Instruction, 4,* 25–42.

West, R. F., & Stanovich, K. E. (1991). The incidental acquisition of information from reading. *Psychological Science, 2,* 325–330.

West, R. F., Stanovich, K. E., & Mitchell, H. R. (1993). Reading in the real world and its correlates. *Reading Research Quarterly, 28,* 34–50.

Willett, J. B. (1988). Questions and answers in the measurement of change. In E. Z. Rothkopf (Ed.), *Review of research in education* (Vol. 15, pp. 345–422). Washington, DC: American Educational Research Association.

Willett, J. B., & Sayer, A. G. (1994). Using covariance structure analysis to detect correlates and predictors of individual change over time. *Psychological Bulletin, 108,* 363–381.

Wood, E. N. (1963). A breakthrough in reading. *Reading Teacher, 14,* 115–117.

Yekovich, F. R., Walker, C. H., Ogle, L., & Thompson, J. (1990). The influence of domain knowledge on inferencing in low-aptitude individuals. In A. Graesser & G. Bower (Eds.), *The psychology of learning and motivation* (pp. 259–278). San Diego, CA: Academic Press.

Zill, N., & Winglee, M. (1990). *Who reads literature?* Cabin John, MD: Seven Locks Press.

8

Creative Expertise: A Life-Span Developmental Perspective

Dean Keith Simonton
University of California, Davis

In this chapter, I dedicate myself to an ambitious, maybe even impossibly grandiose task. I wish to trace the development of expertise across the entire individual life span, from birth to death and everything between. Furthermore, I want to introduce a theoretical (and sometimes even mathematical) model that aspires to explain the main features of this life-span development. At the same time, this model will try to coordinate all the central empirical findings that have accumulated over the past 160 years, since Adolphe Quetelet's *Sur l'homme* of 1835 to be explicit. As if all this were not bold enough, I am going to aim this analysis at a type of expertise that is far more elusive and consequential than what normally passes under that name. To appreciate the nature of this audacious departure, I must first establish a crucial distinction.

In *Walden Pond*, Thoreau (1845/1942) complained that "There are nowadays professors of philosophy, but not philosophers" (p. 39). Likewise in *Man and Superman*, Shaw (1903) remarked that "He who can, does. He who cannot, teaches" (p. 230). Although both assertions may be guilty of exaggeration, and maybe even a little peevishness, they do capture an important difference between two types of experts.

On the one hand, some individuals manage to master all the key facts, theories, themes, and techniques that define the state of the art in their chosen domain. These persons have thereby attained the status of the discipline's bona fide experts. They may teach and disseminate their learning, and they may even practice what they know, as is the case for top-notch doctors and lawyers. Even so, we must always acknowledge a fundamental limitation to their knowledge and skill: They exhibit no more than "received expertise." What they have mastered is what others before them have discovered and developed. To borrow Newton's famous metaphor, they may see farther than the rest simply because they stand on the shoulders of giants. Yet these experts may not be giants themselves. The presence of these experts preserves rather than transforms the field.

On the other hand, other individuals can make major contributions to their field that redefine what are considered to be the domain's central facts, theories, themes, or techniques. Rather than just teach creative writing, they publish innovative works that earn them a Nobel Prize in literature. Rather than merely mastering all the rules of harmony, counterpoint, and rhythm, they devise compositions that attain recognition by breaking all those rules. Rather than memorize all the significant (and insignificant) empirical data of their science, they conceive novel theories that either render those facts trivial or else endow those facts with more profound meanings. These disruptive people are the discipline's creators. We can therefore say that they exhibit "creative expertise." Although these creators may not necessarily be experts in the sense used earlier, they do create what will later become the basis for the future display of received expertise. After Kant wrote his famed *Critik*, others could earn PhDs by discussing his revolutionary epistemology.

Admittedly, I am not putting forward a novel distinction here. This same contrast can be found in many areas of the behavioral sciences. For instance, the distinction is implicit in current computer models of problem solving, which can be divided into expert systems like MYCIN (Buchanan & Shortliffe, 1984) and discovery systems like BACON (Langley, Simon, Bradshaw, & Zytkow, 1987; Shrager & Langley, 1990). Only on rare occasions is there serious discussion of how to bridge these two divergent conceptions of problem solving (e.g., MacCrimmon & Wagner, 1987). In addition, the distinction is at least partially tapped by several psychometric instruments, such as Kirton's (1976) measure of Adaptors versus Innovators. In fact, research has shown that critically acclaimed producers in a field think differently and have a distinctive personality structure in comparison to those peers who can only claim professional expertise in the same disciplines (e.g., Eysenck, 1995; MacKinnon, 1978; Rostan, 1994). Albert Einstein, for instance, did not know more physics or mathematics than his less illustrious colleagues. Indeed, he often exhibited less expertise. What was crucial was not how much he knew, but rather how he organized his knowledge, including how that information meshed with a distinctive style and worldview.

Nevertheless, we must also acknowledge that, like a good many other dichotomous distinctions, this one is probably overstated. A continuum likely underlies the apparent dichotomy. For example, in Kuhn's (1970) theory of scientific revolutions, the scientists who practice "normal science" occupy a sort of middle ground. These scientists do more than just master the paradigm; they also advance it further. The normal scientists even unearth the paradigmatic anomalies that are supposed to set the stage for the creators who propound totally revolutionary paradigms. Nonetheless, the distinction remains useful as a way of indicating the type of expertise that will be the primary focus of this essay. Here I concentrate on those individuals whose creative expertise renders the received expertise obsolete.

Therefore, this chapter develops a formal framework for understanding the emergence and manifestation of creative expertise across a creator's life span. The framework begins by hypothesizing a longitudinal model of creative productivity, and then defines the role of individual-difference variables.

AGE AND CREATIVE PRODUCTIVITY

Before I launch into the model, let me begin with a disclaimer. The theory to be outlined in the following is extremely rough, with many wrinkles yet to be smoothed over. Particularly problematic is that portion of the model that has been mathematically formalized. Although originally trained in the physical sciences, I have a great deal of skepticism about the utility of mathematical models in the behavioral sciences. The phenomena we deal with are simply phenomenally complex. We must remember how difficult the mathematics becomes even to solve relatively simple physical problems, such as the orbit of an electron around a proton. Certain rudimentary questions, such as the three-body problem, have never really been solved, and have stumped intellects as grand as those of Newton and Poincaré. Often the only way we can obtain tractable equations is to impose so many "simplifying assumptions" that we end up with a scheme that is implausible on a posteriori if not a priori grounds.

All these faults—and more—are applicable to what I plan to present here. I do not stop right now because I believe that we can still learn much from simple models so long as they are complex enough to accommodate the central features of the phenomenon that attracts our fancy. The theoretical system that I propose is rich enough in explanatory and predictive power that it forces us to look at the available data in a new way, and even urges us to search for new facts. If someday the model is shown to be fundamentally erroneous, it will have at least obliged all rival models to grapple with a more intricate web of observed relationships. In fact, the constraints imposed by these results already rule out many alternative explanations right from the start. At present, I maintain that the current model, for all its faults, may have the greatest potential for theoretical and empirical development.

That caveat complete, let me begin by specifying the theoretical premise on which the theory is built.

Variation-Selection Theory

At bottom, I posit that the creative process is essentially Darwinian. That is, creativity entails a process of variation and selection. James (1880), Campbell (1960), Skinner (1972), and others have proposed that a similar variation-selection process explicates creative behavior. Of special interest is Campbell's (1960) "bind variation and selective retention" model of creativity. According to this model, the creative mind spontaneously generates ideational combinations in a more or less unpredictable manner; a small proportion of these combinations are then selected for further elaboration, testing, retention, and application. Campbell showed that this Darwinian model was consistent with the introspective reports of creative individuals, such as those of the eminent French mathematician Poincaré (1921). Furthermore, this model was compatible with other Darwinian systems, like evolutionary epistemology and social evolution (Campbell, 1965, 1974; Toulmin, 1972).

More importantly, others have further elaborated Campbell's (1960) variation-selection model of creativity. In a book and in several chapters and articles, I developed this model into what I have styled the "chance-configuration theory of creativity," with a special focus on scientific genius (Simonton, 1988b, 1988e, 1989b, 1993a, 1993b, 1994a). This chance-configuration theory can account for several key aspects of scientific creativity, such as the phenomenon of multiple discovery and invention (Simonton, 1979, 1987b). Kantorovich (1993) added several improvements to my own version, especially by extending it to the output of scientific communities (cf. Simonton, 1994c). Eysenck (1993, 1994, 1995) connected the "Campbell–Simonton" model of creativity with a broad theory of the creative personality that incorporates both experimental and correlational data (cf. Simonton, 1993a). Finally, Martindale (1990, 1994) pushed the Darwinian perspective in a different direction by using it as a foundation for his evolutionary theory of stylistic change in the arts. These and related elaborations promise to help make variation-selection theory one of the most comprehensive and precise frameworks for understanding creative behavior in all of its complexity.

Needless to say, not everyone is enthusiastic about these theoretical developments. Many feel that it places too much emphasis on chance, and that it downplays the role of goal-directed behavior (e.g., Gruber, 1989; Perkins, 1994). Others may maintain that it understates the role of logical and conscious information processing, such as that stressed by those who study creativity from the standpoint of computational models of problem solving (e.g., Weber, 1992; Weisberg, 1992). Because I have addressed these and other complaints elsewhere (e.g., Simonton, 1988d, 1993a, 1994a, 1994b, in press-b), I have no desire to repeat myself here. Instead, I wish to give a thumbnail sketch of how the Darwinian framework helps us grapple with the central question of this chapter.

Longitudinal Model

We begin by proposing a mathematical model that predicts how the output rate of creative products varies during the course of a career (Simonton, 1984b, 1988a, 1989a, in press-a). The model begins with three assumptions:

1. Each creative individual launches his or her career with a certain amount of *initial creative potential* (m). This is a hypothetical count of the total number of products the creator would be capable of producing in an unlimited life span.[1] In concrete but simplistic terms, this individual-difference variable is a multiplicative function of the wealth of concepts a person has acquired within a domain and the richness of their associative interconnections (James, 1880; Mach, 1896; Simonton, 1980a).

2. During the course of the career, this potential is actualized into overt products by the two-step process of *ideation* and *elaboration*. Ideation entails coming up with new ideas by a free-associative, combinatory procedure. Elaboration involves the process of transforming these ideational combinations into completed products. Both ideation and elaboration operate largely by variation-selection mechanisms, although the elaboration process is probably more constrained by consciously applied criteria. In any case, corresponding to each of these two processes is a transformation rate. We must thus speak of an ideation rate (a) and an elaboration rate (b). I have more to say about these two constants in a moment.

3. This conversion of potential to actual productivity begins at the moment a career effectively begins. In other words, if we express productivity as a function of time, or $p(t)$, then $t = 0$ at the career onset. Hence, the age curve that results is defined according to career age, not chronological age. This definition sets the model apart from many rival theories (Simonton, 1988a) and leads to many distinctive empirical predictions (Simonton, 1991a).

Given these three assumptions, we can set up a second-order differential equation that specifies how potential creativity converts into actual creativity (see Simonton, 1984b). The solution to this equation then yields a function that predicts the annual output of finished products as a function of career age, namely, $p(t) = c(e^{-at} - e^{-bt})$, where $c = abm/(b - a)$ and e is the exponential constant. A typical age curve and corresponding equation are shown in Fig. 8.1. This curve has been tested against a large number of data sets, including the data gathered by Lehman (1953), Dennis (1966), Cole (1979), and Zuckerman (1977). The results have been excellent. The correlations between predicted and actual levels of productivity range in the

---

[1]Technically speaking, m should be defined in terms of the number of original ideas a person can produce. Actual output is then a fraction of this value, according to the "least publishable unit" of a discipline (e.g., brief articles vs. monographs, poems vs. novels). Because this nicety has no consequences for our conclusions, I ignore the distinction here.

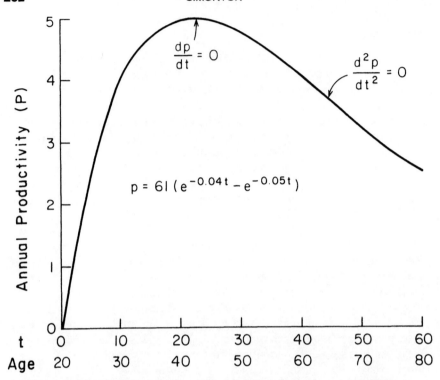

FIG. 8.1. Predicted relation between productivity *p(t)* and career age *t* according to a two-step model of the creative process. From Simonton (1984b). Reprinted with permission from Academic Press.

middle to upper .90s (Simonton, 1984b, 1988a, 1989a). The theoretical curve even gets the fine details right, like the career path's concave downward commencement, its single prominent peak, and its concave upward finish (Simonton, 1984b, 1989a).

Clearly, this theoretically derived age curve passes the first check. It provides a superb summary of the typical career path for a creative career, at least as we can infer from statistics aggregated across multiple careers (and duly corrected for such potential artifacts as the "compositional fallacy"). The model even can accommodate the data from a single career, albeit with less precision. For instance, the correlation between Thomas Edison's output of patents and the productivity predicted by the model is an impressive .87 (Simonton, 1989a).

However, to maximize the correspondence between predicted and observed output, we must make important adjustments in the equation, adjustments that have significant theoretical implications. Specifically, when we fit the curve to career trajectories in different creative disciplines, we obtain best fits by permitting variation in the two information-processing parameters *a* and *b* (Simonton, 1984b, 1988a, 1989a). In some fields, such as poetry and pure mathematics, ideation and elaboration proceed rather quickly (e.g., $a = .04$ and $b = .05$). In other domains, such as history and geology, the two-step procedure moves more slowly (e.g., $a = .02$ and $b = .03$). These differences are only deceptively small. Poets consume their creative potential at over twice the rate as do historians, for example. In addition, small contrasts in ideation and elaboration rates result in large differences in the expected career trajectories. For example, the predicted career peak for historians comes 18 years later than that for poets. Figure 8.2 shows the predicted curves for two hypothetical disciplines with only the slightest difference in the two information-processing parameters (and holding initial creative potential constant).

According to the theory, these contrasts have to do with the nature of the cognitive material that must be manipulated in a given creative enterprise (Simonton, 1989a). The more simple, abstract, or finite the array of concepts that the creator deals with, the faster the information-processing rates. In contrast, the more complex, associatively rich, or unbounded this repertoire, the slower become the same rates. Thus, poetry deals with a smaller range of topics and a more restricted vocabulary than does history. Likewise, pure mathematics handles more refined and restricted concepts than does geology. Moreover, the ideation and elaboration processes are somewhat independent of each other. What is required to elaborate a poem may

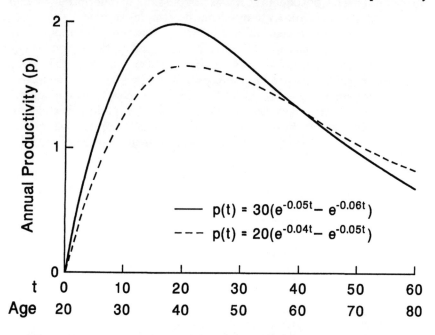

FIG. 8.2. Predicted relation between productivity $p(t)$ and career age t for two disciplines that differ slightly in the rates of ideation (a) and elaboration (b), but with creative potential and career onset identical. From Simonton (1991a). Copyright © 1991 by the American Psychological Association. Reprinted with permission.

be different than what is necessary to perfect a mathematical proof. Accordingly, the two information-processing rates may be freely varied to capture the signature trajectory of various creative activities. For example, two fields may peak at the same career age, yet one may exhibit a rapid postpeak decline, whereas the other displays a more gradual loss in output with age (Simonton, 1989a).[2]

Equal-Odds Rule

So far we have been speaking of total output per age period. Yet many if not most ideas that a creator offers the world have no impact whatsoever. These are the paintings collecting dust in basements, the books that go out of print, and journal articles that receive no citations in the literature. Therefore, we must distinguish the hits from the misses. Only the hits represent genuine creativity, whereas the hits and misses combined together represent unselected productivity. For some time researchers believed that the age curves for exclusive quality differed from those for inclusive quantity (e.g., Dennis, 1966). Yet this conclusion was based on flawed data analyses (Simonton, 1988a). Tabulations of total output from one data set were compared with tabulations of selective output from another data set. Consequently, it was not possible to determine whether any differences were due to contrasts in the samples studied.

However, more recent studies have compared quantity and quality with the same individual creators, and the story comes out quite differently (e.g., Over, 1989; Simonton, 1977a, 1984c, 1985b; see also Quetelet, 1835/1968). The age curves for quality and quantity are basically identical. The former is merely a scaled-down version of the latter. This congruence holds not only for the overall trajectory, but for the period-to-period fluctuations besides. Those periods in which a creator produces the most masterpieces are often the same periods in which that same creator generates the most forgettable pieces.

The same point is made more dramatically by the *quality ratio* (Simonton, 1977a, 1984c, 1985b). This is the ratio of hits to total attempts in consecutive age periods (e.g., 10-year or 5-year intervals). This ratio neither increases nor decreases with age, nor does it exhibit some curvilinear form. This means that the odds of hitting a bull's eye is a probabilistic function of the total number of shots. The more attempts made, the more successes won, but also the more failures suffered. Hits and misses go

---

[2]If the ideation and elaboration rates happen to be identical for a particular discipline (i.e., $a = b$), the solution to the differential equations becomes $p(t) = a^2mte^{-at}$ (Simonton, 1988a). Still, the resulting curve has the same appearance as what we see in Fig. 8.1. I should also mention that although a and b are considered constants for a discipline at a particular point in time, these parameters may change as a creative domain matures and becomes more complex, slowing one or both rates and thereby shifting the peaks toward later in life (see, e.g., Zhao & Jiang, 1986; cf. Lehman, 1953).

together so that the ratio does not vary systematically across the creative career. This result leads to an important empirical generalization: the *equal-odds rule*.[3] The principle holds that quality correlates positively with quantity, so that creativity becomes a linear statistical function of productivity.

This equal-odds rule has two intriguing aspects, one empirical and the other theoretical.

1. Empirically, the rule applies across careers as well as within careers. In any sample of contributors to a particular domain, the variation in total lifetime output will be tremendous (Dennis, 1954a, 1954c, 1955; Lotka, 1926; Price, 1963; Simonton, 1984c, 1988e). Usually the top 10% who are the most prolific account for around half of everything produced. The most prolific have bibliographies or lists of works that are at least 100 times longer than their least productive colleagues. Nonetheless, those who are the most productive are producing both hits and misses. They have more successes only because they have more failures, too. W. H. Auden put his finger on this essential reality when he said, "The chances are that, in the course of his lifetime, the major poet will write more bad poems than the minor" (quoted in Bennet, 1980, p. 15). Hence, whether we are looking across lifetimes or within careers, the equal-odds rule operates.

2. The equal-odds rule is compatible with our overall Darwinian perspective on creativity (Simonton, 1988e, 1993b, 1994a). It is simply the variation-selection principle operating at yet another level of analysis. Just as ideas within a creator's head must undergo selection before they are ready to present to the world, those ideas that the creator decides to offer the world will often endure ruthless selection in the minds of others. Only a subset of a creator's work will actually have an impact. In the sciences, for example, a large proportion of journal articles receive no citations at all by colleagues in the scientific community. What is especially fascinating is that creative individuals are not apparently capable of improving their success rate with experience or enhanced expertise. This longitudinal continuity is consistent with the notion that the variational procedure is ultimately "blind." Creative persons, even the so-called geniuses, cannot ever foresee which of their intellectual or aesthetic creations will win acclaim. All they can do is maximize their "productive success" by maintaining prolific output across the life span.

These two implications aside, the equal-odds rule will soon provide a useful principle for deciphering the course of a creative career.

---

[3]In earlier writings, I referred to this rule as the constant probability of success model or principle (e.g., Simonton, 1988a). This change in terminology was motivated only by a desire for elegance. The underlying concept is unaltered.

Three Career Landmarks

The trajectory of any given creator's career can be described by what I call *career landmarks* (Simonton, 1991a; cf. Raskin, 1936). There are three such critical turning points: the first, the best, and the last masterpiece, hit, or influential contribution. The age at the first hit then marks the real onset of the creative career, when quantity finally produces something of quality. The age at the best hit defines the career peak, when a creator produces that work that most enhances his or her reputation. The age at the last hit indicates when the creative portion of the career has terminated. The creator may evince further output, but this will count as the aftermath of a creative life now spent.

Where are these three landmarks placed during the course of a career? At this point we can only treat the middle landmark, which can be handled without introducing anything beyond the principles we have already established. If quality is a function of quantity, then creators will produce the most hits in those periods in which they are the most prolific. Yet the equal-odds rule applies to the collection of hits as well as to all output regardless of quality. This implies that those periods in which the most hits appear will, on the average, contain that single hit that we can consider the best hit of all. It follows that the single most significant creative product will fall around the same age as the point of maximum output. In other words, we can reinterpret the curve in Fig. 8.1 as expressing the likelihood that a creator's magnum opus will appear at a given age across the life span (see, e.g., Simonton, 1977a, 1980b, 1991b).

Individual Differences: Career Onset and Creative Potential

The foregoing derivation for age at best work is incomplete because it ignores the influence of two individual-difference variables. Furthermore, without accommodating this cross-sectional variation we cannot even begin to specify the longitudinal placement of the first and last career landmarks. Fortunately, these two factors are already an integral part of the mathematical model sketched earlier.

The first variable is a direct consequence of our stipulation that the trajectory be defined according to career age. Although career age correlates very highly with chronological age, the correlation is not perfect (Bayer & Dutton, 1977; Stephan & Levin, 1992). This implies that creators can vary in age at career onset (Simonton, 1991a, 1991b). Some individuals launch their creative enterprises at incredibly youthful ages, whereas others get an unusually late start. Variation in the age at career onset does not alter the shape of the age curve, but only its location within a person's lifetime. For example, those who get a quick start will peak earlier than those who were late bloomers.

The second variable is more subtle but no less essential. According to the model, the career trajectory is founded on the realization of a beginning amount of creative potential, which we designated as m. Yet we must emphasize that this initial creative potential varies considerably across creators (Simonton, 1984b, 1991a, 1991b). Some are essentially "one-idea" intellects, and therefore run out of steam early on. Others are phenomenally prolific in the generation of ideas, and cannot be stopped except by death. In any case, individual differences in m have an interesting consequence for the career trajectory. For persons working in the same discipline, variation in creative potential does not affect the shape of the curve, but it does determine the curve's height. This happens because the parameter that scales the magnitude of annual output is given by $c = abm/(b-a)$. Using the assumption of disciplinary homogeneity to hold a and b constant, c becomes a direct linear function of m (Simonton, 1984b). In concrete terms, this means that the higher an individual's initial creative potential, the faster the average output rate throughout the career. Even though the maximum output rate at the career peak will be higher for those enjoying greater creative potential, the peak age for that maximum output will not vary with individual differences in initial potential.

Now according to both theory and data, these two variables are uncorrelated with each other (Simonton, 1991a, 1991b). Someone high or low in initial creative potential may get either an early or a late start on his or her career. The orthogonal nature of these factors enables us to put forward a typology of career trajectories for creators working in the same discipline. Such a hypothetical typology is graphed in Fig. 8.3. Here the ideation and elaboration rates (a and b) are held constant, whereas the two individual difference variables vary across the extremes, yielding four idealized trajectories: early bloomers with either high or low creative potential and late bloomers with either high or low creative potential.

Given this typology, we can return to the question of where the three career landmarks are placed over a creator's life span. Because the creator's best work appears around the time of peak productivity, it is clear that this is affected solely by individual differences in the age of career onset. Those who commence their careers earlier will peak earlier. On the other hand, the age at best work is not influenced by cross-sectional variation in creative potential. Highly creative persons will produce more masterpieces at their career acme, but that optimum will occur at the same place as it does for anyone else who began their career at the same age and within the same discipline.

What about the first and last career landmarks? Here we must again apply the equal-odds rule. We begin by noticing the difference between the career trajectories for people who differ widely in initial creative potential: Right from the career's onset those with higher initial potential are producing works at a faster pace than their colleagues with lower initial potential. This faster accumulation of total attempts increases the likelihood that those

CREATIVE POTENTIAL

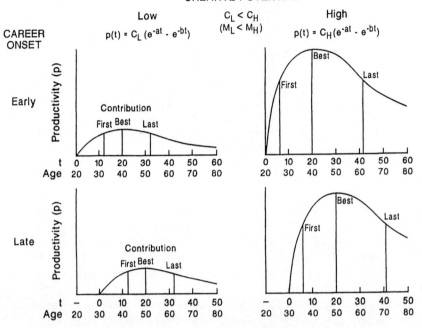

FIG. 8.3. Typology of career trajectories according to early or late career onset and low or high initial creative potential. From Simonton (1991a). Copyright © 1991 by the American Psychological Association. Reprinted with permission.

with higher creative potential will get a hit at an earlier stage in their careers. In contrast, those who can boast less potential will come out with ideas more slowly, and therefore the odds are stacked against them having an early career success.

The same argument applies for the last career landmark. Higher initial creative potential indicates a more prolific output in the later years. This raises the chance of a hit late in life. In comparison, those with lower potential will most likely produce their last important work not long after they produce their best work. Hence, holding other variables constant, the higher a creator's initial potential, the earlier the first landmark appears and the later the last landmark appears, and the middle landmark stays in the same place. On the other hand, a person with very low initial potential will have the first landmark happen so late and the last occur so early that all three landmarks will appear within only a few years of each other. In the extreme case, we have the "one-book author" whose single contribution to human culture represents all three career landmarks at once!

It should now be evident that we have a theoretical basis for providing an operational definition for initial creative potential, a construct that would otherwise have no empirical content. This variable can be directly assessed by (a) the maximum annual output rate at the career peak, or (b) the total lifetime output (introducing controls, when required, for life span and age at career onset). We can also employ a more indirect proxy when necessary, namely the differential eminence of the creators (Simonton, 1977b, 1991a, 1991b, 1992b; see also Simonton, 1991c). This linkage is based on the application of the equal-odds rule to cross-sectional variation in lifetime output: Those who produce the most total works will tend to produce the most total influential works, where eminence is a linear function of the sum total of career hits.

By explicitly introducing both age at career onset and initial creative potential into the analysis, we can reconcile this fundamental fact: Individual differences in productivity account for more variance than does career or chronological age (Over, 1982a, 1982b; Simonton, 1977a, 1991a, 1992b; Stephan & Levin, 1992). More importantly, once we have introduced these two variables, we can derive several specific and distinctive predictions about individual differences in career trajectories (see, e.g., Simonton, 1991a, 1991b, 1992b). To illustrate, the theoretical model exposes itself to Popperian falsification by making the following clear-cut predictions:

1. Total lifetime productivity, the mean output rate per rate annum, and the maximum output rate each correlate negatively with age at first hit but positively with age at last hit (i.e., the signs of six zero-order correlations predicted, three as positive, three as negative).
2. The correlations are zero between age at best work (or age at maximum output rate) and total lifetime productivity, the mean output rate per annum, and the maximum output rate (i.e., six zero-order correlations predicted to be zero).
3. The partial correlations among ages at first, best, and last hit are all positive controlling for total lifetime productivity, the mean output rate per annum, or the maximum output rate (i.e., another nine first-order partial correlations predicted to be zero).
4. The partial correlation between age at first hit and age at last hit is negative after controlling for either age at best work or age at maximum output rate (i.e., two first-order partial correlations predicted to be negative).
5. The time interval between the age at career onset and the age at first hit is negatively correlated with total lifetime productivity, the mean annual output rate, and the maximum output rate (i.e., three zero-order correlations predicted to be negative).
6. The correlations among the output rates for consecutive time units of a creative career are best fit by a single-factor latent-variable model rather than by an autoregressive process (i.e., the correlation matrix for productivity among consecutive decades or half decades will exhibit a highly distinctive covariance structure).

This configuration of predicted zero-order and partial correlations is so unique that it cannot be successfully generated by any other theory of creative productivity that has been proposed to date (for some relevant evidence, see Albert, 1975; Christensen & Jacomb, 1992; Cole & Cole, 1973; Dennis, 1954b; Raskin, 1936; Simonton, 1980b, 1991a, 1991b, 1992b; Zhao & Jiang, 1986; Zuckerman, 1977; Zusne, 1976). For example, this pattern of relationships is inconsistent with cumulative advantage and psychoeconomic models of creative output (Simonton, 1988a, in press-a).

Interdisciplinary Contrasts in Career Landmarks

The preceeding predictions all posit that the ideation and elaboration rates are unchanged. In other words, we are assuming that the individuals under consideration are active in the same discipline. Yet we could also reverse matters, allowing the information-processing rates to vary as age at career onset and initial creative potential are both held constant. By applying the equal-odds rule, we can then make predictions about how the expected appearance of the three career landmarks varies across distinct disciplines. For example, it should be obvious that those disciplines with faster ideation and elaboration rates will tend to have the best works appear at younger ages than is the case for those disciplines with slower rates. In addition, the first career landmark will be placed according to the slope of the curve of ascent at the beginning of the career, and the last career landmark will depend on the slope of the curve of descent. Because these portions of the age curve are a complex function of the specific ideation and elaboration rates for a discipline, the longitudinal model can be easily adjusted to accommodate the particular career trajectories for various disciplines. To appreciate the necessity of this provision, we can inspect Fig. 8.4, which indicates the distinct location of career landmarks in several scientific disciplines (Simonton, 1991a).

It must be stressed that these interdisciplinary contrasts are statistically significant and that they survive control for any differences in the age of career onset (e.g., mathematics vs. medicine). I know of no theoretical model, mathematical or otherwise, that can account for these more subtle features of the creative career.

Needless to say, if we permit a sample of creative experts to vary in their age at career onset, initial creative potential, and domain of creativity, the current theoretical model stands alone in its ability to handle a tremendous diversity of career trajectories.

DEVELOPMENTAL IMPLICATIONS

The proposed model enables us to comprehend a great deal about how creative expertise changes across the lifespan. For instance, the model is useful in addressing the question of how much creativity we can reasonably

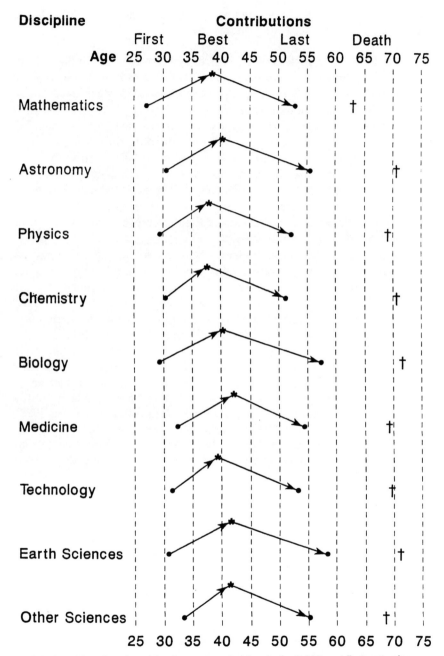

FIG. 8.4. Mean location of the three career landmarks for 2,026 contributors to nine scientific disciplines. From Simonton (1994b). Reprinted with permission from The Guilford Press.

expect from individuals long advanced in years (Simonton, 1990). On this subject the model makes four principal points.

1. Under the parameters of the typical age curve shown in Fig. 8.1, the rate of output of senior citizens will be around half that seen at the career peak, and the rate will still exceed what they achieved during the first decade of their careers.
2. Even so, the creative productivity expected in the final years depends appreciably on the discipline in which the individual is engaged. For those fields with extremely slow ideation and elaboration rates—as in history, philosophy, and most forms of scholarship—the peak occurs late in life and the postpeak decline tends to be negligible.
3. Creators with higher initial potential will have higher rates of output in their final years, and therefore they are more likely to have their last hit appear late in life.
4. Individuals who started their creative careers much later than normal can expect that their career peak will be displaced proportionately, and that they will probably still be going strong in their last years. Indeed, the theory permits the possibility that creators who have exhausted their creativity in one discipline may switch fields, and thereby begin a new career trajectory in another discipline.

Hence, even if some of us might get nervous about the postpeak decline, the model actually supports a rather optimistic prognosis. In fact, many creators have so many factors in their favor that they are capable of producing masterpieces toward the very end of their lives (Lindauer, 1993a, 1993b; Simonton, 1989c). These are sometimes called *swan songs*.

Not only can the theoretical model take our analysis to the creator's last day, but additionally it provides a framework for extending the analysis earlier in the creator's life—even back to the instant of conception. Hence, the model sustains a genuinely life-span developmental treatment of the development of creative expertise. This treatment is founded on the recognition that certain developmental conditions and experiences determine (a) the age of career onset, (b) the choice of creative discipline, and (c) the level of initial creative potential. I cannot possibly offer an exhaustive examination here, so allow me to sketch enough possibilities to make my claims appear more plausible (cf. Simonton, 1992a).

Age at Career Onset

What factors govern the age at which a creative individual's career takes off? Why do some creators bloom early and others late? We cannot begin to answer this question until we recognize that creative potential is not born from nothing. It takes a considerable amount of preparation—knowledge acquisition and skill practice—before the foundation has been laid for constructing a creative career (Ericsson & Charness, 1994; Ericsson, Krampe, & Tesch-Römer, 1993; see also Ericsson, chap. 1, and Sloboda, chap. 4, this volume). It has been estimated that this foundation consists of about 50,000 chunks or patterns relevant to the domain of achievement (Simon, 1986; Simon & Chase, 1973; cf. Richman, Gobet, Staszewski, & Simon, chap. 6, this volume). Assuming that the talented youth is spending several hours per day assimilating this mass, it usually takes about a decade for the basis of creative expertise to become established (Hayes, 1989; Simonton, 1991b)[4] Given this inescapable reality, we can conclude two things.

1. Circumstances that interfere with the required expertise acquisition will delay the moment when the creative career can begin. For instance, studies of talented teenagers have shown how various extraneous conditions involving school, family, or peers can pull the individual away from the requisite practice and study (Csikszentmihalyi, Rathunde, & Whalen, 1993). On the other hand, it could also happen that the youth has the good fortune of living in a supremely supportive environment where nearly all the waking hours can be devoted to talent development (Bloom, 1985). This is often the situation for child prodigies both historical and contemporary (Feldman & Goldsmith, 1986). Mozart and J. S. Mill are prime examples.

2. The earlier the age at which a youth begins this arduous process of expertise acquisition, the earlier the day will arrive when the creative career can be launched. Among the early experiences that can accelerate the onset of talent development is the availability of role models in the domain of future achievement (Simonton, 1975, 1977b, 1988c, 1992b, 1992c; Walberg, Rasher, & Parkerson, 1980). In contrast, others may get a late start simply because they floundered around for years until they discovered a discipline that attracted their fancy. Sometimes it is not until these late bloomers encounter a "crystallizing experience" that they finally latch on to the domain that is to be their destiny (cf. Walters & Gardner, 1986). For example, Anton Bruckner was around 40 when his encounter with the music of Richard Wagner finally sparked his symphonic career. About a decade later, when he was 50, he produced his first hit, and about a decade after that came his best work.

Choice of Creative Discipline

I have not listed and cannot list all the variables that determine the age of career onset; however, one particular omission can be corrected here: the domain of creative activity. Disciplines vary in how early training can begin as well as the amount of training that is required (Simonton, 1986). This

---

[4]However, there exists some evidence that the most gifted individuals may take less time to master the requisite skills and knowledge (Simonton, 1991b; for discussion see Simonton, 1994b; see also Winner, chap. 10, this volume; also compare with findings of Cohn, Carlson, & Jensen, 1985, and Jensen, Cohn, & Cohn, 1989). This imposes an important qualification on the 10-year rule for expertise acquisition. Even so, the difference is not so substantial that they can skip the long period of apprenticeship.

variation is especially apparent when we look at the different levels of formal education that are necessary. For some creative activities, nothing less than a PhD will put a would-be creator in the right position to begin making contributions to a field, whereas other activities may require no more than a high school diploma, or even less (Simonton, 1983a, 1984c). I think we can see this influence operating in Fig. 8.4, such as in the contrast between biology and the medical sciences in the location of the first career landmark.

But what determines the choice of discipline? This simple question probably has a very complex answer. It is possible that some portion of the impetus comes from genetic endowment. This was the doctrine advocated by Galton (1869) in his *Hereditary Genius*. Despite the fact that his definition of intelligence seems most consistent with the notion of Spearman's g, his data analysis and discussion suggest that he actually believed that the inheritance of talent followed more disciplinary lines. After all, the pedigrees tend to be bounded within specific domains of creativity. As an example, the distinguished lineage established for the Bach family contains only musicians and composers, not artists, writers, scientists, or philosophers. More recently, Gardner (1983) argued for seven distinct intelligences, each corresponding to a distinct domain of creative behavior (Gardner, 1993). To some extent these intelligences are rooted in a different neurological substrate, and hence it is possible that there exists a genetic basis. Certainly modern behavioral genetics has done a commendable job documenting the numerous and diverse intellectual and personality traits that feature nontrivial hereditary coefficients (e.g., Bouchard, Lykken, McGue, Segal, & Tellegen, 1990). Even a trait as complex as religiosity may have a genetic component (Waller, Kojetin, Bouchard, Lykken, & Tellegen, 1990). Identical twins separated at birth and reared apart in separate families will nonetheless display uncanny similarities in interests and activities. This concordance provides the context for appreciating the role of the crystallizing experiences that often can set an individual on a specific course of talent development (Walters & Gardner, 1986). This development may consist of the sudden recognition of an intimate match between an innate disposition and the intellectual and emotional demands of a particular domain. Hence, this aspect of talent development could indeed be decided at the moment of conception.

Even so, we must also admit that nature is not the sole factor. Nurture probably contributes just as much if not more to the choice of discipline. In some ways, Johnson (1781) may have been correct in affirming that "the true Genius is a mind of large general powers, accidentally determined to some particular direction" (p. 5). For instance, Galton's (1869) pedigrees might be attributed to the greater accessibility of role models and mentors within a domain where there exists a family tradition of achievement (Simonton, 1983b, 1988c). Nor is this the only possible environmental input. A large number of childhood and adolescent experiences may guide a person with rather general gifts to cultivate a more specialized expertise

(Simonton, 1986). Among these possible influences are socioeconomic class, birth order, early parental loss, and formal schooling and education (Simonton, 1994b).

Level of Initial Creative Potential

We have just affirmed that the choice of discipline is a function of both genetic and environmental influences. The same joint operation of nature and nurture is certainly operative in the development of creative potential as well. On the genetic side, creative potential assumes a high degree of intelligence. This intellectual power permits the individual to acquire the enormous quantity of conceptual and behavioral material that defines the foundation of expertise within a discipline. Yet a large part of this information-processing power can be credited to genetic endowment. Moreover, this endowment may entail both generalized intelligence (Spearman's g) and the more specific intelligences demanded by a particular domain of creative expertise.

High intelligence alone will not suffice, however (Barron & Harrington, 1981; Eysenck, 1995; Simonton, 1985a, 1994b). Creative potential is a function not just of the sheer wealth of disciplinary data, but also of the manner in which this information is organized. If otherwise, the distinction between received and creative expertise would become meaningless. According to the theory, the cognitive material must be profusely interconnected to nourish the free-associative variation process that generates the creative ideas. I would argue that a portion of this associative richness may originate in genetic endowment as well. There is an old tradition that, as Dryden (1681) put it, "Great Wits are sure to Madness near ally'd,/ And thin Partitions do their Bounds divide" (p. 6). This linkage between creative expertise and psychopathology has substantial empirical and theoretical support (e.g., Barron, 1963; Eysenck, 1994, 1995; Ludwig, 1995; Prentky, 1989; Richards, 1981). A mind that is slightly off center, that tends to organize experiences in more inclusive and diffuse categories, will more likely support the kind of ideational variations necessary for the emergence of truly innovative ideas. Because psychopathology itself has a indubitable genetic foundation as well, certain individuals may inherit a proclivity to structure their intellect in the optimal manner for the development of creative potential. I am not claiming here that creators are crazy. On the contrary, the research suggests that these individuals lie on the borderline between normal and abnormal thoughts, precisely as Dryden suggested (Barron, 1963; Eysenck, 1993, 1995; Rothenberg, 1990). Therefore, even though eminent creators tend to come from family lineages with above-average incidence of pathology (Juda, 1949; Karlson, 1970), the creators themselves are usually spared the debilitating consequences of unrestrained mental and emotional illness. Like Goldilocks, they get it just right—courtesy of the particular mix of genes they received from their parents.

After the same fashion, genetic endowment may lay the groundwork for other personality traits that contribute to the development of creative expertise (Eysenck, 1994, 1995). Still, we must allow ample latitude for the influx of environmental factors as well (Simonton, 1987a). Experiences and circumstances in childhood, adolescence, and early adulthood can help shape both intellectual and personality development in ways that favor or disfavor the growth of creative potential. Among the many relevant influences are orphanhood and other traumatic experiences, association with mentors and role models with optimal characteristics, the acquisition of the right amount and degree of formal education, the situation of cultural or professional marginality, and the emergence in a specific political and cultural milieu (see, e.g., Eisenstadt, Haynal, Rentchnick, & De Senarclens, 1989; Ludwig, 1995; Roe, 1952; Simonton, 1975, 1976b, 1977b, 1983a, 1984d). One striking characteristic of these environmental forces is that they often tend to work via complex curvilinear relationships and interaction effects (Simonton, 1976a, 1984a, in press-c). Because the genes can operate this way as well (Lykken, McGue, Tellegen, & Bouchard, 1992), and because genetic and environmental variables can themselves interact in intricate ways (Scarr & McCartney, 1983), the development of creative potential becomes an extremely convoluted phenomenon. It is largely for this reason that the identification and encouragement of creative talent is so difficult. Successful prediction alone would require a regression equation containing hundreds of variables with hundreds more product terms to capture all the curvilinear and interaction effects (cf. Simonton, 1984a, 1985a).

EVALUATION

I have by no means given the current model the attention it deserves. It would take a monograph to elaborate all the theoretical implications and to incorporate all the germane research. Rather than go any further, however, it is probably best for me to acknowledge the model's liabilities. The most crucial deficiency is that its treatment of the career trajectories presumes that each individual represents a closed system. External events may impinge on the precareer phase in the form of developmental influences, but once the career takes off, the environment vanishes (cf. Simonton, 1978). This is obviously wrong. Research has documented a host of extraneous circumstances that can inhibit creative productivity (Simonton, 1988a). Some of these are somewhat impersonal, such as war and competition, whereas others are more personal, such as physical illness and administrative responsibilities (e.g., Roe, 1972; Simonton, 1977b, 1985b; Stephan & Levin, 1992). The model can handle these inputs merely by assuming that they operate as random shocks throughout the life span. Only when we average across many careers do these random shocks cancel out, leaving the pure Platonic forms predicted by the deterministic model.

This issue becomes more serious when we consider another peculiar feature of the model: Initial creative potential is accumulated during the developmental period only to be expended during the productive period of a creator's life. Such a static conception ignores the more dynamic nature of a creative career. Creative individuals can continue to absorb information from their environment, and the very act of publication can evoke stimulating feedback from the external world. For instance, scientists who are embedded in a disciplinary matrix of collaborators, colleagues, associates, and rivals tend to enjoy longer productive careers, an association that may reflect some replenishment of creative potential (Simonton, 1992c). The present model can dispatch this problem, but only with a little inelegance. For example, we can assume that the time pressures of full-time employment and adulthood responsibilities preclude the kind of commitment to expertise acquisition that characterizes the developmental period. Consequently, the resuscitation of creative potential would always remain small relative to the amount of potential that is consumed. In addition, to keep the curves unaltered, we would add that this influx of new ideational material is more or less randomly distributed across the career (an assumption compatible with the equal-odds rule if the main influx comes as feedback provoked by published output). In other words, the realities reveal the simplicities of the theoretical model without necessarily forcing us to reject the model out of hand.[5]

This is not to say that I myself believe the model is "true." On that issue I remain agnostic. To make perhaps an immodest comparison, my attitude compares to that of Maxwell toward his electromagnetic theory. To derive useful equations, he hypothesized a mechanistic model that included some blatantly implausible assumptions. For example, he had to posit a universal ether through which all matter could pass without any resistance whatsoever and yet had the supreme rigidity needed to propagate high-frequency waves! Still, Maxwell's highly contrived model served as an effective scaffolding for building a mathematical edifice that has withstood the test of time.

Not that I expect my own impoverished formulae to endure with the same success as Maxwell's wonderful equations! Far from it! The equations that produced Figs. 8.1, 8.2, and 8.3 are far too simple and the data much too complex to exclude a large number of rival equations. Even in the "hardest" subdisciplines of the behaviorial sciences, such as modern cognitive science, alternative mathematical models can proliferate with virtually no empirical inhibitions whatsoever (e.g., Luce, 1986). Even so, I do maintain that for competing formulations to have a fair shot at overturn-

---

[5]I have not overlooked many other simplifications. For example, the assumption that the ideation and elaboration rates are constant may not be strictly true. Certainly human information-processing speed slows down toward the end of life (Schaie, 1993). Nevertheless, I would argue that these and many other longitudinal changes would not oblige any crucial changes in the predictions generated by the current model.

ing this theory, they must prove themselves compatible with an awesome variety of well-established findings. With respect to the career trajectories alone, alternative schemes must somehow account for individual differences and interdisciplinary contrasts in the productivity curves, including the extremely distinctive pattern of covariances among the three career landmarks. Furthermore, an impressive range of other phenomena should also be explicated, phenomena that have already been explained under the Darwinian model (Eysenck, 1993, 1995; Kantorovich, 1993; Kantorovich & Ne'eman, 1989; Martindale, 1990, 1994; Simonton, 1988e). These include (a) stylistic changes in the arts, (b) serendipity in science and technology, (c) multiple discovery and invention, (d) Planck's principle of innovation acceptance, and (e) the Lotka and Price laws of the cross-sectional productivity distribution. At the present moment, our knowledge base is such as to exclude perhaps all current models besides the one offered here (Simonton, 1994c).

I am not trying to discourage anyone from venturing a rival theoretical account of how creative expertise unfolds over the life span. I merely want to ensure that all alternative proposals capture the full complexity of this behavioral spectacle. It may ultimately happen that my entire theoretical system will look as ridiculous as phlogiston theory now does to post-Lavoisier chemists. Nonetheless, that will occur not because the current model is proven wrong, but rather because a future model is proven more right.

REFERENCES

Albert, R. S. (1975). Toward a behavioral definition of genius. *American Psychologist, 30*, 140–151.

Barron, F. X. (1963). *Creativity and psychological health: Origins of personal vitality and creative freedom.* Princeton, NJ: Van Nostrand.

Barron, F., & Harrington, D. M. (1981). Creativity, intelligence, and personality. *Annual Review of Psychology, 32*, 439–476.

Bayer, A. E., & Dutton, J. E. (1977). Career age and research—Professional activities of academic scientists: Tests of alternative non-linear models and some implications for higher education faculty policies. *Journal of Higher Education, 48*, 259–282.

Bennet, W. (1980, January–February). Providing for posterity. *Harvard Magazine*, pp. 13–16.

Bloom, B. S. (Ed.). (1985). *Developing talent in young people.* New York: Ballantine Books.

Bouchard, T. J., Lykken, D. T., McGue, M., Segal, N. L., & Tellegen, A. (1990). Sources of human psychological differences: The Minnesota study of twins reared apart. *Science, 250*, 223–228.

Buchanan, B. G., & Shortliffe, E. H. (Eds.). (1984). *Rule-based expert systems: The MYCIN experiments of the Stanford Heuristics Programming Project.* Reading, MA: Addison-Wesley.

Campbell, D. T. (1960). Blind variation and selective retention in creative thought as in other knowledge processes. *Psychological Review, 67*, 380–400.

Campbell, D. T. (1965). Variation and selective retention in socio-cultural evolution. In H. R. Barringer, G. I. Blanksten, & R. W. Mack (Eds.), *Social change in developing areas* (pp. 19–49). Cambridge, MA: Schenkman.

Campbell, D. T. (1974). Evolutionary epistemology. In P. A. Schlipp (Ed.), *The philosophy of Karl Popper* (pp. 413–463). La Salle, IL: Open Court.

Christensen, H., & Jacomb, P. A. (1992). The lifetime productivity of eminent Australian academics. *International Journal of Geriatric Psychiatry, 7*, 681–686.

Cohn, S. J., Carlson, J. S., & Jensen, A. R. (1985). Speed of information processing in academically gifted youths. *Personality and Individual Differences, 6,* 621–629.

Cole, S. (1979). Age and scientific performance. *American Journal of Sociology, 84,* 958–977.

Cole, S., & Cole, J. R. (1973). *Social stratification in science.* Chicago: University of Chicago Press.

Csikszentmihalyi, M., Rathunde, K., & Whalen, S. (1993). *Talented teenagers: The roots of success and failure.* New York: Cambridge University Press.

Dennis, W. (1954a). Bibliographies of eminent scientists. *Scientific Monthly, 79,* 180–183.

Dennis, W. (1954b). Predicting scientific productivity in later maturity from records of earlier decades. *Journal of Gerontology, 9,* 465–467.

Dennis, W. (1954c). Productivity among American psychologists. *American Psychologist, 9,* 191–194.

Dennis, W. (1955). Variations in productivity among creative workers. *Scientific Monthly, 80,* 277–278.

Dennis, W. (1966). Creative productivity between the ages of 20 and 80 years. *Journal of Gerontology, 21,* 1–8.

Dryden, J. (1681). *Absalom and Achitophel: A poem.* London: Davis.

Eisenstadt, J. M., Haynal, A., Rentchnick, P., & De Senarclens, P. (1989). *Parental loss and achievement.* Madison, CT: International Universities Press.

Ericsson, K. A., & Charness, N. (1994). Expert performance: Its structure and acquisition. *American Psychologist, 49,* 725–747.

Ericsson, K. A., Krampe, R. T., & Tesch-Römer, C. (1993). The role of deliberate practice in the acquisition of expert performance. *Psychological Review, 100,* 363–406.

Eysenck, H. J. (1993). Creativity and personality: Suggestions for a theory. *Psychological Inquiry, 4,* 147–148.

Eysenck, H. J. (1994). Creativity and personality: Word association, origence, and psychoticism. *Creativity Research Journal, 7,* 209–216.

Eysenck, H. J. (1995). *Genius: The natural history of creativity.* Cambridge, UK: Cambridge University Press.

Feldman, D. H., & Goldsmith, L. T. (1986). *Nature's gambit: Child prodigies and the development of human potential.* New York: Basic Books.

Galton, F. (1869). *Hereditary genius: An inquiry into its laws and consequences.* London: Macmillan.

Gardner, H. (1983). *Frames of mind: A theory of multiple intelligences.* New York: Basic Books.

Gardner, H. (1993). *Creating minds: An anatomy of creativity seen through the lives of Freud, Einstein, Picasso, Stravinsky, Eliot, Graham, and Gandhi.* New York: Basic Books.

Gruber, H. E. (1989). The evolving systems approach to creative work. In D. B. Wallace & H. E. Gruber (Eds.), *Creative people at work: Twelve cognitive case studies* (pp. 3–24). New York: Oxford University Press.

Hayes, J. R. (1989). *The complete problem solver* (2nd ed.). Hillsdale, NJ: Lawrence Erlbaum Associates.

James, W. (1880). Great men, great thoughts, and the environment. *Atlantic Monthly, 46,* 441–459.

Jensen, A. R., Cohn, S. J., & Cohn, C. M. G. (1989). Speed of information processing in academically gifted youths and their siblings. *Personality and Individual Differences, 10,* 29–34.

Johnson, S. (1781). *The lives of the most eminent English poets* (Vol. 1). London: Bathurst et al.

Juda, A. (1949). The relationship between highest mental capacity and psychic abnormalities. *American Journal of Psychiatry, 106,* 296–307.

Kantorovich, A. (1993). *Scientific discovery: Logic and tinkering.* Albany: State University of New York Press.

Kantorovich, A., & Ne'eman, Y. (1989). Serendipity as a source of evolutionary progress in science. *Studies in History and Philosophy of Science, 20,* 505–529.

Karlson, J. I. (1970). Genetic association of giftedness and creativity with schizophrenia. *Hereditas, 66,* 177–182.

Kirton, M. J. (1976). Adaptors and innovators: A description and measure. *Journal of Applied Psychology, 61,* 622–629.

Kuhn, T. S. (1970). *The structure of scientific revolutions* (2nd ed.). Chicago: University of Chicago Press.
Langley, P., Simon, H. A., Bradshaw, G. L., & Zytkow, J. M. (1987). *Scientific discovery.* Cambridge, MA: MIT Press.
Lehman, H. C. (1953). *Age and achievement.* Princeton, NJ: Princeton University Press.
Lindauer, M. S. (1993a). The old-age style and its artists. *Empirical Studies and the Arts, 11,* 135–146.
Lindauer, M. S. (1993b). The span of creativity among long-lived historical artists. *Creativity Research Journal, 6,* 231–239.
Lotka, A. J. (1926). The frequency distribution of scientific productivity. *Journal of the Washington Academy of Sciences, 16,* 317–323.
Luce, R. D. (1986). *Response times: Their role in inferring elementary mental organization.* New York: Oxford University Press.
Ludwig, A. (1995). *The price of greatness: Resolving the creativity and madness controversy.* New York: Guilford.
Lykken, D. T., McGue, M., Tellegen, A., & Bouchard, T. J., Jr. (1992). Emergenesis: Genetic traits that may not run in families. *American Psychologist, 47,* 1565–1577.
MacCrimmon, K. R., & Wagner, C. (1987). Expert systems and creativity. In J. L. Mumpower, O. Renn, L. D. Phillips, & V. R. R. Uppuluri (Eds.), *Expert judgment and expert systems* (pp. 173–193). Berlin: Springer-Verlag.
Mach, E. (1896). On the part played by accident in invention and discovery. *Monist, 6,* 161–175.
MacKinnon, D. W. (1978). *In search of human effectiveness.* Buffalo, NY: Creative Education Foundation.
Martindale, C. (1990). *The clockwork muse: The predictability of artistic styles.* New York: Basic Books.
Martindale, C. (1994). How can we measure a society's creativity? In M. A. Boden (Ed.), *Dimensions of creativity* (pp. 159–197). Cambridge, MA: MIT Press.
Over, R. (1982a). Does research productivity decline with age? *Higher Education, 11,* 511–520.
Over, R. (1982b). Is age a good predictor of research productivity? *Australian Psychologist, 17,* 129–139.
Over, R. (1989). Age and scholarly impact. *Psychology and Aging, 4,* 222–225.
Perkins, D. N. (1994). Creativity: Beyond the Darwinian paradigm. In M. A. Boden (Ed.), *Dimensions of creativity* (pp. 119–142). Cambridge, MA: MIT Press.
Poincaré, H. (1921). *The foundations of science: Science and hypothesis, the value of science, science and method* (G. B. Halstead, Trans.). New York: Science Press.
Prentky, R. A. (1989). Creativity and psychopathology: Gamboling at the seat of madness. In J. A. Glover, R. R. Ronning, & C. R. Reynolds (Eds.), *Handbook of creativity* (pp. 243–269). New York: Plenum.
Price, D. (1963). *Little science, big science.* New York: Columbia University Press.
Quetelet, A. (1968). *A treatise on man and the development of his faculties.* New York: Franklin. (Original work published 1835)
Raskin, E. A. (1936). Comparison of scientific and literary ability: A biographical study of eminent scientists and men of letters of the nineteenth century. *Journal of Abnormal and Social Psychology, 31,* 20–35.
Richards, R. (1981). Relationships between creativity and psychopathology: An evaluation and interpretation of the evidence. *Genetic Psychology Monographs, 103,* 261–324.
Roe, A. (1952). *The making of a scientist.* New York: Dodd, Mead.
Roe, A. (1972). Patterns of productivity of scientists. *Science, 176,* 940–941.
Rostan, S. M. (1994). Problem finding, problem solving, and cognitive controls: An empirical investigation of critically acclaimed productivity. *Creativity Research Journal, 7,* 97–110.
Rothenberg, A. (1990). *Creativity and madness: New findings and old stereotypes.* Baltimore, MD: Johns Hopkins University Press.
Scarr, S., & McCartney, K. (1983). How people make their own environments: A theory of genotype Æ environmental effects. *Child Development, 54,* 424–435.
Schaie, K. W. (1993). The Seattle longitudinal studies of adult intelligence. *Current Directions in Psychological Science, 2,* 171–175.

Shaw, G. B. (1903). *Man and superman.* New York: Brentano's.

Shrager, J., & Langley, P. (Eds.). (1990). *Computational models of scientific discovery and theory formation.* San Mateo, CA: Kaufmann.

Simon, H. A. (1986). What we know about the creative process. In R. L. Kuhn (Ed.), *Frontiers in creative and innovative management* (pp. 3–20). Cambridge, MA: Ballinger.

Simon, H. A., & Chase, W. G. (1973). Skill in chess. *American Scientist, 61,* 394–403.

Simonton, D. K. (1975). Sociocultural context of individual creativity: A transhistorical time-series analysis. *Journal of Personality and Social Psychology, 32,* 1119–1133.

Simonton, D. K. (1976a). Biographical determinants of achieved eminence: A multivariate approach to the Cox data. *Journal of Personality and Social Psychology, 33,* 218–226.

Simonton, D. K. (1976b). Philosophical eminence, beliefs, and zeitgeist: An individual-generational analysis. *Journal of Personality and Social Psychology, 34,* 630–640.

Simonton, D. K. (1977a). Creative productivity, age, and stress: A biographical time-series analysis of 10 classical composers. *Journal of Personality and Social Psychology, 35,* 791–804.

Simonton, D. K. (1977b). Eminence, creativity, and geographic marginality: A recursive structural equation model. *Journal of Personality and Social Psychology, 35,* 805–816.

Simonton, D. K. (1978). The eminent genius in history: The critical role of creative development. *Gifted Child Quarterly, 22,* 187–195.

Simonton, D. K. (1979). Multiple discovery and invention: Zeitgeist, genius, or chance? *Journal of Personality and Social Psychology, 37,* 1603–1616.

Simonton, D. K. (1980a). Intuition and analysis: A predictive and explanatory model. *Genetic Psychology Monographs, 102,* 3–60.

Simonton, D. K. (1980b). Thematic fame, melodic originality, and musical zeitgeist: A biographical and transhistorical content analysis. *Journal of Personality and Social Psychology, 38,* 972–983.

Simonton, D. K. (1983a). Formal education, eminence, and dogmatism: The curvilinear relationship. *Journal of Creative Behavior, 17,* 149–162.

Simonton, D. K. (1983b). Intergenerational transfer of individual differences in hereditary monarchs: Genes, role-modeling, cohort, or sociocultural effects? *Journal of Personality and Social Psychology, 44,* 354–364.

Simonton, D. K. (1984a). Artistic creativity and interpersonal relationships across and within generations. *Journal of Personality and Social Psychology, 46,* 1273–1286.

Simonton, D. K. (1984b). Creative productivity and age: A mathematical model based on a two-step cognitive process. *Developmental Review, 4,* 77–111.

Simonton, D. K. (1984c). *Genius, creativity, and leadership: Historiometric inquiries.* Cambridge, MA: Harvard University Press.

Simonton, D. K. (1984d). Is the marginality effect all that marginal? *Social Studies of Science, 14,* 621–622.

Simonton, D. K. (1985a). Intelligence and personal influence in groups: Four nonlinear models. *Psychological Review, 92,* 532–547.

Simonton, D. K. (1985b). Quality, quantity, and age: The careers of 10 distinguished psychologists. *International Journal of Aging and Human Development, 21,* 241–254.

Simonton, D. K. (1986). Biographical typicality, eminence, and achievement style. *Journal of Creative Behavior, 20,* 14–22.

Simonton, D. K. (1987a). Developmental antecedents of achieved eminence. *Annals of Child Development, 5,* 131–169.

Simonton, D. K. (1987b). Multiples, chance, genius, creativity, and zeitgeist. In D. N. Jackson & J. P. Rushton (Eds.), *Scientific excellence: Origins and assessment* (pp. 98–128). Beverly Hills, CA: Sage.

Simonton, D. K. (1988a). Age and outstanding achievement: What do we know after a century of research? *Psychological Bulletin, 104,* 251–267.

Simonton, D. K. (1988b). Creativity, leadership, and chance. In R. J. Sternberg (Ed.), *The nature of creativity: Contemporary psychological perspectives* (pp. 386–426). New York: Cambridge University Press.

Simonton, D. K. (1988c). Galtonian genius, Kroeberian configurations, and emulation: A generational time-series analysis of Chinese civilization. *Journal of Personality and Social Psychology, 55,* 230–238.

Simonton, D. K. (1988d). Quality and purpose, quantity and chance. *Creativity Research Journal, 1,* 68–74.

Simonton, D. K. (1988e). *Scientific genius: A psychology of science.* Cambridge, UK: Cambridge University Press.

Simonton, D. K. (1989a). Age and creative productivity: Nonlinear estimation of an information-processing model. *International Journal of Aging and Human Development, 29,* 23–37.

Simonton, D. K. (1989b). The chance-configuration theory of scientific creativity. In B. Gholson, W. R. Shadish, Jr., R. A. Neimeyer, & A. C. Houts (Eds.), *The psychology of science: Contributions to metascience* (pp. 170–213). Cambridge, UK: Cambridge University Press.

Simonton, D. K. (1989c). The swan-song phenomenon: Last-works effects for 172 classical composers. *Psychology and Aging, 4,* 42–47.

Simonton, D. K. (1990). Creativity in the later years: Optimistic prospects for achievement. *Gerontologist, 30,* 626–631.

Simonton, D. K. (1991a). Career landmarks in science: Individual differences and interdisciplinary contrasts. *Developmental Psychology, 27,* 119–130.

Simonton, D. K. (1991b). Emergence and realization of genius: The lives and works of 120 classical composers. *Journal of Personality and Social Psychology, 61,* 829–840.

Simonton, D. K. (1991c). Latent-variable models of posthumous reputation: A quest for Galton's G. *Journal of Personality and Social Psychology, 60,* 607–619.

Simonton, D. K. (1992a). The child parents the adult: On getting genius from giftedness. In N. Colangelo, S. G. Assouline, & D. L. Ambroson (Eds.), *Talent development: Proceedings from the 1991 Henry B. and Jocelyn Wallace National Research Symposium on Talent Development* (pp. 278–297). Unionville, NY: Trillium Press.

Simonton, D. K. (1992b). Leaders of American psychology, 1879–1967: Career development, creative output, and professional achievement. *Journal of Personality and Social Psychology, 62,* 5–17.

Simonton, D. K. (1992c). The social context of career success and course for 2,026 scientists and inventors. *Personality and Social Psychology Bulletin, 18,* 452–463.

Simonton, D. K. (1993a). Blind variations, chance configurations, and creative genius. *Psychological Inquiry, 4,* 225–228.

Simonton, D. K. (1993b). Genius and chance: A Darwinian perspective. In J. Brockman (Ed.), *Creativity: The reality club IV* (pp. 176–201). New York: Simon & Schuster.

Simonton, D. K. (1994a). Foresight in insight? A Darwinian answer. In R. J. Sternberg & J. E. Davidson (Eds.), *The nature of insight* (pp. 465–494). Cambridge, MA: MIT Press.

Simonton, D. K. (1994b). *Greatness: Who makes history and why.* New York: Guilford.

Simonton, D. K. (1994c). Individual differences, developmental changes, and social context. *Behavioral and Brain Sciences, 17,* 552–553.

Simonton, D. K. (in press-a). Career paths and creative lives: A theoretical perspective on late-life potential. In C. Adams-Price (Ed.), *Creativity and aging: Theoretical and empirical perspectives.* New York: Springer.

Simonton, D. K. (in press-b). Creativity as variation and selection: Some critical constraints. In M. Runco (Ed.), *Critical creativity.* Cresskill, NJ: Hampton Press.

Simonton, D. K. (in press-c). When giftedness becomes genius: How does talent achieve eminence? In N. Colangelo & G. A. Davis (Eds.), *Handbook of gifted education* (2nd ed.). Boston: Allyn & Bacon.

Skinner, B. F. (1972). *Cumulative record: A selection of papers* (3rd ed.). New York: Appleton-Century-Crofts.

Stephan, P. E., & Levin, S. G. (1992). *Striking the mother lode in science: The importance of age, place, and time.* New York: Oxford University Press.

Thoreau, H. D. (1942). *Walden* (G. H. Haight, Ed.). New York: Black. (Original work published 1845)

Toulmin, S. (1972). *Human understanding.* Princeton, NJ: Princeton University Press.

Walberg, H. J., Rasher, S. P., & Parkerson, J. (1980). Childhood and eminence. *Journal of Creative Behavior, 13,* 225–231.

Waller, N. G., Kojetin, B. A., Bouchard, T. J., Jr., Lykken, D. T., & Tellegen, A. (1990). Genetic and environmental influences on religious interests, attitudes, and values: A study of twins reared apart and together. *Psychological Science, 1,* 138–142.

Walters, J., & Gardner, H. (1986). The crystallizing experience: Discovering an intellectual gift. In R. J. Sternberg & J. E. Davidson (Eds.), *Conceptions of giftedness* (pp. 306–331). New York: Cambridge University Press.

Weber, R. J. (1992). *Forks, phonographs, and hot air balloons: A field guide to inventive thinking.* New York: Oxford University Press.

Weisberg, R. W. (1992). *Creativity: Beyond the myth of genius.* New York: Freeman.

Zhao, H., & Jiang, G. (1986). Life-span and precocity of scientists. *Scientometrics, 9,* 27–36.

Zuckerman, H. (1977). *Scientific elite.* New York: The Free Press.

Zusne, L. (1976). Age and achievement in psychology: The harmonic mean as a model. *American Psychologist, 31,* 805–807.

9

The Childhoods and Early Lives of Geniuses: Combining Psychological and Biographical Evidence

Michael J. A. Howe
Unversity of Exeter

There are a number of reasons for our fascination with geniuses. Their achievements can touch our own lives, as we are reminded every time we listen to a masterpiece like *Tosca,* or read a great novel such as *Middlemarch,* or spend an hour in a major art gallery. For millions of people the Newtons and Einsteins of science have transformed the very manner in which the world is seen to operate. These individuals, and other major scientists such as Galileo and Darwin, revolutionized human thought by shattering old certainties that had rested unquestioned for numerous generations.

The possibility of discovering how geniuses are formed is intriguing, but they appear to be mysteriously different from ordinary people. However, on close examination they turn out to be surprisingly similar to other individuals, in some respects at least. Attending to the similarities as well as the differences not only helps us to understand geniuses better but also make it easier to identify practical insights that can be applied toward encouraging today's young people to be more innovative and creative. Despite the fact that genius is often thought to be inherently mysterious, I am convinced that it is possible to extend our understanding of its origins by following an approach in which findings obtained from psychological research are combined with information taken from biographical sources.

DEFINING GENIUS

Saying precisely what we mean by a "genius" is difficult. There are no universally agreed defining characteristics. When people are deciding whether or not to call someone a genius, what usually happens is that the decision is made largely on the basis of the person's achievements, rather than any measurable characteristics. Calling someone a genius is more of an acknowledgment of what they have done than an assessment of what they are. We say that someone is a genius only if they have made some outstanding creative achievement. In the absence of any great attainment, a person is rarely if ever regarded as being a genius, however clever, artistic, diligent, wise, or insightful they are thought to be (Howe, 1994).

The fact that there is no agreed defining attribute of a genius does not detract from the usefulness of the term, but it does have the consequence of making it very difficult to agree on who is to be called a genius and who is not. There is a small number of individuals who are very widely acknowledged to have been geniuses, and a much larger category of people whose candidacy for inclusion in a list of geniuses would be supported by some people but not others. The first group would include great scientists and artists such as Galileo, Shakespeare, Michelangelo, Newton, Mozart, Darwin, and Einstein. Among the numerous famous names in the second group might be, for instance, Emily Brontë, Trollope, and Marie Curie.

Mixing Biography and Psychology

The science of psychology cannot on its own provide all the resources needed to understand the origins of genius. The contributions of the art of biography are also essential. Biographers are drawn to what is unique about individuals, and they take on the vital job of tracing and putting into perspective the events of people's lives. However, psychological knowledge remains vital, even if those scholars whose experience of witnessing the application of psychology to the enterprise of trying to discern causes and effects in the lives of individuals is limited to the "psychobiographical" approaches that were recently fashionable could be forgiven for doubting this. Despite the fact that most biographers have impressive skills and intellectual resources (see, for biographers' comments on the art of biography and its pitfalls, Cockshut, 1974; Garraty, 1958; Maurois, 1929; Sturrock, 1993), they are not necessarily well equipped with the kinds of knowledge that can make it possible to understand why or how an individual became capable of outstanding accomplishments. Although it is arguable whether the Freudian and related brands of psychology that permeate psychobiographies have ever had much to offer for extending our understanding of the origins of individuals' outstanding attainments, it is clear that modern empirical psychology can provide many kinds of vital evidence.

For example, imagine that a biographer is confronted with the feats of someone like Mozart, who not only began to compose music when he was no more than 4, but by the age of 6 was an accomplished performer on both harpsichord and violin, and was reported in late childhood to have written out the complete score of Allegri's *Miserere*, a lengthy multipart musical composition, after hearing it just twice. Lacking the psychological knowledge that could help explain Mozart's prodigality, it is more than likely that the biographer would reach a conclusion based on one or more of the following three apparently reasonable and widely shared assumptions: (a) that Mozart's early accomplishments were a complete mystery, (b) that he simply possessed an inborn musical gift or talent, and (c) that he inherited his musical ability from his father. However, as someone who had been given the opportunity to survey psychological research into the determinants of exceptional ability would be able to point out, none of those three underlying assumptions is actually justified, and any conclusion that is based on them would be unwarranted.

However, if these three assumptions about the causes of Mozart's early feats are all untrue, how do we explain his accomplishments? Can psychology really help? It undoubtedly can. In the case of all three of Mozart's feats, there exist very strong grounds for saying that remarkable as they were, adequate explanations can be found, and the origins are not at all mysterious. So far as Mozart's early performing skills are concerned, evidence from psychological research shows that they were not out of line with what would be expected in a child of that age who received intensive training and spent a considerable amount of time practising, as Mozart undoubtedly did (Ericsson, Tesch-Römer, & Krampe, 1993; Sloboda, Davidson, Howe, & Moore, in press). Mozart's initial efforts at composing were no more mysterious, and although it is certainly unusual for a young child to engage in any composing at all, his achievements at that age do not seem so remarkable once it is appreciated that none of his more substantial or original compositions were produced prior to his having experienced over 10 years of lengthy musical training (Hayes, 1981). Similarly, his memory feat, although undoubtedly impressive, appears less than miraculous in the light of the fact that research has shown that, for reasons psychological investigations of memory have convincingly clarified, very impressive memory feats are relatively commonplace when they involve the recall of information that is closely related to a person's specialized knowledge and special interests (Chi & Ceci, 1987; Howe, 1989). Because Mozart's father subjected him to an unusual childhood regime characterized by constant exposure to music, there would have been ample opportunities for Mozart to gain the knowledge of music that would have made his memory feat possible.

The suggestion that Mozart must have had an innate musical gift is unconvincing because it begs a number of questions and provides only the appearance of an explanation rather than a genuine one. A statement of that kind can never amount to more than a half-baked explanation unless it is possible to specify precisely what form such an innate gift takes, how its presence is detected and exactly how it operates (Howe, 1990; Sloboda, Davidson, & Howe, 1994). In the absence of that information, the assertion that innate gifts and talents are crucial is virtually impossible to verify or disconfirm, and the arguments that are provided to support such a view often involve circular reasoning. That is not to deny the possibility that some exceptional individuals may have been born with special characteristics that contributed to their special abilities, but simply making the bald assertion that such was the case (without even saying precisely what those characteristics are) and assuming that by doing that one is explaining the person's accomplishments, is not at all helpful. The assumption that an ability can be directly inherited is equally unconvincing. Inheritance simply does not work in that way. Genes are far from being the determining blueprints implied by that assumption, and genetic causation is not the simple, all-or-none process that is implied by the widespread but incorrect view that it is possible for an ability as such to be directly inherited from a relative.

Psychology also places a necessary emphasis on the need to ensure that evidence is as reliable as possible. Research findings draw attention to the importance of verifying apparently factual biographical evidence about a person. The need to do this is indicated by the results of investigations designed to elicit memories of the first years of life. A number of such studies have established that people can remember remarkably little about their early childhoods, with a person's recollections of happenings alleged to have occurred in their first year or two usually being fictitious, however strongly they are believed to be real. Consequently, a degree of skepticism is in order when we read in a biography of Noel Coward, for instance, that before he was 20 months of age, "He had already made his first journey by train . . . during which he had stayed wide awake, staring at everything all the time, which made his mother fear he was a bad traveller. Could this have been the first manifestation of his enduring passion for trains and for travelling in them?" (Lesley, 1976, p. 4).

A biographer who is unaware of certain limitations of human memory may fail to realize that it is entirely possible for an honest person to give a detailed description of an event in the distant past when in fact there is objective evidence that the event could not possibly have happened at all. Mistaken memories are not at all unusual, particularly in the case of autobiographical recollections, and the degree of confidence that people have in the truth of their own recollections is no guide at all to their actual veracity. For instance, for much of his life Jean Piaget retained a vivid and detailed memory of a childhood incident in which someone tried to kidnap him, but later he discovered that the incident he remembered so clearly could not possibly have taken place.

Knowledge of psychological research findings can be equally valuable in connection with the interpretation of those early events that indisputably did occur. It is all too easy for a biographer to make unwarranted assumptions about an event's significance. For example, in the early childhood of Alfred Hitchcock, he once woke up to discover that his parents had left him alone in the house while they went for a walk. The frightened young Hitchcock wandered into the kitchen, where he found a piece of meat, which he ate while drying his tears. Hitchcock's biographer made much of this event: "How did this incident affect Hitchcock? Certainly by imparting a lifetime fear of being alone or in darkness: certainly by inflicting a terror. . . . But the memory also indicates that he knew, even if subconsciously, that food could be his comfort against solitude—an association that has become in recent times a self-evident truth to both doctors and dieters alike" (Spoto, 1983, pp. 17–18).

However, the findings of numerous studies have established that there is a limit to the degree to which single occurrences affect young people's lives (Rutter & Rutter, 1992). It is almost impossible for one incident in childhood to establish habits that persist for a whole life. Long-lasting problems are almost always caused by repeated events or adverse circumstances that persist over a period of time. Similarly with abilities and positive qualities: The findings of investigations studying the long-term effects of training and practice show that people become unusually able not because of the occasional dramatic instances on which a biographer may be tempted to dwell but as a result of repeated and regular activities that provide the numerous hours of training and practice that are indispensable for excellence in virtually all areas of competence (Ericsson, Tesch-Römer, & Krampe, 1993; Sloboda, Davidson, Howe, & Moore, in press).

Plausible as this claim about the possible long-lasting effects of a single event may appear to be, the fact is that particular isolated incidents are rarely all-important, even when they are traumatic. The unnoticed routine background events of a person's life are in many respects far more influential than the more dramatic incidents that we enjoy reading about in biographies.

ASPECTS OF A NEW APPROACH

We can now see that psychological findings make an essential contribution to our understanding of the origins of geniuses' abilities. These findings show that phenomena that may appear to a biographer to be mysterious or inexplicable are not in fact inexplicable at all; they make it clear that some of the so-called explanations that might be suggested by a biographer's ideas about commonsense psychology are far from being adequate, and they establish that single events, even ones that appear to have had a dramatic impact, could not possibly have had some of the effects that they are believed to have had. All the same, the skills and resources possessed by biographers are just as essential as those of psychological researchers, and this becomes apparent when we consider some necessary features of an approach that will help make it possible to understand how exceptionally creative people gain the capabilities that make their achievements possible. Such an approach will undoubtedly depend on psychological research findings, for reasons I have already mentioned, but in addition it will need to have the following five aspects, all of which require inputs of information that can only come from biographical sources.

First, there must be an emphasis on examining the lives of individual men and women. Psychological research usually begins by looking at samples comprising a number of people, and that way of doing things often has much to recommend it, making it possible to arrive at generalizations that apply to people in general. However, the benefits recede and the limitations become pressing when the aim is to understand individuals who are extraordinary, and whose very uniqueness is a primary reason for taking an interest in them.

Second, there are advantages to be gained by taking an approach that, at least initially, is largely descriptive, as is some extent inevitable when there is a large biographical component. It is sometimes necessary to keep a rein on our natural enthusiasm to explain and understand, because it is rarely possible to explain how something happened until we know precisely what actually did happen. It is essential to describe in some detail the lives of particular individuals. Failure to appreciate the necessity to describe things properly before trying to explain them has led psychologists into all kinds of difficulties, but once a good description is available, the job of explaining is often more than half done.

Starting with a descriptive approach (which does not mean simply collecting random facts or denying the importance of explanatory theories) can make it easier to avoid some of the preconceptions and unjustified assumptions that can create barriers to genuine understanding by constraining a researcher's observations and thoughts. If I listen to a young person playing the violin unusually well, I may be tempted to describe her as being "gifted," perhaps without realizing that by introducing that word I am drawn into agreeing with the explanation that is implicit in it, indicating that the player is not just especially competent, but competent for a particular reason, namely that she possesses a musical gift. If I begin to use the word gifted regularly for describing able musicians, I may unknowingly begin to convince myself that it is good musicians' gifts that make them excellent; and if I allow myself to become convinced that the only possible reason for Beethoven's becoming a great composer was that he was born with a special gift for music, I will be largely unable to perceive possibilities and pursue questions other than those that directly follow from that belief, and I will be blind to alternative explanations.

Third, it is important to obtain continuous records of people's lives. In principle, there is nothing to prevent psychological researchers from doing that, but in practice most psychological research involves brief experiments being conducted, or occasional snapshot observations being made on a small number of occasions: Longitudinal research involving frequent observations over a period of years is much more uncommon, partly because it is very expensive. But the real lives of individual people are continuous, and, as we have seen, many of the events that mold a person take the form of everyday happenings that occur frequently and regularly, gradually and cumulatively exerting their effects over periods of months and years. Influences of this kind cannot be adequately assessed by research that is based on occasional observations, or properly encompassed in experimental research. Here it is essential to call on the kinds of data that some biographers have been able to collect, being careful to be sure to give at least as much attention to the regular and routine background events that shape a person's abilities and qualities as to the more dramatic incidents that strike our attention—and sometimes the biographer's—most forcefully. A person's early life is in some respects analogous to a journey that follows a particular route unique to the individual: Having a continuous record of the person's life helps make it possible to trace the route by which the individual has made progress.

Fourth, the approach needs to be one in which emphasis is placed on getting as close as possible to the actual experiences of the individuals whose early lives are being traced. This means more than just taking account of environmental circumstances. With a few exceptions, such as the work of Csikszentmihalyi and his coresearchers (see, e.g., Csikszentmihalyi, Rathunde, & Whalen, 1993), psychologists have looked at people's environments from the perspective of an outside observer rather than that of the individual who is directly concerned. However, as far as the actual person is concerned, what really counts about an event is not simply those qualities of it that could be recorded by an observer but the manner in which it is actually experienced by the particular individual. As Dunn and Plomin (1990) showed in their study of brothers and sisters brought up together, however much the parents strive to produce an environment that is equivalent for all the children in one family, the children's all-important experiences of family life will differ enormously. It is not easy to move away from external measures of environment toward direct assessments of people's experiences, but it is worth making big efforts to do so.

The fifth essential characteristic of an approach that aims to discover how individuals became capable of major creative achievements is that it must consider the whole person, rather than being narrowly concerned with just the intellectual qualities that the individual draws on. Intellect is far from all important, and our knowledge of geniuses and their lives makes it abundantly clear that other influences, ranging from personality and temperament to a person's self-confidence, motivation, and sense of direction, are equally crucial. For example, Darwin had to draw very heavily on attributes of tact, diplomacy, courage, confidence—which grew as his expertise increased, as Sulloway (1985) demonstrated in a quantitative analysis of entries in Darwin's letters—and his pronounced ability to get along with other people. Without these qualities he would never have managed to get along with some difficult individuals whose cooperation he depended on, and he would not have been able to assemble the network of diverse individuals, ranging from scientists and collectors to veterinarians, horticulturists, pigeon fanciers, beekeepers, rose growers, farmers, and horse trainers who he depended on for evidence to support the theory of evolution. Darwin was far from untypical in his needing to have a number of qualities other than his intellectual ones. Although the paths the lives of geniuses have followed are extremely diverse, every genius needs and depends on a range of human qualities.

The approach that I have been taking involves looking at a relatively small number of individuals and trying to describe the routes by which they became capable of making the creative achievements they eventually produced. It is not the only possible approach, but it is my firm impression that examining the lives of individuals reasonably closely and over lengthy periods of time does bring useful rewards. It is important to emphasize that my current interest is not in trying to understand exceptional creative achievements as such but in attempting the rather different task of explaining how someone becomes capable of exceptional achievements. No two geniuses are alike, and the two people I very briefly discuss here, in order to illustrate some aspects of the approach being taken, were different from each other in many ways. However, they did have one thing in common: Both started from extremely unpromising beginnings.

GEORGE STEPHENSON

The British engineer George Stephenson had an enormous influence on the development of steam locomotion and on the railway revolution that made possible. He was born in 1781, in a mining region near Newcastle in northeastern England. He was the second of six children, none of whom went to school because the family was very poor and had to exist on the low wages of Stephenson's father, who worked as an engine firemen at a nearby colliery.

Most of the information we have about Stephenson's early life comes from a biography written soon after his death in 1848 by Samuel Smiles (1857/1881), who is best known for writing a mid-19th century best-seller called *Self-Help*, a book that urges on readers the need for self-improvement and gives examples of the ways in which individuals have managed to achieve that as a result of hard work, perseverance, and strenuous efforts to educate themselves. Smiles was well suited to be Stephenson's biographer, partly because he was working for a railway company when he started writing the book and had a close practical understanding of some of the problems Stephenson had encountered. Smiles talked to number of people who had known Stephenson as a child and young man, and he constructed a picture of a childhood that was not particularly unusual, but in which the young Stephenson displayed a number of signs of being particularly resourceful and displaying initiative, and was a little more ambitious than most of the boys with whom he grew up.

In looking for evidence of early interests and experiences that might have been especially helpful in encouraging Stephenson to acquire skills that he could call on later, one kind of activity that Smiles remarked on deserves attention: It is one that happens, incidentally, to be similar to a childhood preoccupation of Isaac Newton. Smiles reported an account of the young Stephenson, at around 11 or 12, making models of mine engines and machinery out of clay, supplemented by corks and twine and pieces of waste wood. The models were sometimes highly ingenious. One consisted of a complicated apparatus in the form of a miniature winding machine, which was linked to a model engine made from clay from a local bog. Imaginary steam pipes were constructed out of hemlock branches. This model simulated the activity of sending tubs of coal up and down a mine, via a structure made out of pieces of waste wood found in the nearby carpenters' shop. The model coal tubs were made from hollowed-out corks linked together by twine.

A few years later we see the first glimmer of a possibility that this uneducated working man might one day become a proper engineer. Stephenson, still not 18, now had a relatively skilled job as a "plugman" or engine man responsible for keeping a pump engine working and fixing minor defects. Smiles noted that the when an engine suffered a serious breakdown, the engine man's usual response would be to send for the chief engineer. However, Stephenson applied himself so assiduously and successfully to the study of the engine and its gearing—taking the machine to pieces in his leisure hours for the purpose of cleaning it and understanding its various parts—that he soon acquired a thorough practical knowledge of its construction and mode of working, and very rarely needed to call the engineer of the colliery to his aid. His engine became a sort of pet to him, and he never wearied of watching it and inspecting it with admiration (Smiles, 1857/1881).

Stephenson's constant close interest in the detailed working of machines and his delight in persistently giving close attention to their operation, hour after hour, never tiring of observing how the different parts work together, are traits typical of those who become mechanical inventors, even today. He also continued to have the interest in model building that he had first displayed when younger. Sometimes he would carry out small experiments of his own to test ideas that came to him when he was told about scientific findings (Davies, 1975; Rolt, 1960). For a 19th-century engineer, practical activities of this kind would have been crucial to growing competence. For Stephenson, the effects of regularly and frequently engaging for lengthy periods of time in them would have been in some respects not unlike the outcomes of the constant practicing that musicians have to do and the lengthy training and preparation activities that are necessary in order to move ahead in other areas of expertise. Smiles, who unlike some biographers was very aware of the importance for the acquisition of special skills of these undramatic background activities, observed that,

> The daily contemplation of the steam engine and the sight of its steady action, is an education of itself to an ingenious and thoughtful man. It is a remarkable fact that nearly all that has been done for the improvement of this machine has been accomplished, not by philosophers and scientific men, but by laborers, mechanics, and engine men. Indeed, it would appear as if this were one of the departments of practical science in which the higher powers of the human mind must bend to mechanical insight. (Smiles, 1857/1881, p. 10)

However, Stephenson still had a long way to go before he could be more than a skilled workman. A major limitation was that he was totally illiterate: At 18 he could not even write his own name. By this time he had heard about the new improvements to steam engines that had been made by James Watt and others, but because he was unable to read he had no access to the information that he was so anxious to acquire. Even simple arithmetic would have been beyond him, and he would not have been able to decipher the diagrams and plans that are essential to the work of an engineer. His knowledge of the physical sciences was effectively nil.

Although his long working hours gave him very little leisure time, and despite his being barely able to afford the fourpence a week that it cost him to have lessons, at the age of 18, Stephenson began to learn to read and write, and also to perform simple arithmetic, going to classes in a neighboring village 3 nights every week. He did all this with enormous determination. As one of his colearners remarked, Stephenson "took to figures so wonderful," largely because, "George's secret was his perseverance. He worked out the sums in his byhours, improving every minute of his spare time by the engine-fire, there studying the arithmetical problems set him upon his slate by the master. In the evenings he took to Robertson the sums which he had 'worked', and the new ones were 'set' for him to study out the following day. Thus his progress was rapid" (Smiles, 1857/1881, p. 11).

Eventually, his determination and the hard work he invested in his plans to educate himself brought rewards. After demonstrating to his employers on a number of occasions that he had the initiative and competence they were looking for in order to make their mines operate more effectively and more economically, at the age of 32, Stephenson was given a job in which he had considerable leeway to introduce new transport systems in the mines where he was employed. By 1814, a time when there were no obvious reasons for believing that locomotives could be anything other than cumbersome and inefficient machines, Stephenson had become convinced that reliable and economical railway travel was possible. He was also sure that he would play a large part in making that happen. "I will," he accurately predicted at a moment in his life when he had only recently been elevated from being a workman to an engineer, "do something in coming time which will astonish all England" (Rolt, 1960, p. 54). At that time there was a fair amount of interest in the possibility of steam locomotion, and steam locomotives had already been invented, but not ones that were satisfactorily reliable, and enormous developments were still needed to make passenger travel by steam railway a practical possibility. Someone who knew of Stephenson at that time and was aware of the opportunities he had in his job and his reputation for making innovations might have predicted that Stephenson would earn himself a byword in the history of steam locomotion. In fact, of course, he achieved far more than that.

It had taken Stephenson a long time to reach the point of being prepared to make a real contribution as an inventor. He was now well over 30. By that age, Darwin had pieced together the theory of evolution by natural selection, and Dickens, who had written *Pickwick Papers* when he was only 24, had already been famous for several years. Schubert had died before reaching the age of 32. In the majority of cases, the preparatory years of individuals who create major accomplishments broadly correspond with the years of childhood and adolescence, but Stephenson was an exception.

Ostensibly, the task of explaining how the competent engineer eventually became an engineering genius seems even more difficult than explaining how the unschooled boy had become a competent engineer. In Stephenson's case, however, that may not be true, because to a considerable extent his subsequent progress hinged on him happening to be a person with the right qualities, interests, opportunities, vision, insight, and determination to do what was necessary to transform the rudimentary steam locomotives of the time into efficient machines that could be relied on as a form of transport, and also solve a number of other problems, such as ones to do with the rail systems that trains run on, the problems of constructing railways over hilly terrain, and the development of ways to make engine parts to precise specifications. Partly through luck and good fortune, Stephenson, with his abilities and interests and his forceful personality, was as well placed as anyone at the time to make progress on all these fronts. He made himself into the man with the qualities his era required. By this time he was showing the single-mindedness and the strong sense of direction that could be seen in Newton and Einstein and nearly all the great innovators. By 1831, the time of the opening of a line showing that it was possible to construct and operate a relatively long-distance steam railway between two towns, Liverpool and Manchester, which were separated by a number of natural obstacles, Stephenson had become famous, and was henceforth widely regarded as an engineering genius.

Space has limited me to providing a few illustrative glimpses of Stephenson's early life. A fuller account would convincingly demonstrate how it was possible for one person to become a great engineer despite his complete lack of early education. Psychological research into the long-term outcomes of training and practice helps us to see that there were no miracles or mysteries in his progress. The route that led him to success was unusually arduous, and he had to overcome more obstacles than most people encounter. However, an examination of the journey through life by which Stephenson eventually arrived at the stage of being prepared to make a substantial contribution shows that there were no sudden or incomprehensible advances in his capacities. Although he had a striking ability to profit from his experiences, there are no indications that he learned more quickly than another equally highly motivated and similarly self-confident and diligent person would have. There are absolutely no indications that he was able to move ahead without the long preparation, practice, and training that other people have to undergo in order to achieve their goals. Initially, it seems astonishing that a person with his lack of formal education could have gone so far, and the fact that such an achievement is so rare increases our admiration; but on closer examination, his progress does not seem entirely impossible to chart or to understand: To a considerable extent, we can now see how and why Stephenson became capable of the advances he made.

MICHAEL FARADAY

The story of George Stephenson's achievements is an inspiring one, and tempts us to believe that a person can achieve anything, even without formal education. Obviously that is not entirely true: We know, for example, that in the absence of musical training, Stephenson could never have become a composer. In fact, there are reasons to believe that in most areas of achievement a lack of education would have been more of a handicap than it was for Stephenson, and that although limited education may not have held back an early 19th-century engineer, that was partly because until after that time science played a rather small part in the development of steam power and locomotion. Even then, in most other areas of accomplishment, the effects of grave limitations in formal education would have had more serious effects.

In particular, the chances are that someone with Stephenson's very limited education could never have become a successful scientist. An understanding of science has always depended to a much greater extent than early 19th-century engineering did on knowledge that comes from books. Unlike technology and engineering, science is often opposed to common sense and practical experience, and because it is sometimes abstract and counterintuitive, the practical understanding of the everyday world that was so helpful to Stephenson would do little to help a person understand science (Wolpert, 1992). Consequently, the process of learning about science has to involve deliberate study activities that are detached from daily life, making it extremely difficult for a person who is denied books and opportunities for studying abstract topics to acquire a scientific education.

Nevertheless, there are instances of eminent scientists who had very little schooling, apparently contradicting what I have just said. It is instructive to consider an example of a scientific genius who had limited schooling, if only to check on the possibility that I may be wrong to assert that someone with Stephenson's lack of education could never have been a scientist. One such individual was the British scientist Michael Faraday, whose many achievements included the discovery of electromagnetic induction, which made electric engines possible. Faraday came from a very poor family, left school before he was 13, and worked for 7 years as an apprentice bookbinder. He nevertheless eventually became known as a scientific genius (Bence Jones, 1870; Gooding & James, 1985; Pearce Williams, 1965).

However, closer examination reveals that Faraday had some very real advantages compared with Stephenson. For a start, he went to school long enough to learn to read and write. Faraday himself remarked that his school education was very limited, but literacy would have made many things possible for him that Stephenson lacked: Simply being able to read opens doors to various self-education activities. Second, for someone who could read and write, a lack of secondary schooling would not have been anything like the handicap for a potential scientist at the time when Faraday was a teenager (in the first decade of the 19th century) that it would be nowadays, for the simple reason that the education then provided in schools included virtually no science at all. Even for Darwin, who went to a school that was regarded at the time as being a very good one, the curriculum he encountered there included no science and very little mathematics.

Being a bookbinder's apprentice was by no means a bad thing for the young Faraday. For a start, it brought a boy from a poor home into a world of books and the people who read them, because Faraday's employer was a bookseller and stationer as well as a binder of books. As it happened, the employer was a sympathetic and helpful individual who did much to encourage his apprentices' interests. Faraday was not the only of his employees to have gone on to a successful career, a fact that suggests that the atmosphere of the shop was a congenial and stimulating one, and in some respects more so than the classroom environment Faraday would have experienced had his education at school not been terminated so early.

I am not suggesting that leaving school early had no disadvantages at all for the young Faraday, but it is probable that lack of schooling as such might not have been as huge an impediment to Faraday as it might at first seem to have been. Fortunately for Faraday, he was able to continue his education, largely through his own efforts. He certainly had no lack of books to read. Compared with Stephenson, the young Faraday was in a much more favorable situation as far as education was concerned. Being active, energetic, and curious, as well as having plenty of self-discipline, he took advantage of his opportunities. Although he read voraciously, he did not just read, but also went to lectures and classes, and became engaged in a number of activities that would have helped him to gain the knowledge and skills needed by a young scientist. He learned a great deal from a book by Watts (1801) entitled *The Improvement of the Mind*. This is essentially a "how to study" book, written in the middle of the 18th century, and it happens to be an excellent example of that genre. From it, Faraday would have learned a great deal about effective study skills, he would have discovered how to make good use of books and avoid assuming that anything he read in a book must be correct, and he would have discovered how to organize and plan learning activities.

As in Stephenson's case, when Faraday's progress is seen from afar his enormous success despite the lack of schooling seems quite astonishing, but when it is examined more closely in the light of modern knowledge about the acquisition of expertise, the progress he made does not seem grossly superior to what we might expect to observe in a person with Faraday's opportunities and experience, together with his enthusiasm to learn and his (admittedly remarkable) capacity to persevere at his studies. As with Stephenson, there is not overwhelming reason to assume that Faraday learned faster or more easily than others, or that he could dispense with the time and determination that other learners need to invest in their studies. Like Stephenson, Faraday was fortunate at times, first in having such a sympathetic employer, and second, later, in getting employment as an assistant to Humphry Davy, then Britain's most prominent research chemist. To some extent, of course, successful people manufacture their own good fortune, but Faraday was luckier than most. Yet what was most remarkable about the young Faraday was his extreme dedication and persistence.

When we attend to their progress toward acquiring the skills and knowledge that their later achievements built on, with neither Stephenson nor Faraday is there any firm evidence that their rate of learning, in the sense of the ratio of progress to time and effort involved, was particularly exceptional. What does seem to have been exceptional in both of them was their willingness to persist at learning activities, their perseverance, persistence, doggedness, and sheer self-discipline. It is one thing to be curious and keen to learn, as many young people are, but it is another thing to keep at the task of studying, hour after hour, in the disciplined and determined way that is necessary in order to succeed, especially in the absence of the kinds of guidance and support that is provided by schools and educational institutions. So what enabled these individuals to be so persistent, and to keep working at their studies and resisting distractions?

In Faraday's case we can gain some useful clues by combining some research findings with a knowledge of his family background. Some recent research by Csikszentmihalyi and his colleagues (Csikszentmihalyi & Csikszentmihalyi, 1993) has shown that those young people who are good at studying on their own (which many people, including most youngsters, find difficult), and are least likely to dislike the combination of being solitary and attentive that is necessary for studying, tend to be individuals who come from family backgrounds that are not just stimulating and encouraging (especially in regard to learning and education) but also structured and supportive. A child from such a background is likely to learn how to get on with the task of studying, like other jobs, and to acquire the habit of doing so and have a clear idea of what can be expected from others and what is expected of himself or herself. Consequently the child is unlikely to waste time complaining about life being unfair or arguing with brothers and sisters about whose turn it is to do a job, and more likely to be able to count on being given whatever help is needed to enable him or her to do whatever he or she is required to do. Such a person simply gets into the habit of getting on with life's tasks. As we saw earlier, it is those regular and background habitual activities of a person's life, the ones that that tend to be neglected in biographical accounts, that largely determine how successful the individual eventually becomes.

As a teenager, Faraday would have been well supplied with both intellectual stimulation and a structured and supportive background. The interesting work environment of his apprenticeship would have compensated for any lack of stimulation in his home life. As far as support and structure were concerned, there is some anecdotal evidence that his family was unusually close, and, perhaps more importantly, he and his family were members of a small religious sect in which there was considerable emphasis on members giving each other help and support. Other people perceived Faraday as someone who appeared unusually serene, and it is more than likely that his sense of security stemmed partly from his membership of this very close-knit group (Cantor, 1991).

CONCLUSION

When it is possible to examine the early lives of creative people closely enough to gain an idea of how they filled their time and experienced their days, we begin to see how they acquired the skills and knowledge that helped make it possible for them to create the accomplishments and achievements that made them famous. Doing that does not completely explain the achievements, which remain remarkable, even if one agrees with Weisberg (1993) that there is nothing fundamentally special or distinct about those kinds of thinking that are labeled creative, but it does enable us to move some way in that direction. There are no points in either Stephenson's or Faraday's life at which we suddenly encounter inexplicable progress or mysteriously acquired capacities, or at which powers appear that cannot be accounted for without invoking a special innate gift or talent. It is not being claimed that anyone given Stephenson's opportunities, or Faraday's, would have ended up with their accomplishments, but there do seem to be grounds for suggesting that we do not have to assume that there must have been anything inherently remarkable about either of these people. Individuals like this have certainly become capable of astonishing accomplishments, but they have done so as a consequence of their impressive (but not superhuman) personal qualities, their unusual (but not entirely mysterious) dedication to their particular interests, the remarkable lives they have experienced, and a certain amount of good fortune that has helped to ensure a good match between their abilities and the nature of the achievements that happened to be necessary and valued in their time.

REFERENCES

Bence Jones, H. (1870). *The life and letters of Faraday*. London: Longmans, Green & Co.

Cantor, G. (1991). *Michael Faraday: Sandemanian and scientist*. Basingstoke, UK: Macmillan.

Chi, M. T. H., & Ceci, S. J. (1987). Content knowledge: Its role, representation, and restructuring in memory development. *Advances in Child Development, 20*, 91–142.

Cockshut, A. O. J. (1974). *Truth to life: The art of biography in the nineteenth century*. London: Collins.

Csikszentmihalyi, M., & Csikszentmihalyi, I. S. (1993). Family influences on the development of giftedness. In G. R. Bock & K. Ackrill (Eds.), *CIBA Foundation Symposium No. 178: The origins and development of high ability* (pp. 187–200). Chichester, UK: Wiley.

Csikszentmihalyi, M., Rathunde, K., & Whalen, S. (1993). *Talented teenagers: The roots of success and failure*. Cambridge, UK: Cambridge University Press.

Davies, H. (1975). *George Stephenson*. London: Weidenfeld & Nicolson.

Dunn, J., & Plomin, R. (1990). *Separate lives: Why siblings are so different*. New York: Basic Books.

Ericsson, K. A., Tesch-Römer, C., & Krampe, R. T. (1993). The role of deliberate practice in the acquisition of expert performance. *Psychological Review, 100*, 363–406.

Garraty, J. A. (1958). *The nature of biography*. London: Jonathan Cape.

Gooding, D., & James, A. J. L. (1985). Introduction: Faraday rediscovered. In D. Gooding & F. A. J. L. James (Eds.), *Faraday rediscovered: Essays on the life and work of Michael Faraday, 1791–1867*. Basingstoke, UK: Macmillan/Stockton Press.

Hayes, J. R. (1981). *The complete problem solver*. Philadelphia: Franklin Institute Press.

Howe, M. J. A. (1989). *Fragments of genius: The strange feats of idiots savants*. London: Routledge.

Howe, M. J. A. (1990). *The origins of exceptional abilities*. Oxford, UK: Blackwell.

Howe, M. J. A. (1994). Genius. In R. J. Sternberg (Ed.), *Encyclopedia of intelligence* (Vol. 1, pp. 483–488). New York: Macmillan.

Lesley, C. (1976). *The life of Noel Coward*. Harmondsworth, UK: Penguin.

Maurois, A. (1929). *Aspects of biography* (S. C. Roberts, Trans.). Cambridge, UK: Cambridge University Press.

Pearce Williams, L. (1965). *Michael Faraday: A Biography*. London: Chapman & Hall.

Rolt, L. T. C. (1960). *George and Robert Stephenson*. London: Longmans.

Rutter, M., & Rutter, M. (1992). *Developing minds: Challenge and continuity across the life span*. London: Penguin.

Sloboda, J. A., Davidson, J. W., & Howe, M. J. A. (1994). Is everyone musical? *The Psychologist, 7*, 349–354.

Sloboda, J. A., Davidson, J. W., Howe, M. J. A., & Moore, D. G. (in press). The role of practice in the development of performing musicians. *British Journal of Psychology*.

Smiles, S. (1881). *Life of George Stephenson*. London: Murray. (Original work published 1857)

Spoto, D. (1983). *The dark side of genius: The life of Alfred Hitchcock*. New York: Ballantine Books.

Sturrock, J. (1993). *The language of autobiography*. New York: Cambridge University Press.

Sulloway, F. J. (1985). Darwin's early intellectual development: An overview of the *Beagle* voyage. In D. Kohn (Ed.), *The Darwinian Heritage* (pp. 121–154). Princeton, NJ: Princeton University Press.

Watts, I. (1801). *The improvement of the mind*. London: J. Abraham.

Weisberg, R. (1993). *Creativity: Beyond the myth of genius*. New York: Freeman.

Wolpert, L. (1992). *The unnatural nature of science*. London: Faber & Faber.

10

The Rage to Master:
The Decisive Role of Talent
in the Visual Arts

Ellen Winner
Boston College
Harvard Project Zero

In this chapter, I argue for the decisive role of talent in achieving expertise in the visual arts. By talent, I refer to an innate ability or proclivity to learn in a particular domain. I argue that individual differences in innate ability exist, and that high levels of ability include a motivational component: a strong interest in a particular domain, along with a strong drive to master that domain. The same case for talent that I make here for the visual arts can also be made in many other domains. Specifically, I suggest, the case for talent can be made for any domain in which one finds childhood precocity or autistic and/or retarded savants.

It has been argued that hard work is all that there is to exceptional achievement in any domain. For instance, Howe (1990), arguing against the existence of innate individual differences in ability, suggested, "With sufficient energy and dedication on the parents' part, it is possible that it may not be all that difficult to produce a child prodigy" (p. 138). It is suggested that with enough practice and reward for achievement, anyone can reach unusually high levels of performance in any domain. (For further elaboration of this argument, see Ericsson, 1988; Ericsson & Faivre, 1988; Ericsson, Krampe, & Tesch-Römer, 1993; Sloboda, Davidson, & Howe, 1994). Ericsson (chap. 1, this volume) summarizes this argument.

Here are three widely cited pieces of evidence on which a strong environmental view of expertise might rest. The first comes from Roe's (1951, 1953a, 1953b) studies of eminent scientists. Roe found that what predicted outstanding achievement in science was not so much individual differences in intellectual abilities, but rather the capacity for endurance, concentration, and commitment to hard work. This has been taken to show that high achievement is more a function of tenacity than talent.

The second piece of evidence comes from Bloom's (1985) study of eminent people in science, arts, and athletics. Bloom found that none of his subjects achieved expertise without a supportive and encouraging environment, including a long and intensive period of training, first from loving and warm teachers, and then from demanding and rigorous master teachers.

The third piece of evidence comes from Ericsson's studies of adult experts in piano, violin, chess, bridge, and athletics (Ericsson et al., 1993). Ericsson demonstrated that levels of achievement reached in these domains correlate strongly with the sheer amount of deliberate practice in which these individuals have engaged. That is, those who spend more time working on difficult problems over and over in order to perfect them (deliberate practice) are the ones who reach the highest levels. He noted that in music, ballet, and chess, the higher the level of attained performance, the earlier the age of first exposure to the domain, and hence the earlier the onset of deliberate practice.

Each of these pieces of evidence, however, although clearly demonstrating the role of motivation, commitment, and hard work, fails to rule out the possibility that innate talent plays a necessary role in high achievement. First consider Roe's studies. The scientists studied were all high in intellectual ability to begin with. Thus, what these studies really show is that high ability by itself is not enough; they do not allow the reverse conclusion—that hard work by itself is enough to achieve eminence in science.

Second, consider Bloom's study. This study is often taken as strong evidence that eminent adults started out as perfectly ordinary children who had dedicated parents and teachers who motivated them to work long and hard. However, I believe this is a misreading. A careful look at the descriptions of these eminent individuals as children shows that at a very young age, prior to any regimen of training, signs of unusual ability were clearly evident. The musicians recalled being quick to learn at the piano, and both their parents and teachers recognized them as special, as children worth devoting their efforts to. The sculptors recalled drawing constantly as children, usually realistically, and also enjoying working with their hands, building, hammering, and nailing. The mathematicians recalled a fascination with gears, valves, gauges, and dials, and were considered "brilliant" as children. Most of the interviewees said that they learned easily in their chosen domain, but did not learn as quickly in other areas in school. Thus, Bloom's work, like that of Roe, allows us only to conclude that hard work is necessary for the acquisition of expertise, but not that it is sufficient.

Finally, consider our third piece of evidence, the studies by Ericsson and his colleagues. The problem here is that hard work and innate ability are very likely confounded. Those children who have the most ability may also be those who are most interested in a particular activity, who begin to work at that activity at an early age, and who work the hardest at it. One is likely to want to work hard at something when one is able to advance quickly with relatively little effort, but not when every step is a painful struggle. Thus, Ericsson's research, like that of Roe and of Bloom, demonstrates the importance of hard work but in no way allows us to rule out the role of innate ability.

Psychologists would never assert that retardation is due to too little training or not enough drill. No one disputes the biological basis of retardation (with the exception of that due to extremely impoverished environments); and yet some do assert that high ability, the flip side of retardation, is entirely due to hard work. But if biological retardation exists, why not biological acceleration?

In this chapter, I use evidence from the domain of the visual arts to make the case for the role of talent in the achievement of expertise. I review what is known about the drawings of children who draw in advance of their age level, as well as what is known about other characteristics of these children. To avoid begging the question, I refer to children who draw in advance of their age as precocious rather than gifted or talented. I make no assumptions about whether the cause of this precocity is biological or environmental.

At the conclusion of the chapter, I evaluate the evidence that drawing precocity has an innate, biological component. I argue that although it is impossible to isolate ability from practice (because high-ability children always practice), there is converging evidence to demonstrate that practice without ability is not enough to explain expertise. First, high achievers in the visual arts have high ability before they begin to work at drawing extensively. Second, ordinary children cannot be motivated or even forced to work at drawing to the extent that a precocious child willingly does so. Third, precocious drawers display different kinds of drawing abilities than do ordinary children who simply work hard at drawing. I also argue that there are other signs besides drawing precocity that these children are atypical from birth: They are often non-right-handed, they display a variety of visual-spatial strengths, and also tend to have linguistic deficits. This combination of factors suggests a brain-based component of drawing talent that can account for drawing precocity both in autistic and retarded savants as well as in nonpathological children.

The strong role of innate talent, however, does not allow us to rule out the importance of practice and hard work. Through practice, learning occurs. Even the most prodigious show development of their skills, and this development is a function of intense work. I argue that precocious drawers, as well as children who are highly precocious in any domain, differ from the ordinary child in these four respects:

1. They learn more rapidly in the domain.
2. They are intrinsically motivated to acquire skill in the domain (because of the ease with which learning occurs).
3. They make discoveries in the domain without much explicit adult scaffolding. A great deal of the work is done through self-teaching, which, as pointed out by Charness et al. (chap. 2, this volume) and Ericsson (chap. 1, this volume), can be a form of deliberate practice.
4. They not only make discoveries on their own, but often do things in the domain that ordinary hard workers never do—inventing new solutions, thinking, seeing, or hearing in a qualitatively different way.

DOES DRAWING PRECOCITY EXIST?

There have been far fewer reports of reputed drawing prodigies than of prodigies in math, music, and chess. Studies searching for drawing prodigies in populations of schoolchildren have concluded that drawing talent in very young children was far rarer than talent in other domains (Goodenough, 1926; Lark-Horowitz, Lewis, & Luca, 1973). Although it is possible that drawing ability is rarer than ability in other domains, cultural factors could also account for the discrepancy. Drawing ability is far less valued in our culture than is mathematical ability; children who show ability in music are immediately given music lessons; children who show ability in chess join chess clubs and participate in competitions much as do young athletes. Children are not routinely screened for drawing ability as they are for academic ability; nor are they typically signed up for formal lessons as they are in music. When the culture supports a particular domain, talent is more readily recognized and then nurtured; but also, such a culture makes clear what the skills are that need to be mastered for excellence to be achieved (Csikszentmihalyi & Robinson, 1986).

It is likely that many children who draw ahead of their age go unnoticed and thus unnurtured by their parents and their schools. Moreover, we now have numerous reports of children who appear to be prodigies in drawing (Cane, 1951; Gardner, 1989; Goldsmith, 1992; Goldsmith & Feldman, 1989; Golomb, 1992, 1995; Golomb & Hass, 1995; Milbrath, 1987, 1995, in preparation; Paine, 1981; Selfe, 1977, 1983, 1985, 1995; Wilson & Wilson, 1977; Winner, 1996; Winner & Martino, 1993; Zhensun & Low, 1991; Zimmerman, 1992). Thus, early high achievement in drawing is clearly possible. Whether such achievement is as common as high achievement in other domains seems less important than the fact that it does occur.

TYPICAL CHARACTERISTICS OF PRECOCIOUS DRAWINGS

Our knowledge of early high achievement in drawing comes from two sources. One source is the childhood drawings of famous artists (Beck, 1928; Gordon, 1987; Paine, 1987; Pariser, 1987, 1991; Richardson, 1991; Vasari, 1957). The problem with this kind of evidence is that it is so sparse, and we have almost no drawings by artists preserved from before the age of 9. Thus we know nothing about the first signs of drawing in those who went on to become artists. A more informative source is children who have been identified as precocious in drawing by their parents or teachers (see earlier references). These children do not necessarily become artists as adults, but their drawings are at least several years in advance of those of their peers. Both sources of evidence point consistently to the following set of characteristics as typical of precocious drawings.

Recognizable and Differentiated Shapes

The earliest sign of precocity in drawing is the ability to draw recognizable shapes 1 to 2 years in advance of the normal age timetable of 3 to 4 years of age. Whereas children typically scribble until about 3 to 4, precocious children draw clearly recognizable shapes by the age of 2. Figure 10.1 shows a typical 2-year-old's scribble. Figure 10.2 contrasts a precocious and age-typical attempt at drawing apples. Both drawings were made by 2-year-olds. The age-typical child drew a slash for each apple (Fig. 10.2a). For him, a slash stood for anything. The precocious child drew each apple's shape, along with the stem (Fig. 10.2b). For him, the representation had to capture the apple's contour in order to represent an apple. Figure 10.3 shows a fish by another precocious 2-year-old, which also captures the appropriate contour.

Fluid Contour

Whereas 3- and 4-year-olds typically represent humans by tadpoles, with a circle representing an undifferentiated head and trunk (Fig. 10.4), some precocious children draw the human figure with head and trunk differentiated by age 2 (Golomb, 1995). Preschoolers typically draw additively, juxtaposing geometric shapes (e.g., to make a human, they make a circle for a head, an oval for the body, and straight lines for arms and legs). In contrast, precocious children draw the whole object with one fluid contour line (Winner & Martino, 1993; Fig. 10.5).

Precocious drawers draw recognizable, realistic images quickly and with ease. They do not labor over and erase their lines. Picasso was reported to begin drawings from noncanonical places (e.g., drawing a dog starting with the ear), with no decrement in speed or confidence (Richardson, 1991).

FIG. 10.1. Typical scribble by 2-year-old.

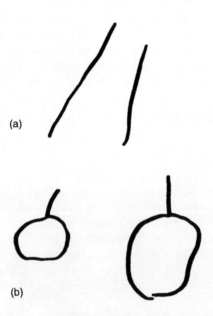

FIG. 10.2. Apples drawn by typical 2-year-old (a) and by Ryan Sullivan, a precocious 2-year-old (b, reprinted by permission of Ryan Sullivan).

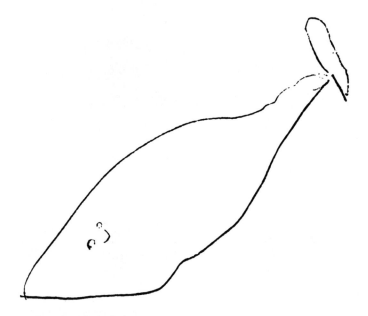

FIG. 10.3. Fish by Eitan at age 2;2. From Golomb (1992). Reprinted by permission of Claire Golomb.

FIG. 10.4. Typical tadpole human by 3-year-old.

FIG. 10.5. Drawing of a girl by Peter, a precocious drawer, at age 4;6, showing a
fluid contour line. Reprinted by permission of Lois Borrelli.

Details

Precocious children do not depict a generic object, but include a rich amount
of detail. For example, one child added gas tanks, axles, grills, bumpers,
headlights, and brake boxes to his vehicles (Golomb, 1992). Another child
drew dinosaurs with scientific accuracy, using paleontology books to acquire
the needed information (Milbrath, 1995). The inclusion of detail is one way
in which the drawings of precocious children achieve realism.

Techniques to Represent Depth

Precocious drawers achieve the illusion of realism not only by drawing
differentiated shapes and details, but also by depicting the third dimension. They use all of the known Western techniques to show depth: foreshortening, occlusion, size diminution, modeling to show volume, and
even the most difficult technique of all, linear perspective. In a comparison
of ordinary and precocious drawers, Milbrath (1995) showed that the
precocious sample used all of these techniques years earlier than did the
normal sample. For instance, foreshortening was used in 50% of the
drawings by Milbrath's precocious sample by age 7 and 8; comparable
levels in the normal sample were reached only by ages 13 and 14, 6 years
later.

Linear perspective is used by precocious drawers sometimes almost as soon as they begin to draw (e.g., the case of Eitan reported by Golomb, 1992, 1995). But the perspective systems used are at first primitive ones, and they are applied locally to separate objects on the page, rather than in a unified fashion to the entire scene (Milbrath, 1987, 1995, in preparation). Nonetheless, the invention of perspectival drawing systems by very young children is astounding to see. Linear perspective is a convention, and it is not an intuitively obvious one (Gombrich, 1960). Typically children in the West do not begin to draw in perspective until middle childhood, and only those who have explicit instruction ever attain true geometric perspective (Willats, 1977).

Perhaps the most extreme example of the untutored invention or discovery of linear perspective is the case of Eitan reported by Golomb (1992, 1995). Eitan's parents report that Eitan consistently resisted instruction and insisted on working on his own. Eitan's first drawings at age 2 were flat and displayed the object from a frontal view (e.g., as seen in Fig. 10.3). However, he was not satisfied with showing only canonical views, because by 2;2 he began to juxtapose different views of the same object, resulting in a feeling of solidity and depth. Figure 10.6 shows his first attempt to show depth. Here Eitan has drawn some kind of a vehicle (perhaps a tractor or a bicycle) but he did not just draw a flat frontal view of the wheels. Instead he gave them a look of three-dimensionality by juxtaposing a side and top view of the wheels.

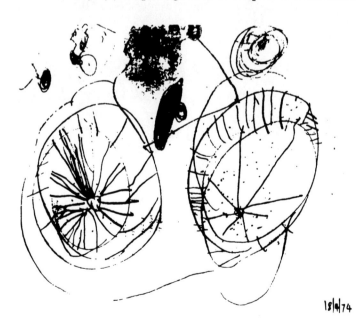

FIG. 10.6. Tractor or bicycle by Eitan, age 2;2, showing a juxtaposed side and top view of the wheels, making them look three-dimensional. From Golomb (1992). Reprinted by permission of Claire Golomb.

Eitan discovered (or invented) three perspective systems:

1. He juxtaposed different faces of an object along the horizontal or vertical axis (horizontal and vertical oblique perspective; Fig. 10.7).
2. He drew the sides of an object with lines diverging out from the frontal plane (divergent perspective).
3. He drew the sides of an object with oblique parallel lines. (Fig. 10.8) By 4, this kind of perspective, called isometric, was his preferred strategy, and was used quite systematically by age 6 (see Fig. 10.9), but he did use converging lines to represent depth at 3;8.

The perspective systems that Eitan used followed a logical progression, identical to the progression followed by ordinary children. However, there are three important differences: the early age at which he began, the rapid speed with which he passed through different perspectival "stages," and the fact that he was entirely self-taught.

Orientation

Precocious drawers vary the orientation of figures, in contrast to the canonical orientation used by ordinary children. For instance, a comparison of drawings by ordinary and precocious children showed that human figures were drawn in three-quarters view only 15% of the time by ordinary

FIG. 10.7. Cement truck by Eitan, age 2;7, showing the side view of the truck, the top view of the hood, and a frontal view of grill and bumper. From Golomb (1992). Reprinted by permission of Claire Golomb.

FIG. 10.8. Truck by Eitan, age 3;7, showing isometric perspective, in which the third dimension is represented by parallel oblique lines. From Golomb (1992). Reprinted by permission of Claire Golomb.

FIG. 10.9. Drawing entitled "Near Accident," by Eitan, age 6;6, showing the systematic use of isometric perspective. From Golomb (1992). Reprinted by permission of Claire Golomb.

children between 11 and 14 years. In contrast, by age 6 precocious drawers used this orientation in half of their figure drawings (Milbrath, 1995). These three-quarter views appeared abruptly between 6 and 7 years. Note that a three-quarters view is a distortion, just as is foreshortening, size diminution, occlusion, and so on. Precocious drawers are willing to distort the size and shape of objects in order to show them as they appear to the eye.

All of the characteristics just described make precocious drawings look exceptionally realistic. The ability to draw realistically at a precocious age also marks the childhoods of those who have gone on to become recognized artists. Gordon (1987) studied the childhood works of 31 Israeli artists and found that all stood out for their ability to draw realistically. Sloane and Sosniak (1985) interviewed 20 sculptors and found that most recalled drawing realistically at a very early age. Many other famous artists' early drawings have been singled out for their advanced realism: for example, Millais (Paine, 1981), Landseer (Goldsmith & Feldman, 1989), Seargent (Cox, 1992), and Klee, Picasso, and Lautrec (Pariser, 1987, 1991). Picasso recalled one of his first drawings in this way: "I was perhaps six. . . . In my father's house there was a statue of Hercules with his club in the corridor, and I drew Hercules. But it wasn't a child's drawing. It was a real drawing, representing Hercules with his club" (Richardson, 1991, p. 29).

Although almost all Western children identified as accelerated in drawing have drawn realistically, Golomb (1991) discovered two artists whose childhood drawings stood out for their aesthetic sense but not for their realism (see also Golomb & Hass, 1995). The childhood works of these two artists showed an advanced sense of composition and color. Admittedly, it is more difficult to demonstrate that a drawing is advanced aesthetically than to show that it is advanced in realism, as the criteria for measuring aesthetics are far less clear than those for measuring realism. Nonetheless, the drawings of these children stood out on fairly clearly measurable dimensions. They were filled with decorative properties; colors were used in a highly expressive manner, and colors and shapes were endlessly and inventively varied. Thus, although an ability to draw realistically may be the most typical and striking characteristic of Western children who draw precociously, exceptional nonrepresentational skill with design, form, and color also occurs in children who draw precociously. Similar cases have been described by Hurwitz (1983), Kerchensteiner (1905), and Lark-Horowitz et al. (1973).

Realism as an early indicator of precocity in drawing may well be culturally determined. In the West, at least from the Renaissance until the 20th century, artists have striven to capture the illusion of space, volume, and depth (Gombrich, 1960). Although precocious drawers probably begin to draw realistically long before they have looked closely at examples of Western realistic art, they have certainly been exposed to illusionist images on billboards, magazines, picture books, and so on. What about children not exposed to such examples?

We have one well-known example, a Chinese painting prodigy who, because she grew up in China, probably saw far fewer examples of Western illusionist images than do Western children (Goldsmith, 1992; Goldsmith & Feldman, 1989; Zhensun & Low, 1991). Yani was spared traditional Chinese drawing instruction because her artist father felt such instruction killed the artistic imagination. However, Yani spent many hours a day in her father's art studio painting alongside her father. Although her father insists that he did not teach her, we really do not know whether Yani received any kind of instruction from her father. We do know that she painted all the time, and she painted way in advance of her years.

Yani's paintings looked nothing like those by Western gifted children. Instead, hers were painted in the allusionistic, impressionistic style of traditional Chinese brush painting (Fig. 10.10). What I think she shares with Western children who draw precociously is the ability to master the pictorial conventions of one's culture. In the West this means mastering the convention of perspective and realism. In China this means mastering the convention of capturing the spirit of objects, not their exact likeness. Thus, like Eitan, Yani was able at an abnormally early age to make pictures that looked remarkably like the adult art of her culture.

THE COMPULSION TO DRAW

So far I have discussed the characteristics of the drawings produced by children who draw at a precocious level. I now turn to a pervasive characteristic of the children themselves: their compulsion to draw.

The children who draw in the manner I have described draw constantly and compulsively. Peter, a precocious drawer, began to draw at 10 months, in contrast to the typical age of about 2 (Winner, 1996). Once he discovered

FIG. 10.10. Painting by Yani, age 5, entitled "Pull Harder!"

that he could make marks on paper, Peter wanted to draw all the time. Soon he was waking up in the mornings and bellowing for paper and markers before getting out of bed. He drew before breakfast, during breakfast, while getting ready for school, while being driven to school, and as soon as he returned home from school. His drawings were of the kind typically produced by precocious drawers—advanced in realism. Peter was particularly skilled at drawing fluid Klee-like figures in a wide variety of moving positions (Figs. 10.5, 10.11, 10.12, 10.13). When friends came over to play, he would bore them by making them pose for him, or by insisting that they draw with him. Peter and Eitan showed the same kind of fascination with drawing reported by Sloane and Sosniak (1985) of sculptors as young children.

The compulsion to draw found in precocious drawers has its parallels in many other domains. That is, any time a child is precocious in a particular activity, that child is also highly interested in and drawn to work at that activity. One can find children who spend hours every day finding and solving math problems; not surprisingly, these children also are precocious

FIG. 10.11. Drawing of girl in bathing suit by Peter, age 3;7. Reprinted by permission of Lois Borrelli.

FIG. 10.12. Drawing of ballerina by Peter, age 4;6. Reprinted by permission of Lois Borrelli.

at math, and able to think about mathematical concepts far beyond the reach of their peers. The same kinds of children have been noted in music, chess, and reading. I have studied a number of these children, and the parallels are striking (Winner, 1996). For example, take the case of Jacob, a child who heard heavy metal music on the electric guitar at age 4 and begged his parents for 2 years to let him play the electric guitar. His parents did not consider this a childlike kind of music, and thus they resisted Jacob's pleadings for 2 years. However, confronted with the intensity of Jacob's interest, they finally bought him a guitar and found him a teacher. At his first lesson, scheduled for 30-minutes, Jacob refused to leave. Whereas most children are relieved that a lesson is over, Jacob did not want it to end. After his second lesson, his teacher was certain that Jacob was a prodigy. He could play back just about anything by ear, he could master complex music seemingly without effort, and he could improvise in a musical manner. Once while on an outing with his father, Jacob passed a group of street musicians. He asked to try their electric guitar and astonished bystanders, who were heard joking that he must be a reincarnation of Jimi Hendrix.

Jacob played his guitar from the moment he got home from school until he had to go to bed. His parents never had to ask him to practice, for there

FIG. 10.13. Drawing of the Clintons by Peter, age 6;1. Reprinted by permission of Lois Borrelli.

was no difference for Jacob between playing for fun and practicing. He set himself challenges and worked on them for hours. Instead of the usual story of prodding the child to practice, his parents had to pry him away from his instrument to eat, sleep, and go to school.

The same phenomenon of precocity linked with drive can be seen in the description of Josh Waitzkin, the child chess player in the book and movie, *Searching for Bobby Fischer* (Waitzkin, 1984). At age 6, Josh watched several games of chess with great interest, and then began to play chess himself. His coach immediately recognized that he had exceptional ability because the very first time he played he used the sophisticated strategy of combining pieces to launch an attack. He was also able to calculate 15 to 20 moves ahead. Like Jacob, Josh showed a rage to master. He could not be stopped from watching and playing chess for hours each day. His father said that between the ages of 6 and 8, he studied chess as intensively as a college student studies for a comprehensive exam.

Now one could argue that all of these examples of children who work so hard and achieve so much simply demonstrate the role of practice in achieving expertise. These children work harder than do typical children and thus naturally they achieve higher levels. However, this kind of argument assumes that the hard work comes first, the high achievement later and it fails on two grounds. To begin with, even the very first productions of precocious children are advanced. The earliest drawings of Eitan and Peter were not normal. They drew recognizable forms by 2; within a few months Eitan was using linear perspective, and by 3 Peter was drawing very complex, fluid figures in motion. The same kinds of claims can be made for precocious children in other domains. As just mentioned, the first time 6-year-old Josh Waitzkin played chess, after having observed the game just a few times, he combined pieces to launch an attack, certainly not a strategy that children normally alight on initially. The second time that Jacob came to his guitar lesson, his teacher decided he was a prodigy. These signs of ability came before any instruction, and before any time for deliberate practice.

Of course, all of these children went on to learn immense amounts about their domain, and this learning was acquired primarily independently. They certainly engaged in what might be called deliberate practice. Where they differed from ordinary children was in the independence with which they worked (they needed little or no tutoring) and the ease with which they discovered the rules of their domain. This difference is one that is attributable to innate talent in the domain.

The second problem with the argument that the hard work causes the high achievement is that it does not explain what motivates these children to work so hard. One cannot even cajole or force a normal child to draw or play music or chess all day, and the children I am talking about insisted on spending their time in this way. Indeed, they often had to be dragged away from their preferred activities in order to eat, sleep, go to school, and be sociable. The interest, drive, and desire to work on something must be part and parcel of the talent. Of course, as I have already indicated, and as Charness et al. (chap. 2, this volume) and Ericsson (chap. 1, this volume) have argued, the daily hours spent working on something lead to improvement that would not occur without the daily work. However, the desire to work so hard at something comes from within, not without, and occurs almost always when there is an ability to achieve at high levels with relative ease.

Because precocity and drive tend to co-occur, it is difficult to determine the relative contribution of each. However, the fact that precocity and drive so often co-occur is not simply a natural confound that befuddles our research efforts. This co-occurence also tells us something of critical importance, namely, that drive (or what I call the rage to master) is an ineluctable part of talent.

Occasionally one finds examples of hard work without what I would call innate talent. I refer to these children as *drudges*, in contrast to those I would call gifted. In the domain of drawing there exists a published record of drawings produced by a child who was obsessed with drawing, who drew constantly, but who never made much progress. This child, Charles, described by Hildreth (1941), provides us with a vivid example of hard work, perhaps one might say deliberate practice, without much innate ability.

Charles produced over 2,000 drawings of trains from the time he was 2 until he was 11, most of them drawn between the ages of 7 and 9. Charles clearly drew 2 to 3 years ahead of his age, but as Figs. 10.14, 10.15, and 10.16 show, although he made some progress, his drawings never reached a level anywhere near to those of Eitan or Peter.[1] True, his drawings became more complex, more realistic, and more controlled. But after age 4, his drawings showed little development, and even at age 11 his drawings were fairly schematic and showed neither Eitan's mastery of perspective nor Peter's ability to capture contours in motion.

Another kind of example of the effects of hard work without talent can be found in any urban preschool and elementary school in contemporary China. Chinese children are given explicit instructions in drawing from the age of 3, when they enter kindergarten; and from the age of 6 they have daily practice in copying calligraphy (Gardner, 1989; Winner, 1989). These children are taught in a meticulous, step-by-step manner how to produce a wide variety of graphic schemas found in traditional Chinese painting: bamboo, goldfish, shrimp, chickens, roosters, and so on. They are taught precisely which lines to make, and the direction and order in which to make them. They learn by copying, but eventually they are able to go beyond copying and draw from life. Whereas ordinary Western children are given virtually no instruction in drawing, and are simply given materials with which to explore and experiment, ordinary Chinese children are given very detailed instruction in drawing as a skill. Thus, the drawings of ordinary Chinese children appear controlled, neat, skilled, and adultlike, whereas those of ordinary Western children appear free, messy, unskilled, and childlike (see Fig. 10.17). It is undoubtedly the instructional regimen imposed on the Chinese child that accounts for the difference.

One can see the same phenomenon in the domain of music. Ordinary Japanese children trained in the Suzuki method of violin begin to play the violin at a very young age and practice every day. These children play in a disciplined, controlled, musical manner at a very young age, and appear on the surface as if they are all musical prodigies.

PRECOCIOUS DRAWERS ARE NOT JUST AHEAD, THEY ARE DIFFERENT

Although Chinese drawers and Suzuki violinists perform at a level that makes them look highly skilled, they are really very different from the kinds of children I described earlier—those who not only choose to draw, play music, or solve math problems, but who insist on doing so, and all the time. Ordinary Chinese children become very proficient at drawing but would

---

[1] I am indebted to Rudolf Arnheim and Claire Golomb for bringing Hildreth's study to my attention as an example of what can be achieved with work but no exceptional talent.

never be confused with Yani. Nor would Suzuki violinists ever be confused with a young Yehudi Menuhin or the Japanese violin prodigy, Midori. Yani far surpasses the average Chinese child in skill and inventiveness, as does Midori the average Suzuki-trained violinist.

Precocious drawers seem to be able to do things with lines on paper that are simply never mastered by ordinary children who work hard at drawing. Here are a few ways in which they differ. First, as already mentioned, they are self-taught. For example, they invent techniques such as perspective and foreshortening on their own, whereas ordinary children require instruction to arrive at these achievements. Second, they show a confidence in their line, and an ability to draw a complex contour with one fluid line.

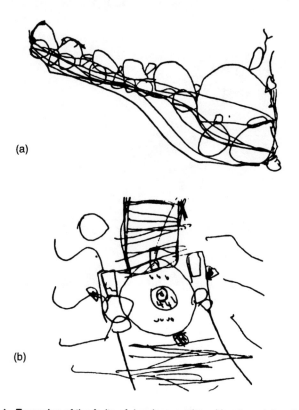

(a)

(b)

FIG. 10.14. Examples of the fruits of drawing practice without much innate talent: All drawings by Charles are from Hildreth (1941). (a) Drawing of train by Charles, age 2, showing tracks and differentiation between engine and passenger cars. (b) Drawing of train by Charles, age 3, showing noncanonical front view, and showing tracks smaller behind the train, but with no converging lines. (c) Drawing of train by Charles, age 4, showing three-dimensional space by vertical positioning (the farther trains are placed higher up). (d) Drawing of train by Charles, age 5, showing differentiated passenger and freight trains. Copyright © 1941 by Kings Crown Press. Reprinted with permission of Columbia University Press.

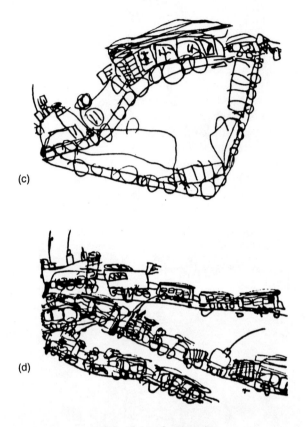

(c)

(d)

FIG. 10.14. Continued.

Ordinary children never arrive at this. Witness Charles' trains (Hildreth, 1941). Third, they can begin a drawing from any part of the object drawn, and draw objects from noncanonical orientations. This ability suggests a strong visual imagery ability (see the following for evidence of this). Strong visual imagery is also suggested by the way in which these children often draw something vividly that they have seen months, even years ago (Selfe, 1995; Winner, 1996). Fourth, these children are highly inventive, and endlessly vary their compositions, forms, and sometimes colors. Note how Eitan varied his perspective systems, and how Peter varied the positions of his figures in motion.

This ability to invent and discover the domain independent of instruction has its parallel in all other domains in which one finds precocious children. Josh Waitzkin discovered the strategy of combining pieces to launch an attack in chess. Musical children start improvising, transposing, and composing on their own; they often have perfect pitch, and can hear errors that others cannot. Bloom's pianists were noted by their teachers to learn with great ease. Mathematical children invent novel ways of solving problems, and ask mathematical questions that ordinary children who work hard at their math lessons, and do well, just do not ask.

In short, precocious children are not mere drudges. They are not ordinary children who know how to work hard. Not only can one not make ordinary children spend hours a day at drawing or chess or math, but even if one could, as in China or Japan, these children do not achieve with instruction what precocious children achieve on their own.

POTENTIAL BIOLOGICAL MARKERS
OF DRAWING TALENT

I have thus far argued for the existence of children who draw at a precocious level, and who are driven to work hard at drawing. I have argued that the drive to work at drawing, and the interest in drawing, is inextricably connected to the precocity. Moreover, the precocity is seen from the outset, and thus cannot be a consequence of hard work.

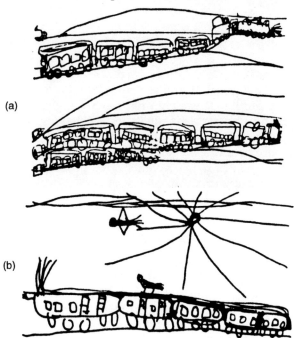

FIG. 10.15. Further drawings by Charles, ages 6 to 9. (a) Drawing of train by Charles, age 6, showing trains receding in distance and diminishing in size. (b) Drawing of train by Charles, age 7, which appears no more advanced than drawing at age 6. (c) Drawing of train by Charles, age 8, in canonical side view. (d) Drawing of train by Charles, age 9, showing technique of diminishing size to suggest depth. Copyright © 1941 by Kings Crown Press. Reprinted with permission of Columbia University Press.

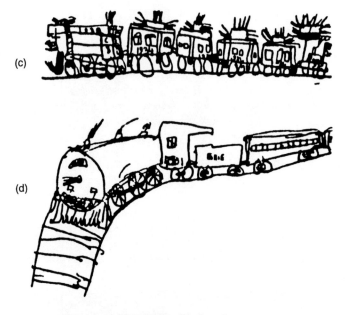

FIG. 10.15. Continued.

I now turn to what I argue are biological markers of talent in the visual arts. The case that I make is that children who show precocity in drawing have a particular profile. These children have a higher than average likelihood of being non-right-handed, and of having visual-spatial strengths along with linguistic deficits. The profile cut by these children can be seen in extreme and exaggerated form in the profile of abilities and disabilities seen in drawing savants. This profile of abilities and disabilities is consistent with the existence of a biological component to drawing expertise.

Higher Than Average Incidence of Non-Right-Handedness

A disproportionate number of adult artists and children who draw precociously are non-right-handed (Mebert & Michel, 1980; Peterson, 1979; Rosenblatt & Winner, 1988; Smith, Meyers, & Kline, 1989). For instance, in one study it was shown that 21% of art students were left-handed, compared to only 7% of nonart majors at the same university; 48% of the art students were non-right-handed (i.e., either left-handed or ambidextrous), compared to 22% of the nonart majors (Mebert & Michel, 1980). No environmental explanation can make sense of this finding: Artists do not need to use both hands when drawing, and even very young precocious drawers show this tendency, often drawing interchangeably with both hands (Winner, 1996).

Non-right-handedness is a marker, albeit an imperfect one, of anomalous brain dominance. It is estimated that about 70% of the population has standard dominance—a strong left-hemisphere dominance for language and hand (yielding right-handedness) and a strong right-hemisphere dominance for other functions such as visual spatial and musical processing (Geschwind & Galaburda, 1985). Those remaining 30% with anomalous dominance have more symmetrical brains (with language and visual-spatial functions represented somewhat on both sides of the brain).

Visual-Spatial Strengths

Anomalous dominance has been argued to result in a tendency toward inborn ability in areas for which the right hemisphere is important (e.g., visual-spatial, musical, or mathematical areas; Geschwind & Galaburda, 1985), and children who draw precociously have been shown to possess other visual-spatial strengths besides the ability to render. There are anecdotal reports of unusually vivid and early visual memories in these children (Winner, 1996).

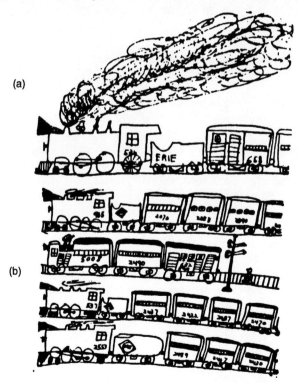

FIG. 10.16. Drawings by Charles at ages 10 and 11: (a) Drawing of train by Charles, age 10, in canonical side view. (b) Drawing of train by Charles, age 11, showing increase in detail, still drawn in canonical side view. Copyright © 1941 by Kings Crown Press. Reprinted with permission of Columbia University Press.

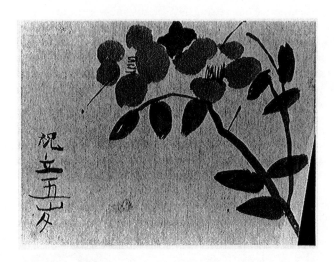

FIG. 10.17. Brush and ink painting by a typical (nonprecocious) Chinese 6-year-old, showing high skill level as a consequence of regular, formulaic, drawing instruction.

There is also experimental evidence for advanced visual-spatial strengths in children whose drawings are unusually skilled. Such children excel in visual memory tasks of various sorts (Hermelin & O'Connor, 1986; Rosenblatt & Winner, 1988; Winner & Casey, 1992; Winner, Casey, DaSilva, & Hayes, 1991). For example, they are better able to recognize nonrepresentational shapes that they have seen before (Hermelin & O'Connor, 1986) and to recall shapes, colors, compositions, and forms in pictures (Rosenblatt & Winner, 1988). They also show superior ability to recognize what is represented in incomplete drawings (O'Connor & Hermelin, 1983), suggesting that they have a rich lexicon of mental images. And they excel in mentally rotating images in three-dimensional space, as do children who are labeled as gifted in math as well as adults who choose math as a college major (Winner & Casey, 1992). Thus, precocious drawers show the kinds of right-hemisphere skills that would be predicted by anomalous dominance. It is perhaps because of strong imaging abilities that these children are able to begin drawings from noncanonical places, and can draw from memory images they have seen long ago.

Linguistic Deficits

Anomalous dominance has also been argued to lead to deficits in areas for which the left hemisphere is important, resulting in language-related problems such as dyslexia (Geschwind & Galaburda, 1985). This hypothesis can be tested either by assessing heightened right-hemisphere abilities in dyslexic children, or by assessing frequencies of dyslexia in children who draw precociously. Both ways of testing the hypothesis yield a clear and consistent picture of an association between visual-spatial ability and language-related learning disorders.

Many studies have shown that on IQ tests, dyslexic children score higher on subtests assessing right-hemisphere spatial skills than on those assessing left-hemisphere sequential skills (Gordon, 1983; Gordon & Harness, 1977; Naidoo, 1972; Rugel, 1974). For instance, they score higher on constructing patterns or puzzles than on recalling sequences of numbers. These findings fit with anecdotal observations of visual-spatial talent in dyslexics (Galaburda & Kemper, 1979).

The same association shows up when either adults or children who draw at high levels are examined for verbal problems. Artists score poorly on tests of verbal fluency (Hassler, 1990), they report more reading problems as children than do other college students (Winner et al., 1991), and they make more spelling errors than do other students (Winner et al., 1991). Moreover, the kinds of spelling errors they make are just those associated with poor reading skills—nonphonetically based errors that do not preserve letter–sound relationships (Frith, 1980; Phillips, 1987). Nonphonetically based errors are ones in which wrong letters are included, correct ones are omitted, or letters are reversed (e.g., physicain for physician); in contrast, phonetically based errors are ones that when sounded out, sound right (e.g., "phisician"). This tendency to make nonphonetically based errors was found by Winner et al. (1991) even when SAT performance was partialed out. This suggests that artistically inclined individuals have problems specific to reading and spelling that are independent of the kinds of abilities measured by the SAT.

Thus individuals who show high achievement in the visual arts have a tendency toward non-right-handedness and also have heightened right-hemisphere skills and lowered left-hemisphere skills. The confluence of non-right-handedness, spatial skills, and linguistic problems has been dubbed a "pathology of superiority" by Geschwind and Galaburda (1985, p. 445). Geschwind and Galaburda argued that such pathologies of superiority were due to the hormonal environment of the developing fetal brain. In particular, either excess testosterone, or heightened sensitivity to testosterone, was argued to slow development of an area of the brain's left posterior hemisphere. Slowing of the left hemisphere was argued to lead to compensatory development of the right hemisphere, and thus to result in the emergence of talents associated with the right hemisphere such as music, drawing, and mathematics. This theory remains controversial (see Bryden, McManus, & Bulman-Fleming, 1994; Schacter, 1994). Nonetheless, there is as yet no other theory that can explain the established fact that ability in drawing is associated both with non-right-handedness and dyslexia. This fact lends support to the claim that children who draw precociously are different from the start.

Drawing Savants

The final piece of evidence that I present in favor of a biological component to drawing expertise is the existence of drawing savants. Savants are people who show prodigious ability in one area, but severe retardation in all other areas. Although such individuals are rare, generalizations about them can be drawn. They are typically found in one of four domains: music (almost always piano), mental calculation, calendar calculation, and visual arts (almost always realistic drawing). There have been numerous attempts to explain the savant syndrome. Environmental explanations appeal to practice and reinforcement (Ericsson & Faivre, 1988). Psychodynamic explanations appeal to a compensatory search for a communication channel when language is lacking. However, I argue here that a biological explanation of these individuals is the only feasible one because of the rapidity with which they acquire the domain, their lack of need for scaffolding, and their drive to master. Moreover, savants can be seen as particularly extreme examples of the pathology of superiority. Savants have a highly developed skill (usually one subserved by the right hemisphere), and are deficient in everything else.[2] The severity of their pathology limits them to a restricted set of domains, and also limits what they can do in these domains.

The most famous drawing savant is Nadia, an autistic child who drew at least from the age of 3;6 on (Selfe, 1977, 1983, 1985, 1995). Her drawings preserved from this age are drawn in perspective, with foreshortening, occlusion, and correct proportion. Her drawings are more advanced than those of any nonpathologically gifted child that we know of (Fig. 10.18), but other autistic children have also been shown to draw at an exceptional level (Park, 1978; Sacks, 1985, 1995; Wiltshire, 1987). These savants resemble precocious drawers. They draw early and a lot, and they also stand out as different from ordinary children in the same ways as do precocious drawers. They discover perspective and foreshortening and other depth techniques on their own, they can begin a drawing from any part of the object, they draw with astounding confidence and fluidity of line, and they can draw from memory objects and pictures they have seen months or years ago.

Heightened drawing ability exists in only a small subset of autistic children (Charman & Baron-Cohen, 1993), and we do not know whether anything else differentiates this subset of autistic children from those who draw at their mental level (Selfe, 1995). Nonetheless, the existence of extraordinary drawing ability in the presence of retardation and autism, and in the absence of any explicit instruction, calls for a biological, brain-based explanation. If the high drawing ability of savants were simply due to the fact they draw all the time (which they do), then one would expect

---

[2]Savantism in calculation, a left-hemisphere skill, can also be explained by Geschwind and Galaburda's (1985) theory. They argued that in addition to compensatory right-hemisphere development, regions next to the left posterior areas may also undergo compensatory development, which would lead to high calculation ability.

FIG. 10.18. Drawing of horse by Nadia, at about age 5. From Selfe (1977). Reproduced courtesy of the publisher Academic Press London Limited.

savants in any domain. All that would be required is compulsive practice. The fact that savants are found only in certain domains suggests that practice cannot be the explanation. Moreover, the intense drive to draw (or play music, or calculate mentally) seen in savants is what leads to the compulsive practice. We have to explain the intense drive for mastery in a domain that we see in savants just as we see in normal children. This rage to master is part of the talent; it does not explain the talent.

CONCLUSION

I have tried to disentangle work from talent in order to argue that talent comes first. Talent leads to hard work, which in turn leads to ever-increasing levels of achievement. It may be useful to think in terms of four logically possible combinations of these two variables.

Most children have neither exceptional talent in drawing nor do they spend much time at drawing. These children never draw particularly well. Some children have no exceptional talent but they work hard at drawing.

The Chinese schoolchildren and Hildreth's train drawer are examples of such children. These children are able to draw at a level considerably beyond their age. Some children have talent but by early adolescence they disengage from their domain of talent, often because of competing demands by school and family (Csikszentmihalyi, Rathunde, & Whalen, 1993). Finally, there are those with both talent and a drive to work that continues undiminished into adulthood. These are the Picassos, the Yanis; in music, these are the Mozarts and the Menuhins; in science, these are Roe's eminent scientists.

What kind of further evidence would one need to conclude definitively that talent plays a decisive role in expertise in drawing or in other areas? Ideally, one would need to take a large sample of young and untutored children, selected at random, and submit them to identical levels of deliberate practice. Three conditions would have to obtain to demonstrate that hard work begun at an early age is all that is necessary to explain the Picassos and Mozarts of the world. First, all of the children must eventually achieve the same levels of expertise with the same levels of work. Second, all children would have to learn in the same way, mastering what is given to them rather than deviating and inventing their own techniques. Third, with sufficient work and time, the levels reached must be as high as those reached by individuals we consider truly exceptional. Only then could we rule out talent as a factor in high accomplishment. I, for one, would place my bets on quite different outcomes: highly differential levels achieved despite the same amount of work; difficulty getting most of the children to work as hard as some of the children; those that work willingly also inventing techniques on their own; and no levels achieved concomitant to those achieved by Yani, Picasso, Mozart, or Menuhin.

ACKNOWLEDGMENTS

Much of this chapter is based on my forthcoming book, *Gifted Children: Myths and Realities;* Basic Books, 1996.

REFERENCES

Beck, W. (1928). *Self-development in drawing. As interpreted by the genius of Romano Dazzi and other children.* New York: Putnam.

Bloom, B. (Ed.). (1985). *Developing talent in young people.* New York: Ballantine Books.

Bryden, M. P., McManus, I. C., & Bulman-Fleming, M. B. (1994). Evaluating the empirical support for the Geschwind–Behan–Galaburda model of cerebral lateralization. *Brain and Cognition, 26,* 103–167.

Cane, F. (1951). *The artist in each of us.* New York: Pantheon.

Charman, A., & Baron-Cohen, S. (1993). Drawing development in autism: The intellectual to visual realism shift. *British Journal of Developmental Psychology, 11,* 171–186.

Cox, M. (1992). *Children's drawings.* London: Penguin.

Csikszentmihalyi, M., Rathunde, K., & Whalen, S. (1993). *Talented teenagers: The roots of success and failure.* New York: Cambridge University Press.
Csikszentmihalyi, M., & Robinson, R. E. (1986). Culture, time and the development of talent. In R. J. Sternberg & J. E. Davidson (Eds.), *Conceptions of giftedness* (pp. 264–284). New York: Cambridge University Press.
Ericsson, K. A. (1988). Analysis of memory performance in terms of memory skill. In R. J. Sternberg (Ed.), *Advances in the psychology of human intelligence* (Vol. 4, pp. 137–179). Hillsdale, NJ: Lawrence Erlbaum Associates.
Ericsson, K. A., & Faivre, I. A. (1988). What's exceptional about exceptional abilities? In L. K. Obler & D. A. Fein (Eds.), *The neuropsychology of talent and special abilities* (pp. 436–473). New York: Guilford.
Ericsson, K. A., Krampe, R. T., & Tesch-Römer, C. (1993). The role of deliberate practice in the acquisition of expert performance. *Psychological Review, 100,* 363–406.
Frith, U. (1980). *Cognitive processes in spelling.* New York: Academic Press.
Galaburda, A. M., & Kemper, T. L. (1979). Cytoarchitectonic abnormalities in developmental dyslexia: A case study. *Annals of Neurology, 6,* 94–100.
Gardner, H. (1989). *To open minds.* New York: Basic Books.
Geschwind, N., & Galaburda, A. M. (1985). Cerebral lateralization: Biological mechanisms, associations, and pathology: I. A hypothesis and a program for research. *Archives of Neurology, 42,* 428–459.
Goldsmith, L. (1992). Stylistic development of a Chinese painting prodigy. *Creativity Research Journal, 5,* 281–293.
Goldsmith, L., & Feldman, D. (1989). Wang Yani: Gifts well given. In W. C. Ho (Ed.), *Wang Yani: The brush of innocence* (pp. 59–62). New York: Hudson Hills.
Golomb, C. (1991). *The child's creation of a pictorial world.* Berkeley: University of California Press.
Golomb, C. (1992). Eitan: The early development of a gifted child artist. *Creativity Research Journal, 5*(3), 265–279.
Golomb, C. (1995). Eitan: The artistic development of a child prodigy. In C. Golomb (Ed.), *The development of gifted child artists: Selected case studies* (pp. 171–196). Hillsdale, NJ: Lawrence Erlbaum Associates.
Golomb, C., & Hass, M. (1995). Varda: The development of a young artist. In C. Golomb (Ed.), *The development of gifted child artists: Selected case studies* (pp. 71–100). Hillsdale, NJ: Lawrence Erlbaum Associates.
Gombrich, E. H. (1960). *Art and illusion.* London: Phaidon.
Goodenough, F. L. (1926). *Measurement of intelligence by drawings.* New York: Harcourt, Brace, & World.
Gordon, A. (1987). Childhood works of artists. *The Israel Museum Journal, 6,* 75–82.
Gordon, H. W. (1983, April). The learning disabled are cognitively right. *Topics in Learning and Learning Disabilities,* pp. 29–39.
Gordon, H. W., & Harness, B. Z. (1977). A test battery for the diagnosis and treatment of developmental dyslexia. *Journal of Speech and Hearing Disorders, 8,* 1–7.
Hassler, M. (1990). Functional cerebral asymmetric and cognitive abilities in musicians, painters, and controls. *Brain Cognition, 13,* 1–17.
Hermelin, B., & O'Connor, N. (1986). Spatial representations in mathematically and in artistically gifted children. *British Journal of Educational Psychology, 56,* 150–157.
Hildreth, G. (1941). *The child mind in evolution: A study of developmental sequences in drawing.* New York: Kings Crown Press.
Howe, M. J. A. (1990). *The origins of exceptional abilities.* Oxford, UK: Blackwell.
Hurwitz, A. (1983). *The gifted and talented in art: A guide to program planning.* Worcester, MA: Davis Publications.
Lark-Horowitz, B., Lewis, H., & Luca, M. (1973). *Understanding children's art for better teaching* (2nd ed.). Columbus, OH: Merrill.
Mebert, C. J., & Michel, G. F. (1980). Handedness in artists. In J. Herron (Ed.), *Neuropsychology of left-handedness* (pp. 273–279). New York: Academic Press.

Milbrath, C. (1987). Spatial representations of artistically gifted children: A case of universal or domain specific development? *Genetic Epistemologist, 25,* 1–5.

Milbrath, C. (1995). Germinal motifs in the work of a gifted child artist. In C. Golomb (Ed.), *The development of artistically gifted children: Selected case studies* (pp. 101–134). Hillsdale, NJ: Lawrence Erlbaum Associates.

Milbrath, C. (in preparation). *Patterns of artistic development.* New York: Cambridge University Press.

Naidoo, S. (1972). *Specific dyslexia.* New York: Wiley.

O'Connor, N., & Hermelin, B. (1983). The role of general and specific talents in information processing. *British Journal of Developmental Psychology, 1,* 389–403.

Paine, S. (1981). *Six children draw.* London: Academic Press.

Paine, S. (1987). The childhood and adolescent drawings of Henri de Toulouse-Lautrec (1864–1901): Drawings from 6 to 18 years. *Journal of Art and Design, 6,* 297–312.

Pariser, D. (1987). The juvenile drawings of Klee, Toulouse-Lautrec and Picasso. *Visual Arts Research, 13,* 53–67.

Pariser, D. (1991). Normal and unusual aspects of juvenile artistic development in Klee, Lautrec, and Picasso. *Creativity Research Journal, 4,* 51–65.

Park, C. C. (1978). Review of "Nadia: A case of extraordinary drawing ability in an autistic child." *Journal of Autism and Childhood Schizophrenia, 8,* 457–472.

Peterson, J. M. (1979). Left-handedness: Differences between student artists and scientists. *Perceptual and Motor Skills, 48,* 961–962.

Phillips, I. (1987). *Word recognition and spelling strategies in good and poor readers.* Unpublished doctoral dissertation, Harvard Graduate School of Education, Cambridge, MA.

Richardson, J. (1991). *A life of Picasso.* New York: Random House.

Roe, A. (1951). A psychological study of physical scientists. *Genetic Psychology Monograph, 43*(2), 121–235.

Roe, A. (1953a). *The making of a scientist.* New York: Dodd Mead.

Roe, A. (1953b). A psychological study of eminent psychologists and anthropologists and a comparison with biological and physical scientists. *Psychological Monographs: General and Applied, 67,* Whole No. 52.

Rosenblatt, E., & Winner, E. (1988). Is superior visual memory a component of superior drawing ability? In L. Obler & D. Fein (Eds.), *The exceptional brain: Neuropsychology of talent and superior abilities* (pp. 341–363). New York: Guilford.

Rugel, R. P. (1974). WISC subtest scores of disabled readers: A review with respect to Bannatyne's recategorization. *Journal of Learning Disabilities, 7*(1), 48–65.

Sacks, O. (1985, April 25). The autist artist. *New York Review of Books,* pp. 17–21.

Sacks, O. (1995, January 9). A neurologist's notebook: Prodigies. *The New Yorker,* pp. 44–65.

Schacter, S. C. (1994). Evaluating the Bryden–McManus–Bulman–Fleming critique of the Geschwind–Behan–Galaburda model of cerebral lateralization. *Brain and Cognition, 26,* 199–205.

Selfe, L. (1977). *Nadia: A case of extraordinary drawing ability in an autistic child.* New York: Academic Press.

Selfe, L. (1983). *Normal and anomalous representational drawing ability in children.* London: Academic Press.

Selfe, L. (1985). *Anomalous drawing development: Some clinical studies.* Cambridge, UK: Cambridge University Press.

Selfe, L. (1995). Nadia reconsidered. In C. Golomb (Ed.), *The development of gifted child artists: Selected case studies* (pp. 197–236). Hillsdale, NJ: Lawrence Erlbaum Associates.

Sloane, K. D., & Sosniak, L. A. (1985). The development of accomplished sculptors. In B. S. Bloom (Ed.), *Developing talent in young people* (pp. 90–138). New York: Ballantine Books.

Sloboda, J. A., Davidson, J. W., & Howe, M. J. A. (1994, August). Is everyone musical? *The Psychologist, 1*(8), 349–354.

Smith, B. O., Meyers, M. B., & Kline, K. (1989). For better or for worse: Left-handedness, pathology, and talent. *Journal of Clinical and Experimental Neuropsychology, 11,* 944–958.

Vasari, G. (1957). *Lives of the artists.* New York: Noonday.

Waitzkin, F. (1984). *Searching for Bobby Fisher: The world of chess observed by the father of a chess prodigy.* New York: Random House.

Willats, J. (1977). How children learn to draw realistic pictures. *Quarterly Journal of Experimental Psychology, 29,* 367–382.

Wilson, B., & Wilson, M. (1977). An iconoclastic view of the imagery sources in the drawings of young people. *Art Education, 30,* 5–11.

Wiltshire, S. (1987). *Drawings.* London: J. M. Dent.

Winner, E. (1989). How can Chinese children draw so well? *Journal of Aesthetic Education, 23*(1), 41–63.

Winner, E. (1996). *Gifted children: Myths and realities.* New York: Basic Books.

Winner, E., & Casey, M. B. (1992). Cognitive profiles of artists. In G. Cupchik & J. Laszlo (Eds.), *Emerging visions of the aesthetic process* (pp. 154–170). New York: Cambridge University Press.

Winner, E., Casey, M. B., DaSilva, E., & Hayes, R. (1991). Spatial abilities and reading deficits in visual arts students. *Empirical Studies of the Arts, 9,* 51–63.

Winner, E., & Martino, G. (1993). Giftedness in the visual arts and music. In K. Heller, F. Monks, & A. H. Passow (Eds.), *International handbook of research and development of giftedness and talent* (pp. 253–281). New York: Pergamon.

Zhensun, Z., & Low, A. (1991). *A young painter: The life and paintings of Wang Yani—China's extraordinary young artist.* New York: Scholastic.

Zimmerman, E. (1992). Factors influencing the graphic development of a talented young artist. *Creativity Research Journal, 5*(3), 295–311.

11

Changing the Agency for Learning: Acquiring Expert Performance

Robert Glaser
University of Pittsburgh

Understanding how expertise is acquired poses a great challenge to learning theory. The authors in this book address the challenge by considering expertise in terms of the learning phenomena involved and the conditions for optimal acquisition of competence. With this work, they begin a new phase in the study of expertise. In most studies of expertise to date, the acquired properties of expert performance have been described. Cognitive task analyses based on performance theory have significantly contributed to these descriptions and to an understanding of the nature of human cognition. Only indirect attempts have been made to infer what the properties of attained expertise might mean for the acquisition of competence. Ericsson and his colleagues have begun now to ask the question that follows cognitive task analysis: What are the conditions of development, learning, and acquisition of expertise?

Given our current state of knowledge, it is an appropriate time to ask this question. In its initial attempts to understand acquired performance, cognitive science set aside study of the dynamics of learning, and only in recent years have questions of acquisition re-emerged. Although learning theory was a prominent and vigorous part of the science of psychology in the middle of this century, the theory of that time was based on analysis of relatively simple performances. Learning theorists expected that principles so generated eventually would be extrapolated to explain complex forms of learning. With the advent of cognitive psychology, however, questions were raised about the nature of what is learned and the nature of the competencies that result from long-term learning and extended experience. Attempts to understand the steady state of attained performance temporarily de-emphasized study of the learning processes by which this performance was acquired and changed. The scientific decision to focus on performance was explicitly acknowledged by Newell and Simon (1972) in the book *Human Problem Solving:*

> Turning to the performance-learning-development dimension, our emphasis on performance again represents a scientific bet. We recognize that what sort of information processing system a human becomes depends intimately on the way he develops. . . . Yet, acknowledging this, it still seems to us that we have too imperfect a view of the system's final nature to be able to make predictions from the development process to the characteristics of the structures it produces.
>
> . . . The study of learning, if carried out with theoretical precision, must start with a model of a performing organism, so that one can represent, as learning, the changes in the model. . . .
>
> The study of learning takes its cue, then, from the nature of the performance system. If performance is not well understood, it is somewhat premature to study learning. . . . Both learning and development must then be incorporated in integral ways in the more complete and successful theory of human information processing that will emerge at a later stage in the development of our science. (pp. 7–8)

At the present time, the study of learning is proceeding on several levels of analysis. At a microlevel, studies are being carried out on the dynamics of memory and verbal learning (Kintsch, 1994), and the neurophysiology of elementary learning processes is being investigated (Squire, 1992). At an intermediate level, there is an active field of machine learning and related studies of artificial intelligence (Langley, 1995). At a molar level, instructional experiments are being carried out on the design of educational and training environments for optimizing learning and improving performance (Brown, 1994; Glaser & Bassok, 1989; McGilly, 1994). It is this molar-instructional level that is the emphasis of my comments here. In this regard, scientists interested in learning theory (and also interested in education, training, and instruction) are designing instructional environments both to understand the improvement of performance and to further define theories applicable to the design of conditions for learning. This "engineering phase" in our science is analogous to other sciences where developments such as the transistor and space flight fostered theoretical advances.

A second emphasis is the relationship between expertise and human competence in general. What we learn about expert performance and its acquisition is applicable to understanding and improving competence in the skills and knowledge learned in school and in the workplace. The objective is for more people to attain competence at higher levels than ever before. To reach this goal, we should be able to design improved environments for learning and to build appropriate assessment tools to measure the criteria of competent performance. As Wagner and Stanovich (chap. 7, this volume) point out, expertise can be defined as relative standing or as mastery of performance criteria, and that neither of these preclude expert attainment by a majority of students. This is an important principle because it makes the work on expertise relevant to standards for education.

Overall, the work reported in this volume has led me to infer a major principle or hypothesis underlying the acquisition of competence, which can be labeled a *change in agency*, that is, a change in the agency for learning as expertise develops and performance improves. Initially, learning involves a significant degree of external environmental support, and as competence is attained, there is an increasing amount of internalized self-regulation that controls the learning situation and the fine honing of performance. The progression can be described in terms of three interactive phases: (a) *external support*, involving early environmental structuring influenced by parental dedication and interests and the support of teachers and coaches; (b) *transition*, characterized by decreasing scaffolding of environmental supports and increasing of apprenticeship arrangements that offer guided practice and foster self-monitoring, the learning of self-regulatory skills, and the identification and discrimination of standards and criteria for high levels of performance; and (c) *self-regulation*, a later phase of competence in which much of the design of the learning environment is under the control of the learner as a developing expert. In this phase, the conditions of deliberate practice are arranged so that performers can obtain feedback on their own performance and so that appropriately challenging situations are available or can be designed. There is very selective use of external support with the performer calling on competitors, performance situations, and the advice of coaches as particularly needed. Given these phases as a framework, we now consider the learning and cognitive processes that underlie the course of acquisition of expert performance.

PROCESSES OF ACQUISITION

Patterns and Organized Structured Knowledge

Pattern-based retrieval serves as a cuing schema for appropriate action in expert performance and is the first process referred to by Ericsson (chap. 1, this volume). A fundamental mechanism proposed in early studies of expertise, pattern-based retrieval reflects the acquisition of well-organized and integrated knowledge that provides a structure for representation that goes beyond surface features. For the development of expertise, knowledge must be acquired in such a way that it is highly connected and articulated, so that inference and reasoning are enabled as is access to procedural actions. The resulting organization of knowledge provides a schema for thinking and cognitive activity. Structured knowledge, therefore, is not just a consequence of the amount of information received, but reflects exposure to an environment for learning where there are opportunities for problem solving, analogy making, extended inferencing, interpretation, and working in unfamiliar environments requiring transfer.

Simonton's notion of initial creative potential, which he defines as a richness of interconnected concepts, relates to structured knowledge. Simonton (chap. 8, this volume) proposes that in the course of becoming skilled, processes of ideation and elaboration occur that enhance knowledge structure and associated chunks and patterns. The properties of this structure are a function of the rate at which associative processes occur and the kind of organizational structures the field or domain allows. Analyses of the kinds of networks that get built up in various fields of knowledge and the kinds of inference and creativity that are entailed would be an important contribution to understanding conditions for improving performance.

Self-Regulation

With increasing attainment of skill there is the ability to interrogate, negotiate, and test a representation so that learning occurs and new levels of performance are attained. In his chapter, Ericsson points out that: "Experts have been found to generate a complex representation of the encountered situation, where information about the context is integrated with knowledge to allow selection of actions as well as evaluation, checking, and reasoning about alternative actions" (p. 15). The learning mechanism here is effective self-monitoring and self-instruction. A significant aspect of this ability to manipulate a representation is the capacity experts have to predict future actions based on their own moves or those of their colleagues or opponents. This strategy entails a coordinate learning process by which the experts provide their own performance feedback on the basis of which subtle changes in their activities are reinforced. Using well-developed representations as a basis for planning, prediction, evaluation, and adaptive refinement is, as Ericsson underscores, a major mechanism in supporting further improvements in performance.

This ability for self-regulation enables experts to leave their coaches and teachers behind and to profit a great deal from practice and serious study by themselves, as Charness and his colleagues point out. Charness, Krampe, and Mayr's (chap. 2, this volume) investigation leads to the conclusion that serious study by one's self is a powerful variable. This finding confirms the significance of skills of self-management, self-regulation, and the design of one's environment in order to optimize learning where the player has control of the amount and duration of study. The player also has control over the quality of the conditions of study and can exercise fine-tuned modification of the situations presented and the feedback obtained. The social feedback aspects of tournament play and analysis of others are not downplayed, but this can be considered as an earlier emphasis, akin to Vygotsky's notion that social learning occurs initially and then becomes individually internalized. The necessity for social interaction continues to be important and will be sought out when necessary but becomes a less-used mechanism of acquisition in certain domains of expertise when one is skilled at designing situations for one's self. Interesting research here would be to examine self-designed learning and to analyze the dimensions of a discipline and areas of skill that make this environmental design easy or difficult.

Self-regulation is greatly facilitated as experts develop automaticity in carrying out fundamental processes and integrated units of performance; this leaves performance time available for higher level processes. Wagner and Stanovich (chap. 7, this volume) remind us of this when they consider the influence of phonological awareness in reading as a significant predictor of rate and level of reading attainment.

Social Feedback. Self-learning involves not only the feedback generated in self-study but also the ability to take advantage of situations in which social challenge and display of the results of one's own activities are made apparent. A role of teachers and coaches is to provide scaffolding for assisted practice in monitoring, the design of situations for self-analysis, and the use of feedback. The coach who does this and then fades out of the picture in order to enable learners to provide these environmental situations for themselves is teaching a most important skill of deliberate practice and self-enhancement of performance.

Starkes, Deakin, Allard, Hodges, and Hayes (chap. 3, this volume) highlight social feedback and consequent self-management in the realm of figure skating. Despite the apparent autonomy of skaters, their training situation is highly interactive. There is a great amount of feedback from coaches and other skaters and constant monitoring and sharing of experiences. This is evident in quotes from skaters such as "Everything is on a silver platter; there are no secrets anymore," and, "All the coaches on the ice . . . are lined up beside me. I am not afraid to share anything with anybody." Although there is a social interaction phase, there also is a consensus among coaches not to babysit the athletes on the ice, and against tutored practice and overlessoning. Here we see the mechanism of fading support to greater self-management.

The fading of self-management in a family context can be inferred in Howe's (chap. 9, this volume) description of Stephenson and Faraday. These men showed the ability to profit from their experiences and from the environment around them. The indication in Faraday's case is that his family background was such that he received the support and then the withdrawal of support necessary to learn self-management. His family environment stressed the importance of ascertaining what is expected from others and what is expected of one's self. Self-learning ability would be enhanced by asking what can I count on myself to do, and when I need to get the help and support of others.

Environment and the Discipline

Use of the situation and the surrounding environment for learning will vary with the friendliness of the environment to providing information. Musicians learn to listen to their playing in order to critique their own performance. Other situations provide more subtle feedback that may be difficult to hear and see, and that require inference and prediction to anticipate performance conditions in which error might occur. The differences in feedback in practice for wrestlers and skaters is apparent in chapter 3 by Starkes et al. The lone skater is able to get feeling and feedback from movements on the ice, whereas wrestlers must work with others on the mat for feedback. The resulting differences in self-regulatory skills, along with an investigation of possibilities of instrumentation for enhancing feedback, would be an interesting issue for future research.

Representation and Procedural Knowledge

Sloboda's (chap. 4, this volume) analysis of the subtleties of musical expressivity suggests learning mechanisms related to representation and procedural knowledge. He points out that the imitation of expression is a difficult technical matter requiring the learning of fine discriminations between the intended musical passage and changes in details that generate the individuality of expression. A representation mechanism is proposed that enables the acquisition of memory for expressive details. Sloboda suggests the transformation of information into an abstracted representation, similar to a stored chunk or pattern, that enables the recovery of performance nuances. Talented performers acquire these patterns that incorporate procedural skills for manipulating, combining, and elaborating appropriate elements of this knowledge. The question for learning is how in the course of practice these knowledge structures and associated skills are enhanced or retarded. In this context, Sloboda suggests the progression of external supports and motivators in early learning and the increasing development of internal resources for self-monitoring later on.

The Self as an Agent for Learning and Conditions of Experience

Acquiring highly competent performance, then, involves a repertoire of ways of learning in which knowledge is used and structured, and performance and its consequences are made apparent in the course of support from a teacher, social support, and self-management. These learning activities can enhance detailed performance feedback, encourage self-explanation, and enable anticipatory analysis of future conditions, such as an opponent's play, and impasses and misleads that can occur in solving problems. Study of self-directed activities, in particular, will contribute to understanding expertise and the capacity for continued learning beyond initial levels. It is important to focus on the experts' ability to observe their activities as if they were outside themselves, to design situations and make predictions and explanations in which this self-observation can occur, or to use people and objects in the environment for this purpose. Learning these skills of self-instruction would involve the scaffolding and fading of support from social situations and coaching.

To further understand the development of expertise, we also need to focus on the situational and social properties of the situation in which people perform. As Patel, Kaufman, and Magder (chap. 5, this volume) point out, qualities of expertise are shaped, for example, by how performance is optimized in complex dynamic environments where expertise is distributed in a convergence of group actions and decision making. Situational, social-management aspects of expertise are emphasized such as communication capabilities, the ability to convey plans and intentions, and the allocation of resources not only for one's self, but for others. How conditions of performance influence the kind of knowledge and skill acquired is especially interesting for understanding learning. Consider the urgency and necessity for accuracy under high-speed conditions where decisions are made by heuristic rules based on symptoms. This is antithetical to decision making based on diagnostic hypotheses where it is possible to develop rich representations as a framework for further action. The situational dimensions of experience, planned or unplanned, shape resulting expertise, and the accompanying ability to transfer and to learn from different encounters.

Winner (chap. 10, this volume) draws attention to conditions of experience with children talented in drawing, and she identifies specific characteristics of their competence such as the ability to differentiate shapes, confidence of line, use of techniques to represent depth, and the ability to adopt various spatial orientations. Precocious drawers do things with lines on a page that are never mastered by other children. Analyses of this kind of development of precocious activity can identify prior knowledge and cognitive ability that can be supported by further learning experiences.

CONCLUDING SUMMARY

The development of structured knowledge is a central feature of cognitive ability in early and later learning, and conditions of learning and experience significantly influence the kinds of knowledge structures that are acquired. Different performance environments foster various forms and uses of knowledge. There is probably a decelerating growth function to this development with stable patterns becoming available for most work, and newer structures appearing less frequently.

Study of the characteristics of environments that optimize structured knowledge is a major research activity for understanding the acquisition of expert performance. We now need to better understand the kind of active learning that fosters connected knowledge and increasing complexities of structure that incorporate abstracted representations and procedural availability. If we consider the goal of improving performance in our schools, we see how easily poorly integrated multiple-choice knowledge is readily transmitted in many educational settings. We need to be explicit about active, constructive problem-solving environments that can be instituted in contrast to common practice, and to examine closely how the environment helps develop structure as students acquire high levels of cognitive competence.

The chapters in this book make it clear that a predominant aspect of the learning process in the acquisition of expertise is self-regulation; this involves negotiating representations, interrogating, monitoring, and adjusting performance. The learning trajectory involves a progression from external and social support to increasing ability for self-regulation. Studies of developing expertise and coaching make this apparent, as do the details of the changing nature of learning techniques used in the course of achievement. Particular attention should be given to the question of how competent individuals design the environment of people and things about them, and use the situations they encounter to improve their performance. It would also be informative to understand the properties of different disciplines and different situations of performance that are more or less amenable to designing conditions for improvement, and that require various kinds of participatory experiences and assisting devices for supporting performance in the course of acquiring competence.

To reiterate the theme, the outstanding feature of acquiring expert performance apparent in the work and thinking reported in this volume is the changing sense of agency in how learning occurs. Initially, the learner depends on others, and with time, begins to increasingly rely on self-mechanisms and on self-judgment about when to engage others as participants and coaches. The amount of time spent by experts in self-learning at later stages of experience is an important lesson for school education. Self-learning and abilities for continued learning are expressed educational goals that we should be able to attain as we learn more about the acquisition of competence.

ACKNOWLEDGMENTS

Preparation of this chapter was sponsored in part by the National Research Center on Student Learning at the Learning Research and Development Center at the University of Pittsburgh and funded by the Office of Educational Research and Improvement (OERI) of the U.S. Department of Education. Additional support was provided by the National Center for Research on Evaluation, Standards, and Student Testing. The opinions expressed herein are those of the author and do not necessarily reflect the views of OERI.

REFERENCES

Brown, A. L. (1994). The advancement of learning. *Educational Researcher, 23*(8), 4–11.
Glaser, R., & Bassok, M. (1989). Learning theory and the study of instruction. *Annual Review of Psychology, 40,* 631–666.
Kintsch, W. (1994). Text comprehension, memory, and learning. *American Psychologist, 49*(4), 294–302.
Langley, P. (1995). *Elements of machine learning.* San Fransisco, CA: Morgan Kaufmann.
McGilly, K. (Ed.). (1994). *Classroom lessons: Integrating cognitive theory and classroom practice.* Cambridge, MA: MIT Press/Bradford Books.
Newell, A., & Simon, H. A. (1972). *Human problem solving.* Englewood Cliffs, NJ: Prentice-Hall.
Squire, L. (1992). Memory and the hippocampus: A synthesis from findings with rats, monkeys, and humans. *Psychological Review, 99*(2), 195–231.

12

Expert Performance
and the History of Science

Frederic L. Holmes
Yale University

As a historian of science I have for many years been studying the work and careers of creative experts in specialized domains of knowledge. Until I began to read the chapters prepared for this volume, however, I knew little about the body of expertise that has been assembled concerning the processes that have enabled my subjects to perform at the levels I have been tracking.

The history of science offers fruitful territory for the exploration and sometimes for the testing of the generalizations concerning expert performance that cognitive scientists are generating. Answers to questions they might ask are not necessarily to be found in the existing historical literature, because it has been written largely with other questions in mind. I do not, therefore, focus here on what historians of science can tell cognitive scientists about their problems, but on how what the latter have learned, and the problems they have posed, can illuminate questions that arise in the history of science, and how this can suggest new directions for scholarship in my field.

During the last decade some historians of science have come to focus much attention on what they sometimes call experimental practice. For examples of the varied approaches to experimentation recently pursued by historians, philosophers, and sociologists of science, see Gooding, Pinch, and Schaffer (1989).

I have resisted this phrase as an overall framing term for the close study of what experimental scientists do, because it has seemed to me to portray experimental science as routine activity at the expense of the creative aspect of experimentation, to suppress the unique aspects of each scientist's activity in his or her laboratory at a special time and place, at a particular phase in the exploration of a specific problem. My own candidate phrase to characterize this mode of activity, which has failed to be adopted by others, is the *investigative enterprise* (see, e.g., Holmes, 1989).

The more sharply defined definitions of practice that are emerging from the studies of cognitive scientists can help historians to clarify the meaning of experimental practice, to differentiate it from other aspects of experimental activity, and to elucidate the role of expert performance of the routine practices of a given field in the emergence of novelty.

A number of historians of science are advocating special attention to the experimental system as a unit of stability in the development of experimental sciences more fundamental than the discipline, the research school, or other categories in which we have sought to localize experimental activity. One of them, Rheinberger (1993), wrote:

> I propose that we move away from the perspective of a more or less well-defined disciplinary matrix of twentieth-century biology . . . toward what scientists are inclined to call their *experimental systems*. Such systems . . . do not respect disciplinary, academic, or national boundaries of science policy and of research programs. Insofar as they orient research activity, they may also prove helpful for the orientation of the historian. Experimental systems have a life of their own. (p. 44)

There is much evidence, from history as well as the present, to support Rheinberger's generalization, but we might ask why it happens. There are clearly disadvantages, as well as advantages, when the means gain priority over the ends. One explanation might be that the capital and other investments in an experimental system create inertias independent of the original intent in setting them up. Another might be that the existence of the system suggests opportunities not apparent when they were first established. It seems to me that the most compelling potential explanation, however, is that the experimental system gives rise to a domain of expert performance.

My detailed studies of three eminent experimental scientists each provide opportunities for the exploration of this theme. Lavoisier developed a repertoire of instruments and operations designed to study the fixation and release of "airs" in 1773. Over the next 15 years the apparatus gradually became more complex and specialized and the problems Lavoisier took up became technically more difficult, but the lineage from the earliest to the latest methods and equipment is clear enough so that his repertoire could well be characterized as an evolving experimental system. I think that Lavoisier's investigative pathway over this decade and a half could fruitfully be examined from the perspective of his sustained practice and continually improving performance at the set of physical skills and cognitive judgments required to master and fully exploit the investigative potential of the system that he had devised (Holmes, 1985).

Krebs was trained in the laboratory of Warburg in the 1920s in the use of a very well-defined experimental system: the Warburg manometer linked to a vessel containing tissue slices in a fluid medium in which the activities of intact cells could survive long enough to measure chemical processes that produced changes in the fluid or gaseous medium. Afterward, Krebs adapted this system to the study of the pathways of intermediary metabolism, and built much of his distinguished early career around the diverse applications of this versatile system. I have reconstructed the day-by-day progression of his research pathway over its first 10 years. I have been aware, and have commented in my narrative in a general way, about the effects of the continuous growth of his experience with this system on the scope of his investigations, but I believe that much more could be done to elucidate, from the perspective of this volume, how Krebs' daily practice in the use of this system, and his concentrated attention on the interaction between repetitive moves and their adaptation to new situations enabled him steadily to improve his performance (Holmes, 1991, 1993).

Bernard's experimental system lay less in a network of instruments and apparatus than in the remarkable surgical skill he applied to master the art of vivisection experiments. Through the rich collection of surviving laboratory notebooks, one might effectively trace, among other things, the effect of continuous practice on the scope and difficulty of the experimental operations he carried out almost daily, during the decade in which he established himself as the leading experimentalist in his field (Holmes, 1974).

The 10-year rule of necessary preparation that the examination of the acquisition of expert performance has revealed (Ericsson, chap. 1, this volume) seems to me important for understanding much more about the patterns of scientific development than merely the obvious one that a long apprenticeship is required in most cases before a scientist is ready to make significant original discoveries. The stability of experimental systems may be, at least in part, explained by the fact that the investment in the skills required to deploy them at a level at which they become powerful investigative tools takes a very long time. The scientist who has acquired such levels of performance cannot easily shift to a different experimental system, even if the new one appears better adapted to the unsolved problems at hand, unless there is a large degree of transfer of skills from one system to the other. It may often seem more practicable to press the old system a little further than to risk an extended less productive period while the scientist attempts to catch up with the levels of performance necessary to make the new system competitive. If that is so, we might also expect a lessening of this effect in laboratories of the present era, in which the principal investigator can more readily hire such skills by adding appropriate experts to the research group than by acquiring them individually.

As a number of the chapters emphasize, expert performance applies to creative reasoning as well as to repetitive skilled actions. If such performance levels also require many years to acquire, then I think we ought to be able to trace improvements in the level of reasoning in the historical activities of scientists whose investigative activities have left dense records such as laboratory notebooks. In following the research trail of Krebs, I sensed what I called a growing maturity during the 7 years that culminated in 1937 in his most important discovery, the citric acid, or Krebs cycle. He not only seemed to focus more persistently on problems at the heart of his subfield of interest, but the short-term patterns of his experimental trail seemed to reflect a deeper understanding of the power and limits of his experimental system. It would, however, be worthwhile to go over this trail again, applying the models and experiences acquired in these studies of expert performance, to see whether my impressionistic sense can be refined and sharpened.

The patterns in the acquisition of expert performance that cognitive scientists have found can also illuminate the later trajectories of scientific careers. Although the old adage that great scientific discoveries are made by people under the age of 30 is no more than that, the lifetime development curves that Simonton has produced verify that scientists normally achieve their most creative, most original successes relatively early in their careers (Simonton, chap. 3, this volume). What happens afterward? Some, of course, are diverted by the responsibilities and opportunities that come with prominence and seniority, others visibly lose momentum. But what of the many who sustain well-disciplined investigative activity, who keep in touch, who remain productive, but who rarely do something in their later careers that overshadows their defining contributions? Is it true that time, age, and long-term immersion in a field eventually inhibit the free play of creativity? Perhaps observations found in these chapters that in music, sports, and other areas where deliberate practice is central, older performers cease to strive for improvement, only to sustain the level they have achieved, is relevant also to experimental science. Although they must continue to learn, there may be a tendency, later in careers, to concentrate more on the exploitation of what one has acquired than on the improvements one could make by devoting more of one's time to gaining new layers of expertise.

The experimental systems and investigative problems with which a young scientist achieves prominence normally do not stay in the forefront of advance for periods commensurate with the length of a scientific career. As new problems and methods emerge, the mature scientist often is left doing good but less exciting work, consolidating what he or she has earlier found, following up further implications and ramifications that are valued but not seen as "breakthroughs," which sometimes appear to the upcoming generation even as backwater work. Why then do the scientists who have tasted the rewards of pathfinding investigation in their early careers not more regularly repeat their successes in the fields that have since displaced from the leading edge those areas in which their previous successes were achieved? Would their accumulated experience not give them advantages over their less practiced colleagues? Undoubtedly this often does happen, but the analyses contained in this volume suggest why it is not the dominant pattern. If the acquisition of expertise is a very long process, then the scientist in midcareer cannot readily transfer the mastery of reasoning and techniques through which he or she excelled in one area to the same level of performance in an area that requires different forms of expertise.

One can find prominent examples of historical figures who have successfully moved from fields in which they scored auspicious early successes to others in which they again did so, and other examples in which figures equally successful in the first field in which they achieved leadership were conspicuously less so in their subsequent moves. It may be instructive to examine the conditions that differentiate these two classes. Among the most famous of the first type was Louis Pasteur, who began with the study of asymmetry in chemical crystals, moved to fermentation, spontaneous generation, and finally the germ theory of disease, achieving greater prominence with each move. The pattern that seems to have underlain his repeated successes was his ability to make techniques and ideas that had worked in one domain central to his pursuit of the next, so that there appears to be strong continuity of approach linking activities in several fields. At least that is how he told it. (Among numerous studies of the career of Pasteur, see especially, Geison, 1995.)

A contrasting figure is Justus Liebig. During the first two decades of his career, Liebig became one of the two or three most influential leaders in the field of organic chemistry that emerged during the period between 1820 and 1840. He combined a deep feel for laboratory practice, insight into the central problems of the field, and a dominating, charismatic personality, to powerful effect. Here, too, I believe we would find improving levels of performance for at least a decade as Liebig's promising early publications matured to the commanding ones of his second decade in the field. In 1840 Liebig moved precipitously from the field of organic chemistry to an inchoate field of physiological, or as he called it, animal chemistry. Here he brought to bear insights from his former field that were not yet familiar to physiologists, and his writings in animal chemistry proved enormously influential for the next 20 years. They stimulated new forms of research that helped to shape an emerging field of energy metabolism. Few of his specific views about the intermediary chemical processes endured in the new field. Looking back, we can easily see why. They were brilliant aperçus, but highly speculative, unable to survive the experimental tests to which they were subsequently subjected (Holmes, 1973).

The contrast between the quality of Liebig's work in organic chemistry and that in animal chemistry is striking. How can we account for it? Much has to do with Liebig's tempestuous personal temperament, his impatience, and his dwindling interest in the long hours in the laboratory that filled his early years as a scientist. I would suggest, however, that much of the explanation lies in the phenomena studied by the contributors to this volume. Moving at midcareer into a field with which he had no long familiarity, Liebig read intensively and quickly identified problems to which his chemical expertise was pertinent; but he could not in so short a time acquire deep expertise in the field of physiology, which provided the matrix into which he inserted his chemical knowledge. The superficiality of his understanding of the physiological aspects of the phenomena to which he could provide unparalleled chemical insight is clearly evident in his writing on the topic, and was immediately spotted by skeptical contemporaries. If the results of these studies of expert performance are generalizable to such situations, then Liebig would have had to invest many years developing a second area of expertise, if he were to perform in animal chemistry at a level matching his earlier performance in organic chemistry.

If these patterns of scientific career development conform well to the findings of studies on the acquisition of expertise, how can we explain those instances in which young scientists seem able to evade the 10-year rule, producing pathfinding discoveries much sooner in their careers? Are these naturally brilliant performers who can arrive at the forefront without undergoing the usual apprenticeship in which others must practice and develop their skills? I have been studying a case that appears anomalous from this point of view. In 1958 two youthful scientists, Matthew Meselson, a graduate student, and Franklin Stahl, a postdoctoral student, produced at Caltech an experiment that has become a classic event in the early history of molecular biology. Known still as the Meselsohn–Stahl experiment, this precocious achievement provided the first persuasive experimental evidence that DNA replicates in the manner predicted by the Watson–Crick double helix model (Meselson & Stahl, 1958). Both Meselson and Stahl have had long and distinguished scientific careers, but for both of them this product of their first independent investigative projects remains what Simonton would call their "greatest hit." Is this case merely a violation of the usual rules for expert performance, an instance where genius overrides the normal patterns of development?

The Meselson–Stahl experiment illustrates, I believe, not merely that rules can be broken, but that science includes a mechanism whereby opportunities exist to bypass the long process of acquisition of expert mastery. The rules and skills that must be learned to practice at a high level may suddenly change, when new techniques are invented. Such innovations open up niches in which those who have developed the novel approaches quickly become the leading experts in their use. This is, in part, what happened to Meselson and Stahl. Their experiment was performed in an analytical ultracentrifuge, a complex instrument they had no experience in using when they began. Early in the work, however, Meselson discovered a new method, density gradient centrifugation, on which their subsequent success was based. Immediately he was the foremost expert in the practice of a new method whose spreading applications became even more important to an emerging field than the famous experiment itself. Far from refuting the general viewpoints underlying the chapters in this volume, therefore, this case of rapid rise to scientific eminence is consistent with them. It illustrates in another way how the insights emerging from these cognitive studies can illuminate the patterns of creativity we find in the history of science.

REFERENCES

Geison, G. L. (1995). *The private science of Louis Pasteur.* Princeton, NJ: Princeton University Press.

Gooding, D., Pinch, T., & Schaffer, S. (Eds.). (1989). *The uses of experiment: Studies in the natural sciences.* Cambridge, UK: Cambridge University Press.

Holmes, F. L. (1973). Liebig, Justus von. In C. C. Gillispie (Ed.), *Dictionary of scientific biography* (Vol. 8, pp. 329–350). New York: Scribner's.

Holmes, F. L. (1974). *Claude Bernard and animal chemistry.* Cambridge, MA: Harvard University Press.

Holmes, F. L. (1985). *Lavoisier and the chemistry of life: An exploration of scientific creativity.* Madison: University of Wisconsin Press.

Holmes, F. L. (1989). *Eighteenth century chemistry as an investigative enterprise.* Berkeley, CA: Office for the History of Science and Technology.

Holmes, F. L. (1991). *Hans Krebs: The formation of a scientific life.* New York: Oxford University Press.

Holmes, F. L. (1993). *Hans Krebs: Architect of intermediary metabolism* (Vol. 2). New York: Oxford University Press.

Meselson, M., & Stahl, F. W. (1958). The replication of DNA in escherichia coli. *Proceedings of the National Academy of Sciences, 44,* 671–682.

Rheinberger, H.-J. (1993). Experiment and orientation: Early systems of in vitro protein synthesis. *Journal of the History of Biology, 26,* 444.

13

Capturing Expertise in Sports

John B. Shea
Geoffrey Paull
Florida State University

It should not be surprising that from its inception sports expertise has been studied separately from mainstream motor learning research. Although both share an interest in skill, the focus of sport expertise has been comparatively broad in comparison to those of motor learning, which have centered almost exclusively on mechanisms responsible for response selection and control per se. In addition, sports expertise has emphasized the importance of ecological validity and has therefore been faithful in its use of actual sports tasks and situations (or at least close approximations) for study. This stands in stark contrast to motor learning researchers who have studied laboratory tasks so reduced in their complexity that any resemblance of skills used in sports is all but lost. These researchers appear to have been faithful to the admonition of Adams (1971) that "The villain that has robbed 'skills' of its precision is applied research" (p. 112). However, one cannot help think that the true villain Adams railed at was empirical and not necessarily applied research. Thus the lack of a theory of expertise may explain the past reluctance of motor learning researchers to pursue sports expertise as a topic of investigation. The general theory of expertise proposed by Ericsson, Krampe, and Tesch-Römer (1993) may provide the impetus for motor learning researchers to approach their research from an expertise framework. In addition, Ericsson et al. provided a paradigm for the complementary study of expertise with actual sports tasks as well as with laboratory tasks.

Ericsson (chap. 1, this volume) has described three approaches by which to study expert performance. These are the historical approach, laboratory approach, and developmental approach. Whereas the historical approach is dependent on available public data, the laboratory and developmental approaches involve greater investigator–subject interaction. The developmental approach typically involves the use of surveys and interviews. This information relates to circumstances existing during the development of skills and/or activities engaged in over an extended period of practice. The laboratory approach emphasizes the detailing of mechanisms underlying expert performance. It seeks causal relationships that allow descriptions of mechanisms underlying skill performance. Ericsson suggests a laboratory methodology (referred to as "capturing") that involves having the expert perform a number of representative tasks. Possible processes responsible for performance are then posited. Verbal reports along with other techniques are then used to eliminate alternative processes until some limited number of underlying processes responsible for performance of all representative tasks has been identified.

The bringing of sports expertise and motor learning research together within one framework has great potential to advance our understanding of motor skill. The long history of motor learning research conducted in the laboratory provides a plethora of hypothetical constructs that need to be operationalized at the application level. For example, the ubiquitous law of practice in which performance improves as a negatively accelerating function is well documented in the laboratory, as well as in the field setting. The attractive characteristic of the laboratory setting is that it offers a way to quickly train subjects to asymptotic performance levels (see Richman, Gobet, Staszewski, & Simon, chap. 6, this volume; Shiffrin, chap. 14, this volume). However, the advantage of being able to train subjects quickly is attained at the cost of losing equivalency in practice time between the laboratory and the field setting. It is impossible to know how many days, weeks, months, or years 150 practice trials in the laboratory will translate to in the actual sports setting (perhaps 10 years?). Sports expertise research can provide this temporal equivalency. There are many more constructs that offer an opportunity for parallel experimentation in the laboratory and the field setting. The need for continuity in this process suggests that it can best be attained through the collaborative efforts of researchers working in the same program.

Our approach to this chapter is to use a brief discussion of the research presented by Starkes, Deakin, Allard, Hodges, and Hayes (chap. 3, this volume) as a starting point for a review of sports expertise-related research from two different laboratory paradigms. These will be referred to as the expert–novice and the expert modeling paradigms. The expert–novice paradigm is congruent with the "capturing" methodology described by Ericsson and consists of selecting a component function of performance (e.g., eye fixation point) that is thought to underlie a sports skill (e.g., batting in baseball, the volley in tennis, and shooting in basketball) and then test expert and novice athletes to determine differences in how they use that component to control performance. The assumption for this comparison is that if performance differences are found, then the component function is an important discriminator for success. The expert modeling paradigm has been pursued by researchers interested in talent identification. This research has used linear regression techniques and has been empirically motivated by the desire to predict achievement in sports. Moreover, this research has been pursued independent of theoretical constructs related to sports expertise. Renger (1993) pointed out that despite considerable research on the topic, there has been little progress in identification of factors that differentiate successful and unsuccessful athletes using this approach. After a reviewing the literature, Renger concluded that this inability to identify factors associated with success in sports can be attributed to theoretical and methodological problems in current research. Fleishman (1972) and his colleagues were able to use this paradigm in the laboratory setting to study individual differences in abilities and task performance. We present selected studies from Fleishman's research as a useful paradigm from which to study expertise in both the laboratory and applied sports settings.

Starkes et al.

A major basis of Ericsson et al.'s theory of the acquisition of expertise has been the defining of components of deliberate practice that are believed to lead to expert levels of performance. These include: (a) the benefits of a coach or teacher, (b) that practice is not inherently enjoyable and perceived as not always relevant to final performances, and (c) there are constraints as to the amount of practice that can be achieved before fatigue impinges on performance. This proposal that a set of general rules governs acquisition of expertise can be contrasted to the view that the greatest precision in explanation will lie with more local or domain-specific rules. Can we expect a musician practicing solo routines to report the same feelings and conditions as a team player working in an interactive, dynamic training environment? Although the components of deliberate practice proposed by Ericsson et al. appear to be accurate, their individual relevance to any particular activity may be determined by the nature of the activity and the environment in which practice is undertaken.

The studies by Starkes et al. clearly fall within the purview of the developmental approach in which a questionnaire was used to obtain retrospective reports about practice regimes from wrestlers and figure skaters. These studies offer broad support for Ericsson et al.'s general theory of expertise, but do suggest limits to the extent any particular rule will apply across domains. Specifically, these studies provide evidence that the characterization of deliberate practice offered by Ericsson et al. may need to be adjusted to admit practice that is considered relevant and enjoyable.

Other conclusions by Starkes et al. are more circumspect. Figure skating coaches were interviewed and asked open-ended questions about the identification of talent, selection of skaters for their program, and the nature of training. They were also asked to rate the relative importance of items on a list of attributes thought to influence success in skating. The presentation of findings for this study consists of a casual discussion in which we are treated to a presentation of descriptive data and illustrative quotes. There is no attempt at a systematic protocol analysis (Ericsson & Simon, 1993) consisting of the classification of comments into response categories and inferential statistical analysis of these.

The authors place importance on the ratings by skaters and coaches of attributes related to success in skating in drawing their conclusions. The ratings of skaters and coaches were analyzed and found to be significantly related. A finding highlighted by the authors was that desire and good coaching ranked first and second, respectively, and that practice ranked only third in importance for both coaches and skaters. This finding appears less impressive when the relatively high and uniform rating of these three attributes for coaches (desire, $M = 10$, good coaching, $M = 9.9$, practice, $M = 9.8$) and skaters (desire, $M = 9.6$, good coaching, $M = 9.5$, practice, $M = 9.4$) is considered in addition to the absence of an inferential analysis of the ranking data. Perhaps it is worth noting that fitness level also received a high rating for coaches ($M = 9.8$) and skaters ($M = 9.0$). This suggests that there might be a relationship of practice and fitness level, and that fitness level might be considered a by-product of the amount of practice engaged in. If one chooses to ignore the likelihood of a ceiling effect being responsible for the obtained rankings, these findings might be explained by the uniform level of expertise of the athletes. That is, a possible reason for practice not ranking higher is that all skaters were at the national level and may train for about the same amount of time. Thus variables other than practice become determining ones. Administering the survey to other skill levels and thus avoiding any effects due to population attenuation might reveal quite different findings.

Finally, we can appreciate the anecdote of Moe Norman the expert golfer, which effectively conveyed the lesson that deliberate practice may be a necessary precursor, but by itself it may not be sufficient for success. However, it is difficult to escape the conclusion that Norman attained his goal of being an excellent striker of golf balls and that deliberate practice adjusted to obtaining this goal was successful. Furthermore, we cannot be certain of the eventual level of success Norman would have attained had he remained on the professional circuit.

The Expert–Novice Paradigm

There now exists sufficient published research to assess the value of any paradigm for explaining expert levels of performance. Certainly in the last 15 years, studies investigating a variety of perception and motor performance abilities have been reported, revealing many factors relevant to the acquisition of high levels of performance across many sports. This experimentation has not, however, progressed to describe any underlying mechanisms responsible for expertise in sport. Although propositional networks associated with declarative and procedural knowledge have been used (Anderson, 1985, 1987; MacKay, 1987) to explain perceptual-motor performance (Allard & Starkes, 1991; Paull & Glencross, in press), there has been little empirical evidence to support their utility in sports expertise.

This short review outlines various approaches to the study of expert levels of skilled behavior. Although not exhaustive of all the studies in the past 15 years, it illustrates the range of factors implicated in expert performance, the usefulness of the information to guide coaches in training athletes for expert knowledge in particular sports, and the need now to substantiate theories that will provide the framework for these empirical endeavors.

Reaction Time. Operating in the short time frames available in many sports situations suggests a cognitive system capable of reduced latencies for motor responses (Starkes, 1987). Simple reaction time (SRT) has been proposed as a measure of speed of cognitive function (Nielsen & McGown, 1985). However, SRT of athletes has not consistently been correlated with their performance level (Abernethy & Russell, 1984; Goulet, Bard, & Fleury, 1989; Nielsen & McGown, 1985). In addition, choice reaction time (CRT) as a measure of the speed of decision making has not consistently differentiated experts from novices (Nielsen & McGown, 1985). CRT, however, has been useful as a measure of cognitive operations when a task relevant to the one of interest is utilized (Goulet et al., 1989). Experts exhibit shorter decision times than novices for relevant stimuli when this is the case.

A difficulty arises in devising relevant tasks to measure decision time when performing in simulations of sports events. Abernethy and Russell (1984) found cricketers viewing films of medium-paced bowling reacted in excess of 300 ms after the ball was released by the bowler. This figure greatly exceeds the 189 ms calculated by Glencross and Cibich (1977) as the decision time available for a batsman facing fast bowling of 140 kph. Adams and Gibson (1989) required cricketers to respond on a push button at the moment of release of a cricket ball bowled by a live bowler. Error scores (response latency) were as high as 160 ms for lower grade batsmen, and averaged about 60 ms for the most expert group. This response was supposed to represent the start of ball flight information and yet this delay encroaches well into the available processing time available in a game. Glencross and Cibich's data for tennis indicate a receiver only has 253 ms to react to a 164 kph serve, but Goulet et al.'s (1989) expert subjects reacted at around 1.5 s across trials of filmed serves. In field hockey, Starkes (1987) tested players on identification of ball location and also tactical decision-making time from photographic slides. Average reaction times of 880 ms and 1,413 ms, respectively, would exceed the time available to a player in many game situations (e.g., defending close to the goal). Baseball batters in elite competition probably have less than a quarter of a second in which to commence a swing to coincide with a fastball pitch (Glencross & Cibich, 1977), but Paull and Glencross' (in press) experiments produced decision times averaging in excess of 400 ms for experts and longer for novices.

Absolute time aside, the expert–novice paradigm has shown differences between decision times for performers from different skill levels. Expert tennis players have been shown to make faster decisions than novices concerning the type of serve displayed in filmed action (Goulet et al., 1989). Abernethy and Russell (1984) found first-grade cricket batsmen make faster decisions concerning the delivery length of filmed bowling than third-grade players. In a study of baseball batting, Paull and Glencross (in press) demonstrated the earlier decision-making ability of expert batters over novices when performing to an interactive video simulation of pitching. These figures for decision times in experimental situations should be used as relative measures that indicate differences in expertise levels of players. Any attempt to infer skill level based on the absolute elapsed time in these experimental situations will not accurately reflect actual performance in fast action sports.

Accuracy.   Laboratory research in which accuracy is the dependent variable has produced findings that have not had a close relationship to actual responses. Results reported for tennis (Buckolz, Prapavesis, & Fairs, 1988; Goulet et al., 1989; Isaacs & Finch, 1983; Jones & Miles, 1978), squash (Abernethy, 1989, 1990a, 1990b), ice hockey (Salmela & Fiorito, 1979), badminton (Abernethy, 1987a, 1988a), volleyball (Borgeaud & Abernethy, 1987; Wright, Pleasants, & Gomez-Meza, 1990), and baseball (Paull & Glencross, in press) all indicate the greater accuracy of experts over less skilled subjects. However, these studies show that errors may occur in up to 50% of trials and that responses may be displaced on a court in the order of many meters. These findings bear little resemblance to actual elite performance. Therefore, findings must be treated as relative indicators of performance and not absolute measures of ability.

Visual Processes.   Many features of athletes' vision have been examined relative to sports performance. The conclusion generally drawn has been that it is not orientation of the eyes or physiological attributes of the visual/ocular system that lead to expert performance (Abernethy, 1988a; Starkes, Allard, Lindley, & O'Reilly, 1994). Rather, it is use of information contained in the visual array that separates expert from less skilled athletes. This "information pick-up" (Abernethy, 1987b) acts in the knowledge base an athlete has for a sport to provide recognition of pertinent information. Increased pertinence of information picked up differentiates expert performers from novices who do not understand the value of the information contained in the visual array.

The purpose of directing the eyes to particular locations in the display is to facilitate the pick-up of information to guide performance. We assume a player directs attention in line with orientation of the eyes, but visual orientation (looking) does not necessarily equate with visual attention (Abernethy, 1988b). It is the active perceiver who benefits, not from the display per se, but the information contained in the display (Broadbent, 1982). Support for this conclusion has been provided by Abernethy and Russell (1987b), who recorded badminton players' eye movements while watching films. In one film, the opponent had body parts occluded to remove these as a source of information about the shot to be executed. Both novice and expert players spent closely an equivalent time fixating the racquet and arm of the opponent when these cue sources were available. When the racquet and arm of the opponent were occluded, experts' error scores were higher than those of novices, who apparently extracted less information from these cue sources and therefore suffered less from their removal. These findings are similar to those of Goulet et al. (1989), who found that expert and novice tennis players use similar visual search patterns in the preparatory stages (ball toss and early arm movement) of a filmed opponent's service. However, experts are more accurate when the preparatory stage was the only information shown to subjects. This agrees with Shank and Haywood's (1987) finding that novice baseball batters fixate both the pitcher's head and arm during the delivery action, whereas experts only fixate the ball's release point.

Investigation of the use of cues provided in advance of the actual onset of information (e.g., a ball in flight) has used filmed displays of performers during delivery actions. Decrement in accuracy scores when advanced cues are occluded from the display are then held to indicate the existence of "telegraphic" cues (Bakker, Whiting, & van der Brug, 1990) that are available in the natural display. Abernethy (1988a, 1990a) and Abernethy and Russell (1984, 1987a, 1987b) utilized this technique in squash, cricket, and badminton. Similar studies have been conducted in baseball (Paull & Glencross, in press), tennis (Buckolz et al., 1988; Goulet et al., 1989; Isaacs & Finch, 1983; Jones & Miles, 1978), volleyball (Wright et al., 1990), ice hockey (Salmela & Fiorito, 1979), and field hockey (Starkes, 1987). The finding of superior expert performance was replicated in all these studies.

The need for more advanced technology to study the effects of visual occlusion on sports performance in natural settings has been addressed by Burroughs (1984) and others (Starkes, Edwards, Dissanayake, & Dunn, 1995: Paull & Glencross, in press). Starkes et al. used liquid crystal occlusion spectacles to study estimation of landing position of the ball in volleyball. Estimates of landing position of the ball were more accurate for skilled than for novice volleyball players. Paull and Glencross (in press) found that prediction of pitch location over the plate from early information in the pitch was more accurate for expert than novice baseball players.

Subjective Probabilities. Whenever alternative events are non-equiprobable, the situation will allow the astute player to set probabilities (expectancies) about forthcoming events in a competition (Abernethy, 1987b). Unlike the reactive visual processes discussed earlier, setting subjective probabilities by a performer is proactive, and works in advance of stimulus onset for an athlete who has developed knowledge for the game, opponents, and the competitive environment. Paull and Glencross (in press) studied the use of this strategy by baseball batters. Before half the trials in their first experiment, information about the progress of a hypothetical game was provided to allow batters to consider what type of pitch would be thrown next. Batters improved the time of their decisions by an average of 60 ms. This was not at the expense of accuracy, as these decisions were more accurate than when no game information was provided.

In summary, many paradigms have been used to examine expert performance of sports skills. The procedures for determining factors relevant to performance of many sports skills have been developed and information from additional sports is accumulating. This information is relevant to understanding the sports of interest, and particularly useful for coaches who can implement specific training to develop the knowledge base in their athletes for the highest levels of performance. It is now appropriate for researchers in the sports sciences to refocus experimental efforts and systematically examine cognitive mechanisms to substantiate theories of expert performance.

The Expert Modeling Paradigm

The method suggested by Ericsson (chap. 1, this volume) for identification of component skills in the laboratory provides a start in theoretical analysis for use of hierarchical regression or discriminant analysis and subsequent testing of predictive validity in the study of expertise in sport skills (Renger, 1993). The previously reviewed studies have used inferential statistical procedures to demonstrate expert–novice differences on component skills presumed to be important for task performance. It is of course very different to show statistically reliable differences between expert and novice performers than to show the meaningfulness of those differences. The use of regression procedures would allow the researcher to determine the relative importance of the component skill they are studying in terms of the amount of variance accounted for in performance of the total skill. This approach would allow the investigation of variables individually or in combination on performance. Moreover, it would allow researchers to develop more comprehensive models for sports expertise by systematically adding new variables to their task and removing those that account for low variance in the criterion measures.

The research program conducted by Fleishman and his colleagues concerning abilities and human performance illustrates the potential benefits of a modeling approach using regression procedures for training purposes. Fleishman (1972) regarded abilities as referring to capacities the individual utilizes in performing a task. According to Fleishman, many of these capacities are learned and develop at different rates. This view differs with that of leading motor learning theorists such as Schmidt (1988), who view abilities as strictly inherited and therefore not subject to change as a result of experience. In addition, Fleishman (1972) recognized the importance of developing a taxonomy of motor tasks based on common capacities necessary for performance rather than a taxonomy based on the structural similarities of tasks (Parker & Fleishman, 1961).

Following an earlier study by Parker and Fleishman (1961), Fleishman and Rich (1963) performed the now classic experiment supporting the changing component abilities hypothesis which proposes that the abilities underlying early performance are not the same as those underlying later performance. This hypothesis makes sense if one believes that subjects change their approach to a motor task as they become more skilled (Pew, 1966). Fleishman and Rich tested subjects for kinesthetic sensitivity and spatial orientation before having them practice 40 one-minute trials on a two-hand coordination task. The two-hand coordination task consisted of keeping a target follower on a small target disk as the target moved irregularly and at various rates around a circular plate. The movement of the target follower was controlled by simultaneous rotation of two handles, one held in each hand. The dependent measure was the total time for each trial that the target follower was in contact with the target (total time on target). Subjects received 40 one-minute trials separated by rest intervals of 15 seconds in duration. At the conclusion of the experiment, subjects' kinesthetic sensitivity and spatial orientation test scores were correlated with their two-hand coordination task scores.

Over half the variance (R^2 = .53) in total time on target was accounted for by the combination of kinesthetic sensitivity and spatial orientation measures. In addition, the correlation between kinesthetic sensitivity and spatial orientation measures was not significant (r = .12), an indication that the two tests measured independent abilities. The 40 two-hand coordination scores were grouped into 10 blocks of four trials each so that the relationship of kinesthetic sensitivity and spatial orientation measures to stage of learning could be investigated. Early in practice the correlation between two-hand coordination and spatial orientation scores was higher (r = .36) than the correlation between two-hand coordination and kinesthetic sensitivity scores (r = .03). Later in practice, however, the correlation between two-hand coordination and kinesthetic sensitivity scores was higher (r = .40) than the correlation between two-hand coordination and spatial orientation scores (r = .01).

Fleishman and Rich provided a somewhat convincing measure of predictive validity by stratifying their subjects into those who had high and low spatial orientation scores (either above or below the group median spatial orientation test score). When practice performance for these groups was compared, it was found that early in practice, two-hand coordination performance was better for the group that scored high than for the group that scored low on the spatial orientation test (this difference was significant, p < .01). However, by the end of practice this difference between the groups was negligible.

Fleishman and Rich went on to stratify their subjects into those who had high and low kinesthetic sensitivity test scores. Performance for these groups diverged with practice. Early in practice, there was no difference in performance between groups, but later in practice, performance was better for the group that scored high than for the group that scored low on the kinesthetic sensitivity test (this difference was significant, $p < .01$). These findings provide evidence that learners change their approach to a task with practice and so the processing structure used to regulate early performance may not be the same as that used later in practice.

Parker and Fleishman (1961) showed that knowledge of the changing pattern of abilities can be used to adjust instructions during practice so that learning is facilitated. Subjects performed 17 sessions of 21 one-minute trials each (357 total trials) on a complex tracking task that simulated flying an aircraft. Briefly, subjects used a hand-held joystick and foot-operated pedals to keep a target dot in the center of an oscillograph display. The performance measures were integrated absolute error and the time during each trial the target dot was kept in the center of the display (time on target). Before practice, subjects were administered a test battery from which two factors were identified as contributing to performance on the complex tracking task. These were spatial orientation and multilimb coordination. Figure 13.1 shows changes occurring in the importance of these two ability factors with practice.

Three groups were compared. One group received no formal instructions throughout practice. A second group received commonsense instructions throughout practice, which approximated typical instructions given to military pilots. A third group received "adjusted" instructions that emphasized the control operations appropriate to the importance of ability factors for performance at a particular time in practice (as determined by findings of the earlier analysis depicted in Fig. 13.1) in addition to commonsense instructions. Figures 13.2 and 13.3 show the integrated absolute error and time on target measures, respectively, for the three instructional groups across the 17 practice sessions. It can be seen that adjusting instructions so they were appropriate for the ability factors important for performance can increase the effectiveness of training beyond that typically given. Further, this procedure was found to result primarily in an increase in the rate of learning but not its basic character.

The foregoing experiments by Fleishman and his colleagues provide a methodology analogous to "capturing" as described by Ericsson (chap. 1, this volume) that can be used to greatly enhance the acquisition of expertise. This methodology would consist of the use of linear regression techniques to identify important component skills (e.g., visual cues, decision making, event anticipation) necessary for performance and then either adjusting instructions to complement the use of these component skills or giving independent practice on these. The underlying assumption for giving independent practice on the component skills is that the total skill will benefit as the result of the improved component skill. However, one caveat to this is that this technique may not be effective if the total skill is comprised of closely interwoven

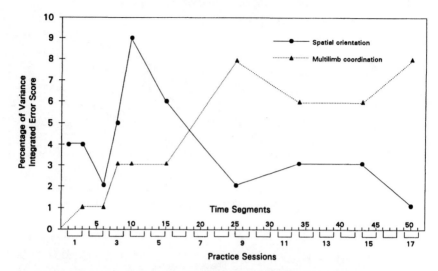

FIG. 13.1. Changes in the correlations between spatial orientation and multilimb coordination with complex tracking task performance across 17 sessions of 21 one-minute trials each (357 total trials). Adapted from "Use of Analytical Information Concerning Task Requirements to Increase The Effectiveness of Skill Training" by J. F. Parker & E. A. Fleishman (1961), *Journal of Applied Psychology, 45,* p. 297.

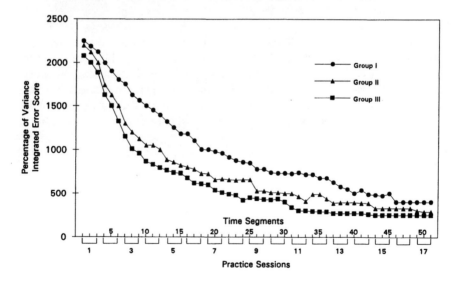

FIG. 13.2. Integrated absolute error measures for three instructional groups (no instructions, commonsense instructions, and adjusted instructions) for complex tracking task performance across 17 sessions of 21 one-minute trials each (357 total trials). Adapted from "Use of Analytical Information Concerning Task Requirements to Increase The Effectiveness of Skill Training" by J. F. Parker & E. A. Fleishman (1961), *Journal of Applied Psychology, 45,* p. 299.

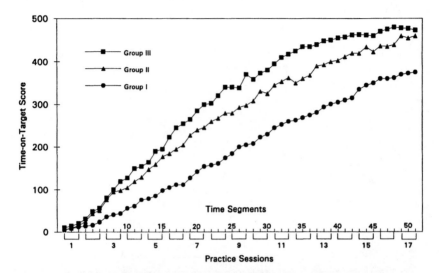

FIG. 13.3. Time on target measures for three instructional groups (no instructions, commonsense instructions, and adjusted instructions) for complex tracking task performance across 17 sessions of 21 one-minute trials each (357 total trials). Adapted from "Use of Analytical Information Concerning Task Requirements to Increase The Effectiveness of Skill Training" by J. F. Parker & E. A. Fleishman (1961), *Journal of Applied Psychology, 45,* p. 299.

components. In this case, the independent practice and improvement of any one component may not effectively transfer to the whole skill. This may be the case unless the supporting structure of the component skills has advanced to the new level necessary to support performance of the improved component. Furthermore, it may be the case that all the component skills can be improved an equivalent amount but that cohesive integration among the components will not be improved. In this case performance of the whole task will not be facilitated. It is conceivable that such practice could even negatively influence performance of the whole skill.

These early studies by Fleishman and his colleagues demonstrate that the expert modeling approach has potential to benefit the training of expert performers in sport. This must of course be demonstrated in the sports setting.

CONCLUSION

Ericsson et al. (1993) proposed characteristics of deliberate practice that lead to expert levels of performance across different skill domains. These include age of commencing practice, the use of a coach or teacher, and the resolve to spend many hours in deliberate practice of the skills required in the performance. Starkes et al. extend understanding of these factors to the sports of figure skating and wrestling. They show, however, that the attributes of deliberate practice may not be uniform across domains of skill. For example, their finding that deliberate practice can be enjoyable differs from previous evidence (Ericsson et al., 1993). Also, the perceived relevance of different factors associated with deliberate practice may differ between figure skaters, wrestlers, and skilled performers in other activities.

These findings may pose a difficulty for a general theory of expertise. This is that actual components of deliberate practice for any skill may be embedded in the domain of that skill. Therefore, the need for an inflexible rendition of a musical score will differentiate the characteristics of that task from, for example, a practice bout between wrestlers. Further constraining a general theory is the need to define expertise. The narrative by Starkes et al. of the golfing talent of Moe Norman illustrates the need to understand the difference between performance of a skill and behavior in competition. The latter must include the multitude of variation occurring in a dynamic environment, and it may be difficult to address this complexity through the capturing methodology proposed by Ericsson (chap. 1, this volume) and the expert modeling approach we have described.

Research under Ericsson's historical and developmental approaches to the study of expertise may reveal factors associated with development of expertise. These approaches, however, will not identify the mechanisms used by experts to regulate their highly skilled actions. Taking the laboratory approach as the means for such investigation, two paradigms have been outlined. Experiments that contrast expert and novice performers have provided good information across many sports about regulating perceptual and motor processes. These experiments have not been consistent in determining the contribution of any component process to actual performance. A more empirical approach would be hierarchical regression or discriminant analysis and subsequent testing of predictive validity (Renger, 1993).

The work by Fleishman and his colleagues (Fleishman, 1972) provides a useful paradigm from which to investigate the perceptual and motor processes underlying expert sports performance. This research demonstrated that the underlying processes for performance may change with practice, and that knowledge of individual differences in the capacity to use these processes allows prediction of final performance level. Fleishman and Rich (1963) showed that subjects high or low in spatial orientation or kinesthetic sensitivity either converged or diverged across practice trials. It is interesting that this occurred in spite of the fact that subjects had the same amount of deliberate practice in the experimental tasks. Although the amount of practice provided in the experiments by Fleishman and Rich (1963) and Parker and Fleishman (1961) by no means approached that which could be attained in 10 years, the findings of these studies suggest perceptual and motor capacities may interact with deliberate practice to determine final level of performance. The resolution of this question will necessitate experimental investigation.

Research in the domain of expert performance is providing exciting knowledge concerning the acquisition of high levels of skill in sport. Although findings to date are refining general notions of deliberate practice into sports-specific descriptions, there may still be a need to provide this as knowledge to coaches and athletes in applied training models. We may be answering the question "how to practice?" and leaving the question "what to practice?" unanswered. Any new paradigm to examine the contribution of any factor and how it interacts with other factors to determine the performance of sports skills should be given consideration.

REFERENCES

Abernethy, B. (1987a). Selective attention in fast ball sports II: Expert-novice differences. *The Australian Journal of Science and Medicine in Sport, 19*(4), 7–16.

Abernethy, B. (1987b). Selective attention in fast ball sports I: General principles. *The Australian Journal of Science and Medicine in Sport, 19*(4), 3–6.

Abernethy, B. (1988a). The effects of age and expertise upon perceptual skill development in a racquet sport. *Research Quarterly, 59,* 210–221.

Abernethy, B. (1988b). Visual search in sport and ergonomics: Its relationship to selective attention and performer expertise. *Human Performance, 1,* 205–235.

Abernethy, B. (1989). Expert–novice differences in perception: How expert does the expert have to be? *Canadian Journal of Sports Sciences, 14,* 27–30.

Abernethy, B. (1990a). Anticipation in squash: Differences in advance cue utilization between expert and novice players. *Journal of Sports Sciences, 8,* 17–34.

Abernethy, B. (1990b). Expertise, visual search, and information pick-up in squash. *Perception, 19,* 63–77.

Abernethy, B., & Russell, D. G. (1984). Advanced cue utilization by skilled cricket batsmen. *The Australian Journal of Science and Medicine in Sport, 16*(2), 2–10.

Abernethy, B., & Russell, D. G. (1987a). Expert–novice differences in an applied selective attention task. *Journal of Sports Psychology, 9,* 326–345.

Abernethy, B., & Russell, D. G. (1987b). The relationship between expertise and visual search strategy in a racquet sport. *Human Movement Science, 6,* 283–320.

Adams, J. A. (1971). A closed-loop theory of motor learning. *Journal of Motor Behavior, 3,* 111–150.

Adams, R. D., & Gibson, A. P. (1989). Moment-of-ball release identification by cricket batsmen. *Australian Journal of Science and Medicine in Sport, 21,* 10–13.

Allard, F., & Starkes, J. L. (1991). Motor-skill experts in sports, dance, and other domains. In K. A Ericsson & J. Smith (Eds.), *Towards a general theory of expertise: Prospects and limits* (pp. 126–152). Cambridge, UK: Cambridge University Press.

Anderson, J. R. (1985). *Cognitive psychology and its implications* (2nd ed.). New York: Freeman.

Anderson, J. R. (1987). Skill acquisition: Compilation of weak-method problem solutions. *Psychological Review, 94,* 192–210.

Bakker, F. C., Whiting, H. T. A., & van der Brug, H. (1990). *Sports psychology: Concepts and applications.* Chichester, UK: Wiley.

Borgeaud, P., & Abernethy, B. (1987). Skilled perception in volleyball defense. *Journal of Sports Psychology, 9,* 400–406.

Broadbent, D. E. (1982). Task combination and selective intake of information. *Acta Psychologica, 50,* 253–290.

Buckolz, E., Prapavesis, H., & Fairs, J. (1988). Advance cues and their use in predicting tennis passing shots. *Canadian Journal of Sports Sciences, 13,* 20–30.

Burroughs, W. A. (1984). Visual simulation training of baseball batters. *International Journal of Sports Psychology, 15,* 117–126.

Ericsson, K. A., Krampe, R. T., & Tesch-Römer, C. (1993). The role of deliberate practice in the acquisition of expert performance. *Psychological Review, 100*, 363–406.

Ericsson, K. A., & Simon, H. A. (1993). *Protocol analysis: Verbal reports as data.* Cambridge, MA: MIT Press.

Fleishman, E. A. (1972). On the relation between abilities, learning, and human performance. *American Psychologist, 27*, 1017–1032.

Fleishman, E. A., & Rich, S. (1963). Role of kinesthetic and spatial-visual abilities in perceptual-motor learning. *Journal of Experimental Psychology, 66*, 6–11.

Glencross, D. J., & Cibich, B. J. (1977). A decision analysis of games skills. *Australian Journal of Sports Medicine, 9*, 72–75.

Goulet, C., Bard, C., & Fleury, M. (1989). Expertise differences in preparing to return a tennis serve: A visual information processing approach. *Journal of Sport & Exercise Psychology, 11*, 382–398.

Isaacs, L. D., & Finch, A. E. (1983). Anticipatory timing of beginning and intermediate tennis players. *Perceptual and Motor Skills, 57*, 451–454.

Jones, C. M., & Miles, T. R. (1978). Use of advanced cues in predicting the flight of a lawn tennis ball. *Journal of Human Movement Studies, 4*, 231–235.

MacKay, D. G. (1987). *The organization of perception and action.* New York: Springer-Verlag.

Nielsen, D., & McGown, C. (1985). Information processing as a predictor of offensive ability in baseball. *Perceptual and Motor Skills, 60*, 775–781.

Parker, J. F., & Fleishman, E. A. (1961). Use of analytical information concerning task requirements to increase the effectiveness of skill training. *Journal of Applied Psychology, 45*, 295–302.

Paull, G. C., & Glencross, D. J. (in press). Expert perception and decision making in baseball. *International Journal of Sport Psychology.*

Pew, R. W. (1966). Acquisition of hierarchical control over the temporal organization of a skill. *Journal of Experimental Psychology, 71*, 764–771.

Renger, R. (1993). Predicting athletic success: Issues related to analysis and interpretation of study findings. *The Sport Psychologist, 7*, 262–274.

Salmela, J. H., & Fiorito, P. (1979). Visual cues in ice-hockey goal tending. *Canadian Journal of Applied Sport Sciences, 4*, 56–59.

Schmidt, R. A. (1988). *Motor control and learning: A behavioral emphasis* (2nd ed.). Champaign, IL: Human Kinetics.

Shank, M. D., & Haywood, K. M. (1987). Eye movements while viewing a baseball pitch. *Perceptual and Motor Skills, 64*, 1191–1197.

Starkes, J. L. (1987). Skill in field hockey: The nature of the cognitive advantage. *Journal of Sports Psychology, 9*, 146–160.

Starkes, J. L., Allard, F., Lindley, S., & O'Reilly, K. (1994). Abilities and skill in basketball. *International Journal of Sports Psychology, 25*, 249–265.

Starkes, J. L., Edwards, P., Dissanayake, P., & Dunn, T. (1995). A new technology and field test of advanced cue usage in volleyball. *Research Quarterly for Exercise and Sport, 66*, 162–167.

Wright, D. L., Pleasants, F., & Gomez-Meza, M. (1990). Use of advanced visual cue sources in volleyball. *Journal of Sport & Exercise Psychology, 12*, 406–414.

14

Laboratory Experimentation on the Genesis of Expertise

Richard M. Shiffrin
Indiana University

The study of the development of expertise is among the oldest topics in psychology. In the last few years particular interest has been directed toward a question crystallized by Ericsson, Krampe, and Tesch-Römer (1993). I would phrase this question as follows: To what degree is the development of the highest levels of expertise a matter of appropriate practice rather than innate talent? There are many domains (such as chess and music) in which it is the popular belief that innate talent is the dominating factor. The alternative view espoused by Ericsson et al. (1993) and many of the contributors to this volume would place all or virtually all of the causal factors in the type and amount of practice carried out. I think the interest in this question is based in part on the importance for society of the truth, and the perception of the truth, of this matter: If it were widely believed that practice were the crucial factor, then choices made by individuals that determine their lifetime professions and avocations might well be different than is now the case.

Many of the presentations in this conference echo earlier work by Ericsson and others suggesting the importance of practice. I found these interesting, intriguing, and thought provoking. Unfortunately, the evidence is at best suggestive, based on observed correlations between amounts and types of practice and achieved levels of expertise. As always in such cases, the observed correlations could be produced by selection effects even were innate talent a critical factor: For a variety of reasons, those people with high talent would be expected to be the ones to pursue their domains of expertise most avidly. Although statistical analyses of the type used by Wagner and

Stanovich (chap. 7, this volume) and formal modeling of the type reported by Richman, Gobet, Staszewski, and Simon (chap. 6, this volume) take a step in the right direction, I believe the establishment of the direction of causality will require laboratory experimentation with appropriate controls. My commentary is limited to a brief discussion of potential tasks and types of laboratory studies suitable for this purpose.

Laboratory studies of the development of expertise have a history as old as experimental psychology. An example I like to quote is the study of the learning of the receiving of telegraphy carried out at Indiana University in the late 1800s by William Lowe Bryan (later to be president of the university), and reported in Psychological Review (Bryan & Harter, 1899). Many of the themes appearing in the present presentations were presaged in that report (see Fig. 14.1).

Student Will J. Reynolds. Tested Weekly By Noble Harter at W.U. Telax. Office. Brookville, Ind.

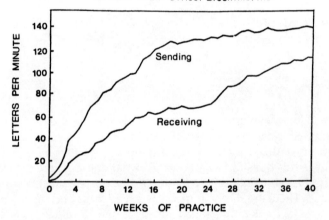

Receiving Rates of Student John Shaw, Brookville, Ind.

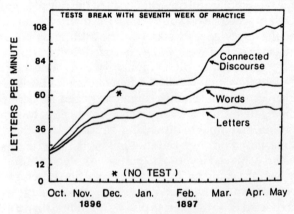

FIG. 14.1. The rates of sending and receiving telegraphy as a function of days of training for two subjects. From Bryan and Harter (1899).

Bryan and Harter argued that skill developed in a series of stages, with plateaus at each level, the plateaus allowing sufficient automatization of a given subskill to allow the next stage of learning to proceed. For example, when letters are received automatically, the receiver can switch resources to analysis of words; when words are received relatively automatically, the receiver can switch processing resources to analysis of meaning, and so forth. Later research cast doubt on the possibility that such plateaus could be observed experimentally, but the basic hypothesis remains plausible to this day (see Shiffrin, 1988, for a more extended discussion).

As with many such studies over the years, the Bryan and Harter study was not particularly well suited to allow assessment of the practice–talent issue. First, despite the many months of practice given the two subjects, performance at the end of the study remained well short of the highest expert levels; Bryan and Harter noted that 10 years was the accepted duration of practice for the highest levels to be achieved. Second, any assessment of the consequences of practice would require knowledge of the rate of approach to asymptotic performance, but the level of asymptotic peformance is unobtainable when training ceases early. Third, individual differences were not a goal of this study, and could not have been, given that only two subjects were trained. These problems are typical of experimental studies of the development of expertise over the last 100 years, and must be addressed in appropriate designs.

The problem of finding an appropriate laboratory design seems formidable: The greatest interest is in expertise developed in tasks representing the peaks of human achievement in domains such as music, reading, chess, sports, and mathematics that require 10 years or more of intensive training to reach the highest levels of competence. To study the practice–talent issue would require large numbers of suitably randomized subjects trained to the highest levels (i.e., for 10 years or more) with little or no dropout of subjects. These requirements do not seem practical for laboratory studies.

One solution might involve retaining complex tasks, but training for only short periods of time. For this to work, we would have to know a great deal about the correlation of variability in performance early and late in training, and such knowledge would probably require extended training studies. In the absence of such studies and knowledge, rate of learning and asymptotic competence are inextricably confounded. Thus such an approach could not presently be recommended.

Let us consider then whether it might not be possible to turn to simpler tasks, ones in which training might proceed more quickly. The hope would be that the lessons learned could be generalized to the more complex tasks of general interest. It must be admitted at the outset that relatively little is known about the training time needed to reach asymptotic performance levels in simple tasks, so it is an assumption that training time will be reduced in simpler tasks. I have some recent evidence demonstrating shorter training times to asymptote for one component of one task; this evidence is reported briefly later in this commentary.

Simple tasks have often been studied, but the learning seen is not often called "expertise." Perhaps the most trivial task imaginable is simple reaction time (RT): A light appears and the subject responds as rapidly as possible. RT improves over a period of learning (a power law learning curve is seen). Would anyone want to call this the development of expertise? Even those who would be willing to do so might not regard the results with much interest, or judge them to bear on the issues under discussion in this book. I would like to suggest that this point of view be reconsidered.

To make this point, let me change the domain from simple RT to a task that is carried out as an Olympic sport, with world championships, acknowledged world experts, and expertise that is developed over years of deliberate practice. This task is marksmanship. It might be hard to find another task this elementary, other than the RT task I just described. What would be wrong with using marksmanship in the laboratory to study the development of expertise? It would be easy to implement, easy to measure the relevant variables, and there would be in the armed services a ready pool of subjects and a probable source of funding. If this task would be worth investigating, then why not simple RT?

Of course I am not trying to get anyone to take up the development of expertise in simple RT, a field that has been more than adequately explored over the last 100 years. Rather I am suggesting that it ought to be possible to investigate the development of expertise in many tasks simpler than music or chess, without subverting or bypassing the major issues of interest. To the contrary, these major issues would become subject to experimental test.

Another approach to the problem of laboratory experimentation on expertise involves initially limiting research to the learning of one subcomponent of a task that is otherwise much more complex. For example, simple RT is a critical component skill in a complex task like the 100-meter dash, where success depends in considerable part on the speed of reaction to the starter's pistol. The idea of building up our understanding of the learning of expertise through the understanding of task components is of course an old one and has been used successfully by Simon and his colleagues in the development of EPAM (e.g., Richman et al., chap. 6, this volume). There are several ways to approach this problem, some involving limiting task complexity, but others involving experimental techniques that allow a task subcomponent to be isolated within an otherwise complex task. An example arises in my own recent research in which I explore a component skill that is important for the development of expertise in reading: the perceptual unitization of the visual characters used to print words.

The task that Lightfoot and I have used to study the perceptual learning of new visual objects involves visual search for novel characters (see Lightfoot & Shiffrin, 1992, for one early report). Figure 14.2 shows the objects to

Novel, Conjunctively Defined Stimuli

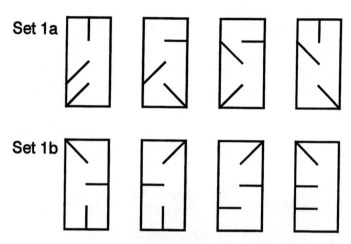

FIG. 14.2. Novel stimuli used in visual search studies by Lightfoot and Shiffrin (1992). Each row of four stimuli was used in different blocks of trials. No internal features (line segments) are shared between rows. Within a row, each stimulus shares exactly one feature with each other stimulus, ensuring that at least two features need to be examined to succeed in the search task.

be learned. These are rectangular frames with three internal line segments that do not touch. Figure 14.3 illustrates the training task.

Subjects viewed a circular display of from one to eight of these characters searching for the presence or absence of a particular target character presented in advance of the trial. In some blocks (CM), using the four stimuli in one row of Fig. 14.1, the target was the same on all trials: One stimulus was always the target and the distractors were chosen randomly from the other three stimuli. In other blocks (VM), using the four stimuli from the other row of Fig. 14.1, the target changed randomly from trial to trial. Four times as many trials per block were given in the VM case so as to equate the number of occurences of given items as targets.

The two rows of stimuli in Fig. 14.1 shared no internal line segments. Within each row, any two stimuli shared exactly one line segment. This design ensures that no one line segment can be used to carry out the search; at least two must be used to locate a target. We hoped that this *conjunction search*, as it is called, would encourage subjects to learn these stimuli as holistic units. We were primarily interested in the slope of the function relating response time to display size, typically interpreted as the comparison time per character. We trained subjects for 50 sessions of about 1,500 trials each.

The results given in Fig. 14.4 show gradual improvements in search rate from 250 ms per object to 80 ms per object after 35 sessions, when improvement stopped and performance remained stable thereafter. The VM group

Visual Search

Positive Trial, Display Size 7

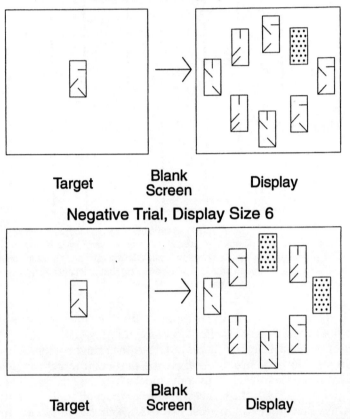

| Target | Blank Screen | Display |

Negative Trial, Display Size 6

| Target | Blank Screen | Display |

FIG. 14.3. Examples of trial displays used in the visual search paradigm of Lightfoot and Shiffrin (1992). Each trial began with the presentation of a target to be searched for. Then a circular display of eight positions was presented with from 1 to 8 characters, and the remaining positions filled with masks. On positive trials the target was present (top row), and on negative trials the target was absent (bottom row). Accuracy was high, and response time was the measure of interest. More precisely, the slope of the function relating response time to display size was the measure of primary interest.

learned faster, presumably because they had four times as many trials per block and items appearing as distractors facilitated learning. However, the final performance level for both groups was identical, and typical of what is seen for attentive, terminating visual search for alphabetic characters. That is, the slope values are near those observed for alphabetic characters, the negative slopes are twice the positive slopes, and although it is not shown in Fig. 14.4, the response time functions were linearly related to display size. We interpreted the learning that occurred gradually over 35 sessions as due to the development of new perceptual units that allowed an object to be compared in one step, rather than feature by feature.

The subjects ran in additional transfer and control conditions, enabling us to learn many things about what had been learned, what factors were necessary to enable the learning, and how such learning could generalize, all questions that would be at least of some interest to those studying the development of expertise. The additional training, however, never improved performance beyond the asymptotic level seen in Fig. 14.4. Thus we have at least one case where a truly asymptotic level

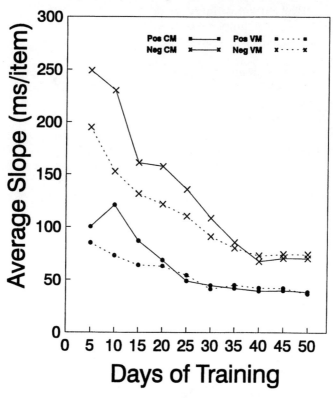

FIG. 14.4. Results from the first study of Lightfoot and Shiffrin (1992): Slopes of the search functions as a function of days of training, for CM and VM blocks, and for negative and positive trials.

ofperformanceforataskcomponent(rateofcharactercomparisoninvisual search) is attainable in 35 sessions rather than 10 years.

The fact that performance reaches a true asymptote could be useful for assessing questions about individual differences versus training. We used only two subjects in the initial studies, because we had a somewhat different set of goals and objectives than would have been the case if we were studying expertise per se. We were concerned with the mechanisms of performance and the rules of learning as exhibited by a typical subject. We were less concerned with such questions as the nature of training, terminal levels of skill, individual differences, motivational variables, and the effects of strategic choice and strategic intervention. Suppose, however, that many subjects had been used, and these had exhibited a range of days of training to reach asymptote, and a range of comparison rates once asymptotic performance had been achieved. The differences in rate of learning might reflect both innate differences and differences due to factors like motivation, type of practice, and strategies. The differences that remain after all subjects have reached terminal levels might well reflect innate differences (although the possibility that the terminal level of performance would be based on the same factors that affect the rate of learning would also have to be considered and explored).

Let me end this commentary on the following cautionary note. Suppose that it is possible with appropriate laboratory experimentation to answer the question posed at the outset, and establish the percent of asymptotic expertise that is attributable to practice. Suppose furthermore that the answer turns out to be quite high, perhaps 99%. For many purposes, this percentage will be high enough that individuals will judge correctly that they can guide their own destinies. This would be true, for example, if individuals wished to become doctors, lawyers, or academics, professions with large numbers of practitioners. However, the remaining 1% could be critical for other professional aspirations, in areas where the number of successful practitioners is extremely small. Some examples might include professional basketball player, chess Grandmaster, classical music concert performer, and other professions for which ability to earn a living, say, would require being in the top fraction of 1% of the population. This may be an obvious point, but it suggests being cautious about the benefits of practice in cases where the target skill level is at the extreme limits of current human performance.

ACKNOWLEDGMENTS

This research was supported by NIMH Grant 12717, a James McKeen Cattell Fellowship, and a Fellowship from EPOS and the University of Amsterdam.

REFERENCES

Bryan, W. L., & Harter, N. (1899). Studies on the telegraphic language. The acquisition of a hierarchy of habits. *Psychological Review, 6,* 345–375.

Ericsson, K. A., Krampe, R. T., & Tesch-Römer, C. (1993). The role of deliberate practice in the acquisition of expert performance. *Psychological Review, 100*(3), 363–406.

Lightfoot, N., & Shiffrin, R. M. (1992). On the unitization of novel, complex, visual stimuli. *Proceedings of the Fourteenth Annual Conference of the Cognitive Science Society* (pp. 147–152). Hillsdale, NJ: Lawrence Erlbaum Associates.

Shiffrin, R. M. (1988). Attention. In R. C. Atkinson, R. J. Herrnstein, G. Lindzey, & R. D. Luce (Eds.), *Stevens' handbook of experimental psychology* (2nd ed., pp. 739–811). New York: Wiley.

15

Costs of Expertise

Robert J. Sternberg
Yale University

Who does not want to be an expert? Experts are respected, valued, and at times even revered, for their expertise. Little wonder that just about everyone wants to be an expert in something, or many things. And people like to imagine themselves as experts in things about which, after all is said and done, they know little.

Curiously, some research has shown that there are costs as well as benefits to expertise (e.g., Adelson, 1984; Frensch & Sternberg, 1989; Hecht & Proffitt, 1995; Luchins, 1942; Sternberg & Lubart, 1995). One such cost is increased rigidity: The expert can become so entrenched in a point of view or a way of doing things that it becomes hard to see things differently. The thesis of this discussion is that this problem applies not only to the experts we study, but to those who are experts at studying experts.

Perhaps the greatest challenge we face, as experts studying experts, is confirmation bias (Lord, Ross, & Lepper, 1979; Wason, 1960): We tend to seek or interpret evidence as supporting what we believe, in the face of inconclusive or even contradictory data. Scientists are not immune to such bias by virtue of their being scientists, and indeed, may be more susceptible to it than others precisely because they believe that their scientific minds and methods protect them from such bias and lead them to seek disconfirmation. Although scientists should approach problems in this way, the evidence is that they rarely do (Kuhn, 1970; Popper, 1959).

The recent controversy over *The Bell Curve* (Herrnstein & Murray, 1994) shows how susceptible scientists are to ideologically based bias. The book itself throughout commits the elementary error of confounding correlation with causation, but so do many of its critics. Thus, scientists are equally susceptible to bias, whether from the sociopolitical left or right.

I believe that some of the work that has been done on the acquisition of expertise shows the same kinds of biases. Elementary inferential errors are made and overlooked in the service of beliefs that many of us would like to hold, regardless of the extent to which they are truly supported by data. The American dream is that if we work hard enough, we, like Horatio Alger, can become whatever we like. The dream is not limited to the United States: Socialist countries have shared with democratic ones the ideal of equality. However, equality of opportunity gets confounded with equality of ability, as research in this area shows. We, as scientists, can as easily confound the two as anyone else.

The evidence in favor of individual differences in abilities is so over-whelming that it would take volumes to summarize it. Indeed, volumes have been taken to summarize it (e.g., Carroll, 1993; Sternberg, 1982, 1994). Moreover, although one can argue as to what proportions of variation among individuals are environmental, what proportions innate, and what proportions interactive, the evidence in favor of some innate contribution is overwhelming (see, e.g., Bouchard & McGue, 1981; Plomin, 1986; Plomin & McClearn, 1993; Sternberg & Grigorenko, in press) and there is no scientific refutation of it at all. I wish to add that my own biases are environmental (see, e.g., Sternberg, 1985), but that I nevertheless recognize the strength of the evidence for the interaction of heredity and environment.

Given the overwhelming evidence for the existence of talent differences, how can studies such as those described by Ericsson (chap. 1, this volume), Ericsson, Krampe, and Tesch-Römer (1993), and Ericsson and Smith (1991) argue so strongly for the overshadowing role of deliberate practice? I believe that they can through a number of factors.

1. *Ignoring contradictory findings.* Work on the acquisition of expertise is able to deal with this annoying issue by largely ignoring the relevant work on behavior genetics, or claiming that there is no evidence that the studies apply at high levels of practice (Ericsson & Charness, 1994). This claim is refuted by the fact that ability tests measure verbal, quantitative, figural, and other abilities that are the results of tens of thousands of hours of practice in the development and utilization of these abilities. We practice reading and listening in the development of verbal skills, for example, about as much as we practice anything. Thus, behavioral genetic work on these abilities is looking at highly practiced skills. The relatively high heritabilities of practiced skills, such as verbal and quantitative ones, need to be reckoned with, as do the findings (Plomin & McClearn, 1993) that heritabilities tend to increase, not decrease with age. On this view, genetic programs help shape people's behavior—perhaps how much they prac-tice—and thus unfold over time. They are not fully in place at birth. Thus, curiously, the amount of practice might be partly under genetic influence.

There are even cases where, I would argue, expertise is negatively correlated with performance. Moreover, any psychologist who teaches upper level statistics can test the negative correlation for himself or herself. My first year teaching multivariate data analysis, as part of an assignment on multiple regression, I asked students a number of questions, including their Math Graduate Record Examination (GRE) score and the number of hours per week they studied for the multivariate course. Later, I gave a midterm exam. The correlation of Math GRE score with midterm examination score was .8; high but not particularly surprising. The correlation of hours worked per week with midterm score was −.8. The result was so depressing I never gave the assignment again. Basically it seemed to show that in a new upper level mathematical course, those with the mathematical ability did not need to work very hard to do well, whereas those without the higher level of ability did not do so well even when they worked hard. Of course, there are alternative interpretations of the results, such as that those with lower math ability thought they put in more hours than they did, or that those with lower math ability put in time, but it was not well spent. However, as one who struggled for hours and hours as an undergraduate studying for a midterm in real analysis only to receive a grade of 38%, I can sympathize with those who worked to no avail. Without the ability, hours of practice can be for minimal or no rewards.

2. *Rendering views nondisconfirmable.* Of course, one could claim that the practice in verbal, mathematical, or other tasks is not deliberate, but then we merely end up in a situation where a view—that deliberate practice is necessary and arguably sufficient for expertise—becomes unfalsifiable by virtue of any expertise that contradicts such a claim being labeled as nondeliberate. We need careful conceptual and operational definitions to avoid ruling out of our domain any findings that do not suit us.

3. *Confounding of correlation with causation.* The existence of a correlation between high levels of expertise and high levels of deliberate practice says nothing about causal mechanisms. The correlation could approach 1, without deliberate practice playing any causal role at all in the formation of expertise. I am not arguing that deliberate practice is unimportant, but rather, that we should remember from elementary statistics that correlation does not imply causation. There are alternative interpretations of this correlation, as discussed later. It is also important to remember that expressing correlational data in forms that do not use actual product–moment correlations does not change the correlational nature of the data. Many researchers explicitly recognize and even state the need not to confound correlation with causation, but nevertheless still theorize that deliberate practice is causal with respect to expertise.

4. *Nonexistence of control groups.* As stunning as the confounding of correlation with causation is the absence of control groups from this research. Without control groups, one can conclude nothing, as we learned in introductory psychology. Why? Because we do not know how many people

have had as many hours of deliberate practice as the experts, but have failed to come anywhere near to the experts' levels of proficiency. For example, many of us know, and some of us may be, parents who started working with their children as infants to develop their intellectual skills, and who have supported and monitored the intellectual development of their children at all points in their development, only to find that they do not make it into Harvard or anything close. But if we only studied students at Harvard, or perhaps Harvard and Brown, we would no doubt find their parents, on the whole, to have been a highly supportive lot, with some correlation between amount of support and achievement.

I am particularly sensitive to the question of control groups because my own work has been, in part, in the teaching of intellectual skills. Any number of programs have made false claims for their effectiveness by giving pretests and posttests to treated subjects, and conveniently ignoring the issue of control groups (see Nickerson, Perkins, & Smith, 1985).

Obviously, it is hard to get adequate control groups in the area of the acquisition of expertise, because we cannot not easily assign people randomly to groups, and random assignment is the key to adequate control. However, this difficulty does not obviate the need for such groups and for adequate sample sizes to draw conclusions.

5. *Ignoring of dropout effects.* Most people who want to become experts—whether as violinists, skiers, physicists, or whatever—do not make it. They drop out along the way. They try and discover that, for whatever reason, it is not the way for them to go. I know, because as soon as I made the transition from high school to college, I found that I could not realistically compete as a cellist in the much stiffer competition I found in college compared with high school. Eventually I, like many others, decided that my time would be better spent elsewhere.

The result of this dropout effect will be a correlation between deliberate practice and expertise, but it is caused in part by the self-recognition that one may not be cut out to be a concert cellist, Olympic skier, or whatever. In other words, greater talent may lead to more deliberate practice, and vice versa. Deliberate practice may be correlated with success because it is a proxy for ability: We stop doing what we do not do well and feel unrewarded for.

In general, we are more likely to spend the time doing things we enjoy—that we find intrinsically motivating (Deci, 1972). The things we enjoy are also those on the basis of which we are most likely to make our creative contributions (Amabile, 1983; Sternberg & Lubart, 1995). The point, quite simply, is that hours of deliberate practice, in a retrospective study, are hopelessly confounded with talent, motivation, and other variables. Hours of deliberate practice is a proxy for a number of things, not just a measure of time spent wisely.

6. *Choosing domains to maximize fit of data to theory.* Why was Mozart so damn good? Did Einstein practice thinking a lot? What made Picasso so good so young? How about Galois, or our own Vygotsky, both of whom

died very young but are superstars in their chosen fields of mathematics and psychology? Why were the people who were chosen for this volume as experts on expertise chosen, when there are many others who might also lay a claim to such expertise? Did these experts in this book practice more or harder at their craft of psychology? Has even one psychologist found anything close to a perfect correlation between hours seriously worked and recognition for expertise by the field?

The practice view cannot begin to account for the success of extraordinary achievers in the creative domains, and as far as I can tell, its exponents have not made a serious effort to do so. One can say, of course, that creative problem solving is no different from any other problem solving, as do Richman, Gobet, Staszewski, and Simon (chap. 6, this volume) or as did Langley, Simon, Bradshaw, and Zytkow (1987), but such theoretical disagreements cannot adequately account for the very early extraordinary creative expertise of the Mozarts and Einsteins, not to mention many of the people who attended this conference. Indeed, what Mozart did as a child most musical experts will never do nor be able to do in their lifetimes, even after they have passed many times over the amount of time Mozart possibly could have had for deliberate practice as a child.

The bottom line is that we often forget that for every "expert" psychologist invited to such a conference for his or her expertise, there are hundreds and perhaps thousands of others who, too, had hoped to be labeled as expert academics, but did not make it, no matter how hard they tried. We do not gain the recognition that gets us invited to prestigious conferences just by working hard, as many noninvited psychologists would attest to. More importantly, the contributions of a Mozart will not be accounted for by graphs of how many hours he practiced composing.

7. *Ignoring common sense.* Common sense belies the deliberate practice view, as do open eyes and ears. For example, the conference on expertise from which this volume is drawn was fairly typical in that the presentations were far from paragons of outstanding teaching. Most of us, chosen for expertise in research on expertise, are not expert teachers and never will be, no matter how many times we practice our lectures (see Sternberg & Horvath, 1995). Nor, for that matter, are we likely to be as distinguished for our common sense as for any expertise (see Sternberg, Wagner, Williams, & Horvath, 1995). At the same time, every single person at the conference, I would venture to say, has seen young assistant professors who, after just one semester of teaching, are far better teachers than we ever will be, despite their having had far less opportunity to practice teaching (in a focused or any other way) than we have. It is not practice that made them so, nor much more practice that has left most of us no more than ordinary as teachers.

Our children also serve as a control group of sorts in a sometimes painful natural experiment. Thanks to the effects of statistical regression, many of our children will not have the academic success we may have wished for them. We work to see them go to Harvard or Yale, but then see many of them become rejects from the elite schools that we had hoped to see in their future. No matter how much we push them, we are unable to overcome the laws of statistics, in this case, of regression. And we discover that without the ability and motivation, they just do not put the time into the focused practice (i.e., homework, studying for tests, writing papers) that they would need to ever have a crack at the elite schools.

Psychologists like to bash folk theories (Sternberg, 1995). Of course they do: What good would psychology be if all it did was to restate the obvious? Yet, in the process of bashing folk theories, we can become so entrenched in our own narrow world that we become victims of groupthink (Janis, 1972). We fail to see the evidence all around us—scholarly and common-sensical—that people differ in their talents, and that no matter how hard some people try, they just cannot all become experts in the mathematical, scientific, literary, musical, or any other domains to which they may have aspired.

We have a number of ways to reinforce our own groupthink mentality. We preach to the converted, or circulate our work to those who basically agree with us, or simply ignore those who disagree. We find sympathetic editors, or evaluators who have the same vested interests we have and will reinforce our own point of view. They enable us to say we talked to colleagues who agree, and indeed they did, as they had the same axe to grind. Or we come up with ad hoc, untested, and often untestable counter-explanations that fly in the face of common sense, but accomplish the goal of maintaining our normal science.

Experts on expertise are not exceptions to the rule; they are the rule. Dunn and Plomin (1990) spoke of how, just a few decades ago, it was virtually impossible to get funding for research on siblings that considered hereditary factors, whereas now it is difficult to get funding for research that is environmentally oriented. We scientists are as susceptible to fads and follies as anyone else. The acquisition of expertise is an important topic. It deserves the attention it is getting, and so does deliberate practice. How-ever, it is unfortunate that we, as psychologists, feel the need to counter extreme positions, such as the extreme biological view dating back to Galton (1892), with the equally extreme environmental views represented by the view that deliberate practice is everything, or almost everything. Perhaps we will always be imprisoned within Heglian dialectics (Sternberg, 1995), but maybe we can speed them up, and stop making the mistakes of the past. Do we really need to repeat the errors of behaviorism with a neobehaviorism that changes the terms, but leaves the concepts intact? I hope not. But to move on, we have to have the courage to take reflective and often moderate positions, that, although perhaps receiving less media or even scientific attention, better resemble the truth we seek.

The truth is that deliberate practice is only part of the picture. No matter how hard most psychologists work, they will not attain the eminence of a

Herbert Simon. Most physicists will not become Einstein. And most composers will wonder why they can never be Mozart. We will be doing future generations no favor if we lead them to believe that, like John Watson, they can make children into whatever they want those children to be. The age of behaviorism has passed. Let us move beyond, not back to it.

ACKNOWLEDGMENTS

The work reported herein was supported under the Javits Act program (Grant #R206R50001) as administered by the Office of Educational Research and Improvement, U.S. Department of Education. The findings and opinions expressed in this report do not reflect the positions or policies of the Office of Educational Research and Improvement or the U.S. Department of Education.

REFERENCES

Adelson, B. (1984). When novices surpass experts: The difficulty of a task may increase with expertise. *Journal of Experimental Psychology, 10*(3), 483–495.

Amabile, T. M. (1983). *The social psychology of creativity.* New York: Springer.

Bouchard, T. J., Jr., & McGue, M. (1981). Familial studies of intelligence: A review. *Science, 212,* 1055–1059.

Carroll, J. B. (1993). *Human cognitive abilities.* New York: Cambridge University Press.

Deci, E. L. (1972). Intrinsic motivation, extrinsic reinforcement, and inequity. *Journal of Personality and Social Psychology, 22,* 113–120.

Dunn, J., & Plomin, R. (1990). *Separate lives: Why children in the same family are so different.* New York: Basic Books.

Ericsson, K. A. & Charness, N. (1994). Expert performance: Its structure and acquisition. *American Psychologist, 49,* 725–747.

Ericsson, K. A., Krampe, R. T., & Tesch-Römer, C. (1993). The role of deliberate practice in the acquisition of expert performance. *Psychological Review, 100,* 363–406.

Ericsson, K. A., & Smith, J. (Eds.). (1991). *Toward a general theory of expertise: Prospects and limits.* Cambridge, UK: Cambridge University Press.

Frensch, P. A., & Sternberg, R. J. (1989). Expertise and intelligent thinking: When is it worse to know better? In R. J. Sternberg (Ed.), *Advances in the psychology of human intelligence* (Vol. 5, pp. 157–188). Hillsdale, NJ: Lawrence Erlbaum Associates.

Galton, F. (1892). *Hereditary genius* (2nd ed.). London: Macmillan.

Hecht, H., & Proffitt, D. R. (1995). The price of expertise: Effects of experience on the water-level task. *Psychological Science, 6*(2), 90–95.

Herrnstein, R., & Murray, C. (1994). *The bell curve.* New York: The Free Press.

Janis, I. L. (1972). *Victims of groupthink.* Boston: Houghton Mifflin.

Kuhn, T. S. (1970). *The structure of scientific revolutions* (2nd ed.). Chicago: University of Chicago Press.

Langley, P., Simon, H. A., Bradshaw, G. L., & Zytkow, J. M. (1987). *Scientific discovery.* Cambridge, MA: MIT Press.

Lord, C. G., Ross, L., & Lepper, M. R. (1979). Biased assimilation and attitude polarization. The effects of prior theories on subsequently considered evidence. *Journal of Personality and Social Psychology, 37,* 2098–2109.

Luchins, A. S. (1942). Mechanization in problem solving. *Psychological Monographs, 54* (6, No. 248).

Nickerson, R. S., Perkins, D. N., & Smith, E. E. (1985). *The teaching of thinking.* Hillsdale, NJ: Lawrence Erlbaum Associates.

Plomin, R. (1986). *Development, genetics and psychology.* Hillsdale, NJ: Lawrence Erlbaum Associates.

Plomin, R., & McClearn, G. E. (Eds.). (1993). *Nature, nurture and psychology.* Washington, DC: APA Books.

Popper, K. R. (1959). *The logic of scientific discovery.* London: Hutchinson.

Sternberg, R. J. (Ed.). (1982). *Handbook of human intelligence.* New York: Cambridge University Press.

Sternberg, R. J. (1985). *Beyond IQ: A triarchic theory of human intelligence.* New York: Cambridge University Press.

Sternberg, R. J. (Ed.). (1994). *Encyclopedia of human intelligence.* New York: Macmillan.

Sternberg, R. J. (1995). *In search of the human mind.* Orlando, FL: Harcourt Brace College Publishers.

Sternberg, R. J., & Grigorenko, E. L. (Eds.). (in press). *Intelligence, heredity and environment.* New York: Cambridge University Press.

Sternberg, R. J., & Horvath, J. A. (1995). A prototype view of expert teaching. *Educational Researcher, 24*(6), 9–17.

Sternberg, R. J., & Lubart, T. I. (1995). *Defying the crowd: Cultivating creativity in a culture of conformity.* New York: The Free Press.

Sternberg, R. J., Wagner, R. K., Williams, W. M., & Horvath, J. A. (1995). Testing common sense. *American Psychologist, 50,* 912–927.

Wason, P. C. (1960). On the failure to eliminate hypotheses in a conceptual task. *Quarterly Journal of Experimental Psychology, 12,* 129–40.

Author Index

Subject Index

Stephenson, George, 262–267, 269, 307
Support
    external, 305
Suzuki method, 31, 288–289
Swan songs, 242

T

Talent, 57, 76–77, 107–126, 172–175, 271–298,
    337, 339
    biological markers, 292–297
    identification of in skating, 93
Teams
    cognition, 142
    decision-making, 137–161
    vs. groups, 137
    interaction, 135, 146–161
Templates, 178–179
    slots, 179
10-year rule, 10, 173–174, 177, 315, 339
Think-aloud protocols, 34, 41–42, 171
Tower of Hanoi problem, 181

Twin studies, 108–109

U

United States Chess Federation (USCF),
    55–56

V

Variation-selection theory, 230, 246–248
Verbal reports, 34, 41–42
Visual arts, 271–298
Visual search, 340–342
Visual-spatial strengths, 273, 293–295
Vocabulary, 172

W

Work
    vs. deliberate practice, 20–21
    environments, 129–161